Hastening Redemption

Hastening Redemption

Messianism and the Resettlement of the Land of Israel

ARIE MORGENSTERN
TRANSLATED BY JOEL A. LINSIDER

OXFORD
UNIVERSITY PRESS
2006

OXFORD
UNIVERSITY PRESS

Oxford University Press, Inc., publishes works that further
Oxford University's objective of excellence
in research, scholarship, and education.

Oxford New York
Auckland Cape Town Dar es Salaam Hong Kong Karachi
Kuala Lumpur Madrid Melbourne Mexico City Nairobi
New Delhi Shanghai Taipei Toronto

With offices in
Argentina Austria Brazil Chile Czech Republic France Greece
Guatemala Hungary Italy Japan Poland Portugal Singapore
South Korea Switzerland Thailand Turkey Ukraine Vietnam

Published by Oxford University Press, Inc.
198 Madison Avenue, New York, New York 10016

www.oup.com

Library of Congress Cataloging-in-Publication Data
Morgenstern, Arie.
[Meshiḥiyut ve-yishuv Ereẓ Yisra'el. English]
Hastening redemption : Messianism and the resettlement of the land of
Israel / Arie Morgenstern; translated by Joel A. Linsider.
p. cm.
Includes bibliographical references and index.
ISBN-13 978-0-19-530578-4
ISBN 0-19-530578-7
1. Jewish messianic movements. 2. Judaism—Palestine—History—19th century.
3. Jews—Palestine—History—19th century. 4. Palestine—History—1799–1917. I. Linsider, Joel A. II. Title.
BM615.M6713 2006
296.3'36—dc22 2005023269

9 8 7 6 5 4 3 2 1

Printed in the United States of America
on acid-free paper

Preface

The early nineteenth century was a time of enormous and varied change in the life of the Jewish people. Among the Jews of western Europe, the battle for civic equality gathered force, as did the tendency to blend into the surrounding gentile society. Paralleling these trends were the development of the Enlightenment (*Haskalah*) movement and the appearance of the movement for religious reform. Jews began to be absorbed into European culture and even to assimilate and convert. In eastern Europe, meanwhile, the Jews' political situation declined. Governmental persecution and oppression increased and grew harsher, as part of an effort to convert the Jews and forcibly assimilate them into the surrounding society.

That same period also saw the beginning of a slow, covert effort to create a renewed center of Jewish life in the Land of Israel. As a practical matter, the beginning of that movement can be seen in the *aliyah* [immigration to the Land of Israel][1] of thousands of Jews during a brief, thirty-year period. The internal driving force for that *aliyah* was tied to a messianic awakening that affected broad segments of traditional Jewry in the Ottoman Empire, North Africa, and eastern Europe. The messianic aspirations were directed toward the six-hundredth year of the sixth millennium (5600/1840), which the *Zohar* (an important kabbalistic text) had identified as the year of Israel's redemption. This *aliyah* was accompanied by a significant change in the relationship between the people of Israel and the

1. [*Aliyah*, lit. "going up," is the term for immigration from the Diaspora to the Land of Israel. In later usage, it also refers to successive waves of immigration in the modern period, such as "the First *Aliyah*" in 1881. One who carries out *aliyah* is an *oleh* (fem., *olah*; pl., *olim*).—***translator***]

Land of Israel. Jews, as well as gentiles interested in events in the Ottoman Empire in general and the Land of Israel in particular, became ever more conscious of a strengthening bond between the Jewish people and its historical homeland.

Particularly prominent among the immigrants who reached the Land of Israel in the early nineteenth century was a group led by disciples of the Ga'on R. Elijah of Vilna ("the Vilna Ga'on"); in 1813, they numbered 511 souls. The group's members sought to ensure the realization of the redemption by means of human action—primarily *aliyah*, the fulfillment of the commandment to dwell in the Land of Israel, but also an effort to renew classical rabbinic ordination and the building of Jerusalem.

Historians until now have not comprehensively examined the expectations associated with the year 5600/1840. We find references to those expectations primarily in the writings of R. Judah Ḥai Alcalay and in accounts of his life; the year 5600 also is mentioned in passing in several studies that depend on late sources of questionable reliability. The dearth of studies grows out of the very nature of the subject itself: messianism had always been a matter best not spoken of, and the Sabbatean false-messiah debacle during the seventeenth century only strengthened the taboo on dealing with it. We therefore lack written documentation of the messianic awakening that preceded the year 1840, and we may assume that once this bubble of messianic expectation, like its predecessor, had burst, efforts were made to suppress all recollection of the embarrassing episode and the little that might have been daringly written down before 1840 was later destroyed.

The absence of contemporary documentation reflects more than the Jews' self-imposed suppression of information. External factors to be taken into account include the lack of Hebrew printing houses in centers of Jewish population, especially in North Africa, and the heavy censorship imposed by the Russian authorities on Hebrew printing in Russia and Poland. A messianic movement tied to the Land of Israel, which was then under Ottoman rule, would likely be regarded as hostile to the Czarist government. Fear of Russian censorship and government persecution almost certainly led to the destruction of thousands of letters between the Jewish community in the Land of Israel and its members' native lands, and only a few of those letters have come down to us. And the overall flow of events, wars, and persecutions to which the Jews of Russia-Poland and the Land of Israel have been subjected through the years brought about the loss of this type of historical source.

But despite this scarcity of sources, material discovered in the latter part of the twentieth century permits us to reconstruct this important episode in the life of the Jewish nation and its settlement in the Land of Israel during the first half of the nineteenth century. The sources on which this book is based are contemporaneous with the period under consideration. Some were not known until recently, even though they were preserved in public and private archives throughout the world; some were concealed and made available to researchers only during the last twenty years but until now have not been used in a comprehensive and probing manner. I am referring in particular to *Iggerot ha-Peqidim ve-ha-Armarkalim mei-Amsterdam* ("Letters of the *Pekidim* and *Amarkalim* [Clerks and Administrators] in Amsterdam" from 1826 to 1870.[2] The book is based as well on parallel and complementary sources, such as the journals of the missionaries sent by the London Society for Promoting Christianity Amongst the Jews ("London Society"), established in London in 1809 and active then in the Land of Israel, and on rare books, manuscripts, and printed matter from the period under study.

Since this is first use of these materials, something should be said about them. At the end of World War II, a closed and sealed wooden chest was found under a bridge in Amsterdam. When the chest was opened, it became clear that it contained a portion of the rich archive of the Organization of *Peqidim* and *Amarkalim* in Amsterdam ("Clerks' Organization"). In the chest were fifteen large, bulky packets of copies of letters sent from Amsterdam to tens of Jewish communities throughout western Europe and to Jewish centers in eastern Europe and the Ottoman Empire, along with hundreds of copies of letters sent to individuals, communities, and funding organizations in the Land of Israel during the years 1826 to 1870. The Clerks' Organization was established in 1809 and engaged in the raising of funds for the Jews of the Land of Israel; for many years it was headed by the banker and Jewish mystic Ẓevi Hirsch Lehren, and it was he who wrote most of the letters.

The letters deal with a wide range of subjects—some quotidian, others related to the most important questions affecting the Jewish world of the nineteenth century. Naturally, the letters encompass considerable material on how funds were raised, transferred, and distributed to individuals and community organizations in the Land of Israel. But they provide as well a wealth of information on the governance of the *yishuv* (the Jewish settlement in the Land of Israel), on its communities and charitable funds, and on relationships among and within them. They include data on economic conditions and issues, and they consider such matters as *aliyah* to the Land of Israel and departure from it, Torah study versus secular learning, the attitude toward productivity and modernization, the way of life in the Land of Israel, and intellectual streams within Judaism throughout the world. Since the Clerks' Organization was a transcommunal association, we learn much from the letters about what was happening in hundreds of communities throughout Europe: their ties to the Land of Israel; the *Peqidei Qushta* (Clerks of Istanbul), who supported the Sefardi communities in the Land of Israel; the organization of *Roznei Vilna* (Nobles of Vilna), which supported *aliyah* by the Ga'on of Vilna's disciples (known as the *Perushim*, literally, "those who withdrew," after their dissociation from the Hasidim) and their community organization; the courts of Hasidic *ẓaddi-*

2. The letters appear in two different sources. The larger source, extant in manuscript only, is *Iggerot ha-Peqidim ve-ha-Amarkalim mei-Amsterdam* (Letters of the *Peqidim* and *Amarkalim* [Clerks and Administrators] in Amsterdam). It comprises fifteen volumes, of which the first has been lost; the manuscript is housed at the Yad Izhak Ben-Zvi Library in Jerusalem. It is referred to here as *Iggerot ha-Peqidim* (Letters of the Clerks). The second source is a three-volume printed edition of volume 2 of the manuscript, edited by J. J. and B. Rivlin. It is referred to here as Rivlin and Rivlin, *Letters of the Clerks*.

qim and communal rabbis; magnanimous patrons and community functionaries; and the House of the Rothschilds and Moses Montefiore. They likewise contain information about the Clerks' Organization's ties with royal courts and with the foreign ministers and consuls who were active then in Jerusalem and the coastal cities of the Land of Israel, Syria, and Egypt.

The letters of the Clerks' Organization offer great potential for productive research, making them the most important historical source for study of the Jewish *yishuv* in the Land of Israel during the first half of the nineteenth century. Before their discovery, research on the *yishuv* during that period was based on a random, nonconsecutive collection of several dozen isolated documents. The lack of sources precluded any solid understanding of the historical context, and the flawed understanding of the *yishuv*'s inner motivation during that period fostered anachronistic generalizations. The letters of the Clerks' Organization, turned over to the library of Yad Izhak Ben-Zvi in Jerusalem, open a new age in the historiography of Jewish settlement in the Land of Israel during the nineteenth century.

Much can also be learned from the journals of the missionaries who worked in the Land of Israel under the auspices of the London Society. These journals, discovered after the Six-Day War in Christ Church in the Old City of Jerusalem, were copied and printed in part in missionary newspapers in London, beginning in 1812. Except in some limited, extraordinary cases, however, they have not been used until now in historical study.[3]

The characteristic religious sermonizing of these diaries makes them difficult to read and research, but the historical accounts they incorporate have great importance—not only because of the journals' reliability, but also because they document matters of faith and messianism, subjects that the Jews themselves preferred not to treat in writing. What distinguished the London Society during the first half of the nineteenth century was, among other things, the belief of its members that the redemption of Israel would precede the redemption of mankind and that the return of the Jews to their historical homeland signaled the fulfillment of the prophecies about the return to Zion. In light of their interest in the subject, they document the *aliyah* movement and the factors that brought it about, as well as the Jews' viewpoint with respect to the Messiah. Their understanding of Jewish belief reflects the fact that many of them were converts from Judaism and thus fluent in the languages spoken by Jews, familiar with the Jewish way of life, and not far removed from direct contact with Jews. Their reports were not contrived; they involved no intermediaries and were recorded directly on the day of the event described or very soon after. Many of the facts referred to in the diaries are confirmed by parallel sources, including the Letters of the Clerks.

3. For logistical reasons, the extracts from these materials and some others are quoted not in their original English but in English retranslations by the translator of this volume of the renderings that appeared in the Hebrew version of the book.

To study the nature and substance of the messianic beliefs that held sway in the years leading up to 1840, I examined hundreds of books and manuscripts encompassing discourses, eulogies, wills, Torah commentaries, community records, and contemporary letters. Embedded in these sources are messianic allusions and implications, for only by writing obliquely could the authors evade the censors and, occasionally, avoid deliberate eradication of the written material. The need to reduce matters to writing arose in particular after 1840, when the community of believers suffered a crisis of faith. To calm the waters and hearten the despondent, it was necessary for the rabbis, spiritual leaders, and preachers to account for the Messiah's failure to appear. Thanks to these efforts, we possess important evidence regarding the expectations for the year 5600/1840 and the nature and effects of the crisis of faith that ensued. Of the books printed in Jerusalem during the 1840s, two by R. Aviezer of Tiktim, one of the *Perushim* who had immigrated to the Land of Israel, are particularly noteworthy. Also deserving of mention are two essays on the subject by R. Moses Turgeman, a leader of North African Jewry, and the collections of letters and Torah insights by R. Eliezer Bregman, who immigrated to the Land of Israel from Germany in 1834, became one of the *yishuv*'s leaders, and engaged in series of important activities.

This study makes use as well of important documents published by earlier scholars. Their pioneering work, which laid the groundwork for any study of the *yishuv*'s history during the period in question, remains invaluable, notwithstanding the decisive importance of the newly discovered material described above.

Since this book was published in Hebrew in 1985, its subject has generated controversy among modern Jewish historians.[4] Indeed, the academic disputes over the historical significance of the events described here and their contribution to the historiography of the Jewish *yishuv* in the Land of Israel have to a degree fostered my continued research in the field.

Additional sources found in old and new archives and in private collections during the last ten years have shed further light on the messianic concepts of Jews and of millennial Christian groups, and more attention has been directed to the wide geographic range of messianic awakenings in the Jewish world. New aspects of the subject have been considered in connection with modernization and secular education and the beginning of the backlash against them within the *yishuv*. An effort has been made to examine the question of demographics in a critical manner, through the use of reliable data; and the door has been opened to renewed consideration of organizational and social issues.

Nineteenth-century Jewish messianism is a far-reaching subject, and this

4. Much of the controversy reflects the erroneous concept that the Ga'on of Vilna and his disciples, unlike the Hasidim, were confirmed rationalists, opposed to all messianist notions. According to that concept, which until now has held sway among scholars, their sole motive for immigrating to the Land of Israel was to study Torah there.

book can encompass only its highlights.[5] The bibliography appended here will enable the reader to locate more studies written in the wake of the present book. In particular, I want to note "The Disciples of the Ga'on of Vilna, Sabbateanism, and the Jewish Essence" (Hebrew), a revolutionary study by Prof. Judah Liebes, the noted authority on Kabbalah; it appeared in the philosophy and Kabbalah journal *Da'at*, nos. 50–52 (2003). According to Prof. Liebes's discoveries, R. Menaḥem Mendel of Shklov, the Ga'on of Vilna's disciple, regarded Shabbetai Ẓevi as the false "messiah," who had stumbled and fallen down among the *qelippot* (the "husks," kabbalistic imagery for the forces of evil). The Ga'on himself, meanwhile, was the true messiah, known as "the reviving serpent" (*naḥash* in Hebrew, the numerical value of whose letters equals that of *mashiaḥ*, messiah), who had come to repair Shabbetai Ẓevi by revealing the secrets of the Torah and, later in the process, through the settlement of the Land of Israel by his disciples.

This English edition is published through the generosity of the Shalem Center, which provided me the opportunity, as a senior fellow, to continue my research into eighteenth- and nineteenth-century Jewish messianism. My thanks go to my friends Dr. Yoram Hazony and Dr. Dan Polisar, the leaders of the Center, and its dynamic general director, Mr. Yishai Haetzni. Thanks also to my English translator, Joel Linsider.

My gratitude is extended as well to the staffs of the following libraries and research institutes: Rozenthaliana Library in Amsterdam, Jews' College and the British Museum Library in London, and the Bodelian Library at Oxford. Thanks also to the staffs of the Central Archive for Jewish History in Jerusalem; the library of Yad Izhak Ben-Zvi; and the National and University Library in Jerusalem: the Manuscript Institute, the Institute for Photocopies of Hebrew Manuscripts, and the Rare Books Department. A special thanks is due to many private collectors who made their information and collections available to me, including Mr. Salo Mayer of Amsterdam, R. Abraham Shischa Ha-Levi of London, R. Samuel Gur, and the family of R. Barukh Horwitz of Jerusalem. Thanks also to the staff of Yad Izhak Ben-Zvi and its general management, who brought the original Hebrew version of this book to publication in 1985 with love and dedication.

Finally, thanks to my beloved wife Leah, who happily suffered not only the adverse economic effects of my lengthy studies but also the burden of my constantly talking to her about what I was working on and the discoveries I had made, which seemed to me more important than anything else. Her wise counsel helped me greatly.

Jerusalem
Adar II 5765—April 2005 A.M.

5. Since 1985, I have published some twenty additional studies related to the subject. They appeared in various periodicals and have been collected in my book, A. Morgenstern, *Redemption Through Return: The Vilna Ga'on's Disciples in the Land of Israel, 1800–1840* (Hebrew) (Jerusalem, 1997).

Contents

Translator's Note

This work quotes extensively from documents more or less contemporaneous with the events recounted. Few of those documents have previously been translated into English, and the extracts from them are newly translated here. The book also quotes from other primary sources and classical Jewish texts, some of which are available in English. Where previous translations of those materials are used, they are cited; in most instances, however, the translations are my own. In translating biblical verses, I relied heavily on the Old JPS and New JPS versions (*The Holy Scriptures* [Philadelphia: Jewish Publication Society of America, 1917]; *The Tanakh* [Philadelphia: Jewish Publication Society of America, 2d ed., 1999]).

In transliterating Hebrew terms and titles, I aimed for a balance between precision and readability. I have used the following conventions:

’ = *’alef*
‘ = *‘ayin*
ḥ = *ḥet*
k = *kaf*
ẓ = *ẓadi*
q = *qof*

Where *’alef* and *‘ayin* appear at the beginning or the end of a word, they are not represented unless needed for clarity.

Although I transliterated the titles of Hebrew primary works, I translated the titles of Hebrew secondary works, on the premise that the English reader will find the meaning of the title more useful than an often lengthy Hebrew transliteration. (I used the translated titles that appear in the works themselves where available and otherwise translated the titles myself.) In all cases, however, the information provided should be enough to permit an interested reader to locate the cited source.

Hastening Redemption

I

Background of the Early-Nineteenth-Century Messianic Awakening

The world has surely collapsed and fallen to pieces and changes appear in the world each day. My wisdom and understanding, along with anyone with eyes in his head, can see that day of the Lord is near, when He will direct His attention to His people.

—R. Hillel of Kovno, *Hillel ben Shaḥar*

Emancipation and Messianic Faith: Reformers Versus Traditionalists

The beginning of the Modern Period in human history is characterized by a series of political and social revolutions that befell Europe, beginning with the French Revolution of 1789. The French Revolution's ideas regarding the equal rights of citizens aroused all of Europe and substantially changed the face of European society. In the wake of the Revolution, wars broke out that engulfed the countries of western, central, and eastern Europe and wrought changes in their forms of governance.

The Jews constituted a religious and ethnic minority in all the countries of Europe, and their fate was profoundly affected by each local government's attitude toward the revolutionary ideas of liberty, equality, and fraternity. The controversy over "reforming the situation of the Jews" and the Jews' right to civic equality engaged thinkers and policy-makers in every European country. The question was answered in various ways, from ringing endorsement of Jewish rights to absolute negation of the idea. In France, for example, a law enacted in 1791 granted the Jews full equality as citizens; in Russia, meanwhile, the Jews were suppressed and persecuted mercilessly.

But it was not only the legal status of the Jews that underwent change during this period. There were transformations as well in their self-image and in the intensity with which they considered substantive questions related to their existence as a nation and their standing among the nations. The dramatic improvement in the Jews' standing in some countries of Christian Europe, and the awakening in others of the old anti-Semitism in new garb, re-ignited messianic expectations unknown since the demise of Shabbetai Ẓevi's messianism.[1] Events that suggested alteration of the world order had always aroused messianic expectations among the Jews, and they accordingly had more than academic interest in them at such a time. The world order was undergoing change before their very eyes, and they regarded these decisive and intense developments as events of the sort the sages had said would precede the Messianic Era.[2]

The possibility that Jews might attain equal civic rights for the first time in the history of Christian Europe compelled Jews and gentiles alike to consider their religious and national distinctiveness. The principal question presented was whether the Jews, once granted the rights of citizens, would be able to assume all the associated obligations as well or whether, conversely, their religion entailed a unique political aspect that precluded them from taking upon themselves all the obligations of citizens of their countries of residence, including a sense of full fraternity with the gentiles. Two fundamental Jewish ideas were seen as obstacles to granting the Jews full civic rights: that of chosenness, which obligates Jews to separate themselves from gentiles; and that of the Messiah, which, by invoking the hope to return to Zion and reestablish the kingdom of the Jews in their historical land, seems to conflict with loyalty to a European homeland.

The extended consideration of these questions led to the emergence of two principal approaches to contemporary Jewish belief in the Messiah: that of the reformers and that of the traditionalists. The reformers, in turn, were themselves of two sorts. The extremists, associated with radical reform groups, sought fundamental change in the idea of the Messiah. In their view, the very process of granting equal rights to the Jews represented the beginning of the Messianic Era. The attainment of equality could cure the ills of human society, for all individuals would be regarded as having equal status, and the nation of Israel could find its own repair through involvement in that process. In their opinion, the Jews' integration into society should be advanced by blurring any features that served to distinguish the Jews. Accordingly, they saw no continuing significance to the historical Jewish homeland; they substituted France and its mountains for Jerusalem and its hills, and they exchanged the Jordan River for the Rhine.

The more moderate reformers did not dare to repudiate the messianic idea outright; instead, they attempted to move it from the national plane to the universal. They sought to divest the Jewish messianic belief of its longing for the return to Zion, for construction of the Third Temple, and for reestablishment of the kingdom of Israel; in place of those elements, they gave prominence to the idea that in the Messianic Era, all mankind would recognize God's sovereignty and achieve worldwide peace and happiness. Proponents of this position saw the traditional messianic belief as an obstacle to the Jews' integration into gentile society; accordingly, they tried to get rid of the uniquely Jewish features that interfered with that integration.

The traditionalists, in contrast, rejected none of the ideas associated with the Jewish belief in the Messiah. In their opinion, faith in the Messiah and the expectation that Israel would be redeemed in its Land were not at odds with the possibility of Jews being loyal to the countries in which they resided. Their civic obligations did not conflict with their religious distinctiveness. Even their hope to be redeemed in their historical Land did not clash with their devotion to their lands of residence: inasmuch as the redemption would take place in the distant future, beyond the horizon, it was not something actual; its realization was not practical. Traditionalists distinguished between loyalty to the historical homeland and loyalty to the actual, contemporary homeland by assigning each to its own historical era. The future one, associated with the distant days of the Messianic Era, was not something practical; it pertained to the domain of belief. The contemporary one, in contrast, pertained to actual existence, and it was the one in which the Jews were obligated, as a practical matter, to show political loyalty. Moreover, by authority of the Three Oaths that God had imposed,[3] Jews were forbidden to do anything to realize or advance the time for their return to their Land and the establishment of their kingdom. It followed that the Jews' expectation of redemption in their Land did not contradict their loyalty to their lands of residence—not only because the expectation was anchored to an historical era different from the present one, but also because they were strictly forbidden to take any action to fulfill that expectation.[4]

Traditionalist circles could not fail to notice the upheavals, the wars, the disputes over the rights of Jews, and the gathering strength of the *Haskalah* (Enlightenment) movement and Reform in western and central Europe. As already mentioned, the sages' comments in the Talmud and *midrashim* about the events that will lead up to the Messiah's coming are diverse and even contradictory. But their common denominator is that all speak of extraordinary events or situations. And since the period under consideration was one of numerous upheavals, both in the state of the world at large and in the situation of the Jews, it is hardly surprising that Jews "daily awaiting the Messiah's arrival"[5] would find in contemporary events indications of the sages' observations on the period designated as the "Footsteps of the Messiah" (*iqveta de-meshiḥa*).

That the traditionalists saw the spread of the Reform movement as itself signaling the approach of redemption is an astonishing feature of nineteenth-century Jewish life. No Jewish movement rivaled Reform in its effort to undercut the traditional messianic concept, yet it was in just this rejectionist stance that traditionalists found an indication of the coming redemption of Israel. The notion rests on the talmudic comment that the Messiah's arrival will be preceded by a dramatic religious and moral decline. Insolence will prevail, and the younger generation will rebel against the authority of its elders;

but it is this very decline that will bring the hoped-for messianic upheaval in its wake:

> It was taught in a *baraita*: R. Judah says, the generation in which the son of David will come will be one in which the [scholars'] meeting place will be turned over to harlotry. . . . The wisdom of the scribes will decay, those who fear sin will be despised, the face of the generation will be that of a dog, and truth will be absent. . . . Young men will humiliate the elders . . . brazenness will abound . . . and the entire kingdom will turn to heresy.[6]

In his early-nineteenth-century homiletical and halakhic writings, R. Wolf Hamburg expresses the view that the Reform movement's success offers no evidence whatsoever of its truth. On the contrary, its success demonstrates its falsity: in traditionalist eyes, the phenomenon of absolute alienation from Judaism signifies that we are in the period of the Footsteps of the Messiah.[7] Hamburg elaborates on this idea at length in his book *Qol Bokhim*, a eulogy for Meshullam Zalman Cohen. The book is not a typical eulogy, neither admonishing the audience nor sermonizing to it. Instead, the eulogy has an apologetic strain, in which the author explains the ways of providence with respect to the prospering of the wicked—that is, the Reform movement's success despite its rebellious doctrines.[8] Hamburg bases his explanation on a difficult passage in the talmudic tractate *Sanhedrin*: "The son of David [i.e., the Messiah] will not come until a fish will be sought for one who is ill but will not be found." He suggests the fish symbolize scholars; the success of the reformers will bring about a scarcity of great Torah scholars in Israel:

> And the son of David will not come until great sages are sought to reprove the generation and set it straight and to heal afflictions of the soul, but none are to be found. . . . And see, from the time the yeshivas were closed, the [divine] abundance was diminished and glory and life have been taken away . . . and the son of David will not come until a fish is sought for one who is ill, and everyone, God forbid, will be culpable . . . and there will be a great calamity in the Footsteps of the Messiah.[9]

Some twenty years later, in his book *Simlat Binyamin*, Hamburg again directs his attention to the all-embracing religious decline that took place under the influence of the Reform movement. In his view, the reformers undercut the three central pillars on which the world rests—Torah, worship, and acts of kindness. Such extremism shows that we are close to the turning point, to the end of days. As he puts it:

> But it appears to me that the prophet was speaking of the present time, nearing the time for redemption, for they [the sages] said, "if you see a generation subject to great tribulations, go and examine the judges of Israel," that is, our contemporary parents and teachers,

> who cause many to stumble regarding Torah and the commandments. . . . For on account of our many sins, the foremost people of the generation, the teachers, have repudiated the three pillars of the world: they have repudiated young students of Torah; they have repudiated prayer, which stands in the place of the [sacrificial] service, by not reciting the silent prayer; . . . and they have even repudiated the pillar of acts of kindness, for the principal aspect of the commandment [to do kindness to the deceased] is to act as pallbearers and escort the deceased to burial, but the wicked of our time seek to have [the deceased] carried on horse or donkey. . . . The rabbis and teachers of our time have repudiated good things that strengthen students of Torah, and they only waste money on having gentiles sing and on lighting white wax candles, in the manner of the nations of the world, and they actively deny the coming of the Messiah who will restore the order of [sacrificial] service to Zion and Jerusalem.[10]

Ẓevi Hirsch Lehren, leader of the Clerks' Organization in Amsterdam, similarly lived and worked under the influence of messianic tension, and he, too, saw the spread of the Reform movement and its ascendancy within Jewish communities as a sign of approaching redemption: "From this, one can perceive that salvation is near. For this exile of the *shekhinah* [God's presence] appears palpably in the appointment of one of our culpable enemies as rabbi and teacher. And on account of our many sins, *asherot* [pagan deities] have already been set up in some places in Germany, and what will be the end of it in all our holy communities?"[11] Elsewhere, in reacting to the reformers' success, he says: "All of this shows that we are close to the set time of redemption, and salvation is near."[12]

The traditionalists saw further evidence of the approaching redemption in the changes taking place in society at large. The improved attitude of the Christian world toward the Jews, manifested in their emancipation within the countries of western Europe,[13] constituted a sign that the redemption was near. A book published in England in 1795 considers the approaching year of redemption on the basis of various End-reckonings; but, along with those End-reckonings, the author's proof that the End-time was approaching rests as well on historical events to which he himself was witness, including the age of liberty that ensued after the American Revolution. He writes:

> And you shall know today and keep in mind [cf. Deut. 4:39] that in the year 5543 [1783], which represented the end of years, there was proclaimed peace and liberty for the residents of the land of America; and from there the light of liberty was ignited and spread to the French state. And the Earth was illuminated by its glory to remove idols from the Earth. . . . And it continues to gain strength and to progress, providing light until the day when the kings gather and pass together, nations roaring and kingdoms shaking from the blood of the dead and imprisoned and from the violent campaign of the

> enemy. . . . But what is written after? "Nations, acclaim His people, for He will avenge the blood of His servants . . . and atone the Land of His people" [Deut. 32:43].[14]

Another work, *Hilkhot Yemot ha-Mashiaḥ* (Laws of the Messianic Age), written in Germany in 1822, also interprets historical events in a messianic vein. It treats the reports from America as if the United States were preparing to establish a Jewish kingdom within it:

> And the proof that now is the time of redemption is that now, matters are to be found in the world. . . . In North America, known as the United States . . . the government has determined that when 35,000 Jewish souls arrive, they will be permitted to establish a state . . . and it turns out that there will be a Jewish kingdom in a settled land. . . . When God, may He be blessed, grants that this endeavor on our part succeeds, I will ascribe to it the verse [Isa. 65:17], "For I am creating a new Heaven and a new earth."[15]

It is well known that Ẓevi Hirsch Kalisher, in a letter to Baron Rothschild, likewise cites the achievements of the age of emancipation and the Jews' integration into the European economy as proof that the time set for the redemption is drawing near: "And in my eyes, it is clear that the light of dawn has begun to shine, for God has granted us that princes of Israel have become prominent in the world, such as the House of the Rothschilds and others like them . . . whose name goes forth from one end of the world to the other. . . . And, so, in every European state there are to be found notable Jews, important in the eyes of the government."[16]

Theological Significance of the Wars After the French Revolution

The emancipation and the changes that took place in the governance and social structure of western and central European states were brought about by the French revolutionary wars. These wars, which produced a fundamental reordering of Europe, were understood as allusions to the workings of providence in matters beyond the normal human horizon: wars are not randomly visited upon the world; rather, the Holy One Blessed Be He brings them about for specific reasons. Europe was engulfed in conflict for twenty years following the French Revolution, and the wars were so intense, and the ensuing political and social changes so fundamental, that the traditionalists regarded them, beyond any doubt, as the referent of the talmudic statement "wars, too, are the beginning of redemption."[17] For obvious reasons, the Jews were precluded from committing these ideas to writing, but even the few sources we have provide evidence of their wide circulation.

In the diary he kept during the 1809 siege of his city, Rabbi Moses Sofer of Pressburg describes the dreadful effects of its heavy bombardment by French artillery. Though exercising deliberate caution, he directs his attention to the Jews' sharing in the wartime suffering and the theological meaning of that suffering: "Now, one of the most likely times for redemption is when Israel is at the greatest depths, a point than which there is no lower. Then he will look willy-nilly into the face of his Messiah . . . and thereby [fulfill] 'look upon the face of your Messiah' [Ps. 84:10]—look for the good, and for the year of redemption."[18] Soon after, he returns to the subject and discourses on it: "And now, my brethren, please see and look how many great troubles and hardships were visited upon us during this present war, the full force of suffering. . . . And the holy *shekhinah* is in exile, and the Torah is diminished, and His great Name is desecrated through our many sins; but if we pray for the deliverance of our souls and our redemption, then war will be the beginning of the redemption."[19]

It thus appears that a religious Jew in difficult circumstances fortifies himself with a faith suffused with hope for the messianic future that will bring an end to all the present tribulations. That future is ready to take shape, for the very fact that Israel's share of suffering has become so great signifies that things will soon change for the better. At the same time, transformations are occurring on a worldwide scale, suggesting Israel's involvement in the changing arrangements.

The concept that global change accompanied by dramatic events signifies Israel's approaching redemption reverberates in a discourse delivered in New York on 9 May 1798 by *Ḥazzan* Gershom Mendes Seixas. Seixas formulates his attitude toward the wars in Europe on the basis of the talmudic statement that "adversity comes to the world only for the sake of Israel" (*Yevamot* 63a). In his opinion, the wars themselves clearly indicate that the days of the Messiah are taking shape and approaching, and the sign is reinforced by the two contemporaneous upheavals—the American War of Independence and the French Revolution: "When we consider the current situation and war-related circumstances, as well as the deterioration and ruination of human morals throughout almost the entire world, we come willy-nilly to believe that the days of the redemption's radiance are taking form and coming and that our God will reveal His will to again gather the dispersed remnant of Israel."[20]

The sharpest expression of the view that the French Revolutionary Wars constitute a sign of the approaching messianic age can be found in a Hasidic tradition about Menaḥem Mendel of Rimanov:

> At the time of the First Napoleonic War, the *rebbe* R. Mendele wanted to make that war into the War of Gog and Magog [an eschatological confrontation]. He pleaded in his prayer that he [Napoleon] would be victorious in battle in order to bring about the redemption. And he said that in his opinion, it was good that Jewish blood be spilled, and that from Pristik to Rimanov they walk knee-deep in Jewish blood, so that it would be the time for our redemption.[21]

Not everyone saw the Napoleonic Wars, with all their fearsomeness and all the Jewish blood they claimed, as a sign of Israel's approaching redemption.

A few sources record that some religious leaders of the age engaged in disputes over the notion. But the very fact of this intellectual confrontation confirms the existence of a view, described above, that was willing to regard the blood price imposed on Israel by the wars—even though they were not Israel's wars—as a sign of the approaching redemption.[22]

Napoleon's military campaigns in Egypt and the Land of Israel in 1798 also were seen by many as evidence that the Footsteps of the Messiah were upon them. The believers were undeterred by the historical fact that the campaign in the Land of Israel was firmly tied to strategic considerations, as Napoleon sought to overcome British hegemony over Mediterranean commerce and to broaden the areas conquered by France.[23] In their view, God's providential direction of history operates through natural events, but particular events in and of themselves do not always represent the intended purpose; rather, they bring in their wake some other event, not yet apparent to the human eye, that turns out to be decisive in achieving the true purpose. *Ḥazzan* Seixas of New York saw Napoleon's campaign in the Land of Israel in that light: "The recent [*ḥadashim la-beqarim*; cf. Lam. 3:23] events [Napoleon's conquest of the Land of Israel] that unfolded in an orderly fashion, one after another, in the spiritual and physical worlds, constitute clear and reliable evidence of the truth of God's word . . . that the great and exalted day is taking shape and approaching."[24]

Even though the historical reality is that Napoleon's true goal was the conquest of Egypt, and that he accordingly proceeded through the coastal cities of the Land of Israel and made no attempt to conquer Jerusalem, his campaign was accompanied by rumors of his intention to turn over Jerusalem and the Land of Israel to the Jews and to assist them in renewing the kingdom of Israel. These rumors appear to have been fed by redemption *midrashim* telling that, at the End, the Christians will rule over the Land of Israel, overthrow the Muslim rulers, and deliver dominion over the Land to the Jewish nation.[25] The rumors told as well of a particular decree issued by Napoleon on 20 April 1799, in which he promises that, following his victory, he will return the Land of Israel to the Jews and help them establish their state there. Investigators differ on whether Napoleon actually issued such a decree,[26] but whether he did or not is of little import for the present inquiry. What matters is that the excitement was generated and the question raised.

Napoleon's expedition to the Land of Israel and all that it entailed were marvelously consistent with the Jews' expectations for the role of Christians in the process of Israel's redemption, as foretold in the *midrashim*. The Jewish imagination was energized by the image of the dazzling military commander, apparently sympathetic to the Jews, who invades the Land of Israel and challenges the Ottoman rulers' hold on it. His image, activities, and expedition gave rise to legends that comprised a bit of truth wrapped in an abundance of wishful thinking. Here, too, we are concerned not so much with historical truth as with belief—a belief so firm that it subordinated reality to its needs. Thus, for example, the Jews wanted to believe that Napoleon's expedition to the Land of Israel was undertaken as a venture in its own right, to conquer the Land

and turn it over to the Jews. Beyond that, they wanted to believe that in invading the Land of Israel, Napoleon battled for Jerusalem and conquered it.

Echoes of such an invented "reality," subordinated to belief, can be heard in an account by Menaḥem Mendel of Kamenetz, who visited Jerusalem in 1834. In describing the cemetery, he writes: "Still standing there among them is large marble pillar with the form of a hand at its top, known as *yad avshalom*. And when Napoleon, King of France, did battle on the Mount of Olives, its fingers were broken off of it by the cannons."[27]

Napoleon's expedition to the Land of Israel aroused similar religious expectations among Christians. Even as the expedition was being planned, the French press published assessments of its chances for success and wrote sympathetically of the possibility that Jewish settlement in the Land of Israel would ensue: "It is known how much importance [the Jews] assign to their ancient homeland and the city of Jerusalem. They are dispersed throughout the world because of persecutions that have gone on now for eighteen hundred years, yet they still look toward the Land of Israel. . . . They will come there from the four corners of the world if only given the sign."[28]

In Germany, too, Napoleon's eastern expedition generated excitement. A pamphlet that appeared in Berlin in 1799, containing a disputation between a Christian theologian and a Jew, had the Jew uttering these lines: "All the newspapers speak as one about Bonaparte's conquest of this holy place [Jerusalem] and add, almost seriously, that he conquered it *for the Jews*."[29] Another pamphlet, which appeared in Nuremberg in 1800, notes that Napoleon's expedition to the Land of Israel aroused messianic hopes among the Jews, as well as eschatological hopes among Christians. According to one commentator, the liberty the Jews will henceforth enjoy will no longer take the form of equality granted in exchange for assimilation; rather, it will be their actual national redemption.[30]

In Protestant England as well, Napoleon's expedition to the Land of Israel gave rise to theological deliberations over Israel's return to its land. These assessments commingled religious expectations with political considerations. The power that helped the Jews return to their land and establish their national state there would gain a grateful and loyal ally in the East, reaping abundant political and economic benefits. Accordingly, it was argued, England should hasten to take advantage of political opportunities by forming alliances to prevent France from harvesting that entire fruit in the wake of Napoleon's expedition.[31] The Protestant theologians saw the worldwide array of events as natural causes directed by divine Providence to the fulfillment of "Israel's return." The exact time of Israel's return to its land might remain uncertain, but there could be no doubt that it was near:

> Never have there been so many reasons as now to assume that it is not far off. We live in dreadful times. We and our forebears have seen wars, but never since mankind learned to shed blood has there been a war like the present one, in which nations shell one another to smithereens on account of ideologies and principles simultane-

> ously linked to religious institutions and civil governments. The most shocking events transpire in quick succession. The "great Babylon" is shaken to its foundations; Rome itself feels the upheaval's blast; and its political-ecclesiastical government is terminated in an instant. The kingdom of the beast conceals itself and proceeds in darkness. The Turkish power has been attacked with great seriousness and is weakened by its own violence; it is now exhausted and weakened in all its parts to the point that it must ask its (hitherto) longest-standing enemy to support its shaky throne.[32]

There can be no doubt that the interest publicly shown by Christians in Napoleon's expedition to the Land of Israel and in the ensuing new prospects for Israel's return to the Land stirred the Jews themselves to see in the contemporary events signs of their approaching redemption.

Influence of International Uprisings and Conflicts on the Messianic Notion

After Napoleon's defeat in 1812, Europe calmed down as it recovered from the shockwaves that had overtaken it. The Jews' hopes that world events were heralding the approach of their redemption were nearly extinguished.[33] But a new wave of international uprisings and conflicts soon inundated Europe, reigniting the tendency to see world events and transformations as a sign that the redemption was near.

July 1830 witnessed a new uprising in Paris. Under its influence, a rebellion against Holland broke out in Brussels, and an independent kingdom of Belgium was declared. The Dutch king, Wilhelm I, failed in his efforts to subdue the rebellion forcibly. At the same time, the Poles rose up against Russia, but that rebellion was put down by the armies of Czar Nikolai I. In the wake of the Polish rebellion's suppression, a severe cholera epidemic overtook Europe, leaving its mark on the era.[34] Once again we are witness to events extraordinary both in their substance and in how they transpire and to political upheavals and transformations concentrated in time, place, and magnitude.

Ẓevi Hirsch Lehren, possessed of a powerful messianic faith, believed that no worldly decree was issued without a precursory supernal decree. On 24 June 1831, he writes: "The earthquake that has now come upon the world in several countries, and the manner in which the fear of government has declined and descended to the dust—who can be sure that this does not entail preparation for the coming of King Messiah, for God, may He be blessed, thereby shows the worldly kings that He alone appoints kings and kingship is properly His. And the shoot of David will sprout and his glory will be raised up, and the kingdom will be restored to Jerusalem."[35] Lehren comments as follows on the political and economic crisis in Europe at that time: "The page is too short to contain the account of the scandals and burdens brought about by the levies to raise armies in order to be fortified against the nation [the

Belgians] who have rebelled against His Majesty the King, [but] our eyes look heavenward, for all this is a good sign for Israel that the year of redemption and salvation has drawn near, may that be [God's] will speedily in our days, amen."[36]

Soon after, Lehren writes:

> It appears to me from world affairs that the year of redemption and salvation is near, for the rebellion against kingdoms that has gone on from the year before last year until now is no insignificant matter [*lo davar reiq hu*; cf. Deut. 32:47]. And I have said already from the beginning of this year, that if the entire world thought as I do and as do many flawless ones who similarly think that we have attained the days of the Messiah, who will reveal himself speedily in our days, and if they were to return to God with all their hearts and all their souls, then we would already have been redeemed. But on account of our many sins, many [people] attribute everything to natural events, in the way of the world, and they pay no attention to the fact that we have already reached the afternoon preceding the onset of the Sabbath. May God have mercy . . . and ease for us the tribulations of the Messiah [lit., "birth pangs of the Messiah"; suffering that is expected to precede his coming], and may we soon attain the repose and the assigned inheritance [cf. Deut. 12:9].[37]

In 1833, Lehren details for Israel of Shklov, a leader of the *Perushim* in Safed, the woes that have brought about a diminution in the funds sent to the Land of Israel. One difficulty was the serious harm inflicted by the cholera epidemic that began to rage in Europe in the summer of 1832. It claimed many lives and left many orphans needing to be sustained by the community.[38] Moreover, the ensuing quarantine prevented merchants from traveling from city to city, thereby impairing the Jews' livelihoods and increasing the number of poor people who also had to be supported by the community. Yet another misfortune was the lengthy war waged by his country, Holland, in the context of the Belgian battle for independence. The war widened and spread; France and England came to the aid of the Belgians and made war against Holland to compel it to grant Belgian independence. Lehren expresses concern that the war might expand even further if Russia and Prussia were to carry out their threats to intervene on Holland's side. Still, he concludes optimistically: "Perhaps, in the meanwhile, redemption will grow out of this."[39]

In winter 1832–1833, Lehren again expresses concern about a flare-up of war on a wider scale. Czar Nikolai I seemed likely to back the Turkish authorities in going to war against Muhammad Ali (the pasha of Egypt, who was being insubordinate to his Turkish overlord), and it was possible that additional governments would join in the war. Such a war would be unique not only in its dimensions but also, primarily, in its possible theater of operations—the Land of Israel—and Lehren takes comfort in the power of Providence to direct events: "Perhaps it is the time of the End and from it, and through it, redemption and salvation will grow."[40]

Russia's Persecution of Its Jews as "Tribulations of the Messiah"

Until the second half of the eighteenth century, few Jews resided in Czarist Russia. The entry of Jews into Russia's borders was forbidden, primarily for religious reasons. After the second and third partitions of Poland in 1793 and 1795, the number of Jews within the boundaries of Czarist Russia increased to about one million, representing the largest concentration of Jews in Europe.

The Jews in Russia found themselves in a situation very different from that of their brethren in central and western Europe. The latter suffered as a result of the revolutionary wars, but the suffering was not particularly directed to them as Jews; rather, it was the fate of the populace at large. And even the confrontation between Jews and gentiles over emancipation did not entail government intervention in the Jews' autonomous and religious lives. The Jews of Russia, in contrast, were repugnant to the authorities by reason of their very ethnic distinctiveness. In order to turn them into "useful citizens" of the society and state, the authorities sought to forcibly assimilate them. To that end, they enacted special decrees, imposing discriminatory and oppressive rules and coercive mechanisms.

The program of coercion and custodianship against the Jews in Russia became manifest in the time of Czar Alexander I, with the Jewish Statute of 1804. The statute eased the burden imposed on the Jews with respect to some state interests, particularly by granting them permission to own real property and to settle in remote, sparsely populated areas. But it was more onerous than previous arrangements insofar as it forbade the Jews from living in villages as lessees; it gave them three or four years to leave their villages and move to urban areas.[41] On the eve of his death in 1825, Alexander I issued an order expelling the Jews from the regions of Mohelov and Vitebsk; another order forbade Jews from living within fifty kilometers of the western border, claiming that in those areas they engaged in smuggling.

The harshest decree to which the Jews of Russia were subjected, known as the Cantonists' Edict, pertained to the military draft. It was first proposed at the start of the nineteenth century, but Jewish intercession managed to prevent its being carried out. On 26 August 1827, however, Nikolai I brought those deferrals to an end. Implementation of the decree profoundly shook Russian Jewry. In contrast to the Austrian military draft, which grew out of an emancipation-based concept of imposing on the Jews equal civic obligations corresponding to their equal civic rights, the Russian military draft reflected the idea that Jews had to be assimilated into society. To that end, it was necessary to do away with every feature that distinguished them, to convert them from their religion, and to employ coercive methods. The military draft could serve as an excellent melting pot. Tearing the Jew away at a young age from his family and Jewish environment; removing his outwardly Jewish features, by steps such as shaving his beard and side curls and confiscating his prayer shawl, phylacteries, and sacred books; and introducing him to a strange way of life, characterized by a strict militaristic doctrine—all of these measures were designed to ensure that only a few young men could maintain their Judaism. And not only were the young Jews placed in a strange, rigid context; they were subjected as well to an array of pressures, including harsh psychological and physical torments that one could escape only by agreeing to convert.[42]

The edict's malicious intention may be evident most clearly in its imposition on the Jewish community of the obligation to see to it that the draft quota was met; the matter was not seen simply as one between the government and the affected individuals. As a result, the Jewish community found itself on the horns of a harsh dilemma. It recognized that unless it strove mightily to produce the requisite number of draftees in a timely fashion, it would by its own hand seal the fate of all the Jews under its protection, for its inability to comply would subject the Jews to renewed attacks by the government. In order to meet the quota but avoid the painful task of selecting the draftees, the Jewish community used the "services" of criminal elements still known in Jewish history as "the kidnappers." As the time for the draft approached, they would snatch children from among the poorer elements of the populace, and they were determined to meet the quota even if the boys they seized were of tender years.

Many of the draftees converted,[43] either because they had been removed from their Jewish environment while still young, before their Jewishness had taken proper shape, or because they succumbed to the torments and coercive measures to which they were subjected. Those who succeeded in maintaining their Judaism did so secretly, fearing harassment by the authorities, and even they were transformed by their experience in fundamental ways. Twenty-five years of military service, of spiritual distance from everything Jewish, tore them away from the old Jewish world. When they returned to their communities, they were regarded as lost: "The cantonist label affected our children negatively not only during their military service but even when they returned to their parents' homes. They wanted to find respite after their harsh labors and after suffering much anger and bitterness; but, for understandable reasons, they could not be reunited with and joined to the source from which they had been hewn."[44] Many other draftees refused with all their might to free their bodies from torment by converting; they breathed their last and died for the sanctification of God's Name.[45]

How did a believing Jew understand the overall effect of these edicts? How did he view the oppression of the Jewish people in the Diaspora? Did he see it as a natural outgrowth of gentile hatred of Jews, or, perhaps, did he look beyond the human vision of natural, historical causes? Did he attribute the Jewish people's unique status to deeper, hidden, inner reasons, reasons grounded in a Providence striving to realize its program through human history?

Here, too, the believing Jew manifested his inclination to assign transcendent meanings to unique events in Jewish history. Caution, of course, precluded reducing much to writing and led those who dared to write to express themselves obliquely. Still, their meaning is unmistakable. Hillel of Kovno, in his book *Hillel ben Shaḥar*, reacts to the 1798 military draft of Austrian Jews, and we may regard his comments as applying, a fortiori, to the harsher Russian draft: "A new misfortune, greater than any that has arisen or been seen since we became a holy nation, is the kaiser's decree to take men for service as soldiers, . . . destroying both body and soul by denying the opportunity to sanctify God's name by dying rather than transgressing."[46] In his opinion, this misfortune afflicted the Jewish people on account of its failure to empathize with the sorrow of the *shekhinah*'s exile and to have pity on Jerusalem the desolate. In order to bring home the edict's horrors, he cites the admonition, from the depiction in Deuteronomy of the curses the Israelites will bear if they violate God's commands, that "your sons and daughters will be given over to another nation . . . and you will be powerless" (Deut. 28:32). In his words:

> We do not sense the sorrow of the Holy One Blessed Be He and His *shekhinah*. Therefore, He brought this sorrow upon us, namely, "your sons and daughters are given over to another nation." In other words, yesterday, you regarded your sons and daughters as a holy nation, dressed in Jewish garb, wrapped in a fringed garment, crowed with phylacteries, with side curls and beard, but in the space of an instant they are given over to another nation, in gentile garb, with shaved side curls and beard, and your eyes see it . . . and you are powerless to save them.[47]

He concludes: "Without doubt, it is the sparks of the tribulations of the Messiah."[48]

In considering the oppression of the Jews of Russia, his own land, Hillel of Kovno cautiously speaks of edicts in general, without specifying their nature. Sometimes, he argues again that the divine purpose of the harsh edicts is to stir the people to penance, so that the redemption of the Jewish people might ensue. In formulating that concept, he relies on a talmudic statement: "R. Eliezer says: If Israel repent, they will be redeemed; if not, they will not be redeemed. R. Joshua said to him: If they fail to repent they will not be redeemed? Rather, the Holy One Blessed Be He will establish for them a king whose edicts will be as harsh as Haman's, and Israel will repent and return to the right path."[49]

Hillel of Kovno attributes the same purpose to the edicts of his time: "For it is my opinion and understanding, and all with eyes in their heads will see, that the day on which God will attend to His people is near. . . . Then God will attend to the heavenly host, casting down the angel that torments us. That is to say, he will attend and command terrestrial kings to impose harsh and wicked edicts . . . as they [the sages] of blessed memory say, it is promised that there will rise up a king as harsh as Haman."[50] Continuing in the same vein, he concludes explicitly that the torments are "tribulations of the Messiah," which will be followed by the redemption: "The Holy One Blessed Be He prepares for them a king as harsh as Haman. . . . When the fury of that fire pours down in those oppressive times, there will be no day more accursed. . . . Without a doubt, it is the spark of the tribulations of the Messiah, . . . and when the fire of His rage subsides, our House of Splendor will be built, as it is said, 'by fire I will in the future rebuild it.' "[51]

Hillel of Kovno confidently ties the three elements together: repentance is an inevitable consequence of the harsh straits in which the Jewish people are living; the redemption without a doubt will follow it, "but repentance on account of fear should not be fled, when they oppress us through subjugation to worldly kingdoms, and all wealth is lost, may that be God's will, speedily and in our day; and each day we look forward to the time when we will cry out to the Lord our God."[52]

But it was not enough to view the oppressive decrees leveled against the nation of Israel as part of the historical redemptive process, and hope for the future could not suffice to ease the Jews' suffering. The present woes were too horrific to serve as a source of consolation by being part of a process that would turn out well. Yet, the Jews could do nothing concrete to ease their present lot. Subject as they were to edicts and persecutions, their only recourse was to spiritual action, such as fasting, praying at the graves of pious men and of ones' parents, and giving charity. Nevertheless, with the discovery of the Letters of the Clerks, we find that the Nobles of Vilna turned to Ẓevi Hirsch Lehren and asked him to make use of his access to the western European royal courts to generate international pressure on Nikolai I to revoke the edict.[53] But these efforts, for all their audacity, invoked no novel procedures. They were grounded in traditional Jewish concepts with respect to both their overall view of the circumstances and the practical possibility of confronting the difficulties.

The Persecutions and a Changed View of "Pressing for the End"

In the early nineteenth century, a change took place in the traditional concept held by groups identified with disciples of Rabbi Elijah, the Ga'on of Vilna. The change itself, no less than the traditional concept, was grounded in the fundamentals of Jewish belief, and it dealt with the relationship between Israel and the nations of the world.

On the traditional view, the Jews were bound by the Three Oaths that God had imposed to bear the burden of the Diaspora and to refrain from any effort to escape their situation. But the Cantonist Edict cast in stark relief the oaths' limiting condition, which forbids Israel from rebelling against the nations or striving to hasten its redemption only as long as the nations do not subjugate Israel to an unreasonable degree: that is, as long as they grant it autonomy and permit it to maintain its Judaism. The oppressive, anti-Jewish measures imposed by the Russian authorities were so extreme as to annul the force of the three-fold oath: the decrees did not just deny true religious autonomy to Jews; they were intended as a way to terminate Jewish existence. Accordingly, the Jews were freed of the prohibition against pressing for the End and "scaling the wall"; beyond that, they were obliged to stand up for their right to religious existence and to act to emerge from under the hand of those who threatened to wipe them from the face of the earth. To that end, it was permissible, fitting, and even obligatory to press for the End.[54]

This ideology is articulated in a letter sent in late 1830 by Israel of Shklov, a leader of the *kolel* (community organization) of the *Perushim* in Safed, to the Ten Tribes.[55] Because the troubles in which the Jewish people finds itself are too harsh to bear, he asks them to try to hasten the End, through abundant prayer and pleading before the Holy One Blessed Be He and by crying out and acting to stir the redemption: "Let them engage in much prayer and crying with their pure and holy souls; let them dress royally and enter the inner chamber before the King, the King of kings, the Holy One Blessed Be He, and in their awesome audiences in the holy sanctuaries, before and within, for the waters have reached the neck [cf. Ps. 69:2], and, if not for our sake, let Him act for His. . . . And may He remember our fathers Abraham, Isaac, and Jacob and have mercy and gather our exiles and build our holy and magnificent house."[56]

The Three Oaths forbade the special spiritual activity that the Ten Tribes were requested to undertake for the purpose of influencing God to change the depressed lot of the Jews, but the force of the prohibition on pressing for the End had expired. The new situation in which Israel found itself required, many came to believe, that it rend the heavens with its cries, for when the Torah was being desecrated by the gentiles and its survival was endangered, it became necessary to act for God's name.

The request to undertake spiritual activities for the purpose of pressing for the End, set in the context of the harsh circumstances in which the Jews of Russia found themselves at that time, can be understood on the basis of the ideological conception described above. What is less understandable is the need to resort to the Ten Tribes in this context. Why did Israel of Shklov, the head of the organization of the *Perushim* in Safed, pin all his hopes on the spiritual activity of the Ten Tribes and look specifically to them to undertake these actions? At first glance, it appears that he and the members of his group should enjoy a higher standing than the Ten Tribes with respect to spiritual activity; for while the image and location of the Ten Tribes remained shrouded in mystery, he himself, and the members of his group, were legatees of the Ga'on Rabbi Elijah; they resided in the holy Galilee, and they could engage in activities at the graves of the holy men—great rabbis of all generations—who are buried there. But it stands to reason that Israel of Shklov looked to the Ten Tribes because their image was tied to various aspects of the redemption. He suggests they were graced with a unique capacity to influence heavenly activity related to all manner of extreme circumstances in which Israel might find itself. As concrete examples, he cites two episodes in which Jews in difficult straits were helped by the Ten Tribes.[57] And, Israel of Shklov writes in his epistle, reports have recently been received about the discovery of traces of the Ten Tribes. To be sure, this was but a single report; still, it was enough to arouse the hope that there might now be a reasonable opportunity to establish contact with them. He writes that in 1829, emissaries from Safed went to Yemen and met a member of the tribe of Dan, who recounted to them the wonders of the Ten Tribes and their distinguished and marvelous status. Additional and precise details could not be obtained, however, for while he was speaking, the man mysteriously disappeared.[58]

The confluence of extraordinary events requiring radical explanation with something able to hint at that explanation tends to strengthen the belief that the explanation is, in fact, the one that is sought. In other words: the fact that persecution of Russian Jews during this period became so intense as to annul the ban on spiritual activity directed toward hastening the End coincided with the emergence of an opportunity to engage in just such activity by invoking the Ten Tribes, and that juxtaposition strengthened Israel of Shklov's belief that a decisive change in Israel's fate was at hand and that it was poised in the doorway to the messianic age.[59]

That and more: according to the sages of blessed memory, the very discovery of the Ten Tribes constitutes proof that Israel is at the threshold of redemption, for it allows for realization of the hoped-for process of gathering the exiles and returning dispersed Israel to its source:

> For that purpose, they relied on the words of our holy rabbis, the *tanna'im*,[60] who taught us . . . and, similarly, our master, the *tanna* R. Simeon bar Yoḥai [to whom authorship of the *Zohar* is traditionally ascribed] revealed to us in his holy *Zohar*, that at the time of the Footsteps of the Messiah, some of our brothers of the Ten Tribes will be discovered. . . . When in the future the Holy One Blessed Be He gathers Israel in, He will first gather the Tribe of Manasseh, . . . The Ten Tribes previously exiled beyond the River Sambatyon, whom the exiles of Judah and Benjamin are destined to join and bring back, so they may together attain the days of the Messiah and the life of the world-to-come.[61]

The Enlightened Rule of Muhammad Ali in the Land of Israel: A Sign of the Approaching Redemption

The Jews placed great messianic hopes in Muhammad Ali, who rebelled against the Ottoman authorities and ruled in the Land of Israel from 1832 to 1840. In contrast to Napoleon, whose expedition to the Land of Israel took no permanent root, Muhammad Ali's appearance produced a more enduring presence. He was involved with the Land, sympathetic to its Jewish inhabitants and their religious needs, and concerned about the Land's economic development and its residents' interest in security. The Jews who anticipated the redemption saw in his enlightened rule not a Muslim government but a European-Christian one, and, in reliance on the *Zohar* and the *midrashim*, they understood his appearance not merely as a change in sovereignty but as a reversal of religious-messianic significance.

According to the *Zohar*, the Muslims were granted sovereignty over the Land of Israel as a reward for observing the commandment of circumcision, and it is that merit of theirs that delays Israel's return to the Land and reestablishment of its sovereignty: "And the Children of Ishmael [i.e., the Arabs] are destined to rule over the Holy Land for an extended time, while it is empty and lacking perfection, and they will impede the Children of Israel's return to their place until the merit of the Children of Ishmael is recompensed."[62] Because a premature effort by the Jews to seize sovereignty over the Land from the Muslims might cause prosecution on high, the Holy One Blessed Be He, according to a complementary midrashic source, will bring about a Christian conquest of the Land from the Muslims, so that it will be the Christians from whom the Jews regain it: " 'And the swine'—that is Edom, 'for it does not chew the cud'—for another kingdom does not follow upon it. And why is it called the swine [*ḥazir*]? Because it returns [*meḥazeret*] the crown to its owners, as it is written, 'Saviors will ascend Mount Zion to judge the Mountain of Esau [i.e, Edom], and sovereignty will be the Lord's (Obad. 1:21)."[63]

Of course, there was a contradiction between the Muslim faith of Muhammad Ali as an individual and his enlightened "Christian-style" regime,[64] but that did not prevent believing Jews from ascribing religious-messianic meaning to the change in government in the Land of Israel. Echoes of that concept can be heard in the writings of Ẓevi Hirsch Lehren:

> His exalted majesty judged well, for it is good for the people of the Land of Israel to live under the Egyptian king. . . . But days will come when they will speak of what God has commanded, for it is not a simple thing in our eyes, and there is room here to question whether the aforesaid king is, in fact, Ishmaelite, in which case there is no ignoring the words of the holy *Zohar* that because of the request of Abraham our father, peace be upon him, that "if only Ishmael live" [Gen. 17:18], our Holy Land was given to him. But if he [Muhammad Ali] is not Ishmaelite, a doorway of hope is opened that he has come only to clear the way to the kingship of Israel.[65]

Muhammad Ali authorized the Jews to repair their synagogues, a step seen by many Jews as signifying the start of the redemption. Lehren expresses gratitude for the news and extends greetings: "May God augment His kindness to his nation and speedily enable us to sense the true salvation and complete redemption, for we now have great need for it."[66]

Gentiles living in the Land of Israel report in a similar vein on the effects of these changes with respect to religious ceremonies. According to them, the Jews saw this revolutionary phenomenon as messianic in and of itself, for only a short while earlier, under the previous regime, a Jewish community official nearly lost his life while trying to carry out minor repairs at the synagogue, which was now being renovated. The Jews, of course, still believed the Messiah would come miraculously; yet when they compared their present situation with what preceded it, they saw the change itself as proof of the Messiah's footsteps.[67]

It appears that the rule of Muhammad Ali, even more than the other events described above, was seen by Jews as a sign that the redemption was near. In contrast to the various negative developments, understood to be "tribulations of the Messiah," Muhammad Ali's enlightened rule in the Land of Israel was not a passing event but a permanent state of affairs. The change in government represented a fundamental change in circumstances, and the new situation appeared to be gaining stability. An echo of the strong sense that this change was substantive and religiously significant in a messianic sense can be found in the letters of Eliezer Bregman. On 2 March 1835, he writes from Jerusalem:

> And the Ishmaelite gentiles are subjugated and greatly cast down, and the Jews, in contradistinction, especially the Ashkenazim, are, with the help of God, may He be blessed, raised to a high level. . . . And from reliable people it is heard that not in a long while (perhaps not since the time of our holy rabbi [R. Judah the Prince, late second to early third century C.E.]) have the Jews in the Land of Israel experienced, blessed be God, such great tranquility. It has reached the point where it reasonable to say that with supernal grace the beginning of the redemption has already arrived, and speedily and in our days may the Redeemer come to Zion.[68]

In an ensuing letter, Bregman writes: "In any event, the laws of the present king are very good, with the help of God, for the children of His people, so it may be said without exaggeration that through supernal grace, the beginning of the future redemption has already arrived, may it come speedily and in our days."[69]

The ideas expressed here flow not only from the situation and events but, primarily, from direct experience of developments in Jerusalem—the place where the redemption of Israel is to take shape. It is that which makes these expressions of faith in imminent redemption as powerful as they are.

Appendix: A Text on Messianism

These nine lines translated below constitute the only Jewish source describing the great fire at the Church of the Holy Sepulcher in Jerusalem on 12 October 1808 (Hoshana Rabba 5569). The fire, which destroyed the church structure and weakened its great dome, was taken by the Jews as a sign that the time was "close to the coming of our righteous Messiah." Earlier fires at the Church of the Sepulcher had likewise aroused messianic hopes, and this was no exception. The nine lines are written on the inside cover of the book *Minḥat Ya'aqov* (Polonnoye, 1802), acquired at an unknown time by the rabbi of Altona, Jacob Etlinger. My thanks to Judah Horowitz for providing me the photocopy of the source and allowing its publication. (The translation is by the translator of this volume.)

> A great event that took place in the holy city of Jerusalem (may it be built and established speedily and in our day), for the rabbi R. Naḥum of Zamost came to us from Jerusalem and told us that on the day of Hoshana [Rabba] of the year 5569 [1808], may it be blessed, before dawn, a fire descended from Heaven and the appalling house of idolatry, the prime source of impurity, was destroyed, [and it was]

a wonder or by means of magic or by means of wisdom, for it itself gave forth fire, and God judged it by fire, and several of their houses were burned along with several priests and treasures of kings and emperors that had been there from ancient times, [though] they maintained guards there, about sixty men, never stopping by day or night. And the cloister was made of marble, with a roof of iron, but it nevertheless was burned—destroyed, destroyed to its very foundation—and was left dust and ashes. And for the Jews, there was light and joy, and they all went up on the rooftops to rejoice, for they also had a tradition from the people of Jerusalem that when the foregoing impurity was burned, the time of our righteous Messiah's coming would be near. And they wrote to the Sultan [requesting permission] to rebuild its ruins, and he replied that because He had shown from the heavens His great fire, and He had light in Zion, it was not possible to rebuild it while we in the Holy Congregation of Tiberias still had among us worry over the land. And bless God that for the Jews, there was comfort and relief.

2

Belief in 5600 (1840) as the Year of Redemption

I am the man who has seen the world, and it is all chaos and without form. . . . Some of the people dwelling on it have sought to reckon [the time for] our redemption and the deliverance of our souls in many ways on the basis of initial letters of words, final letters of words, acronyms, numerical values of letters, various calculations and combination after combination to purify, clarify, and brighten the time of the End of Days.

El'azar N. David, *Ahavat David*

Talmudic and Kabbalistic Sources for the Belief in the Year 5600

The historical background for the early-nineteenth-century messianic awakening varied from place to place. It was not, in any event, the sole factor responsible for the awakening and certainly not the decisive one. Logic suggests that if different causes bring about similar effects in places that differ in their political environments and attitudes toward the Jews, some other common denominator, immanent and spiritual in its nature, must be in play. Indeed, the messianic awakening throughout the Jewish world during this period drew primarily on two sources, one talmudic and one derived from the *Zohar*. These sources set the redemption not at some inchoate future time but at a specifically defined date: A.M. 5600. The sources do not make the time of redemption contingent on historical events or other circumstances; rather, they determine it categorically.

These sources were of enormous credibility for religious Jews. The words of the Talmud, as part of the Oral Torah, had determined the beliefs and opinions of the Jewish nation from time immemorial, and they continue to do so among wide circles of Jews to this day. The *Zohar* similarly possessed an aura of sanctity, and what it said or hinted at was regarded in those circles as actual prophecy.

The talmudic source is the statement of R. Dosa in tractate *Sanhedrin* (99a):

> "Rejoice greatly, daughter of Zion; raise your sound, daughter of Jerusalem; behold, your king comes to you, righteous and redeemed is he, yet poor and riding on a donkey" (Zech. 9:9). . . . R. Eliezer says, the days of the Messiah will be forty years. . . . R. Dosa says four hundred years, for it says in one place, "And they will work them and torment them four hundred years" (Gen. 15:13), and it says elsewhere "Cause us to rejoice for as long as we were tormented, for the years we experienced evil" (Ps. 90:15).

In other words, given that the world will endure six thousand years,[1] the days of the Messiah will begin four hundred years earlier, in 5600 (1840).

The kabbalistic source is a passage in the *Zohar* on the Torah portion *Vayeira*, sec. 117:

> When the sixth millennium [of creation] will arrive, after six hundred years of the sixth millennium the gates of wisdom above and the founts of wisdom below will open; and your [biblical] sign for this is 'In the six hundredth [year] of Noah's life' [cf. Gen. 7:11, referring to the opening of the fountains below and the sluices above as the flood began] . . . and the Holy One Blessed Be He will raise up the congregation of Israel from the dust of exile and remember her.[2]

To be sure, other passages in the *Zohar* and in the *midrashim* ascribe the ability to hasten the redemption to various extraordinary events in human history; but these two mutually reinforcing sources determine that the world is already situated at the doorway to the messianic age, even without any involvement of external historical events. Accordingly, there is no doubt that these passages decisively influenced the belief of the pious Jew, who tended to see the various historical events as bearing out his basic messianic faith.

Until the recent discovery of new historical sources, it was mainly Judah Ḥai Alcalay who was known to have expected the redemption in the year 5600. That belief was the basis for Alcalay's idea of the Messiah, and it formed the cornerstone of his later concept, based on messianist activism. In his writings, Alcalay refers dozens of times to 5600 as the year of redemption. He says, for example: " 'And I will remember for them the covenant with the ancients' [Lev. 26:45]. Covenant [*berit,* spelled *b-r-y-t*] is equivalent [in the numerical value of its letters] to twelve [*y-b*] and six hundred [*t-r*]; that is, if they are deserving and I appoint for them twelve tribes, the redemption can come in 600 [that is, 5600, years typically being represented without the thousands figure]."[3] And elsewhere: "If we perform the will of the Holy One Blessed Be He, we weaken the power of the Satan . . . and the redemption will come at the end of days, which is 5600."[4]

At several points in his writings, Alcalay notes that the belief in the year 5600 is widely held; he writes, for example: "The year 5600, commonly spoken of for many years, in reliance on the statement of R. Dosa."[5] And, elsewhere: "Now it has become clear, my brethren, that this 5600, which is spoken of by everyone, is true and settled."[6] In commenting on the Jews of western Europe in his booklet *Qol Qorei* (1848), he says: "Their eyes were raised toward the year 5600, and they had support from the holy *Zohar, Parashat Vayeira*. . . . And all the signs and wonders mentioned in the holy *Zohar* . . . they would anticipate every day."[7] On the basis of these passages, Jacob Katz determined that "in all the Balkan lands, and so, too, in all the lands of eastern Europe, the opinion was widespread that the approaching year 5600 was the year of redemption."[8] But Alcalay's references to the extent of the belief in 5600 were doubted, for they were unsupported by primary sources; his account was at most that of an individual, demonstrating no belief except his own. His viewpoint was regarded as idiosyncratic, just like the claim of Ẓevi Hirsch Kalisher, "his twin brother," that the redemption would come in the wake of sacrifices being brought on the Temple Mount.[9]

But newly discovered contemporary sources confirm that 5600 as the year of redemption was not merely one individual's idiosyncratic belief. As will be shown below, the references to the wide range of the belief in 5600 are grounded in fact, and, beyond that, we have here something greater still—a clear messianist awakening, a mass movement that encompassed a large number of people throughout the Jewish world in both East and West, in Europe and in Asia. Alcalay himself did not realize the full extent of the belief. He also was unaware, and accordingly did not mention, that the belief in 5600 as the year of redemption brought about the immigration of thousands of Jews to the Land of Israel in the early nineteenth century and was the dominant motive for *aliyah* throughout that period.

Belief in 5600 in Persia and Kurdistan

That the belief in 5600 extended to the Jewish Diaspora in Persia and Kurdistan is evident from a pamphlet entitled *Qol Mevasser* (A Voice Brings Tidings),[10] written by Matthias ben Samuel Mizraḥi [or "ha-Kohen"], a native of Shiru'an in northern Persia.[11] The pamphlet, which is not a unitary composition, lacks continuity of ideas and logical structure. It is a collage of the author's visions and reflections reduced to writing over a period of years; accordingly, it is quite repetitious.

The author has a strong inner sense of being destined to fulfill a heavenly mission. That sense is fed, he says, by periodic dreams in which he envisions himself being dispatched on such a mission: "For the dream speaks with me mouth to mouth,"[12] and "As I have heard beyond the veil."[13] He sees himself as the bearer of a divine charge—to disseminate the belief in the approaching arrival of the redemption and to take steps to advance it: "In my dream on . . . the tenth of the month of Nisan, at the time of *tiqqun ḥaẓot*, I heard them say of me 'You will arise and have pity on Zion, for it is the time to be gracious to her, the time has come' [Ps. 102:14]."[14] On another occasion he was told in a dream: " 'Awake, awake, for your light has come' [Isa. 51:17, 60:1], and at this verse I awakened several times and I heard them saying of me, 'You will arise; speak to them.' "[15] And elsewhere he tells of being addressed as follows: "Know that you are my first-born son, for you have come to this lower world only to learn and teach the mystery of determining leap years, for that work will be completed only by you."[16]

The regular procedures for declaring leap years bear not only on the proper identification of sabbatical and jubilee years but also on the enumeration of years for purposes of calculating the End. Against this background, the author sees himself as an emissary charged with disseminating both the process for declaring leap years and the time of the End, which depends on it. Indeed, Matthias never tires of preaching the belief that the redemption will commence soon, in the year 5600, and he strives in his writings to cite numerous sources on which that belief can be grounded. Moreover, he does not rest content with the dissemination of his ideas; like one destined to fulfill a mission, he urges the community of believers to do more than passively await the redemption. He calls on them to undertake activities that have the capacity to hasten the redemption and ensure its realization. For example, he presses the traditional demand for repentance, for it can arouse the compassionate feelings of the Holy One Blessed Be He: "Let each man help his fellow so as to climb the ladder of repentance, and through the weeping they will come to cry, and a crying child will immediately be pitied, and the King Messiah will be revealed to you, together with Moses and Elijah, called the Tishbite."[17] Moreover, in order to raise the *shekhinah* from her dust, he demands strict observance of the *tiqqun ḥaẓot* custom established by the kabbalists: "At six hundred years into the sixth millennium, there will be the complete redemption . . . and this mystery requires raising the *shekhinah* from the deep pit to the high rooftop. . . . It is necessary to raise her by means of good deeds, to awaken at the middle of the night and perform *tiqqun ḥaẓot*."[18]

Matthias does not impose these demands only on others. He reports being commanded, in one of his visions, to arise and journey to Safed: "And I saw in a dream that they were saying of me with great force, why are you sleeping here? Arise and go immediately to Safed (may it be built and established speedily and in our days, amen)."[19] It is fair to assume the author's familiarity with the tradition that the redemption will begin in Safed.[20] There is no proof that he fulfilled his vow and emigrated to the Land of Israel, but it is significant that he intended to emigrate to Safed as a step that would advance the redemption or give concrete expression to his faith that the redemption would originate there.

Matthias recounts that his harsh living conditions kept him from studying Torah in an orderly way: "I never studied in the manner of school children; rather, I ran hither and yon and from city to city. . . . I learned from my teachers only the Pentateuch and the Prophets; and having gone into exile these twenty-four years, I forgot even that."[21] Nevertheless, it is apparent that he was well versed in the allusions underlying the belief in 5600 as the year of redemption; he knew of R. Isaac Luria ("the Ari"; a leading kabbalist in Safed) and his life[22]; and he was familiar with kabbalistic literature. He bases his remarks on the *Zohar,* on *Sefer ha-Yeẓirah,* and on *Idra Rabba* and *Idra Zuta,*[23] but he also attempts to prove the belief in 5600 through original homiletics. For example, he knows of the *Zohar*'s comments in *Parashat Vayeira* 117, but he mentions it only as background: " 'And they bowed down to my sheaf' [Gen. 37:7]—this refers to the future, when the time comes for the kingdom of the House of David, in [5]600; then all the kingdoms will come and bow to the King Messiah, as alluded to by the [5]600 of Noah."[24] He writes further on the same subject: "It alludes to the six hundred [years] of the sixth millennium, when the sons of Moses are revealed. . . . When there remain four hundred years of the sixth millennium, the world will be restored to its original might . . . and the King Messiah will be revealed to you, together with Moses and Elijah, called the Tishbite."[25]

In his efforts to establish a basis for believing that the redemption will occur in the six-hundredth year of the sixth millennium, Matthias makes extensive use of *notariqon* (acronyms and wordplay) and *gematria* (the drawing of inferences from the numerical values of words). For example, on the verse "the people saw that Moses tarried [*boshesh,* spelled *b-sh-sh*] [in descending from Sinai; Exod. 32:1]," he comments: "When is the time of wonders? When there remain four hundred years of the sixth millennium. . . . Do not read *boshesh;* rather, read *be-shesh,* at six hundred (years), Moses will be revealed."[26] Elsewhere he says: "At six hundred [years] of the sixth millennium, the full redemption will take place; accordingly, the letter *waw* was given as a sign to Jacob, and to no other."[27] The episode of crossing the River Yabboq, in which Esau's angel wrestles with Jacob,[28] likewise forms a peg on which to hang a calculation of the End: "The secret of the 112 Jubilee cycles from the creation of the world to the year six hundred of the sixth millennium."[29] And the author finds further support for the belief in the significance of the year 5600 in a variety of verses, such as "It alludes to six hundred of the sixth millennium, and that is, 'it came the turn [*tor,* spelled *t-r* = 600] of Esther, daughter of Aviḥayil' [Esth. 2:15]"[30] and "And this is a sign: 'today the world was born [*harat,* spelled *h-r-t* = 5,600].' "[31] He sees yet another hint in the name of the King Messiah mentioned in Isa. 9:5—"Then peace will come to us, as hinted at by '*sar shalom* [prince of peace],' the Messiah's name—*sar shalom,* at six hundred."[32]

To broaden the base for his argument, the author bends verses at will. He treats King David and King Saul interchangeably in order to draw a parallel between the term *qeẓ ha-yamin* (the End of Days) and *ben ha-yemini* (the Benjaminite): "How long will Rachel weep for her children [cf. Jer. 31:15]? Until six hundred in the sixth millennium . . . until 5600, when immediately there will be revealed to them the son of Qish the Benjaminite [King Saul, of the tribe of Benjamin, one of Rachel's two sons] and that will be the End of Days."[33]

The *gematriot* that Matthias devises on his own are fairly simple. When he counts years, for example, every word or phrase bearing possible messianic significance becomes fair game. Accordingly, he uses the phrase *ḥevlei mashiaḥ* (tribulations [birth pangs] of the Messiah, spelled *ḥ-b-l-y m-sh-y-ḥ*) as warrant for fifty years, relying on the numerical value of ***ḥ-b-l-y*** *m-sh-y-ḥ;* elsewhere, he uses it as a basis for forty-eight years, relying on the numerical value of the acronym ***ḥ****-b-l-y* ***m****-sh-y-ḥ*.[34] In 5574 (1814), he associates the twenty-six years remaining until 5600 with the numerical value of the letters in the Tetragrammaton[35] and the 426 years remaining until the end of the sixth millennium with the numerical value of "they followed" (*tukku,* spelled *t-k-w*) in "they followed in your footsteps" (Deut. 33:3).[36]

Matthias began to record his visions and ideas in writing in 1802,[37] and he intended to complete the composition in 5590 (1830): "And to your holy mountain you will gather the letters in 5590."[38] In planning to complete the pamphlet ten years in advance of 5600, he seems to have had in mind a latent allusion to the beginning of the End in the letters representing that year. These ten years are the doorway to the Messianic Era, which would begin in 5600: "There remain ten years between 5590 and 5600, between sacred and profane."[39] His view that the year 5590 would be the opening of the Messianic Era apparently is based on the numerical value of sacred (*qadosh,* spelled *q-d-w-sh*), 410. In the context of the world's six-thousand-year existence, the Messianic epoch (the sacred) would last 410 years, and it follows that the year 5590 is the start of the redemption.[40]

Because of the importance of 5590, Matthias directed his *gematriot* to that year as well; he did so yearly from the time he began to compose the essay. In 1802 (5562), for example, he referred to the verse: "He told His people of the might of his deeds" (Ps. 111:6); the numerical value of "might" (*koaḥ,* spelled *k-ḥ*) is twenty-eight; added to 5562 it equals 5590. The author no doubt pursued *gematriot* and acronyms alluding to the year in order to reinforce his personal faith in the significance of 5600 and to impress it firmly on his heart and those of his readers—particularly given his sense of bearing a heavenly mission to disseminate belief in the approaching redemption. Because of the "torments of Exile," Matthias wandered from place to place and from community to community, and it is fair to assume that he was not universally popular with the communal leadership. Still, his wanderings gave him the opportunity to spread his ideas widely, and, as an itinerant prayer leader, he may also have had the occasion to address the worshippers.

That Matthias in fact disseminated his views in writing is demonstrated by the existence of another of his manuscripts, *Ḥishuvei Qeẓ,* now in the Israel National Library.[41] The manuscript is incomplete; only a few pages survive. *Ḥishuvei Qeẓ* resembles *Qol Mevasser* in its content but is not identical; it includes ideas that do not appear in *Qol Mevasser,* showing that we have here not a fully wrought manuscript as much as notes of visions that were assembled into a pamphlet.

Moreover, the author did not work on his own. He says that his two brothers assisted him, and he speaks of the three of them as emissaries to reveal the mysteries of the redemption: " 'As in the days when you departed the land of Egypt' [Micah 7:15], Aaron, Ḥur, Joshua, and Moses are an acronym for 'brothers.' [The first letters of *Aharon, Ḥur, Yehoshu'a,* and *Mosheh* form the Hebrew word *aḥim,* brothers.] He revealed the latter to us openly; now, in our generation, he alludes to two messiahs."[42] Elsewhere he says: "One from the city—that is Moses . . . and two of a family—it alludes to two messiahs, hinted at in the wording 'Mizraḥi brothers.' "[43] Each of the brothers was active in a different city. Matthias himself worked in Qazbin; his older brother Abraham, who greatly influenced him,[44] worked in Gil'an[45]; and his younger brother Jacob worked in Shiru'an.[46] But the geographic range of his ideas appears to have been wider, reaching beyond the confines of northern Persia. In his pamphlet, he mentions the distant places he visited. Late in 1811, he reached the lands of Kurdistan and the city of Salm'az;[47] elsewhere he notes that in 5572 (1811–1812) he visited Basra, in Iraq;[48] and in 1830, he evidently visited the city of Sina.[49] In 1815, he and his brother Abraham were in Teheran, at the royal court, on an undisclosed mission; in 1816, he was in the Persian city of Qubiẓ[50] and his own city of Qazbin;[51] in 1830, he was "the holy congregation of Ẓuram, among the cities of Gorgustan;[52] and in 1831, he visited Qushtantina (Istanbul).[53] The author does not always explain the reason for his wanderings. He occasionally attributes them to the travail of the Exile or the need to flee creditors,[54] but he regards the cause of his wanderings as far less significant than their consequence, which is the opportunity to address new audiences and use his discourses to instill ideas of the End: " 'For the matter has been decreed by God' [Gen. 24:50]."[55]

Were the Jewish communities in these regions prepared to absorb and adopt this concrete messianic faith? Were they equipped to deal with these tidings as truth, as part of their religious understanding? Apparently, they were. Only a soil saturated with the study of Kabbalah and the *Zohar* could produce "prophetic" figures such as Matthias and his brothers. Moreover, it must be recalled that several messianic sources within the tradition read that the start of the redemption depends, among other things, on the discovery of the Ten Tribes, whose hidden location is to be found somewhere in the East. That notion was ubiquitous in the region and heightened the spiritual alertness with which the Tribes' appearance was awaited. In this part of the world, locating the Ten Tribes was no mere academic matter; periodically, the region was visited by travelers who had actually set out to find them. These quests regularly revived the question and maintained interest in it. The embers of belief in the redemption were fanned as well by rabbinic emissaries from the Land of Israel who would reach these out-of-the-way places.[56]

Matthias's pamphlet provides an extended description of the people of the Shiru'an community, from which it is plain that the seeds of belief in the year 5600 were not sown on virgin soil. The community, he tells, numbered sixty families, encompassing about fifty to sixty schoolchildren. Its members lived an intensely religious life, observing the 613 commandments punctiliously and supplementing them with kabbalistic customs such as the recitation of *tiqqun ḥaẓot.* Following the Sabbath dinner they would study *gemara,* the *Zohar,* the

Bible commentaries of Naḥmanides, Ibn Ezra, and *Qav ha-Yashar* or other books such as *Shefa Tal, Ma'aseh Rav, Oẓerot Ḥayyim, Eẓ Ḥayyim, Emeq ha-Melekh, Pardes Rimmonim,* and *Miqdash Melekh.*[57] According to Matthias, the residents of his own town did the same. That said, it should be noted that the author refers to variations in the communities' degrees of religious intensity, particularly between the communities of northern Persia and those of Kurdistan.[58] But that does not detract from the force of messianic beliefs in all the communities he visited.

Taking account of the full array of pertinent factors, we cannot escape the conclusion that the belief in 5600 played an important part in the spiritual lives of the Jews of northern Persia and Kurdistan. A primary factor was Matthias's influence and energy, for he saw himself as God's emissary to disseminate the belief in 5600. His eagerness to search out proofs and authority for this belief, his devotion to the issue, and his active efforts to disseminate the tidings both in writing and orally over the course of many years all made him a crucial figure. The title of his pamphlet—*Qol Mevasser* (A Voice Brings Tidings)—is itself evidence of his self-perception and goals, as are the existence of an additional manuscript and, in particular, the extent of the geographic area over which he and his brothers ranged. A second factor was the substantial degree to which Jewish communities in the region were open to the receipt of messianic notions. Given their considerable involvement with the *Zohar* and other kabbalistic books such as *Emeq ha-Melekh* and *Miqdash Melekh,* the belief in the year 5600 was not seen as exceptional; and it was in the eastern lands, more than anywhere else, that seekers of the Ten Tribes were active. A third factor is the parallel and supplementary evidence for the belief in 5600 provided by the reports of Christian missionaries active among the Jews in these regions. These accounts, to be considered further below, reinforce and confirm the accounts in Jewish sources.

End-reckonings could already be found as part of the mystical teachings in the talmudic and midrashic literature, but engaging in them was not generally accepted, lest the reckonings be proven false. The audacity to break that taboo could be mustered only in a period of messianic awakening, when the subject had become immediately pertinent. Accordingly, engaging in End-reckoning and in fixing the time of the redemption—and, even more, reducing those matters to writing—constitute unparalleled proof of how seriously the matter was taken and of its being so immediate that the masses saw its realization as imminent. In turn, the End-reckonings themselves reinforced the general sense that the widely anticipated time was at hand.

Belief in 5600 in Morocco and the Land of Israel

A manuscript from Titu'an, Morocco, contains a collection of texts, two of which refer to the approaching year of redemption. The two sources are shrouded in mystery, both having reached the writer via oral accounts. The rumors described in both texts originated in the Land of Israel, which could enhance their importance and reliability in the reader's eyes.

One text begins with a description of its Land of Israel provenance: "In the year 5590, there was found in the Land of Israel, may it be built and established speedily in our days, an inscription written in gold on stone."[59] The mysterious details of the inscription's discovery afford its content a superhuman aspect; it describes a divine cosmological plan for the stages of redemption that are to unfold between the years 5590 and 5598 (1830–1838). According to the plan, Israel plays an entirely passive role in the redemption process; the active portion has an apocalyptic quality. It says:

> 5590—The memory of the children of Israel will awaken [the Hebrew word has the same spelling as the representation of the year, *t-q-ẓ*]; there will be wars in three lands: Africa and Italy and France.
> 5591—Fiardo [an unknown reference] will arise in Rome as in [unknown abbreviation].
> 5592—There will be great wars throughout the world.
> 5593—All will be mixed up with one another.
> 5594—Thunder and rage and darkness and gloom will occur throughout the world.
> 5595—The three aforesaid lands will be burned, and Rome and its environs will be turned to blood.
> 5596—Gog and Magog will arrive.
> 5597—The entire world will recognize [unknown abbreviation] of the King of the world, the Holy One Blessed Be He.
> 5598—He will gather his community and God will be King over the entire world, etc.
>
> And this was told to me by a certain Jew from the city of Arbat, may God protect it, in the year "enter its gates with thanks" [Ps. 100:4; marked letters in the Hebrew have a numerical value indicating 5595] here in Tanja, may God protect it.[60]

That the rumor of the divine redemptive plan was transmitted orally all the way along the Mediterranean coast from the Land of Israel to Arbat and Titu'an says much about the story's wide geographic range.

The second source in the manuscript from Morocco likewise deals with a supernatural event, one that took place at the Jewish people's holiest site—the Temple Mount. Central to the story, which took place in 1835, is a description of a divine revelation in which a voice from within the Holy of Holies declares the news that the redemption will take place in two years:

> We heard a rumor from a certain scholar who passed our way, named R. Abraham Isho, may God protect and redeem him, in the year "whom I held from the ends of the earth" [Isa. 41:9; marked letters in the Hebrew have a numerical value indicating 5596

> (1836)], here in Tanja, may God protect it. Namely, that on the New Moon of Tammuz 5595 [28 June 1835] the people of Jerusalem saw at the Temple something like a candelabrum of gold and of silver, but they did not sense it[s significance]. The next day, they looked and saw something similar, but they failed to see the truth of the matter. On the third day, the gatekeepers heard a noise going forth from the Ark's foundation stone, and they wanted to enter but could not, and from a distance they saw that they had seen truly on the first two days. In addition, they saw the image of Jews reading [the *shema'*] and praying there. They went and told the king. The king then came with his officers to observe the matter; they looked carefully, and they saw that what had been said was true. What did the king do? He called in the magicians, who saw by means of their practices that a voice was going forth from the foundation stone saying in two years, the savior of the Jews will be in Zion. And the Jews living in the Land of Israel likewise heard a voice going forth from the Temple saying, in two years, God will be King, etc. Completed.[61]

Three accounts paralleling this source appear in historical documents of a very different nature—a fact that shows the story to have spread over a wide area. One account appears in the diary entry of the apostate missionary F. C. Ewald for 11 January 1836. Ewald reports from Tunis on a rumor that reached there from Jerusalem via Oran (Algeria). When he inquired into the excitement generated by the rumor, he was told that a letter had been received at the home of one of the chief rabbis in Tunis from a rabbi in Oran, based on information the latter had received from Jerusalem, telling that the sounds of an earthquake had been heard in the mosque built on the ruins of Solomon's Temple. The Muslims who went in to see where the sound was coming from fell on their faces and died. Others who came after them met the same end. Afterward, the Jews were summoned, and when they entered, they heard a voice saying, "Repent, House of Israel, for in two years the Messiah will come."[62] Ewald adds that the Jews there were filled with joy and believed that their redemption was at hand; he concludes the entry with the hope that the will of God be so.

A second account was committed to writing in the Land of Israel, nearer the site of the event, so it can be assumed to be freer of the embellishments that naturally accrue to reports of this sort, particularly in an age suffused with messianic expectations. This version of the story lacks the words uttered by the prophetic voice, but it has other historical details that the writer ties to the supernatural event—specifically, the authorization given the Jews to renovate the Sefardic synagogue in Jerusalem. The writer, Joseph Mansfeld, tells his relative in Kalish that the Sefardim recently dispatched rabbinic emissaries from the Land of Israel to the West to raise funds for construction, an effort that was to be completed in time for the Passover festival. He describes the event as follows:

> A wondrous event known for certain to have transpired in Jerusalem on the Sabbath night before the festival of Shavuot in the year 5595

> [1835] [should be 5594 (1834)] at the most sanctified place, the place where, in past times, they saw the foundation stone, where the Muslims have built a great mosque. . . . On the aforesaid Sabbath night, the watchman heard the sound of an earthquake and a great cry from within the mosque. The watchman began to beat a drum as an alarm calling the entire brigade guarding the mosque to assemble, and when they had gathered, they opened the mosque and heard from within the sound of a mighty and terrible earthquake, so much so that the soldiers fled for their lives in fear. They told of having seen the image of a candelabrum of fire above the site of the Temple. A reliable person in Jerusalem told me that he, too, had seen the fire, though not in the form of a candelabrum but in the image of a great comet. After a few weeks, the pasha summoned the leaders of the Sefardim and authorized them to build a synagogue in Jerusalem, for since Nebuchadnezzar's destruction of Jerusalem, the Jews had been barred from building a synagogue. That edict was observed until today . . . but now, with the cancellation of Nebuchadnezzar's edict, the Sefardim immediately dispatched emissaries to Babylonia, Egypt, and all their regions . . . to gather money for the construction of a synagogue in Jerusalem.[63]

A third parallel account can be found between the lines of a letter from Sila Bregman to her parents. The letter bears the date 20 Iyyar 5595 (19 May 1835)—earlier than "the Sabbath night before the festival of Shavuot in the year 5595," as Joseph of Anisfeld puts it, thereby demonstrating that the event at issue had occurred in the previous year, 1834. Its account is based on word of mouth, not on first-hand observation, even though it was written in Jerusalem, where the events took place. Sila Bregman writes: "The Turks say thus, that a certain stone, at the site of the Temple's Holy of Holies, which had always floated in the air, fell to the ground—and that is a sign of the coming of the Messiah."[64]

The historical kernel of these three accounts seems associated with two events: the earthquake that befell Jerusalem on 25 May 1834 and went on for some three days; and the *fellahin* rebellion and its suppression by Ibrahim Pasha, which took place around the same time and entailed the use of cannon. Echoes of these events are to be heard in a letter to Ẓevi Hirsch Lehren from the heads of the community organization of the *Perushim* in Jerusalem: "On the sixteenth day of the preceding month of Iyyar, a horrific event occurred here in the holy city, and the ground raged and shook, and the beams moved, and most of the houses here were damaged, some of them destroyed and collapsing. . . . And blessed be He Whose kindnesses never end, even with respect to another casualty that took place through the wickedness of the villagers who rebelled against their king, the king of Egypt."[65] The Greek monk Spyridon reports that several churches were severely damaged by the earthquake,[66] and John Nicolayson's diary tells that part of the Temple Mount's inner wall, adjacent to the mosque, also was damaged.[67]

In the aftermath of all this, Ibrahim Pasha allowed the Christians to repair the damaged churches, and, according to Spyridon's account, he likewise granted the Sefardic Jews permission to repair their four rickety synagogues. The Jews saw that grant of authority as an extraordinary, logically inexplicable event, for over the course of hundreds of years, they had been forbidden to make even minor repairs to the synagogues in Jerusalem. This exceptional event provided fertile ground for the growth of wonder-stories and messianic embellishments of the episode. In sum, it appears that the stories in the two primary sources, transmitted via letters or rabbinic emissaries all the way to Morocco, were enhanced with a messianic aura in order to augment or corroborate the messianic tension.

While the manuscript from Titu'an speaks of a "divine program" disseminated in various versions among groups of Jews in North Africa, an entirely different source describes the existence of a belief in 5600 among Jews of North African origin living in the Land of Israel. The document, a manuscript known as *Pi Mosheh* (The Mouth of Moses), was composed in Jerusalem in the latter half of 1840 (i.e., toward the end of 5600) by Moses son of Jacob Turgeman, the leader of the Mughrabi Jews in Jerusalem during the 1840s.[68] The unpolished wording, the repetitions, and the various formulations of the introductory remarks show the author's spiritual turmoil. That alone shows we have here not some merely academic treatment but a manuscript reflecting the controversies raised by the belief in 5600.

The author deals with End-reckonings, but underlying his calculations is the belief in 5600. On the surface, it seems odd to deal with the question during the course of that very year; but when we consider the author's motives, we see that he was alarmed by the community's absolute, uncompromising belief that 5600 would be a year of extreme, historic upheaval, of "to be or not to be"—that is, if the Messiah comes, all well and good; if not, we will accept Jesus as Messiah—and saw the risk that the belief embodied more danger than blessing. He expresses that concern several times in the composition: "I heard the calumny of many who disparage the End in the Zohar . . . saying that if the Messiah fails to come in the year 5600 . . . he will never come, and they will leave the community. . . . There is an obligation to bring back those who go astray."[69] Elsewhere, he states explicitly: "I heard the calumny of many . . . that if the Messiah does not come in 5600, he will never come, . . . and some of them left the community for the Christian religion."[70] All this suggests not only a widely shared belief that the Messiah would come in the year 5600 but also the dependence on that belief, for many, of their Judaism itself.

As leader of the Mughrabis, Moses Turgeman felt a sense of responsibility for his community. He attempts to discharge the dangerous tension and instill a new meaning into the concrete messianic belief:

> To disabuse those who err with respect to the End-reckoning mentioned in the *Zohar, Parashat Vayeira* . . . who take the view that the End in the Zohar is the year 5600 and if he fails to come at his time, he is a fraud, and faith is lost. . . . And I, when I heard this, I

> stood trembling and my stomach roiled, and I girded my loins like a man to free our people of this pitfall . . . so they would not be ensnared in a place where God's name is desecrated . . . and would not take heed of falsehoods ([spelled *sh-q-r,* equivalent in value to] 5600) concerning the End that they themselves fabricated on the basis of their error in understanding the foregoing words of the *Zohar.*[71]

He recognized the gravity of his effort to reinterpret the belief in 5600: "I am not unaware of my limited worth . . . for I am slow of speech and slow of tongue [cf. Exod. 4:10]."[72] But the purpose for which he writes sanctifies the act: "For I will not forbear to speak. . . . It is obligatory to restore those who err . . . so that this not be a stumbling block for them . . . in that they act defiantly with regard to the Torah, perverting the texts for us in accordance with the falsehood of 5600."[73]

This sort of effort on Moses Turgeman's part required superhuman legitimization, capable of determining the *Zohar*'s simple meaning. He claims that the true meaning of the *Zohar*'s words was conveyed to him in a nighttime dream by no less than the *Zohar*'s author himself: "I have come to write what R. Simeon bar Yoḥai (may his memory protect us, amen) said to me in a dream. . . . I dreamt that R. Simeon bar Yoḥai said to me . . . I heard only the sound of words but I knew that it was R. Simeon bar Yoḥai speaking with me."[74] His fear of the dangers associated with the belief in 5600, and the revelation he received in his dream, instilled in him a sense of divine mission to explain to the believers the true place of the year 5600 in the redemptive process: "And now God has sent me to bring news to the humble and heal the broken-hearted . . . with respect to the true End. . . . Pay no heed to words of falsehood . . . to numerological calculations devised by their whims . . . for they know not that the words of the *Zohar* regarding the true End are obscure and sealed. . . . And I travailed and found the little [understanding] I achieved not through any wisdom within myself but through God's kindness to me and the merit of [my] ancestors."[75]

Turgeman continues with various End-reckonings, all of them based on the premise that 5600 is only the point of departure, to which he then adds a particular number of years. The reckonings are not all identical. Some are within five years of 5600; others are fifty years' distant. He does not negate the importance of 5600, but he sees it as simply one step in the divine cosmological plan:

> That is, the End will be in the seventh [century] after ten years of it have gone by, that is, in the year 5610 [1850]. For that encompasses [the letter] *tav*—400—and [the letters] *resh, dalet,* and *vav* [200 + 4 + 6 = 210] years [omitting, as customary, the thousands figure] . . . to fulfill what is said [Micah 7:15] "as the days of your departure from the Land of Egypt [where the Israelites dwelt 210 years] I will show him wondrous deeds," for then will be fulfilled "until Shiloh comes" [Gen. 49:10], [alluding via] *gematria* to Moses, for the year

> after it is 5611 . . . "Moses commanded the Torah to us" [Deut. 33:4; the numerical value of the letters of the word "Torah" is 611].[76]

Turgeman presents a prodigious number of complicated reckonings based on the destruction of the two temples and the prophecies of Daniel and reaches a conclusion regarding the stages of deliverance: "If so, the End will be in 5605 [1845], and, at that End, the heavenly signs will be seen and the Messiah will be revealed in the Galilee. . . . But this Messiah [son of Joseph] will not redeem Israel . . . and in the year 5611 [1851], the Messiah [son of David] will be revealed and will wreak vengeance on the nations and will gather the dispersion of Israel, and after twenty-eight years the war of Gog and Magog will ensue and God will be King over all the Earth."[77]

Recognizing that the sages of blessed memory decreed a ban on engaging in End-reckoning, Turgeman feels obliged to explain his actions: "But in these times, which are near to the days of the Messiah and when the lights have already begun to open, there is no prohibition. On the contrary, there is an obligation to reveal this teaching for preparation and instruction, for by that merit, the Messiah will come."[78] Had the earlier generations known how distant they stood from the End-time, they would have been unable to withstand the sufferings of Exile. But now, Turgeman claims, the time is near, and there is no concern about revealing the End.

Turgeman's reference to the year 5600 as a signpost for End-reckoning has a certain apologetic element. It appears that he himself believed in 5600, and only during the course of that year, or perhaps after it had ended without the appearance of the "waving banner" heralding the arrival of the Messiah, did he claim that the year encompassed, in essence, only one stage of the redemption. Although he does not acknowledge that view, his writings attest to it. They are set forth in the manuscript *Pi Mosheh* and in another, more organized, composition, *Ḥibbur al Shenat 5600* (Essay on the Year 5600).[79] Turgeman presents no substantive or doctrinal position at all, nor does he describe the process of redemption or the factors that help bring it about, such as repenting, studying Kabbalah, or performing *tiqqun ḥaẓot*. His book's central subjects are the End-reckonings for the years 5605–5610–5611, and his principal goal is to wean the multitude from their belief in 5600 as the year of redemption. But it is precisely that fact—that many indeed believed in 5600—that is important for us.

Belief in 5600 Among the *Perushim* in Eastern Europe and the Land of Israel

Several sources tell of the spread of the belief in 5600 among the disciples of the Ga'on R. Elijah of Vilna in eastern Europe. Not all of them report the belief approvingly, but even the sources in which dissenting views are expressed provide useful evidence of the doctrine's spread. We have, for example, writings of Menasheh of Ilya, a disciple of the Ga'on of Vilna known for his rationalist approach and his opposition to involvement with Kabbalah. Despite this outlook, Menasheh of Ilya was close with the leading supporters of *aliyah* by the Ga'on's disciples, as attested by his friendship with Shemariah Luria, the son-in-law of Hillel of Shklov, a member of the Ga'on's family who immigrated to the Land of Israel in 1832.[80] Apparently referring to a confrontation with a group of Lithuanian scholars against the background of the belief in 5600, Menasheh of Ilya writes as follows:

> Anyone who abounds in stupidity and firmly clings to a false [Heb. *sh-q-r,* having a numerical value of 600] belief is holy in his own eyes. But anyone who wishes to use his mind to inquire whether there is substance to his words is said to be of the mixed multitude [cf. Exod. 12:38], whose nature and origins preclude belief. But Jews are believers, the sons of believers, . . . and it is well known what happened in this regard in the time of the false messiah Shabbetai Ẓevi, may his name be erased, and we still have not escaped him and his legacy, a root sprouting gall and wormwood [cf. Deut. 29:17]. . . . In any event, the implication of our remarks . . . is that one should agree with true intellect . . . and that Torah and commandments should not contradict straight intellect.[81]

It can be inferred from this description that the belief in 5600 was widespread. Those individuals who dared to deny or dispute it were stigmatized as weak of faith; meanwhile, affirmation of the belief elevated the believers' self image to the point of sanctity. The divide between the camps was profound: believers referred to skeptics as "a mixed multitude"; Menasheh of Ilya characterized believers as "a root sprouting gall and wormwood" because of the belief's Sabbatean taint. Manasseh goes on to sharply attack the gullible fools who shroud their words in mystery, "saying that this is in accordance with secret [teachings], as is the practice these days, instead of probing with the human intellect."[82] In contrast, he points favorably to those who study the Torah's commandments, as well as human beliefs and doctrines through the use of their intellects. In his view:

> The fools' beliefs have wrought grave damage, and troubles have come upon us on account of the belief in several false prophets and messiahs, . . . particularly since it is well known to all that these words [that one who does not believe is of the "mixed multitude"] went forth from the false messiah, Shabbetai Ẓevi, may his memory be erased, to strengthen his faction and to scare them away from questioning him and his vile actions, and there were many fools who believed him. . . . In any event, it is fitting to be chastened by that experience and no longer allow oneself to be led astray after alien ideas.[83]

The sharpness and extreme tone of the mutual recriminations show that the debate over the belief in 5600 raged at least some ten years in advance of that date, and, perhaps, even long before then, around the time that the disciples of the Ga'on of Vilna immigrated to the Land of Israel.[84] The harsh differences of opinion regarding the issue, and the camps generated around it, attest to its centrality and importance in the religious life of the traditional Jewish leadership of the time.

Another account, corroborating that of Menasheh of Ilya, describes the existence of the belief in 5600 within the academy of the Lithuanian scholarly class. Its source is in the Volozhin yeshiva, founded by Rabbi Ḥayyim ben R. Yiẓḥaq of Volozhin, the leading disciple of the Ga'on of Vilna. The apostate Benjamin Bary tells of the practice at the Volozhin yeshiva, when he was a student there, of using the interval between the Saturday afternoon prayer and the evening prayer at the departure of the Sabbath to discuss the details of the Messiah's advent. The Ga'on's remarks in his commentary on *Sifra de-Ẓeni'uta,* which allude to the End-year known to the pious,[85] were accepted as absolute, unquestionable truth, and the inquiry was limited to the circumstances that would attend the Messiah's arrival in 5600.[86]

The messianic expectations for the year 5600 seem to have been held as well by large groups within the *kolel* of the *Perushim* in the Land of Israel, second-generation disciples of the Ga'on of Vilna. Evidence to that effect is provided by Aviezer of Ticktin, one of the scholars of the Jerusalem *Perushim,* who immigrated to the Land of Israel in 1832.[87] In contrast to Moses Turgeman, Aviezer of Ticktin claims that he and others had accepted the belief in 5600. In his book *Sha'arei Ẓedeq le-Zera Yiẓḥaq,* he explicitly writes: "And now we come to resolve and explain the words of the holy *Zohar,* at *Vayeira* 117 . . . and why what is explicitly written there regarding the year 5600 did not come to be."[88]

In addition to attempting the justify the belief in 5600, Aviezer of Ticktin sought to buttress the faith of those caught up by despair on account of their hopes having been dashed. After constructing an array of proofs to confirm that the expectations for 5600 had been justified, he went on to explain that the year would bring merely the start of the redemptive process, which would be completed only in 5606. The five intervening years, he claimed, were years of testing, and, accordingly, might well be very difficult. Aviezer based his comments on fundamental concepts of Lurianic Kabbalah along with *gematriot* and wordplay. He transformed every numerological or other allusion to 5600—represented by the letters *h-t-r*—into an allusion to 5605, represented as *r-t-h.*[89] By deferring the designated time, he was attempting simply to prolong the hope as much as possible and to avoid at all costs the crisis unfolding before his eyes. This approach appears prominently in his reading of various verses in the Song of Songs, which kabbalists and students of the Ga'on of Vilna saw as reflecting the song of the future redemption. One such verse states that "the blossoms are seen in the land; the time of singing has arrived, and the voice of the turtledove is heard in our land" (Song of Songs 2:12). Aviezer interprets it as follows: "This was [the situation] only on high, but it had not yet come to pass below. . . . 'The blossoms are seen in the land' refers to the beginning of blossoming, which remains in the supernal land, but people do not know of it. But 'the voice of the turtledove is heard in our land' means that when the year *h-t-w-r* [5606; the letters are the spelling of the Hebrew words 'the turtledove'], that is, five [*h*] thousand and six hundred six [*t-w-r*] years, arrives, then this will be heard in our land as well."[90]

Belief in 5600 Among the Eastern European Hasidim

The belief in 5600 as a possible time for the Messiah's advent spread among the Hasidim as well. The earliest report we have of the stance of prominent Hasidim on the matter is to be found in a discussion among "the Holy Grandfather" of Shpola (R. Aryeh Leib) and four other *ẓaddiqim*—Leib "the Rebuker" of Polonnoye, Leib ha-Kohen of Berdichev, Meshullam Zusha of Hanipoli, and Mordecai of Neshkhiz—on the subject of the redemption, the Messiah, and the end of the Exile. Hasidic tradition tells that the Grandfather of Shpola arose and said: "Master of the Universe, I hereby shake hands with you [i.e., affirm] that rebukes and torments will no longer lead Israel to return and better itself, so why should you torment them for naught?"[91] The tradition goes on to recount the emotional reaction of the *ẓaddiqim*: the Grandfather of Shpola broke down sobbing, and his guests sobbed along with him. He then recovered and spoke, basing his words on the conclusion reached in the passage from the *Zohar* presented above:

> Now, I have seen great authorities who wrote down a time for the coming of the Messiah, this one such and that one such. . . . But I can disclose only this, that the Messiah's sanctuary remains closed by a great and awesome closure. . . . But it is said in the *Zohar* that in the year six hundred of the sixth millennium, the gates of wisdom will be opened, and this closure will then be opened as well, and the gate of the Messiah's sanctuary will be ready to be opened. But I do not see who can open it except the Lord Himself, may He be blessed, in all His glory.[92]

Another Hasidic source, attributed to Jacob Ẓevi Yellish of Dynow, a disciple of the Seer of Lublin, teaches: "It is the future redemption, may it come speedily and in our days, whose arrival we hopeful ones anticipate and await each day. . . . But the *Zohar* mentions several End-times and the last of them is the six-hundredth year of the sixth millennium, and it appears impossible for it to be delayed beyond that even a bit. Thus, after the end of five thousand and six hundred years, all these matters will be resolved, and our righteous Messiah will surely come."[93] In support of his view, Yellish cites God's statement to Moses, at the time of the first redemption (i.e., the redemption from Egypt), that "*now you will see* what I shall do to Pharaoh" (Exod. 6:1). He maintains that statement in fact alludes to the final redemption, destined to come in the year 5600. He sees the word "now" (*'attah*) as hinting that the redemption will come "in its time" (*be-'ittah*), and he takes "you will see" (*tir'eh,* spelled *t-r-'-h*) as an anagram for letters representing the year 5600 (***h*** [five] ***'alafim*** [thousand] ***t-r*** [six hundred]).[94]

The use of *gematria* to determine the time of the redemption was an accepted practice within the traditional world. Hasidic groups also interpreted the verse "I shall grant rain for your land at its [proper] time" (Deut. 11:14) in that connection: the numerical value of the letters in the words "rain for your land" (*metar arẓekhem*) is equal to that of the letters in "six hundred years" (*t-r shanim*); accordingly, the verse can be read "I shall grant the year [5]600 as the time of redemption 'in its time.' "[95]

Oral tradition likewise attests to the belief in 5600 among the Polish Hasidim:

> In the year 5600, there was great excitement among the Jews of Warsaw and within Jewry in general. The yearning for redemption found its release. Everyone, including great scholars of Hasidic doctrine, believed that the Messiah would come that year. This belief was based on the *Zohar—Bereshit, Parashat Vayeira,* p. 117. . . . The belief was so strong that a *ẓaddiq* like Abraham of Buczacz, author of *Da'ut Qedoshim,* kept white clothes by his bedside, as well as servant who stayed awake all night with a ram's horn, so that the servant could awaken him upon the Messiah's coming and so that he could immediately greet him. . . . When the year 5600 passed without the Messiah having come, he took gravely ill on account of his grief, and he departed [this world]. In Warsaw, they established watches whose members stayed awake all night in order to be able to herald the Messiah's advent. For the same reason, many sold their possessions for a pittance. These groups were called *Tarnikes.* Jacob Gesundheit, one of Warsaw's great scholars and later its rabbi, feared that the sect would grow powerful and endure for generations, as had similar sects throughout history. He therefore mounted the podium of the central synagogue and avowed that the Messiah would not come in the year 5600.[96]

We read of a similar attitude toward the spread of the belief in 5600 in *Yemot ha-Mashiaḥ,* a collection of sayings by the *admor* of Munkacz, Ḥayyim El'azar Shapira. In the course of recounting the messianic aspirations for redemption in the year 5666 (1906), he considers as well the belief in 5600. He writes:

> I understand more than my elders [cf. Ps. 119:100], for I heard in the name of our master, the holy *ga'on,* the angel and holy one, our master R. Shalom of Belz, may the memory of the righteous be for a blessing, regarding the year 5600 . . . that a voice went forth through Israel that a hint was found in the holy *Zohar* regarding the verse 'in the six hundredth year of Noah's life . . . ' [Gen. 7:11]. Then the holy rabbi of blessed memory proclaimed and announced at the beginning of the year not to consider that year in any way to be the

> year of redemption, and his righteousness served him well to save Jewish souls from apostasy, God forbid.[97]

The practical preparations to greet the Messiah that are reflected in these accounts attest to the force of the belief in 5600 among the Hasidim of eastern Europe.[98]

Belief in 5600 Among the Jews of Western Europe

The earliest evidence for a belief in 5600 within western European Jewry can be found in the writings of Jacob Emden. Despite his merciless persecution of Sabbatean sects and beliefs, Emden entertained his own messianic expectations, tied to himself and his descendants. In his book *Torat ha-Qana'ut,* he bases an estimate of the End-time on a passage in the *Zohar* that complements the one in *Vayeira* 117 that speaks of 5600. He writes: "In any event, in the opinion of *Sefer ha-Zohar* on *qan ẓippor,* it is clear the true End-time is deferred until after 608 years of the sixth millennium."[99]

Another early source can be found in *Binah le-Ittim,* printed in London in 1795. Its author, Elyaqim ben Abraham, considers the various End-reckonings in which the year 5600 occupies pride of place as the year of redemption. His own End-reckonings are based primarily on calculations related to jubilee periods (of fifty years each), but when all is said and done, he relies on the passage in the *Zohar, Vayeira* 117. He writes: "And their numbers add up to 112 jubilee periods, which equal 5,600 years, at which time the attribute of wisdom will shine, as is said in the *Zohar* on *Vayeira.* . . . Thus, we hope that within the time of this jubilee period, which began five years ago [in 5550 (1790)], the End of days for all generations will come, and redeemers shall go up to Zion."[100]

That Jews in Prague shared the belief in 5600 is evidenced as early as 1800 by a reference in El'azar ben David [Plekelsh's] book, *Ahavat David.* He there attacks the remnants in the city of the Frankist sects, who had hoped for the Messiah to come that year; in doing so, he attacks the belief in 5600 as well. In my judgment, his remarks are directed not only at the Frankist minority in Prague but also at other, broader groups:

> Now I know that just as they went mad over this year [5560 (1800)], there will be other periods and times, with their hidden and perverse allusions, of which people will say the year has come, and they will cite indications and raise up signs, [said to be] from secrets of the sage and wise. Thus [they do] regarding the year 5600, may it come upon us for good; they find an allusion in the *Zohar,* in these words: "In six hundred years . . ." I therefore have written these discourses as a decree and remembrance within the congregation of Jeshurun, so they will know unto the last generation and the allusions not lead you astray . . . for the matters are hidden and sealed up until the wondrous time.[101]

Plekelsh offers proofs, from the Zohar and from analysis of *gematriot* and wordplay, that all these calculations are baseless and that the redemption is dependent on one thing only—Israel's repentance and return to the ways of the Torah: "*And the End and the final exile have no set time;* rather, all depends on repentance."[102] He sharply attacks the study of Kabbalah; in his view, those who engage in it do so because they lack all talmudic and halakhic erudition, even of the simplest sort, and therefore prefer to deal with legends and the *Zohar.* He claims the time of redemption is unknown, and even the Holy One Blessed Be He has not articulated, as it were, a statement revealing the hidden time: "For it is written that 'the day of vengeance is in my heart' [Is. 63:4]; the heart has not revealed it to the mouth."[103]

Further evidence for the belief in 5600 within western European Jewry appears in the writings of Ẓevi Hirsch Lehren, head of the Clerks' Organization in Amsterdam. His close contacts with communities throughout western Europe, and particularly in Holland, Germany, and France, enabled Lehren to gather information and impressions regarding intellectual trends, and he conveys them in his letters.[104] He sometimes speaks of the belief in 5600 as a personal matter, but at other times, he characterizes it as much more widely held. In the spring of 1831, upon his return from an extended visit to Germany, he explicitly refers for the first time to the belief in 5600 as a widespread phenomenon: "But the salvation, as simple and near as our hopes, is the coming of our Messiah, and we implore the Holy One Blessed Be He that the salvation not be distant. Many of the fully faithful have said that it will not be delayed beyond the year 5600, may it come upon us for good."[105] While dealing with the question of paying off the debts of the *kolel* of the *Perushim* in the Land of Israel, something very difficult to accomplish, he takes comfort in the belief that the problem will be finally resolved with the Messiah's advent in the year 5600: "Now this year [5593 (1832–1833)] is a sabbatical year, as we know, and there remains only one more sabbatical cycle until 5,600 [years] are completed. We hope for redemption every day and to quickly see the appearance of an auspicious time."[106] And, to similar effect: "May it be [God's] will that the redemption be complete sooner [than the time for paying off the debts], for each day we anticipate being redeemed, and the kindnesses of Heaven will not be later than the year 600 (omitting the thousands figure)."[107]

Evidence for the belief among the Jews of Germany is to be found in a draft of a book by Moses Hess, who mentions that he was aware of the year 5600 being considered the year of the Messiah: "According to an early Jewish prophecy, the Messiah was supposed to come that year, to unite the dispersed Jews and gather them to the Land of their fathers. That was combined with the well-known [blood-libel] events in Damascus. But after more precise inquiry into the matter, I came in good time to the conclusion that, notwithstanding the prophecy of redemption in 1840, the Jews are further from the goal of political rebirth than at any other time."[108] Hess himself did not endorse the belief in 5600; he meant only to use it to galvanize the Jews into working for their political revival. But what is important for our purposes is that the belief was widespread among the Jews of Bonn and Cologne, and, even more important, that a large public of enlightened Jews was aware of it.

In his book *Simlat Binyamin,* written around 5600, Abraham Benjamin Wolf Hamburg of Fürth, one of the leading orthodox rabbis in Germany, refers to the expectations for the year 5600: "And now it is 600 years into the sixth millennium and the guarantee of Elijah, the angel of the covenant, will be fulfilled. And in the year 5600, the coming year for life, there will be respite [*noaḥ*] from our frustrations caused by the people who disparage the footsteps of Your Messiah . . . and behold, the Lord will create windows in the Heavens so we may return to Jerusalem."[109] Like the others, Hamburg relies on the *Zohar* passage on "the six hundredth year of Noah's life," the primary source for the belief in 5600, and he ties it to the reformers harassing him in the Fürth community, "who disparage the footsteps of Your Messiah."

In England, we find a reference to the belief in 5600 as early as 1814. That year saw the publication in London of *The Restoration of Israel,* containing a polemical defense, actually written in 1811, of the bases for the Jewish messianic faith in contrast to the Christian. The author—a rabbi of Hungarian provenance named Joseph Crooll, who served as a Hebrew instructor at Cambridge University—did not share his fellow Jews' tendency to avoid debate with Christian theologians over matters disputed between the two religions. Crooll attacks the idea that Jesus of Nazareth was God's Messiah, as the Christians claim, and he presents an opposing concept in which the messianic age remains in the future. In doing so, he relies on Scriptural references, wordplay, and *gematria.* Crooll arrays the historical epochs hinted at by the word "Adam" in a symmetrical structure. In his view, the word's three letters (*a-d-m*) allude to three touchstones in human history: **A**dam, **D**avid, **M**essiah. From the creation of Adam to the birth of David took 2,854 years. From the birth of David to the coming of the Messiah will take another 2,854 years, meaning that the Messiah will come in the year 5708 (1948). Accordingly, it is implausible that Jesus is the Messiah. At the same time, Crooll sees it as possible that the Messiah may come earlier and appear in the year 5600 (1840).[110]

By their nature, these remarks are more theological explanations than depictions of the degree to which belief that the Messiah would come in the year 5600 had permeated a particular community. Nevertheless, they contain nothing to negate the assumption that, in addition to Crooll, a sizable Jewish public shared the belief in 5600.

Two additional pamphlets by Crooll, printed in England in 1829, contain not only repeated comments about the Messiah's expected appearance in 1840 but also a forceful attack on the London Society for Promoting Christianity Amongst the Jews and on the Christian nations of Europe generally.

In *The Fifth Empire,* Crooll claims the activities of the London Society transgress God's command that obliges the nation of Israel to preserve its distinctiveness and remain separate and apart from the other nations of the world. He maintains that no society or nation has arisen capable of declaring and succeeding in a war against God. Accordingly, the society's efforts to convert the Jews will be unavailing.[111] In his view, the ensuing ten years will see dramatic events in the world, reaching their peak in A.M. 5600—that is, in 1840.[112]

In his pamphlet *The Last Generation,* Crooll piercingly calls the nations of Europe to account for their persecutions of the Jews, describing the coming epoch as the great judgment day. In that trial, God—according to Christian belief, Jesus their messiah—will pose deeply penetrating questions to the European nations: Why and wherefore did they spill Jewish blood? Had he not commanded them to love their enemies? What did the Jews do to them that all united to torment them in a constant, systematic fashion? Why did they not fulfill my command to be merciful to all humans?[113] Before me, God will claim, stand tens of thousands of Jews demanding that I render justice, and justice must be done.[114] I myself, Jesus will say, was born Jewish; why, then, did you scorn my name? Crooll adds a warning that if Jesus in fact is God, he must be a God of justice, and one dare not attempt to arouse his mercies in the hope that he will not apply the law in its full rigor.[115] God's trial will clearly vindicate the Jews and realize their hope to return to Zion, but Gentiles, Crooll says, should not look forward to the day of God, for it will be for them a day of revenge and payback.[116] Crooll calls on the Christian nations to repent speedily, before it is too late. *The Last Generation* concludes with that call to the nations to change their attitude toward Israel, which is destined to be redeemed only eleven years hence.[117]

Missionaries' Accounts of the Jews' Belief in 5600

We considered earlier the paucity of Jewish sources that treat the belief in 5600, in contrast to the numerous extant sources on the Shabbetai Ẓevi episode; the demise of Shabbetai Ẓevi's movement had shrouded the subject in silence. Christian sources, however, offer many accounts of the belief in 5600. They appear in the diaries and reports of missionaries sent by the London Society, who were active in Jewish communities in the Land of Israel and the Diaspora. In the wake of their extended contacts and debates with Jews regarding matters disputed between the two religions—redemption and the Messiah—they did a good job of documenting the Jews' feelings, beliefs, and aspirations.

The Jews' misgivings about written accounts of the belief in a concrete redemption did not extend to oral expressions. To be sure, the quality of the Jews' argumentation cannot be ascertained through the missionary sources, which tried to emphasize the superiority of Christian theological claims by deliberately playing down those of the Jews; but that in no way beclouds the fact that the sources on the Jews' belief in 5600 come from a far-ranging geographic area. The question itself, to be sure, was not one of leading interest to the missionaries, and it occupies only a very small place among the many subjects treated in their diaries. But the tendentiousness of these sources does not detract from their reliability regarding historical facts, and their accounts can often be verified and confirmed by comparison with other contemporaneous sources. The diary entries contain many precise references to even the most minor details, for they apparently were written on the day of the events described rather than later, on the basis of memory. They document facts and impressions derived from their authors' personal contacts and tell of the authors' oral debates with their interlocutors. The reports, as distinct from the evaluations, are generally accurate and reliable, and their abundance attests to the range of the belief in 5600 within the Jewish communities in the Land of Israel and in Asia, Europe, and North Africa. Only a few, however, include descriptions of the theological roots of the messianic belief and take the trouble to anchor it in Scripture.

The accounts were written largely by missionaries active in the Land of Israel. The London Society directed its primary effort there, on the surmise that the Land of Israel would become the focus of increasing Jewish immigration and, accordingly, an important venue for their work. The missionaries without doubt were operating on the basis of a millenarian religious belief and out of a powerful faith in the return to Zion and the fulfillment of the prophets' vision for the future of the nation of Israel.

The earliest account from the Land of Israel was written by the missionary John Nicolayson on 13 October 1827. He tells of meeting in Alexandria with an elderly Jew from Hebron who had come to Alexandria as a rabbinic emissary or as a fundraiser on his own behalf. In the course of a debate on the question of the Messiah, the Jew claimed that, according to a talmudic tradition, the Messiah would appear within twelve years.[118] On 31 December 1831, the missionary S. Farman writes that "all" the rabbis of Safed say that the Messiah will come in another eight years, claiming that opinion is supported by the Kabbalah. Farman goes on to report that a Jew named Finchy, who served as the British vice-consul in Safed, told him to await the Messiah's coming in another eight years, as the rabbis had promised; if the Messiah had not come by then, Finchy would move to London and take on the Protestant religion.[119] Relating these remarks in the name of their author makes the account personal, not anonymous, and correspondingly trustworthy. The incident suggests that the belief in 5600 was not confined to individuals or to a particular segment of the community; rather, it was widespread in many circles. It would be unreasonable to assume that a belief accepted by the rabbis would not spread throughout all groups.

Nicolayson's reports are highly authentic. When he describes an encounter, he includes numerous details that facilitate identifying the participants. On 28 February 1833, he was staying in Safed and met intermittently with the head of the Hasidic *kolel,* Gershon Margaliot, and with three Sefardic rabbis from Jerusalem who had come to the Safed home of the Bekhor family. In the course of a lengthy conversation on the messianic era, conducted in Arabic, they told him they were convinced that the Messiah anticipated by all would come within eight years.[120] On 18 March 1833, Nicolayson notes in his diary a theological explanation for the belief in 5600 that he had heard directly from Naftali of Safed, with whom he had discussed the Messiah's coming. Naftali claimed that the belief was based on the numerical values of the words for "horn" (*qeren,* spelled *q-r-n,* equal to 350) and "lamp" (*ner,* spelled *n-r,* equal to 250); together, they come to 600. These words appear in a psalm concerning the King Messiah that reads: "There will I cause David's horn to sprout; I have provided a lamp for my anointed one" (Ps. 132:17).[121]

We find similar accounts in the reports of the Scottish mission that traveled through the Land of Israel, Turkey, Russia, and Romania during 1839, and it is significant that the reports of the various missionary groups bear out one another. On 8 May 1839, members of the Scottish mission report how impressed they were by the degree to which belief in 5600 had spread among the Jews of Jerusalem. They note that many Jerusalem Jews powerfully feel hope in the Messiah's coming, and that many believe it will come to pass in the year 1840, for that year is the conclusion of the period determined in the *Zohar.*[122]

The Jews of Beirut likewise believed that the redemption was close at hand. On 7 March 1832, Nicolayson tells that the local Jews are unwilling to accept Christian claims about Jesus as the Jews' Messiah because they hope for the speedy advent of their own Messiah.[123]

Regarding the situation in Turkey, we have reports by the Scotsmen A. E. Bonar and R. McCheyne. On 20 December 1839, they write that the local Sefardic Jews manifest absolute devotion to talmudic Judaism; all of them, without exception, have messianic hopes, and many have set the year 1840 as the time of the Messiah's coming.[124] About one month later, Bonar and McCheyne reach Bucharest, from which they report speaking with Jews who believe the Messiah will come soon, and who claim that many in Izmir and other parts of Turkey think he will appear next year.[125]

On 15 September 1839, Bonar and McCheyne report from Russia on a wealthy *admor* (R. Israel of Ruzhin) with many disciples, who is accompanied by a band whenever he sets out on a journey. According to their account, a guest room in the *admor*'s house had already been set aside for the Messiah, and a special horse and carriage had likewise been prepared. They recount as well, in the name of some Jews, that the Rebbe of Navoritch had admonished the Jews against putting too much faith in the Messiah's coming in 1840 or soon after, lest they go to pieces if he fail to come. These two reports suggest that the belief was so palpable and powerful as to entail a real danger that its failure to come to pass could provoke serious dislocation and extreme reactions.[126]

Reports from Poland also tell of firm belief in 5600. From Posen, we hear that, as early as 1827, a local rabbi had sought to dissuade a Jew from converting to Christianity by arguing that the Messiah's coming was at hand and would take place no later than 5600.[127] It was still thirteen years before the anticipated date, but the belief had so taken root that people saw the upheaval attendant on the Messiah's coming as a certain solution to various personal problems.

The missionary L. Hoff tells of the powerful faith in 5600 in the Lublin region. He directs his attention primarily to the strong influence of the Hasidim, who, like many other Jews, anticipate messianic events in 5600 and forcefully reject Christian doctrines.[128]

Reports from the Romanian town of Seret tell of people expecting the Messiah's advent or other dramatic events.[129] Similar accounts are heard from the town of Jasi.[130]

From the port city of Memel, the missionary J. G. Bergfeldt reports in 1836 that the Jews claim, on the basis of talmudic sources, that the Messiah's advent would be no later than within the next three years. Noting that the attention of many Jews is directed toward the final time, he adds that many of them acknowledge that if their hopes are not fulfilled, they will be obliged to forsake their messianic hope.[131] This fateful clinging to a belief in the Messiah's imminent advent seems to have made a powerful impression on the missionary, and he concludes his remarks with the hope and wish that the Jews' expectation will, in fact, be fulfilled.[132]

From England, we have an 1823 reference to the belief that the Messiah would appear in 5600. The London missionary newspaper *Jewish Expositor* attributes it to Rabbi Crooll, mentioned earlier, in the context of his response to the Christian claim that the Messiah had already come. As already noted, Crooll's comments are more theological explanation than factual observation. But that does not contradict the premise that a large community of believers in London stood with Rabbi Crooll and that it was their presence that prompted him to brazenly discuss, in a missionary journal, theological matters that Jews regarded as the deepest of secrets. Rabbi Crooll explains that the belief in the Messiah's advent in 5600 has its roots in the *Zohar,* considered one of the most important books of Jews throughout the world.[133] He goes on to explain that the *Zohar*'s author, R. Simeon bar Yoḥai, lived about sixty years after the destruction of the Second Temple and fixed the time for Israel's redemption as A.M. 5600; inasmuch as the present year is 5583 [1823], another seventeen years remain until the awaited time.[134] In his view, not only is the *Zohar* accorded great esteem by Jews all over the world; beyond that, the *Zohar,* and the signs to appear before the year 5600, provides the basis on which every person will be able to tell that the year of redemption has, in fact, arrived.

The reaction of the missionary journal's editors sheds light on what motivated the London Society to pursue this subject. In their judgment, two factors constitute a heavenly sign, from the Protestant point of view, that the redemption is near: the belief of the Jews themselves in the Messiah's imminent advent, and the very founding of the society, whose purpose was to help Jews return to Zion and there recognize the true Messiah. The editors emphasize that not in 1700 years have Christians had so positive an attitude toward the Jews, to the point of being ready to assist them in returning to Zion.[135]

Missionaries in North Africa likewise report on a belief that redemption would come in 5600. On 21 February 1829, the missionary Farman wrote from Tunis of conversations with Jews regarding their harsh circumstances, in which their hopes for the Messiah were discussed. It became clear to him that they believed mightily that the redemption would take place within twelve years, with the Messiah's expected advent.[136] A few years later, we hear another account of the Jews of Tunis, this time from the apostate-missionary J. C. Ewald. On 10 April 1836, he describes a debate with two Jews over the interpretation of biblical passages that Christians construe as referring to the coming of the Messiah. Though claiming to be erudite Talmud scholars, the two Jews could not understand what the prophetic words alluded to. When Ewald explained that, in his opinion, it could be proven from the passages that the Messiah had already come, one of the Jews replied that the Messiah was not expected to come for another six years.[137] Ewald adds that he reminded the Jews that the rabbis had previously performed various End-reckonings, but that none had come to pass. According to Ewald, the Jew avoided further discussion but promised to bring the argument to the rabbis of the yeshiva.[138]

In 1836, Ewald reports from Tripoli on a theological debate with a Jew concerning the Messiah. This Jew, like many others, based his belief in the year 5600 on the passage in the *Zohar.* He claimed that R. Simeon bar Yoḥai, in the *Zohar,* interpreted the verse "Gladden us for as many days as you have afflicted us, for the years we have seen evil" (Ps. 90:45) to mean that since the world was to endure six thousand years, the Messiah would come in 5600, leaving a period of four hundred years, equal to the number of years during which the Israelites were enslaved in Egypt, during which he would gladden the Jews. The Jew saw a corroborative sign in a contemporary event—the cholera epidemic that had broken out in North Africa.[139]

Echoes of the belief in 5600 could be heard from as far away as Persia. An investigator named A. Grant informs us in 1840 that Persian Jews, like Jews in other parts of the world, anticipate the coming of the Messiah that year.[140]

The members of the London Society, who were active throughout the world, appear to have been impressed that the belief in 5600 was not confined to a limited area or to isolated individuals; rather, it encompassed large parts of the Jewish world. Some reports convey the impression of dealing with a mass movement. On 3 May 1839, the missionary newspapers carried a report, based on the account of C. Bursen, the Prussian ambassador to the Vatican, of a general sense of expectation, throughout Germany and Poland, directed toward an event that would soon come to pass and restore the Jews to the land of their fathers.[141] The missionary T. Grimshaw contends that, while touring the European continent in 1839, he received several accounts of large numbers of Jews preparing to emigrate from Poland and Germany and settle in the Land of Israel. Moreover, throughout Europe and in Asia one could find a general belief that the period of redemption was at hand and was awaited by all. Grimshaw himself encountered the phenomenon when he visited Rome and Leghorn.[142]

In 1840, Grimshaw again took up the subject, reiterating his impression of how widespread the belief in 5600 was within the Jewish world. He asserted that faith in the redemption of Israel and the anticipation of its imminence were universal among the Jews, and its fulfillment appeared to be near. This anticipation was not unique to a particular place or a particular land; rather, it permeated the entire Orient: Izmir and Constantinople, Egypt, Syria, the Land of Israel, Poland, and Germany. The belief was accompanied by the impression that the time of the Messiah's advent has come. The year 1840 has been decreed by the rabbis, on the basis of chronological calculations, to be the time this event would take place. Grimshaw says he examined these facts through personal contacts and investigation during the course of his most recent visit to the Orient and could not recall such unanimity. The tide of emigration to the Land of Israel has begun. "I am going," an elderly Jew told him, "to see the coming of the Messiah with my own eyes. I hope to be a visual witness to it. And if I am proven wrong, my comfort will be that I will at least be buried in the land of my fathers." He adds that he heard many similar expressions and that nine hundred Polish Jews sought the permission of the Russian czar to go up to the Land of Israel; only bureaucratic pitfalls prevented that request from being granted.[143]

3

Immigration to the Land of Israel, 1808–1840

It should be known to you that from other lands, worthy people are actually streaming to the four holy cities (may they be built and established speedily and in our days, amen), [people] of all social strata and all ages, children and elderly, among them octogenarians and older.

Eliezer Bregman, letter from Jerusalem dated 22 Kislev 5595 [24 December 1834], in *Yis'u Harim Shalom*

Messianic Impetus Versus Great Hardship

The years 1808–1840 saw enormous growth in the Jewish community in the Land of Israel; according to several reports, the community doubled in size.[1] That development is perplexing, given the harsh living conditions in the Land of Israel during the early years of the nineteenth century.

For one thing, the political situation was unstable, and governments were subject to upheaval and collapse. The government was ineffectual vis-à-vis local power centers; the Jewish minority lived an insecure life, subject to attack by the gentile populace; and the roads to the four holy cities (Jerusalem, Hebron, Tiberias, and Safed) were impassable and dangerous. Economic conditions also were poor. The impoverished local populace—*fellahin* as well as city dwellers—were economically backward, and commerce was undeveloped. That the Ashkenazim knew no Arabic made it even harder for them to maintain positive relations with the local populace.[2]

In addition to its political, social, and economic difficulties, the

Land suffered from periodic natural disasters—epidemics and earthquakes. The abysmal sanitary conditions claimed many victims, especially among the Jewish immigrants, who had not adapted themselves to the Land's climate, congested living conditions, and poor sanitation.[3]

Not only did the unbearable living conditions afflict the local populace; they also deterred potential immigrants, caused some to depart,[4] and tended to impede the growth in those years of a significant Jewish population in the Land of Israel. If, despite all this, the Jewish population doubled over the course of the thirty years leading up to 5600, it must have been because of the breadth of the *aliyah* movement, which encompassed thousands of highly motivated immigrants sharing a sense of mission. The sources available to us show a consistent stream of immigration during those years, and some mention the motivation for that *aliyah*—to await, in the Land of Israel, the Messiah's advent in the year 5600. These *aliyot* encompassed, to various degrees, all segments of the Jewish Diaspora, from North Africa, Syria, Turkey, Persia and Yemen to Russia, Poland, Hungary, Germany, Holland, and England.[5]

With Muhammad Ali's conquest of the Land in 1831, the Jewish *yishuv* in the Land of Israel became more firmly established and self-sustaining. The Jews' juridical status vastly improved and their economic options were broadened, and both contributed to a significant strengthening of *aliyah* in that period.

The demographic mix of the immigrants indicates a high degree of motivation. They were a heterogeneous group, encompassing not only prominent scholars but also common folk and tradesmen (especially among the immigrants from North Africa, Russia, and Poland), wealthy individuals with considerable property, and young families with numerous children and infants.[6] One might well ask why parents caring for small children and infants would exchange the familiar environment of their native land for life in a place so strange, harsh, and remote. The conditions came as no surprise to them; they recognized from the outset that they would be subject to peril and would have to battle daily for their very existence. Moreover, the journey itself was so costly as to be within the means of only a few. All this suggests that in most instances, the immigrants were moved by a profound messianic faith and sense of mission; only that sort of motivation could have impelled them to undertake the effort. And that is as true of the wealthy immigrants as of the young parents: they certainly could not have seen *aliyah* as a good investment of their assets. On the contrary, some of them put their money into houses and land and into loans to communal organizations and even to churches and monasteries. They were concerned about their economic existence but, at the same time, sought to put down roots and build new lives in the Land of Israel. It follows that they believed they were emigrating at the dawn of a new age.

Immigration of the Vilna Ga'on's Disciples

Descendants of the Vilna Ga'on's disciples in the Land of Israel maintain a tradition of an assembly convened in Shklov in 1806 with the goal of organizing the *aliyah* of the Ga'on's disciples to the Land of Israel as part of the process of the return to Zion.[7] (The year on the Hebrew calendar was 5506, variously presented as having the numerical value of the letters in "Messiah son of Joseph," "Bring us to Zion Your City," and "Awaken, O north, and come, O south.") According to this tradition, the assembly was headed by Benjamin Rivlin and his son, Hillel Rivlin, wealthy residents of Shklov and cousins of the Ga'on.

Examination of hitherto unstudied writings by the Vilna Ga'on's disciples shows a factual basis for this tradition; one cannot regard this *aliyah* as wholly lacking in organization. We hear an echo of that organization in *Amud ha-Yemini*, a book by Abraham ben Asher Anschel, preacher in the Minsk community. In his introduction, the author writes that he is publishing the book in order to earn funds to support his own *aliyah*:

> When my heart roused me to approach the sanctified place, to knock on the doors of its palaces and bestir myself to find refuge in the pleasant land, . . . I therefore formed and immediately carried out the intention of publishing this, my book, to provide me the resources to carry out my goal [of immigrating to the Land of Israel] . . . each person as his heart moves him . . . so I might be led in circles of righteousness and be mighty as a lion and swift as an eagle . . . that I might be privileged to arrive in our land and in His holy city.[8]

He yearned to immigrate not on his own but together with his associates, organized as a secret society with the goal of *aliyah*, and "to stand with those joined by a powerful bond to leave their native land."[9] As noted, however, he lacked the financial resources required of those joining in the *aliyah*: "I longed for it and hoped for it from afar, and how mighty was my desire for it, and my soul yearned greatly, I, like them, all of us sons of one man [the Vilna Ga'on; for the phrase, cf. Gen. 42:11], hewn from one place, but what can I do for my family, for the food is gone from our bins and the children are weak."[10] The writer goes on to describe the magnitude of the enterprise involved in *aliyah* as an organized group, requiring substantial expenditures on the part of its members, as well as courage and sacrifice:

> Praise to God our begetter . . . Who left us a remnant on earth. He instilled in the hearts of our brethren, the members of our covenant, [the will] to abandon all their pleasantries and delights . . . each day, new ones. They travel and circulate throughout the land in which their fathers dwelled, dedicating their silver and gold to God and taking their lives in their hands to abandon their native land, they

> who dwell in a land not their own, [and intending not merely] to dwell [temporarily] there [in the Land of Israel] but to settle there, and set out on the sea and allow their hearts no sadness or fear . . . to arrive at the holy land, which is great, and to become part of God's estate.[11]

Among those issuing approbations for the book are listed three leaders of the *aliyah* organization—Ḥayyim of Volozhin; Abraham Abele Pasweller, the chief rabbinic judge of Vilna; and Saul ben Joseph of Vilna. The book itself was printed in 1811, but the approbation is dated to the summer of 1809, when the *aliyah* movement of the Vilna Ga'on's disciples was at its peak.

The journal of the Brody community tells of a typical emigrant, who calls to mind the description in *Amud ha-Yemini* of those who "travel and circulate," raising money here and there to cover the many travel expenses, and who "take their lives in their hands to abandon their native land" in order to join the group of immigrants so as "to become part of God's estate." The individual is Jacob Yeka Frenkel of Breslau, who arrived in Brody in late spring 1811 en route to the Land of Israel, in order to collect money from his debtors to cover his *aliyah* expenses: "Directing himself to go up to Jerusalem, the holy city and make his residence in the holy land, and after journeying from Breslau to here, the holy community of Brody, he tarried here to collect debts owed to him by members of our community, but he did not succeed in collecting all his debts."[12] That event, alluded to in the community journal, undoubtedly involved a wealthy individual, and we find that he in fact reached the Land of Israel; his name is mentioned in the *Pinqas Ẓefat* (Safed Journal), passages of which are cited by Rabbi A.L. Frumkin in his *History of the Sages of Jerusalem.*[13]

Important evidence for a broad and organized immigration effort that began no later than 1806 can be found in *Sha'arei Ẓedeq* by Abraham Danzig, father-in-law of one of the Vilna Ga'on's children. The book was directed to the immigrants and had a very practical purpose: clarification of the provisions of Jewish law (*halakhah*) that pertain to the Land of Israel nowadays, so that the immigrants would find it easier to fulfill the commandments contingent on the Land,[14] which they would have to begin observing. The author writes: "If a man who enters the king's court without knowing its customs thereby commits a capital offence, how much more so does one who wishes to dwell in our holy land without knowing all the laws that prevail there? . . . And I therefore gathered up all the laws pertaining to this and called it *Sha'arei Ẓedeq* [Gates of Righteousness], after Jerusalem, which is called righteousness. And if, God forbid, I am not privileged to immigrate to there, I will fulfill the laws applicable there through this study of them."[15]

Danzig must have been confident that numerous immigrants would provide a solid market for his book, for he otherwise would not have bothered to write a work exclusively for them and of such little practical use to Diaspora Jews. Moreover, the book's publication, which entailed considerable expense, required not only the author's confidence but also the publisher's. In the chapter on priestly gifts and tithes, the author writes: "It thus appears the coming year of 5572 [1811–1812], may it be a good year, is a sabbatical year. . . . Accordingly, in the years 5573 and 5574, we set aside the priestly gift, the first tithe, and the second tithe . . . and the year 5579 is a sabbatical year, and in the year 5580, the cycle begins anew, and so on. May it be God's will that we merit the ingathering of the exiles."[16] This expresses the author's inner sense, undoubtedly influenced by the *aliyah* movement taking shape before his eyes.[17]

That large groups of Jews were inspired to go up to the Land of Israel brought about an examination of the associated practical halakhic problems, and the records of that examination, in turn, help us appreciate the magnitude of the awakening. Danzig maintained that not everyone should be allowed to emigrate; rather, rules should be set that define who is permitted to join the *aliyah* movement: "But not everyone who wishes to invoke God's name and go up should do so. Even though a *mishnah* near the end of tractate *Ketubbot* [says that] all may go up, etc., that refers specifically to one capable of sanctifying himself there and purifying himself to serve God always with his whole heart, and who is clean of hands and pure of heart [cf. Ps. 24:4]."[18] He favored precluding *aliyah* on the part of those likely to become wards of the community and permitting only the wealthy to emigrate: "One incapable of supporting himself there and needing to become dependent on the community, and who, outside the Land of Israel, supports himself by his own labors, is no doubt better off living outside the Land of Israel."[19] But it appears that matters beyond the prospective *oleh*'s character traits and financial standing concerned the halakhic sages who attended the birth of the *aliyah* movement. They were asked as well about the proper course of action for young people whose parents opposed their emigration; they replied that "it is necessary to examine whether one who has a father and mother who prohibit his emigration is obligated to heed them."[20]

The nature of the scheming required of the *olim* can be read between the lines of the introduction to *Sha'arei Ẓedeq*. It appears that those who wished to emigrate needed to take the risk of deceiving the government in order to obtain authorization "from the court of our lord, his exalted majesty, in the form of a passport."[21] Danzig tells that three great disciples of the Vilna Ga'on—Sa'adiah of Shklov, Ḥayyim Katz of Pekarawi, and Hirsch—had succeeded in doing so some years earlier, and he vowed to do the same in 1804.[22] From the depictions cited below we see that, despite the need to conceal from the government the true purpose for which many were journeying to the Land of Israel, and despite the dangers inherent in organizing *aliyah*, the *aliyah* of the Vilna Ga'on's disciples was, in fact, an organized effort.

First and foremost, we must keep in mind that they emigrated in homogeneous groups, something that in itself suggests organization. Each group that joined with its predecessors significantly increased the number of people in the community of *Perushim* in the Land of Israel; by 1813 they numbered 511 souls (equal to the numerical value of the letters in the word *ashrei* [happy])—a huge number for those days.[23]

The first account of such a column of *olim* dates from 1808. The members of the group, led by Menaḥem Mendel of Shklov, settled in Tiberias, which was already home to a core of individual disciples of the Vilna Ga'on who had immigrated.[24] In 1809, a second column of immigrants arrived, led by Sa'adiah of Shklov, and at the end of that year, a third group set out for the Land of Israel, under the leadership of Ḥayyim ben Tobias and Israel of Shklov. When they arrived, the community of *Perushim* numbered about 150 souls, exclusive of the new arrivals.[25]

Several additional columns of immigrants appear to have reached the Land of Israel before the great epidemic's outbreak in 1813. In a letter from the Nobles of Vilna, dated 25 Adar 5571 (21 March 1811) and given to Abraham Danzig, their emissary to the cities of Germany, we hear of plans to dispatch groups of immigrants during 1811: "The matter occurring at the proper time, for in those days and at this time, several esteemed and leading members of our community will be journeying to our holy land, important men, notables [lit., *Efratim*; cf. Ruth 1:2], confident people, and, with God's help, they will reach there soundly."[26] One of the columns that set out in the spring of 1811 included Abraham Solomon Zalman Ẓoref of Kaidan, then a young man of twenty-six, his wife Hannah, and their three children.[27] We know from records of the Clerks' Organization that he immigrated with a group headed by Elijah Bialystoker, one of the leaders of the community of *Perushim* in Safed during the 1820s.[28] We know as well of an additional group that immigrated in 1813, apparently led by Solomon Zalman Shapira, a prominent disciple of Ḥayyim of Volozhin; he was accompanied by his wife, his daughter, and his young son-in-law, Aryeh ben Yeraḥmiel, who later became a trustee of the *kolel* of the *Perushim*.[29]

Disciples of the Vilna Ga'on known to have immigrated to the Land of Israel with other groups of immigrants include Gershon Harkavy and Ḥayyim ben Pereẓ ha-Kohen of Pinsk. Harkavy, who was extremely wealthy, had studied in the Vilna Ga'on's academy for an entire year. We have part of a letter he sent from Constantinople during the intermediate days of a festival, probably Passover, in 1819 while en route to the Land of Israel. When he reached Safed, he acquired the study hall of the local *Perushim* and purchased vineyards, the income from which went to support the members of the *kolel*.[30] Ḥayyim ben Pereẓ was chief judge of the rabbinic court in Pinsk and, as recounted in a letter from Israel of Shklov to Ẓevi Hirsch Lehren, apparently came to the Land of Israel in 1826 as leader of a large group of immigrants: "We were privileged in that this winter, together with the rabbinic emissary from Vilna, there came to our community a unique individual, a *ga'on* of our generation, renowned for righteousness and piety, namely, the rabbi, the *ga'on*, the great, renowned, honorable, holy in the grandeur of his name, Ḥayyim, may his lamp shine, chief judge and head of the academy of the community of Pinsk and its environs. . . . He settled here in the holy city and the land shone with his glory."[31]

That the groups of immigrants were headed by rabbis, prominent individuals, or rabbinic emissaries from the Land of Israel itself also shows that the *aliyah* had an organizational structure. To limit difficulties and pitfalls en route, the groups would set out in the spring and aim to reach the Land of Israel at the end of the summer. The Nobles of Vilna would send charitable "funds of blessing" with them, for distribution to the members of the *kolel* in the Land of Israel.

A dispute arose between the residents of Safed and those of Jerusalem over an effort by the latter to attract new immigrants. We hear of it in a letter from Israel of Shklov to Solomon Pach: "They all suspect of us that we will send [representatives] from Jerusalem to Constantinople to sit at the crossroads and direct important people to Jerusalem."[32] That characteristic description attests to the constant, almost fixed stream of immigrants and to the effective organization that dealt with it.

Immigration from Bohemia and Galicia

In several important studies, based on Austrian governmental records, N. M. Gelber has pointed out that Jews from Hasidic circles in Bohemia and Galicia also immigrated to the Land of Israel in noticeable numbers. According to these sources, *aliyah* to the Land of Israel gained force in 1811. On 9 November of that year, the kaiser's secret service in Vienna asked the police to look into what was motivating the Jews of Galicia to emigrate to the Land of Israel, whether the emigrants included people of means, and what steps might be taken to combat the emigration. The police compiled a list of thirty families and six single men who had emigrated as a group, among them a Jew named Gershon Margoliot who had taken 15,000 gold ducats with him.[33] Gershon Margoliot is Gershon of Skalit, who, after arriving in the Land of Israel, became an official of the *kolel* of the Hasidim in Safed; he was related to Zalman Ephraim Margoliot of Brod, the patron of the Hasidim in the Land of Israel.[34] In other contemporary records, the Vienna police mention a column of fourteen emigrants who departed for the Land of Israel via Odessa. On 15 February 1812, a report on the migration of numerous Jews from Galicia to the Land of Israel was presented to the kaiser's court in Vienna. The report noted that while their papers portray the Jews as pilgrims, their movement was, in fact, a migration in every sense of the word. In 1826, reports again describe the emigration from Galicia of numerous Jewish families who had taken large sums of money with them.[35] On 6 March 1826, a law was enacted forbidding secret emigration and the removal of monies to the Land of Israel.[36]

To be sure, the connection between the year 5600 and these *aliyot* does not mean that all the immigrants were motivated by messianism. Some sought to overcome their economic straits by becoming eligible for charitable distributions in the Land of Israel (referred to as *ḥaluqah*); they either associated themselves with the organized groups or emigrated as individuals. An echo of these nonmessianic *olim* can be heard in Ẓevi Hirsch Lehren's remarks on the immigration of Polish Hasidim in the late 1820s. In his role as head of the Clerks' Organization, Lehren sought to confine both *aliyah* and the provision of *ḥaluqah* to worthy people:

> Some complain that there are those who leave Poland for the Land of Israel (may it be built and established) because they cannot make a living in Poland, and they become dependent on the community [in the Land of Israel]; and if that is so, nothing is achieved through all that is done for the good of the Land of Israel (may it be built and established), for despite all that, the greater the resources, the greater the number that consume them. So what is the benefit of everything done for the good of those residing in the Land of Israel (may it be built and established), if there is no restriction on those who may enter?[37]

Lehren, who had always opposed *aliyah* in principle, did not make himself the spokesman for those immigrants who were motivated by ideological-messianist considerations. And the immigrants themselves, for reasons readily understood, preferred to conceal their motives and did not commit them to writing. What, then, impelled the immigrants, and how can we obtain information about their motivations? As noted in the preceding chapter, the missionaries' journals are a valuable resource, providing reports on the movement of many Jews from throughout the Diaspora to the Land of Israel and on their motives. The fear that deterred Jews from writing about this subject did not burden the missionaries, and the factors warranting confidence in their reports regarding the expectations for the year 5600 have already been presented. There is no reason not to rely similarly on their reports with respect to *aliyah* and its motivations.

Immigration From Poland and Russia

Three early, external sources mention a migration of Jews from Russia and Poland during 1808–1814 and refer, incidentally, to the migrants' motives. In one, a letter by a Russian merchant from Riga dated 5 March 1811, the writer recounts his son's visit to Crimea the previous summer. En route home via Odessa, the son heard that many Jewish families had gone through that port town. While traveling in Poland, he asked an Ashkenazi Jew where the migrants were headed, and the Jew replied that they were going to the Land of Israel to settle there, for they had a sense that the Messiah would soon appear. The Jew went on to tell that wealthy Jews were raising funds to help cover the travel expenses of their poor brethren.[38] Finding his son's report of great interest, the writer asked a friend living in Vilna to inquire about the migration movement and its underlying causes. After a few days, he received the following reply: "There exists among the Jews a desire to return to the land of their fathers. Some do so for economic reasons, for commerce today is depressed. But many do so because of an expectation that the Messiah will come within eight years. Others tell me that within fifteen years, no Jews will remain in Russia."[39]

This Riga merchant's letter came into the possession of a Christian clergyman, who decided to look into the rumors on his own. In May and June of 1811, he toured two cities with sizable Jewish populations and was told by Jewish leaders that over the preceding two years (1809–1811), several hundred Jewish families had emigrated from Poland to the Land of Israel. When he inquired about the purpose of the migration, he was told that "the Jews hope that the words of the Prophets will soon come to pass and God will gather the remnant of His people from all the corners of the world; and they accordingly want to anticipate the Messiah's appearance in the Land of Israel."[40] The writer notes that after an extended period in which the rabbis had erred in their efforts to determine the time of the Messiah's arrival, the Jews were now convinced that he was finally coming. He adds that the areas from which Jews were emigrating are the Brody region of Poland, and Vilna, in Lithuania.[41]

A second letter, written in 1814, reached the London Society from Russia and reported that the pace of Jewish migration to the Land of Israel was down from its previous level. The writer tells that of the twenty thousand or so Jews in Vilna and Lithuania, only eighteen families had left for the Land of Israel in 1814. Conversations with Jews about to depart made clear to the writer their belief that the Messiah's appearance in the Land of Israel was nearing.[42] This is a particularly important document, evidencing the substantial *aliyah* movement on the part of the Vilna Ga'on's disciples and its ensuing noticeable decline—attributable, in my view, to the reports reaching Russia about the severe epidemic that afflicted the Galilee in 1813 and that wiped out most of the immigrants.

In October 1820, the missionary J. Moritz reports on a Jewish family from Yekatrinaslov that sold its home and immigrated to the Land of Israel with considerable wealth. According to Moritz, some regarded this unusual step as an expression of the Jews' hopes and aspirations to return to Zion, but he saw it simply as a typical instance of Jews going to the Land of Israel in order to die there and be spared the travails of posthumous "underground rolling" to the Land in anticipation of the final resurrection (*gilgul meḥillot*).[43] His comments reflect the accepted, traditional understanding of the motives for *aliyah*, but he does not hesitate to mention the extremely novel alternative understanding, albeit with a certain degree of skepticism. Over the course of time, that view would recur and become based not only on reports of various missionaries but also on remarks by the *olim* themselves. In February 1821, missionaries from Odessa report on an extended stream of Jewish migration to the Land of Israel, motivated by a belief that the Messiah would soon arrive.[44]

In 1838, Benjamin Mordecai Navon notes that more than fifteen years earlier (in 1823), Ashkenazim had come to live in Jerusalem, "they and their children and their wives and their infants . . . and they came here, to the holy city, to settle, and they also purchased houses and lands."[45] There can be no doubt that the immigration of young families burdened with small children and their purchase of houses and lands are important evidence that the *aliyah* was not for the purpose of dying and being buried in the holy land but of establishing roots there.

In a June 1821 summing-up by the London Society, the missionary Moritz refers to data on an extensive migration of Jews to the Land of Israel. That suggests to him that the Near East is destined to become an important locus of missionary activity.[46]

It seems that a steady stream of *aliyah* continued as long as living conditions were reasonably secure. And so, when the stream dried up in the wake of wars that involved Turkey, the change was noted and reported in missionary sources. For example, it was noted that, following the outbreak of war between Turkey and Greece in 1822 and the ensuing naval blockade, the previously large number of Jewish immigrants to the Land of Israel was diminished. Similarly, the war in 1822–1823 between the Farḥi brothers of Damascus and Abdullah Pasha, ruler of Acco, interrupted the immigration of Jews to the Land of Israel and even caused Jews to flee the Galilee. The interruption, however, was only temporary; in May 1824, the missionary W. B. Lewis reports on immigrants streaming to Safed and Jerusalem, and he adds that their immigration was tied in great degree to anticipation of the Messiah's coming. In contrast to Moritz, Lewis does not draw inferences as to the motives for the immigration; he simply documents what he heard from the Jews themselves, and, since he was close to developments within the Jewish community, it is fair to regard his reports as quite reliable. Beyond that, as a missionary he claims that it is necessary for the mission to be in the Land of Israel at such a time, in order to persuade the Jews that they are in error and to explain to them that the Messiah—Jesus—has already come, and that they would be well advised to acknowledge as much.[47]

Immigration From the Ottoman Empire and North Africa

From the start of the nineteenth century to the conquest by Muhammad Ali, numerous reports by missionaries tell of growing immigration to the Land of Israel of Jews from the reaches of the Ottoman Empire and from North Africa. These reports forcefully convey the Jews' own awareness that this was neither the traditional *aliyah* of the elderly hoping to be buried in the Land of Israel so as to avoid "underground rolling" nor *aliyah* attributable to love for the Land or its sanctity. It was, rather, the *aliyah* of young families with rather different purposes.

The first evidence of early-nineteenth-century *aliyah* by North African Jews appears in a letter sent to London from Malta on 15 October 1816. The letter considers the exodus of Jews from Algiers as a consequence of the persecutions there in 1804. The writer tells that the Jews left for other parts of North Africa, particularly Tunis, but he adds that the more pious of the emigrants went to the Land of Israel, mainly to Jerusalem, regarding the persecutions of 1804 as a heavenly sign that the time of redemption was drawing near. He notes that these first immigrants went alone and that their families joined them only later.[48]

An 1815 report from Jerusalem by the Christian traveler William Turner tells of *aliyah* from Constantinople, Izmir, and Salonika: "An elderly Jew called on me this morning and informed me that, in the past, the sole motivation of the Jews coming here was to die in the Land of their forefathers, but, more recently, many young people, impoverished by Turkish oppression . . . spend their last 500 piasters on moving their wives and families to the Holy Land. . . . They come from all parts of the Orient, but the largest number come from Constantinople, Izmir, and Salonika. Last year, 300 came from the former two cities."[49]

Aliyah from North Africa during that period is described in the missionary Joseph Wolff's notes from Beirut, dated 21 June 1828. Wolff had gone to the port in Beirut to greet the *olim* arriving there en route to the Land of Israel; he tells of going on deck and being delighted at the sight of fifty Jews from Tunis and Tripoli who were standing there, bedecked in phylacteries and wrapped in prayer shawls. Their wives and children stood at their sides, all intending to go up to Jerusalem and there await the coming of the Messiah. When Wolff addressed them in Hebrew, they declined to talk with him, saying only that they were going up to Jerusalem to await the redemption of Israel.[50]

In July 1829, Wolff reports on one hundred Jews who had arrived by ship at the port of Jaffa. His report is confirmed by missionary sources in Constantinople, which tell of numerous ships being chartered by Jews for the purpose of transporting them to the Land of Israel. The account goes on to report that many more Jewish families from all over the world are preparing to immigrate to the Land of Israel and that they attribute their *aliyah* to their anticipation of the Messiah's coming, Whatever their motive, a large number of Jews have immigrated to the Land of Israel.[51]

In July 1831, the missionary S. Farman reports as well that several families arrived from Russia in order to await the Messiah in the land of their fathers, and he adds that a wealthy Jew from Gibraltar had arrived for the same purpose.[52]

Immigration During the Time of Muhammad Ali

The *aliyah* movement grew markedly with Muhammad Ali's conquest of the Land of Israel at the end of 1831 and the liberal policies toward the Jews that ensued. First, residents of the Galilee who had fled during Abdullah Pasha's reign of terror returned.[53] In 1831, we hear of the *aliyah* and settlement in Safed of the printer Israel Back and his family, and in 1832 we learn of increasing immigration by Russian Jews. The latter movement was so extensive that Israel of Shklov expresses concern about being able to support the *olim* "who immigrated in great numbers from that land to the Land of Israel, and it is very likely they will double the number there already, and he worried over whence their help would come."[54] The same source reports on a ship that went down near Constantinople with fifty-four immigrants on board, among them "renowned, God-fearing men and certain notables"; all but one drowned.[55] It appears that the immigrants of this period included renowned Diaspora supporters of the *kolel*s in the Land of Israel, including Hillel of Shklov, Shemariah

Luria of Mogilev, and a group of forty leaders of the Vilna community organization, some of them quite wealthy.[56] In 1832, we find a reference to the *aliyah* of Uri Orenstein, together with his aged father, his wife, and his three children[57]; late that year or early the next, the *zaddiq* Abraham Dov Ber of Averitch emigrated with a group of his family members[58]; during the summer of 1833, Menaḥem Mendel of Kamenetz emigrated from Odessa with another eighty Jews on board an Italian ship[59]; and in the fall of 1833, the *ga'on* Ḥayyim ben Avigdor of Pinsk reached the Land of Israel, together with the group of immigrants from Vilna known as *movilei ha-berakhah* (bringers of the blessing).[60]

The impressive dimensions of the *aliyah* movement came to Lehren's attention in the fall of 1832. Relying on a statement in the book *Tuv ha-Arez̤*—"at the time of the End, those residing in the Land of Israel will increase in number to several thousands"—he regarded the increased number of immigrants and the addition of seats to the study hall as a sign of the approaching redemption.[61]

The *aliyah* movement appears to have been so massive that even the Nobles of Vilna became concerned about its effect on the well-being of the existing Jewish community in the Land of Israel. They accordingly issued a statement that even those people worthy of living in Jerusalem should not rely for their sustenance solely on the charitable distribution provided by Vilna, "which has diminished greatly, lest they be regarded as spoilers . . . and lest the large number of immigrants put an end to study and worship on the part of newcomers and veteran residents alike."[62] The proclamation called on the immigrants to organize support groups comprising their relatives in the Diaspora, but it warned that even such support groups should not be relied on in a time of political upheaval and oppression by the Russian authorities. Under these conditions, the Nobles of Vilna favored *aliyah* only on the part of the elderly, who are "free of worldly desires and unaffected by material considerations," and, they concluded, "the masses should not dare to immigrate, for they will not partake of the righteousness of the Land."[63] The proclamation seems have been ineffective, and, in a letter sent to Lehren in 1834, Aryeh Ne'eman similarly saw a need for steps to limit *aliyah*, "for the Land is being transformed into cities of refuge."[64] It is fair to assume that the misgivings of Israel of Shklov and Aryeh Ne'eman about the magnitude of the *aliyah* grew out of their continual concern about raising adequate funds to support the *kolels* and to cover their growing debts. They appear as well to have been made uneasy by the ill-fated effort at *aliyah*, in the early eighteenth century, of a group led by Judah Ḥasid. At the same time, the community itself was likely delighted by the increased immigration, for each new group's successful arrival bolstered the community's self confidence. That viewpoint is expressed in comments by E. Bregman: "The Ashkenazim at all times abound in kindnesses to one another and to all who join them. They are not parsimonious vis-à-vis the new arrivals, for, they say, 'On the contrary . . . , the greater the increase in the number of those dwelling in the Holy Land, . . . the greater [God's] bounty.' "[65]

Muhammad Ali's conquest of the Land of Israel from its Ottoman rulers, and his institution of a liberal regime vis-à-vis the Jews, reinforced the messianic expectations of Jews throughout the Diaspora and encouraged still more *aliyah*. Among the areas affected were the lands of North Africa.

On 22 December 1832, the missionary John Nicolayson writes in his journal of the arrival in Beirut of 180 people from Oran, who had spent two months at sea. He ties the motivation for their *aliyah* to their recognition of the Land's sanctity and their anticipation of the Messiah's imminent arrival.[66] Nicolayson adds that he met them in the Beirut hostel but failed to sell them scriptural texts.[67]

In August 1833, the missionary F. C. Ewald reports on the departure from Tunis of two groups of immigrants, comprising about one hundred elderly men and women[68]; he tells that more than three hundred Jews gathered at the port in Tunis to see their relatives off. In July 1834, he reports from Malta on the presence of a group of thirty-eight Jews from the interior of Morocco. After arriving in Malta by way of Gibraltar, they chartered an Austrian ship to bring them to the Syrian shore. The group included a distinguished Sefardic Jew, Señor Immanuel Israel, along with his wife and two daughters; according to Señor Immanuel, numerous families from Sayel, Arabat, and Tu'an were set to arrive shortly in Gibraltar to join the expedition, and a considerable number of Jews had moved eastward, intending the reach the Land of Israel. Ewald attributes the present interest in *aliyah* to expectation of great events, and he suggests that Muhammad Ali's conquest of the Land and establishment there of an enlightened government signified the time for renewed settlement of the Jews in the land of their fathers.[69] In the preceding year as well, Ewald adds, he had been told by a Jew that God is working wonders with respect to the redemption of the Jews. Because the Jews are now free and enjoy rights equal to those of other residents in the Land of Israel, they await the great event that is soon to come, "for it is time to be gracious to [Zion], for the appointed time has come" (Ps. 102:14).[70]

During 1834 and part of 1835, the missionary Joseph Wolff lived on the island of Malta, where he witnessed the Jews' emigration to the Land of Israel; he writes of noticing frequent columns of Jews en route from Morocco to Jerusalem via Malta.[71] A late-1834 report of the London Society tells of three thousand Jewish families that had already reached the Land of Israel, driven by the notion—mistaken, in the London Society's view—that the Messiah son of David was about to appear and renew the kingdom of Israel.[72] Wolff's accounts, which underlay the society's report, may well have been exaggerated, for he hoped to move the society to establish a large, permanent missionary presence in Jerusalem, but there is no reason to question the basic premise of mass *aliyah*.

In the spring of 1834, we hear of two families of German origin planning to immigrate to the Land of Israel in order "to increase settlement of the holy land."[73] Both families—those of Eliezer Bregman of the city of Zahl and of his friend, El'azar Dov, spiritual leader of the Hochberg community—maintained contact with Lehren, and his comments make clear that they, too, were motivated by active messianic expectations: "And I rejoiced that there was such news and such an increase in the number of people going up to the Land. God is pleased by their efforts; may the redemption succeed and be hastened and may the Messiah come quickly, speedily and in our day, amen."[74] In the summer of 1834, the Bregman family—Eliezer, his wife and five small children, his parents, and another single young man, Luzi (Eliezer) Halberstadt of Fürth—began their journey, taking considerable property with them; in late fall, their ship reached the Syrian coast. In his letters, Eliezer describes the heterogeneity of the immigrants: his ship also transported twenty-two North African Jews—men and women, children and elderly, and even four pregnant women—as well as forty-eight people from Moldavia and Wallachia.[75]

Bregman tells of another ship that had come from Constantinople a few days before his own arrival, bringing eighty people[76]; he adds: "It should be known to you that from other lands, *worthy people are actually streaming to the four holy cities* . . . [people] of all social strata and all ages, children and elderly, among them octogenarians and older."[77] Commenting on the efforts of Jews worldwide to support their brethren in the Land of Israel, Bregman warns against the erroneous notion that those efforts are limited to Ashkenazim; substantial funds, to be sure, are being provided by Russian and Polish Jews, but most of the funding is from eastern Jews: "The stream of Sefardim in these four holy cities is far greater, and they live more comfortably, for their relatives and friends are numerous."[78] North Africa is not the only source of Sefardic immigrants; Bregman tells of an organized group of fifty Jews that arrived toward the end of 1835 from Aleppo, in Syria. They affiliated with a group of twenty people from their community already in Jerusalem and established an independent congregation near the North African Jews' neighborhood.[79] In late summer 1835, Lehren tells of an acquaintance of Moses Sofer of Pressburg, who "set out in a small ship from Constantinople to the Land of Israel and brought with him prominent leaders from Wallachia along with much wealth, but by the end of Adar had still not arrived. It was rumored that they had been killed and drowned at sea . . . or that the ship had broken up."[80]

On 9 April 1836, the missionary Wolff tells of two Yemenite Jews from the city of San'a, the brothers Shalom and Barukh, sons of Zechariah, who had reached Suez by ship from Jedda. They arrived in torn and tattered clothes, and were getting ready to go up to Jerusalem. They told Wolff that they entertained no thoughts whatever of returning to Yemen, expressing the hope to see the Messiah in their lifetime. Failing that, they would die in the Land and be there when the righteous Messiah arrives.[81]

In July 1837, Ewald reports from Tunis on the *aliyah* of numerous Jews from all over the world. Most, he says, are motivated by superstitions growing out of what they are told by rabbinic emissaries from Jerusalem.[82] Other reports tell of immigrants from Odessa and Vilna, whose residents accompanied rabbinic emissaries on their return to the Land. On 17 December 1834, the survivors of a ship that had left Odessa on 20 August arrived in Safed. Among the travelers were Hasidic rabbinic emissaries from Safed and Tiberias, as well as a renowned magnate, Solomon of Kishinev. According to the account of another immigrant, Joseph Mansfeld of Kalish, Solomon's property that went through customs at the port of Beirut encompassed nine large trunks, containing six thousand gold coins, silver and gold utensils, diamond rings, furs, and books.[83]

We hear in summer 1838 of thirty immigrants setting out for the Land of Israel, among them "small boys and girls" (perhaps boys rescued from the forced military service of Czar Nikolai I). They join up with the bearers of the funds sent by the Nobles of Vilna for distribution in the Land of Israel. Lehren writes of them:

> It is surprising that you agreed, in your wisdom, to the journeying last summer of three bearers of blessing, who were a fruitful vine like Joseph [cf. Gen. 49:22], along with thirty souls. There would be no problem were the funds raised in their country for the Land of Israel on the increase; one could say that as the wealth increases, so, too, do those who consume it. But because of our many sins . . . why should some thirty souls (may God save and protect them) be added to take away the livelihood of those who dwell in the Holy [Land]? . . . It is one thing for elders, advanced in years, who want to live out their days in our Holy Land (may it be built and established) [to immigrate], or for known scholars who wish to become even wiser in the atmosphere of the Land of Israel, . . . but it does not seem right to us that young boys and girls, having no wealth of their own, should go up to the Land at this time.[84]

The traveling missionaries Bonar and McCheyne report on a significant increase in the Land of Israel's Jewish population during the reign of Muhammad Ali, particularly from 1832 to 1837. During that time, they say, many Jews came from the Barbary Coast of North Africa and settled primarily in Safed and the coastal towns. Later, in 1838–1839, the rate of *aliyah* tapered off, but a stream of immigrants nevertheless continued. Bonar and McCheyne attribute the pause in *aliyah* to the severe epidemic to which much of the local population, Jews included, succumbed during those years. The unfamiliar climate, cramped living quarters, and wretched sanitary conditions impaired the immigrants' ability to withstand the epidemic and contributed to their mortality rates.[85] These factors discouraged potential immigrants; and the continuation of a stream of *aliyah* in the face of such negative conditions, as reported by the Scottish missionaries, bears inquiry.

After gaining the confidence of the Jews and becoming familiar with prevailing Jewish practices and thought, Bonar and McCheyne suggest the Jewish immigration to the Land of Israel grows out of several factors: the elderly come to be buried there, because of the belief that burial in the Land of Israel has virtues that go beyond the mere avoidance of "underground rolling"; others come because of the belief that those living in the Land of Israel have a direct and better link with the *shekhinah* [God's presence, said to dwell in the Land of Israel]. But, they continue, greater weight is placed now than in the past on the expectation that the Messiah will appear in the Land of Israel, and many Jews are influenced by the sense that the critical time is approaching.[86]

With the epidemic's abatement at the end of 1839, immigration to the Land of Israel again grew in intensity. Bonar, who had previously described the pause in *aliyah* during the epidemic, now reports that an officer on one of the ships sailing to the Land of Israel had told him that between November 1839 and February 1840, he transported some sixty Jews to the Land of Israel on each sailing.[87]

Some large groups' efforts to emigrate were frustrated by factors beyond their control. One such group planned to set out from Morocco, apparently because of the messianic expectations for the year 5600. Rabbi Joseph Mesas recounts that "in the year 1840, the *aliyah* movement was again aroused and my father (may the memory of the righteous be for a blessing) was again moved to emigrate with a large column [of emigrants], but the matter became known to the town's governor, who forcefully held them back, for they included gold- and silversmiths and tailors needed by the townsfolk, inasmuch as the Arabs were not at all trained in those crafts."[88]

Natural Calamities That Impaired the Growth of Jewish Settlement in the Land of Israel

The ongoing stream of immigrants to the Land of Israel during the years between 1808 and 1840 suffered from time to time the severely adverse effects of the harsh living conditions there. The lack of clean, potable water and of adequate drainage and sewerage, along with the cramped living quarters, promoted the outbreak of epidemics—particularly of cholera, which is spread by pollution. In the absence of physicians, of medicines, and of ways to abate the underlying causes, it was difficult to control the epidemics, and they claimed many victims. The missionaries then active in the Land of Israel refer to the epidemics in their reports, considering both their effects on the Jewish community and the possibility of dispatching missionary-physicians to the Land of Israel. Their reports indicate a sharp decline in the growth rate of the Jewish community in the Land of Israel; Bonar emphasizes that despite the large numbers of arrivals, the epidemics' frightful toll was preventing them from becoming more numerous.[89] McCheyne likewise asserts that even though the Jewish community in the Land of Israel had grown apace since Muhammad Ali's conquest of the Land, the epidemics of 1838–1839 had killed many and caused the number of Jews living in Jerusalem to decline.[90] In sum, according to these missionaries, the number who perished in the epidemics exceeded the number of new immigrants and the natural growth of the community combined.[91] Both the high mortality rate on the one hand and the large number of immigrants on the other are referred to in a letter by the missionary G. W. Pieritz; he reports that a Jewish Jerusalemite told him that because of the high mortality during the preceding four years, most of the city's current residents were new immigrants.[92]

During 1813–1814, an epidemic raged in parts of Syria and spread to the

Galilee; it claimed the lives of many new immigrants affiliated with the *kolel* of the *Perushim*.[93] Among the victims were many members of Israel of Shklov's family: his wife Henya, who died on 3 June 1813; his son-in-law Joel, on 25 July; his daughter Leah, on 10 August; his son Naḥman on the very next day, 11 August; and, two days later, on 13 August, his daughter Esther and son Ze'ev Wolf. Later, his parents—R. Samuel and Malkah—also died.

The dreadful torments endured by Israel of Shklov and his family, as well as his ability to withstand them, were far from unique. In the introduction to his book *Pe'at ha-Shulḥan*, he describes the full measure of his suffering:

> And many people fled in columns to the deserts and forests. I, too, together with my family, journeyed to the holy city of Jerusalem (may it be built and established), and, en route, the loveliness of my home, the wife of my youth, the modest, God-fearing Henya (may her memory be bound in the bonds of life) died on the fifth of Sivan. I buried her en route, in the holy city of Shefar'am (may it be built and established speedily and in our days). And when I reached the holy city of Jerusalem (may it be built and established) with my family, I found fear and darkness in all quarters, death entering through our windows [cf. Jer. 9:20]. And there I was doubly afflicted because of my many sins; my sons went forth and are no longer, delightful young men, the delights of my heart. First, the plague began and claimed my eminent son-in-law . . . Joel . . . on the twenty-seventh of Tammuz, at the age of seventeen years, and, after him, my modest daughter Leah (may Eden be her resting place) died on the fourteenth of Av at the age of eighteen years. She left a nursing infant, the child dear to me, my eminent grandson, our honorable teacher the beloved R. Elyakim, and I suffered greatly to raise him to the age of twenty years, when he, too, was taken from me on the night following a festival in [1834]. And after that, my delightful son Naḥman died on Friday, the fifteenth of Av. My delightful daughter Esther died on the fourteenth of Av, and, after that, my delightful son, the pure of mind, Ze'ev Wolf (may his memory be for a blessing) died on Sunday, the seventeenth of Av, at the age of fourteen years. I then received bad news from the holy Galilee that my master, my father, the rabbi eminent in learning and fear of God, occupied in performing God's commandments, our honorable teacher Samuel (may the memory of the righteous be for a blessing) had died, along with my mother, my nurturer, the righteous Malkah (may Eden be her resting place). And I was as one lying in the midst of the sea in the aforesaid burning fire, and my friends and fellows avoided me and I lied on the roof crying and pleading before our Father in Heaven, and my modest little daughter Shaindel, may she live, was lying by me, and my tears ran down my cheeks, my eyes poured forth water on account of all I had suffered, and my agony was as great as the sea.[94]

In April 1827, plague broke out in the regions of Beirut, Damascus, and Aleppo.[95] It seems to have spread to Acco and Safed "to the point that death also entered through the windows of the aforesaid holy city, and because of our many sins, many precious souls were taken, and those who escaped confined themselves to their houses and courts so as to avoid proximity with afflicted people, and some fled from the city to rocky caves and dusty burrows, some of them cast as dung on the face of the field."[96] The description of their travails, incorporating the sharp imagery of the biblical prophets, reflects an unimaginable reality: on the one hand, a group of ill, suffering people, whose lives are in the balance, given over to isolation and quarantine, with no one coming and going; and, on the other, a group that removes itself, despite pangs of conscience, from anyone affected by the epidemic, becoming isolated within the city and effectively exiled through its efforts to escape the epidemic's grasp. Tiberias closed its doors to them, lest they infect the city.[97] The quarantine policy may have been harsh, but it was effective in controlling the epidemic and limiting mortality. Israel of Shklov claims that, having learned from the bitter experience of the earlier epidemic, he established a quarantine regimen for the members of the *kolel* of the *Perushim*; as a result, it suffered only twelve deaths, including infants and women who declined to observe the quarantine. In contrast, three hundred members of the *kolel* of the Hasidim perished, as did a like number of Sefardim.[98] The epidemic appeared to be abating in late summer 1827, but, after a few months, it regained force.[99] In May 1828, the missionary Wolff reports on an epidemic in the Beirut area; in that instance, as well, quarantine was applied. He tells that people visiting his home were careful to avoid hand-to-hand contact with others, lest disease germs be transferred. According to his account, the epidemic spread to the Land of Israel: in Jaffa and Gaza, half of the residents were afflicted, and in Jerusalem, fifteen people died each day.[100] Lehren recounts that over 250 souls perished in the epidemic[101]; among them was the first immigrant from Holland, Ozer Emmerich, who died on 28 September 1827).[102]

The reports on the epidemics and associated sacrifices reflect a particularly cruel environment, in which widespread loss of life to illness is a part of the normal scene. And even where a report is dry and laconic, it resonates with indescribable daily suffering. In July 1831, there are indications of a cholera epidemic in Acre.[103] In September of that year, there are reports of cholera in Jerusalem and Hebron as well. Reports from Egypt tell of an epidemic claiming hundreds of lives each day.[104] In the spring of 1832, an epidemic broke out in the Galilee; Israel of Shklov reports about one hundred deaths in Tiberias.[105] In fall of 1833, plague broke out in Jerusalem and spread to the Galilee; "many died of it until Hanukkah."[106] A cholera epidemic erupted in Jerusalem after the festival of Shavuot in 1837; it claimed an estimated two hundred lives.[107] July 1838 saw a particularly severe outbreak of plague in Jerusalem; it continued, with some remissions, for the better part of a year and, on 2 June 1838, took the life of Hillel Rivlin of Shklov.[108] The missionary-healer Dr. A. Gerstmann reports that many of the ill were saved by the care the missions provided; he adds that living conditions accounted, at least in part, for the epidemic's severity. Quarters in Jerusalem were horrendously cramped, three or four families sharing one small, dark, damp, unventilated room.[109] This time, though, precautions were taken: houses containing the sick were quarantined, and food could be brought only by individuals who had survived an epidemic.[110] Nevertheless, in spring of 1839, the epidemic still raged in Jerusalem, the city remained under quarantine, and mortality was high.[111]

Another appallingly destructive natural disaster was the earthquake of 1 January 1837. In a few short minutes, Safed and Tiberias were reduced to mounds of rubble and thousands of residents were killed and buried under the debris. An eyewitness in Tiberias tells that "he and four others were on the road . . . when the earthquake began. Suddenly the ground opened and closed again, and two members of his party disappeared. He ran home in panic and found that his wife, his mother, and two other family members had perished. The next day, when he excavated the site at which his two companions had disappeared, he found them dead but standing erect."[112] Another eyewitness from Tiberias, who had been in the field shepherding her goats, describes what she saw from the mountaintops:

> I heard a noise like that of a powerful storm, the ground shook underneath me, rock fragments fell from the mountains. . . . I gazed on the city walls: great gaps had opened in them, the towers shook. . . . Suddenly, it appeared as if the entire city had tilted toward the sea, and, a minute later, I saw nothing except a thick, dark dust cloud that covered the entire city; after that, one heard a sound like that of thunder in a cyclone and cries of terror and woe from thousands of mouths. . . . Throughout the night, I worked to roll the stones from atop the bodies of my children. My fingers ran with blood, no one helped me, and I had to give up my effort to find my children; they are buried here beneath the debris. My husband, too, I never again saw. . . . Yet we could not leave this city, so precious to us even in its destruction; here we will live, and here we will die.[113]

This account by an ordinary person expresses, in simple terms, the determination to become firmly rooted in the place despite the intense collective catastrophe. There can be no doubt that, beyond her religious faith, her remarks convey the powerful existential motivation of the Jewish populace in the Land of Israel and the sense of mission impressed on their hearts. The traveler Edward Robinson adds that in Safed, "as in Tiberias, the disaster fell with great weight and full force on Jews of humble fortunes" (in contrast to members of other faiths). He attributes that disproportionate effect to the poor location of the Jewish neighborhood, on the steep mountainside:

> Many died instantly under mounds of debris; many more were swallowed up and died pathetic deaths, before they could be pulled from their ruins; some were extracted after five or six days, covered with wounds, only to linger for a few hours in torment. . . . And this is what could be seen during the weeks following the disaster: every-

> where the wounded, the dying, and the dead, unprotected, unsupervised, and with no place to rest their heads; on all sides, "wounds, bruises, and festering sores, not pressed, nor bandaged, nor soothed with oil" [Isa. 1:6]—such sights were described to us by eyewitnesses in indescribable grief and sometimes overcome by nausea.[114]

The total destruction wreaked by the earthquake, and the impression it made, are described as well in the letter of Aryeh Ne'eman, who witnessed it with his own eyes:

> In the Upper and Lower Galilee, all the houses were destroyed . . . and the mountain was overturned onto them. . . . In a single instant, the precious lives were taken and ascended heavenward. . . . And since the day the Holy Temple was destroyed, there has not been such a destruction, in which the holy cities of Safed and Tiberias were destroyed to their very foundations. Fourteen synagogues here in the holy city of Safed were destroyed, their crowns cast down to earth, along with the crown of the holy Torah and the best of the city's holy people, whose homes were their graves. . . . And we hired laborers to take away the stones so as to remove the dead for burial, and we found among them the righteous rabbi our master, the rabbi R. Eliezer, son of our master the rabbi Mordecai of Slonim (may Eden be his resting place), and the rabbi renowned for acts of kindness, our master the rabbi R. Joseph of Tscherkovo (may Eden be his resting place), wearing his *tefillin* and holding a book of *midrash*, which he was expounding before the congregation.[115]

He describes the impression made by the catastrophe on the survivors:

> And our brethren who remained alive live in tents, where rain falls on them, with no clothes and no covering, without even shoes on their feet . . . this one with a broken arm and that one with a broken leg; this one sitting and crying and that one wailing and keening over his dead. Sounds of lamentation are heard on all sides, and people would give their all to bury their dead, and they remain shrouded in hunger in all the courtyards. . . . There is no adequate description of the grief and woe, hearing the groans and sighs of the sick, for whom there is no medicine, no physician, no balm, and no dressing.[116]

Edward Robinson estimated that about fourteen thousand Jews perished in the earthquake,[117] but that figure is overstated. According to Israel of Shklov's data, the number of Jews who died was just over two thousand.[118] He provided the following details in a letter to Moses Sofer of Pressburg: in Safed, 144 members of the *kolel* of the *Perushim* were killed, as were 500 members of the Hasidic *kolel* and 1,000 members of the Sefardic *kolel*; in Tiberias, 112 Sefardim and 280 Hasidim were killed.[119]

About one and one-half years after the earthquake, Robinson visited the area and reported that "in the Jewish quarter, many houses were rebuilt in a makeshift manner . . . and we found pathetic Jews still roaming around the ruins." Still, he offered the following assessment: "After a few more years, the earthquake's aftermath may no longer recognizable in Safed. For that is the oriental way of life. Earthquakes and wars periodically wash over the land, laying waste to cities and villages; yet the residents, rooted in the land, rebuild their cities and go on with their lives."[120]

In a document written in the latter half of the nineteenth century, Aryeh Ne'eman briefly recounts how the *Perushim* established their settlement in the Land of Israel despite the hardships and suffering they regularly faced:

> And several thousand souls were immersed in this enterprise from [1802], when settlement began in our organization in the Upper Galilee, and from [1816], when our organization began its settlement here in the holy city [of Jerusalem]. On account of the great epidemic [that continued for] two successive years, [1813] and [1814] in Safed (may it be built and established), God save us from it . . . [many died], and they ascended heavenward, and of the great men there remained only the pious one, the kabbalist, our teacher, the rabbi Menaḥem Mendel, a disciple of the Ga'on, knowledgeable in the hidden wisdom (may the memory of the righteous and holy be for a blessing) and the rabbi, the *ga'on*, our teacher the rabbi Israel (may the memory of the righteous and holy be for a blessing), author of *Taqlin Ḥadtin* (*New Shekels*). . . . And between then and 5600 [1840], the community suffered four epidemics (God protect us) and was afflicted by cholera three times. . . . And in [1838] and [1839], there was a plague in which those who had survived the earthquake ascended heavenward, and our hearts trembled at the suffering that came over us.[121]

Poverty, Insecurity, Political Instability, and Other Limitations on Growth

The growth of Jewish settlement in the Land of Israel was adversely affected as well by political instability and by the arbitrary attitudes toward the Jews of the local rulers and populace at large, particularly between 1819 and 1831. Even though the stream of immigration continued during those years, the Jewish population fell—both because Jews were expelled and because they fled the hardship. David Joseph Ayash portrays the hardships borne by the Land of Israel's residents and the resulting emigration from the Land: "For these days, we are not free to do that [i.e., to immigrate to the Land in tranquility] but only in distress and suffering, and it is plausible to return to live outside the Land . . . as we have heard, so we have seen on a daily basis."[122]

The period of political calm and security for the Jews in the Land of Israel came to an end in late summer 1820. On 9 August of that year, Ḥayyim Farḥi, treasurer to the governor of Acco, was murdered by his master Abdullah Pasha, "enemy of all the Jews" (cf. Esth. 9:24).[123] There ensued a period of continual oppression and heavy taxation in the Galilee and in Jerusalem. On the Sabbath of 12 August 1820, Abdullah Pasha arrested all the Jews of Safed, claiming that Farḥi had concealed from the authorities the presence in the Land of thousands of Jews on whose behalf taxes had not been paid.[124] The Jews suffered even as passive bystanders to dealings between the governmental authorities and non-Jews, such as the suppression in 1821 of the Greek rebellion against Turkey.[125] The Jews of the Galilee were harmed by the war between Abdullah Pasha and the rulers of Damascus, and many were forced to flee the Land in November 1823.[126] In Jerusalem, the Sefardim suffered punishment on account of another community's offense: a rebellion of the *fellahin* against Mustafa Pasha, the governor of Damascus, had broken out in February 1825. With the rebellion's suppression, heavy fines were levied on the local population, including the Greek Orthodox and the Sefardic Jews of Jerusalem.[127] After the rebellion's renewal in June 1825, Jerusalem was besieged and succumbed, and Jews fled the oppressor.[128] Later, in October 1826, Sultan Mahmoud directed Abdullah Pasha to go to Jerusalem and subjugate its inhabitants. A force of two thousand besieged the city, and seven cannons shelled it from atop the Mount of Olives.[129] When the city was again overpowered, its residents were turned over to the authorities to be brutalized, and Nathan Neta, son of Menaḥem Mendel, tells that many Jews fled Jerusalem. Wealthier Jews in particular were imprisoned so that their money could be extracted from them.[130] It was in these circumstances that Menaḥem Mendel of Shklov died on 28 February 1827.[131]

Conflicting reports regarding the situation in Jerusalem reached Beirut in October 1827. Some told of Jerusalem's conquest by the Pasha, but others, diametrically opposed, recounted that the city's residents had succeeded in neutralizing the Pasha's forces.[132] The unrest and on-going warfare between the Pasha of Damascus and the Jerusalem populace continued into 1828. As usual, heavy fines were levied on Jerusalem's Jews, and the Sefardic community came under intense pressure and nearly collapsed altogether after having had to borrow huge sums of money.[133]

In February 1829, things took a turn for the better. At the start of that year, the Jew Rafael Farḥi, imprisoned since 1823, was released and appointed prime minister in the Damascus province; another Jew, a member of Farḥi's family, was appointed secretary to the governor in Jerusalem. The Jews' standing improved markedly, to the point that even the Turkish officials in Jerusalem, including the local military commander, began currying favor with them.[134] But even Muhammad Ali's ascendancy, generally a good time for the Jews, had its low points—including the *fellahin* rebellion of 1834 and the Druse rebellion of 1838—when *aliyah* was reduced and some Jews even emigrated from the Land of Israel.[135]

In April 1836, Nicolayson reports from Beirut on his surprising encounter with several Jewish families en route back to eastern Europe—an extraordinary phenomenon, in his view. He tells of being surprised, on a visit to the [Beirut] hostel where Jews from Poland and Russia are usually to be found, to find many Jewish families who had arrived there from the Holy Land for the purpose of returning to their countries in Europe. On being asked to explain, they responded along these lines:

> The persecutions [in our native lands] and the hope for the coming of the Messiah brought us to the Holy Land, but poverty and disillusionment are returning us to Europe. Some of the possessions and furnishings that we brought with us from Europe were pillaged and destroyed by the *fellahin* during the rebellion [of 1834]. We received only scanty support from out brethren in Europe. To avoid leaving the Holy Land, we attempted to make do with one meal a day to sustain our families, but even that degree of support began to fade. Despite that, our wives strove mightily not to leave, and they expressed full satisfaction and agreement with the Talmud's statement that as long a person is able to make do with one meal a day and that meal includes bread, he is forbidden to leave the Holy Land. But we, the men, could not accept that. And so we sold the remainder of our possessions and came here in order to sail to Constantinople.[136]

Nicolayson adds that those leaving the Land of Israel told him of their concerns about financing the remainder of their journey. Their brethren in Turkey and Russia, they said, willingly support immigrants traveling to the Holy Land; but they deny support to emigrants from it and even harass them in every possible way and demean them for having deserted the kingdom of Israel. Nicolayson writes of an elderly person in the group of emigrants who told him that but for his concern about suffering a fate similar to that of Moses' scouts (in Num. 13–14), he would disclose to his brethren in Europe the whole truth about conditions in the Land and would suggest they remain in their homes, to "enjoy the flesh-pot" and not to go up to the Land and "reap the wind."[137] When Nicolayson tried to persuade the emigrants to reverse their course, relying on the Jewish claims regarding expectation of the Messiah, he realized that though the intense messianic expectation had brought them to the Land three years earlier, they were now indifferent to it, and some had nearly abandoned all hope. He adds that the desolate Land's barrenness, especially in contrast to Europe's fertility, also contributed to the chilling of their attitude to the Land of Israel and all the promises tied to its existence. Nicolayson tried to encourage and fortify them, reminding them of the biblical prophecies dealing with the future glory of Jerusalem, but they remained indifferent. Regarding the Messiah, they said: "On the contrary, let him come and redeem us from servitude and from torments, and then we will believe in him."[138] When Nicolayson left the hostel, he met additional families who had left the Land of Israel; some were so poor that they had made their way to Beirut on foot.[139]

Lehren, too, refers to economically motivated emigration from the Land; he tells of debtors who fled to escape obligations they simply could not meet.[140]

The most renowned emigrant was Shemariah Luria, who had come to the Land of Israel in 1832 and left in 1834. The reasons for his departure are somewhat obscure, but the sources suggest he failed to find the economic opportunities he had hoped for.[141]

Not only was there emigration from the Land of Israel; there also were impediments to immigration. The epidemics afflicted both residents of the Land and immigrants en route, in Syria, in Egypt, and in the quarantine camps throughout the Land's coastal towns. We also know of at least four instances in which boats carrying immigrants were lost at sea, and it is fair to assume, given the communications technology of the day, that there were others of which we have no reports.

And yet, despite all these negative factors—including the flight of Jews from the Galilee or Jerusalem, the imposition of heavy fines on the communal organizations, and the immeasurable growth of their debts—*aliyah* went on. It continued even in the face of the Turks' suppression of a *fellahin* revolt at the end of 1826, when the Jewish population was a target of the Turkish authorities' drive for revenge.[142] The harsh living conditions described above did not cut off the steady stream of immigration that continued through the period; and notwithstanding all the hardships and disasters, the Jewish population in the Land of Israel grew by some five thousand people between 1808 and 1840. It follows that substantial immigration must have gone on in the face of the harsh, discouraging conditions; and, if that was the case, the countervailing positive factors that motivated immigration must have been quite powerful. Moreover, the immigration of young families with small children, and of famous, wealthy people, demonstrates that *aliyah* was not for the purpose of living out the end of one's life in the Holy Land, so as to die and be buried there, but for the purpose of building and establishing a new life, either by investing in property or by raising a new generation.

The Montefiore Census of 1839: In the Aftermath of the Earthquake and Epidemics

The Montefiore census of 1839 confirms these conclusions regarding the *aliyah*'s magnitude and demographics. It appears that the Jews at first did not realize why Montefiore had arranged for the census, the first of its kind within the Jewish community in the Land of Israel in the modern era. In their innocence, they thought its purpose was only to facilitate distribution of *ḥaluqah* funds he had brought, and they accordingly were willing to be counted—in contrast to Montefiore's later censuses, in which a segment of the populace declined to participate for religious reasons.

The census is particularly valuable because it provides a comprehensive picture. It comprises not anonymous statistics but lists of names affiliated with the various communal organizations. It refers as well to peoples' ages, family circumstances, year of immigration, and—albeit in less detail—occupations and economic conditions.

According to the census data—which were analyzed by Joseph Meisel[143]—the Land of Israel in the summer of 1839 was home to 6,547 Jews, residing in twelve areas: the four holy cities of Jerusalem, Safed, Hebron, and Tiberias; the four coastal cities of Sidon, Haifa, Acre, and Jaffa; and four agricultural settlements (Shefar'am, Shekhem, Peqi'in, and Jermaq). Other data derived from the census include the following:

Some 68 percent of the Jews in the Land of Israel had been born outside the Land.[144]
Some 74 percent of the Jews in the Land of Israel originated in the Muslim world.[145]
About 60 percent of the Jews in the Land of Israel had immigrated during the years 1830 to 1839.[146]

That last datum leads to the conclusion that during the period in question, the reign of Muhammad Ali, there were great waves of immigration, and about six thousand Jews reached the Land.

The data regarding the Jews' age distribution are of particular interest, for they directly contradict the notion, blindly adopted in the literature, that the movement of Jews to the Land of Israel during the first half of the nineteenth century was "an *aliyah* of the elderly."[147] The census identifies age brackets for 4,044 Jews out of the total of 6,547:

Ages 1–9: 1,153 people; 28.37 percent
Ages 10–19: 712 people; 17.52 percent
Ages 20–29: 377 people; 9.27 percent
Ages 30–39: 460 people; 11.31 percent
Ages 40–49: 603 people; 14.82 percent
Ages 50–70: 691 people; 18.79 percent

In other words, 45.89 percent of the people, about half of the population being considered, were below the age of 20.[148]

4

Process of Redemption Envisioned by the Vilna Ga'on's Disciples

If in Second Temple times we did not find God manifesting His might to the congregation of Israel through patent and public miracles . . . how very much more so will [such miracles] not be manifest in the third redemption; rather, in the future, the event will be conducted in accord with the natural order, not a miracle.

Judah Edel, *Afiqei Yehudah*

Figure of the Vilna Ga'on

The Vilna Ga'on's disciples, known as the *Perushim*, occupy a special place among the groups of immigrants who reached the Land of Israel in the early nineteenth century. They are distinguished primarily by their tie to a charismatic spiritual leader and to the unique conception of Israel's redemption associated with his name.

The Ga'on Rabbi Elijah ben Solomon Zalman of Vilna (1720–1797)[1] defies easy characterization. A genuine prodigy, he discoursed at the age of six and one-half years before rabbis and great scholars in the Vilna synagogue and had already shown extraordinary erudition and insight. Even at that early age, he had a thoroughgoing knowledge of both the Written and the Oral Torah, and before he reached the age of bar mitzvah, he had begun to study Kabbalah.[2] In his youth, he acquired an all-embracing scientific knowledge, which he applied to the better understanding of passages in the Oral Torah. His absolute command of all of biblical and rabbinic literature made him one of the leading Torah sages of all time. His disciple Israel of Shklov writes of him:

> He knew thoroughly the entire Torah given at Sinai, all the Prophets and Writings, and how the Mishnah and Oral Torah were encompassed within them. In his old age, he no longer had any uncertainty regarding any particular *halakhah* or passage in the entire Torah. He knew the entire Oral Torah and all the decisors, down to the most recent commentators on the *Shulḥan Arukh*. He clarified them all, drawing light from the darkness of errors and refining them into fine flour, free of chaff. [He knew as well] the hidden wisdom, all we have of the books of the *Zohar* . . . and he studied and thoroughly knew the writings of the Ari [Rabbi Isaac Luria, an important kabbalist], may his memory be for a blessing, and the various methods of scriptural interpretation, including the mysteries. . . . Only two serious matters among the secrets of the Torah contained in the *Zohar* were difficult for him.[3]

His disciples' attitude toward his genius in both Torah and science can be heard in the words of Elijah Rogoler, chief judge of the Jewish court in Kalish: "In our times, we see our holy rabbi, the divine *tanna* [a term usually applied only to sages of the Mishnah], our master, the rabbi Elijah of Vilna, recognized by all as one in comparison with whom all past sages and professors are as [insubstantial as] garlic skin. They cannot at all match him in any of the seven liberal arts, and they acknowledge that his mind is not that of flesh and blood but of a very awesome godly man. . . . All who see him, and all his disciples who poured water over his hands [in service to him] attest that this is not at all one born of woman."[4] Evidently, his students had difficulty in explaining his vast achievements exclusively as the product of intellectual endeavors. His disciple Ḥayyim of Volozhin writes that the Ga'on experienced an "ascent of the soul" each night and studied at the "celestial academy," where the mysteries of creation and the Torah were revealed to him.[5] Israel of Shklov, who attended the Vilna Ga'on during the final months of his life, likewise refers to the superhuman dimension of the Ga'on's character: "And there were revealed to him mysteries of our father Jacob, and Moses our Teacher, peace be upon him, and [the prophet] Elijah. . . . And we are sending a few of his books, holy with mysteries, and some of the secrets he discovered, which until his advent had been concealed from all who live."[6] People close to the Ga'on and succeeding generations alike saw in his character a supernatural phenomenon with a messianic mission related to the discovery and dissemination of the truths and mysteries of the Torah and to the charting of a practical course for the redemption of the Land and people of Israel.

This view of the Vilna Ga'on was shared by all his disciples, from the rationalist Menasheh of Ilya to the mystic Menaḥem Mendel of Shklov. Menasheh of Ilya writes: "It appears that God has sent us an angel and a holy one from the heavens, the renowned Ga'on, our teacher Rabbi Elijah, may the memory of the righteous be for a blessing, who began the process of restoring the crown of Torah to its earlier glory . . . until matters attain perfect repair (*tiqqun*) and we become worthy of experiencing light and divine bounty through our righteous Messiah."[7] Menaḥem Mendel of Shklov, meanwhile, attributes his own immigration to the Land of Israel and his activity in its settlement to his being the Ga'on's disciple: "And [God] brought me to the home of our lord, master, and teacher, the pious Ga'on of Vilna, rabbi of the entire Diaspora, and God caused me to find favor in [the Ga'on's] eyes and attend him with all my strength. . . . And his merit and that of my fathers . . . stood me in good stead to bring me to the Holy Land."[8]

A book written on the one-hundredth anniversary of the Vilna Ga'on's death conveys all the foregoing elements of his personality, especially his heavenly mission to change the world by disseminating the true method of Torah study and by settling the Land of Israel: "And [God] sent us from on high an angel-like man, garbed in holiness, to plant the tree of life on earth and in its inhabitants. . . . And had not Elijah His chosen one stood in the breach, the Torah would have been forgotten within Israel. And second in holiness was his love for our Holy Land, an unbounded love. . . . He is the foremost one of Zion and Jerusalem, laying the foundation for the settlement of our Holy Land, and his disciples streamed after him, may their merit protect us, Amen."[9] It is hardly surprising, therefore, that this "angel-like" man, seen as a supernatural phenomenon, enjoyed absolute authority and that his interpretations and his understanding of the redemptive process, however opposed to the traditional conception, were accepted as the words of the living God.

The Ga'on never took the trouble to write up his commentaries and ideas in any organized way; he would jot down his commentaries as elliptical and allusive marginal notes. Most of his teachings were committed to writing by his inner circle of disciples, on the basis of his oral remarks or of his notes that they later interpreted. Accordingly, our examination of the Vilna Ga'on's concept of redemption must make use of his disciples' writings and of the traditions reduced to writing during the first half of the nineteenth century. Menaḥem Mendel of Shklov speaks not only of a tradition that he received directly from the Vilna Ga'on but also of that tradition's development into a structured system based on fundamental principles that he learned from the Ga'on: "And I attended him with all my strength, and for the entire one and two-thirds years that I was with him, I never budged from him. . . . And I left his tent neither by day nor by night; where he went, I went, and where he lodged, I lodged, and my hand never left his at all, and he opened the door of wisdom for me. . . . And my ear also heard and understood what he said to others and on this I built great and profound structures."[10]

The Ga'on's Destiny as Understood by His Disciples

In his commentary on *Sifra di-Ẓeni'uta*, the Ga'on concludes that the name and mission of every person on earth are alluded to in the Torah: "And the rule is that all that was, is, and ever will be is included within the Torah, from 'In the beginning' [Gen. 1:1] to 'in the sight of all Israel' [Deut. 34:12]. And not only the generalities but even the details of each and every species and each individual person, and all the events of his life, from the day of his birth to his end."[11] When asked by one of his critics where his own name was alluded to in Scripture, the Vilna Ga'on cited the phrase "a full and honest weight" (Deut. 25:15); the Hebrew for "a full weight" (*even shelemah; e-b-n sh-l-m-h*) is an acronym for Elijah son of Solomon (*E[liyahu] b[e]n Shelomoh*).[12] In his book *Emunah ve-Hashgaḥah,* Samuel Moltzen of Slutsk refers to that statement, adding a related comment that he had heard from Isaac Margaliot, chief judge of Shczoczin, who had heard it attributed to the Ga'on by Ḥayyim of Volozhin: Deuteronomy, the fifth book of the Torah, contains ten weekly portions, each of them relating to one century of the sixth millennium since the creation of the world. That the foregoing allusion to the Ga'on's name appears toward the end of the sixth of those portions (*Ki Teiẓei*) implies a connection to the sixth century of the sixth millennium. The ensuing portion—*Ki Tavo*; "When you come to the Land"—symbolizes the promise of the seventh century in relation to the sixth: that is, the return to the Land beginning in the year 5600.[13]

These authentic sources lend credence as well to the central themes in the eulogy of the Vilna Ga'on by his cousin, Benjamin Rivlin of Shklov. The biblical passage cited above as alluding to the Vilna Ga'on's name is followed immediately by the account of Amaleq's attack on Israel and Israel's obligation to wipe out all memory of Amaleq. According to Benjamin Rivlin, wiping out the memory of Amaleq implies the triumph of faith over apostasy, as the Torah is propagated, and he sees the Vilna Ga'on's mission with regard to disseminating Torah as tied to that allusion. Moreover, the ensuing weekly portion, as already noted, speaks of the Israelites coming to the Land, thereby alluding to the Vilna Ga'on's second mission—bringing about the immigration of his disciples to the Land of Israel, as a means of taking earthly action to stimulate redemption from on high (*it'aruta de-le-tata*; "awakening from below").[14]

The Vilna Ga'on himself set out to immigrate to the Land of Israel and wrote to his family while en route. The letter reveals a bit of the Ga'on's personal side, not otherwise disclosed because he tried to avoid pausing in his Torah study: "I ask you not to be troubled at all . . . and not to worry, for there are people who travel for years in order to earn money, leaving their wives behind and wandering in poverty, but I, praise God, am traveling to the Holy Land that all hope to see, the delight of all Israel and the delight of God, may He be blessed, desired by all celestial and terrestrial beings, and I am traveling in peace, God be blessed."[15] For reasons unknown, the Ga'on abandoned his journey and turned on his heel; upon his return, the documents say, he paid back the loans he had taken to pay for the journey.[16]

The Ga'on's disciples accounted in various ways for his failure to attain his goal of immigrating to the Land of Israel. One suggested that "the Ga'on, may his repose be in Eden, was a spark of Moses our teacher, peace be upon him, and Heaven therefore denied him permission to enter the Land."[17] Moses, the chosen spiritual leader sent by God, had the mission of distinguishing Israel as the nation of Torah and preparing it for its entry into the chosen land. He completed his task at that point, leaving it to someone else to actually bring the Israelites into the Land. Similarly, the Ga'on's mission was to be the agent of providence, charged with disseminating Torah and thereby initiating the final stage in the redemption of the Jewish people on its land, but he himself did not lead them there.

But though the Ga'on himself never settled in the Land of Israel, his decision to set out for there resonated loudly among his disciples. Their descendants have a widespread though still undocumented tradition that the Ga'on in his will instructed his disciples to immigrate to the Land,[18] and Ẓevi Hirsch Lehren writes of that directive as something well known. In a letter dated in 1837, he speculates on Abraham Solomon Zalman Ẓoref's motives for *aliyah*, for Ẓoref, in contrast to other immigrants, was not carrying out the Ga'on's directive: "I am surprised by one who says [Ẓoref's] mission was in accordance with the Vilna Ga'on." In Lehren's view, Ẓoref never attained the status of a distinguished scholar and was not a member of the group of immigrants who saw themselves as carrying out the Ga'on's will; rather, he was part of the group led by Elijah of Bialystok, serving as the latter's personal attendant, "but not as a colleague and certainly not undertaking a mission."[19]

Some years ago, there came to light a manuscript by Aryeh Ne'eman, who immigrated to the Land of Israel in 1813 and served for many years as a trustee of the *kolel* of the *Perushim* in Jerusalem. The manuscript mentions two previously unknown facts related to the *aliyah* of the Vilna Ga'on's disciples: that the initiative began in 1800, only two years after the Ga'on's death, and that the individual who initiated the project was none other than his eminent disciple, Ḥayyim of Volozhin, hitherto known only for his moral, organizational, and economic support for this *aliyah*. Aryeh Ne'eman writes as follows:

> In [1800], God directed His attention to the holy lands and a spirit of purity aroused itself within the heart of the righteous one, foundation of the world, the true genius, our master Rabbi Ḥayyim, may his memory be for a blessing, of Volozhin, an eminent disciple of our lord, master, and teacher, rabbi of all the Diaspora, our master Rabbi Elijah of Vilna, may the memory of the righteous be for a blessing, may his merit protect all Israel. He raised up the banner of Torah in Israel, establishing yeshivas throughout Russia, and he began to marshal plans for opening the gates of the Holy Land and then secretly dispatched from among the disciples of the Ga'on, the pious one, may his memory endure to the life of the world to come, the righteous one, foundation of the world, our master Rabbi Mendel, may the memory of the righteous be for a blessing, a student of the aforesaid Ga'on, together with his son.[20]

To be sure, Aryeh Ne'eman makes no explicit reference to the Vilna Ga'on's will, but that does not undermine the tradition with respect to this matter, which tends to be confirmed by logical inference: the fact that Ḥayyim, even before undertaking his efforts to establish the yeshiva in Volozhin (in late 1802), devoted considerable energies to organizing *aliyah* on the part of the Ga'on's disciples—and, in particular, the fact that he sent several leading disciples to the Land of Israel, rather than having them involved in establishing "the World of Torah"—suggest that the moral inspiration for this *aliyah* must have been a desire to carry out the Ga'on's will.

Sense of the Approaching End-Time

As noted earlier, the Torah portion of *Ki Tavo* was taken as alluding to events in the seventh century of the sixth millennium, anno mundi. The portion contains a series of curses that will befall Israel if they fail to observe the laws of the Torah, and Samuel Moltzen, who worked at collecting the Vilna Ga'on's teachings, saw a necessary connection between the misfortunes described in the scriptural passage and the return to the Land of Israel: "Accordingly, those with insight can easily come to the opinion that the many disasters and misfortunes that have befallen us in this world during this seventh century are alluded to in the curses of the portion '*Ki Tavo.*' "[21]

The connection between the many misfortunes befalling Israel and the approaching redemption is examined at several points in the Vilna Ga'on's writings as well. In his commentary on the Book of Esther, he considers the remarks that appear toward the end of the mishnaic tractate *Sotah* on the period of the final redemption and the troubles that will accompany it. In the Ga'on's view, the troubles signify the end of the period of exile: "Rather, all of the difficulties that Israel suffers in the exile bring the salvation closer . . . and, therefore, all the curses are for their good, to hasten the redemption."[22] Hillel of Kovno, a contemporary of the Ga'on and one of the signatories on the epistle of the Ga'on's disciples in Safed,[23] likewise determines that the troubles befalling Israel in his time constitute an indication that the redemption is imminent: "The root cause of the exile's length is that we have not taken it upon ourselves to taste the taste of exile . . . for without exile, there is no redemption."[24] It appears to be the abundance of torments that will hasten the End, as Hillel of Kovno says elsewhere: "And when a spirit of magnanimity is aroused from on high to redeem us . . . but repentance is denied us, then God will call on the heavenly host . . . which is to say, He will also call on terrestrial kings and direct them to undertake harsh and wicked persecutions."[25] It is not repentance that is determinative, however, but the time—that is, the time for redemption that was set from the outset. Samuel Moltzen, following traditions attributed to the Vilna Ga'on, compares the start of Israel's redemption to a seed that starts to sprout precisely when it is most dried out. So too Israel: when the woes inflicted on it by the nations reach their pinnacle, then the reversal will begin, and with the help of those very nations, Israel's redemption will commence through natural processes. As he put it:

> And just as a seed planted in the earth when it is dry and almost totally lost and destroyed will come back and grow, and the moisture and soil and fertilizer that prevailed over it from the beginning, drying it and putting an end to it, will [now] continue to instill their strength in it to cause it to sprout and grow even more than before

> . . . so we have found of the Jewish nation, "Instead of copper I will bring gold . . ." [Isa. 60:17] and "strangers shall build your walls" [Isa. 60:10].[26]

It seems that the very fact of the Vilna Ga'on's appearance on the stage of history was taken as proof that the End was approaching, for his disciples, as already noted, believed he had been sent for that purpose: "For as it appears, the duration of our exile implies that the footsteps of our Messiah are near, and that it is necessary to clear a path before him, the path of truth. . . . And as it appears, God sent us an angel and holy one from heaven, the renowned Ga'on, our master Rabbi Elijah, may the memory of the righteous be for a blessing."[27] The Ga'on's commentary on *Sifra di-Ẓeni'uta* likewise contains hints that the time of the Messiah's coming is no longer in the category of a secret: "But I adjure the reader by the Lord God of Israel not to reveal this."[28] In *Ma'ayanei ha-Yeshu'ah*, Moses Katzenellenbogen recounts a tradition his father had received from the Ga'on, implying that the Ga'on saw the starting time for the redemptive process as determined and known, at a point three generations after his own time:

> And so you find concerning the days of the Messiah that they will rebel only as a result of eating and drinking and tranquility, as it is said of them, "Jeshurun grew fat and kicked; you grew fat, and thick, and gross" [Deut. 21:15]—these [three terms] refer to the three generations that precede the days of the Messiah. . . . And I received from my late father, may Eden be his resting place, who had received it from the pious Ga'on, our rabbi Elijah of Vilna, may the memory of the righteous and holy be for a blessing, the time at which those three generations would begin.[29]

That the Ga'on saw the onset of the End-time as close by is important in and of itself. For our purposes, however, it is even more important that his disciples and their cohort had a strong inner sense that the onset of the End-time was indeed approaching. They saw themselves as sent to move the concept of redemption from the realm of the potential to that of the actual. The sense of the imminent End suffused their beings, and it served as a powerful inner motivation for all their efforts related to *aliyah* and to settlement of the Land.

Redemption Is Not Contingent on Repentance

The Talmud and *midrashim* consider the subject of redemption from varied points of view. In tractate *Sanhedrin*, a sage of Elijah's academy (*tanna de-bei Eiliyahu*) states: "The world endures for six thousand years—two thousand of chaos, two thousand of Torah, and two thousand of the Messiah's era."[30] In this *tanna*'s view, human history follows a preordained divine plan, progressing toward the higher good that will exist at the end of days. The *tanna* fails to comment, however, on whether the transition to the Messiah's era depends on earthly human actions, and, in the Talmud's ensuing consideration of his statement, a dispute arises regarding the nature of that age: Does it come about simply because the pre-set time has arrived, or is it contingent on human repentance? In other words, does the redemption depend on the End or on repentance? "Rav said, 'All the set times are passed, and the matter depends solely on repentance and good deeds.' . . . Rabbi Eliezer says, 'If Israel repent, they are redeemed; if not, they are not redeemed.' Rabbi Joshua said to him, '[Is it really the case that] if they do not repent they are not redeemed? Rather, the Holy One Blessed Be He sets up a king whose decrees are as harsh as Haman's, whereupon Israel repents and returns to the better way."[31]

In stark contrast to this traditional concept, we find among the early-nineteenth-century disciples of the Vilna Ga'on absolutely no reference whatsoever to any call for repentance as a factor that will hasten the redemption. The few texts in our possession show that their system offers no prospect of hastening redemption, for the generations become progressively less worthy. Accordingly, the redemption will come "in its time"—that is, at the time fixed by God at the outset. In his commentary on *Sifra de-Ẓeni'uta*, the Vilna Ga'on adopts the view presented in the Talmud[32] by Rabbi Joshua ben Levi, declaring: "Know that all these days [of creation] allude to the six thousand years, which are six days [cf. Ps. 90:4; "For a thousand years in Your sight are as a day"] . . . and all the details within those six days come to pass during the six thousand years, each at its ordained day and time, and from this you will know the time for redemption, which will be at its time [even] if, God forbid, they are not worthy."[33]

This idea recurs in the tradition of the Vilna Ga'on's disciples. Samuel Moltzen writes: "But the final End depends not on repentance but on kindness, as is written (Isa. 48:11), 'For My sake, for My sake, will I act' and also on the merit of the patriarchs. And that is the meaning of 'He recalls the pious acts of the patriarchs and brings redemption to their children's children for the sake of His Name.' "[34]

Moses Katzenellenbogen reports his father's recounting that he had learned from the Vilna Ga'on that the redemption in and of itself is not contingent on repentance; rather, repentance bears only on the nature and quality of the redemption and on how it progresses. In other words, if the Jews repent, their redemption will proceed through love, without the birth pangs of the Messiah, as described in Isa. 54:7—"For a brief moment I abandoned you, but with great love I will gather you in." If, however, they fail to repent by the time of the End, the redemptive process will nevertheless go forward, for its primary purpose is to sanctify God's name in the world; but it will entail harsh torments for Israel, as described in Ezek. 20:33–44—"If not, I will rule over you with a mighty hand and an outstretched arm and poured out wrath . . . and with a mighty hand and an outstretched arm and poured out wrath I will gather you in from the lands in which you are dispersed. . . . And you will know that I am the Lord when I do with you for the sake of My Name."[35]

In his book *Margaliyot ha-Torah*, the Ga'on's great disciple Ẓevi Hirsch of

Samyatitsch likewise includes explicit statements regarding the possibility that the redemption will come "at its time" even with no repentance whatsoever: "The redemption has three aspects: [First,] if they repent, He will hasten it out of love. [Second,] even if, God forbid, they are all still guilty, [it will come] at its time. And the third aspect is that the Holy One Blessed Be He will bring them back [in repentance] willy-nilly, by setting over them persecutions as harsh as Haman's."[36] A similar idea appears in the writing of another of the Ga'on's disciples, Pinḥas of Palitsk, who took the view that just as the redemption from Egypt did not take place through the merit of observing of the Torah's commandments—for the Torah had not yet been given—so, too, the future redemption would not be contingent on Israel's observance of the Torah but would come about by reason of the patriarchs' merits: "Even though they then lacked the merit of the Torah, which they had not yet received . . . nor did they have the merit of the Holy Temple, . . . He caused the End to skip over the mountains [i.e., to approach quickly] by reason of the patriarchs' merit."[37]

That Israel's redemption is not conditioned on penitence is conveyed as well in several loose pages found in a book of discourses by an unnamed student of Ḥayyim of Volozhin.[38] The preacher asked why God turned the staff Moses would toss down before Pharaoh into a serpent, of all things [cf. Ex. 4:3]; for God had cursed the serpent (in Eden), and how could God now assign it any role all in the process of Israel's redemption from Egypt? The preacher responds with the talmudic passage telling of the snake that helps the doe bear her young:

> The doe has too narrow a womb [to permit it to give birth; therefore,] when it crouches to give birth, I prepare for her a dragon that bites her belly so it grows slack and she gives birth (*Bava Batra* 16b). So, too, Israel; because they are unable to repent so as to hasten their redemption, the Holy One Blessed Be He sends them a serpent, that is, a harsh and cruel king, who bites them, and the redemption grows out of their ensuing cries. The object of the parable is that Israel's womb is too narrow to bear a righteous one; the children have come to the crisis point, and there is no strength by which to give birth—meaning, to give birth to the redemption by means of repentance. So the Holy One Blessed Be He prepares for us a serpent, that is, a harsh king, and brings about the sprouting. And so it was for Moses, who saw that his generation was not worthy—"and you were naked and bare" [Ezek. 16:7, applied metaphorically to the generation of the Exodus, which lacked the merit of having observed the commandments]—and Moses found it hard to believe [that they would be redeemed], so God showed him a serpent, that is, the harshness of the bondage, as a result of which the Israelites sighed and cried out to God.[39]

Ḥayyim of Volozhin's anonymous student adds that at the time of Mordecai and Esther, the Jews likewise had lost all ability to repent, and only Haman's harsh decree brought them to the point of crying out to God—a cry of pain, not of repentance. He concludes: "We now are like them, and we anticipate a king like Haman."[40]

An important historical document, reflecting intellectual currents among the Jerusalem *Perushim* and describing their view of the connection between repentance and redemption, appears in Aviezer of Ticktin's book, *Sha'arei Ẓedeq le-Zera Yiẓḥaq*. The writer rebukes his readers—his colleagues in the *kolel*—over their responsibility for the Messiah's failure to arrive as anticipated in 5600. He calls on them to repent, which they had not tried to do before 5600, and to be especially punctilious regarding three of the commandments: proper observance of the Sabbath, loving one's fellow with all one's might, and the renewed recitation of *tiqqun ḥaẓot*. His words of rebuke shed light on the Jerusalemites' understanding of the place of repentance in the redemptive process. Their viewpoint was not simply theoretical but had a practical side as well; Aviezer writes: "Do not hasten to comfort yourselves by saying why should we expend the great effort of crying out and praying to God, for we lack the strength and God will certainly bring about salvation even without our arousing it, for God knows all, and the final End will come in any event."[41] Nor is this an isolated incident. Elsewhere in his book, Aviezer disputes the view of the Jerusalem *Perushim* regarding the nature and significance of the woes afflicting the Jews. According to that view, these tribulations form one of the proofs that they are, in fact, living in the age of the "footsteps of the Messiah." Aviezer agrees, but he objects to the corollary implied by his colleagues' concept: namely, that these harsh tribulations suffice to atone for their sins and that, accordingly, there is no need to go beyond them and repent: "This, too, should not enter your minds, that because of the servitude to the governments of the world that we endure throughout this bitter exile, they [the tribulations] will serve as atonement for our transgressions and that there is no need to arouse our own repentance, inasmuch as the sins are of themselves atoned for.[42]

Aviezer of Ticktin protests as well against the *Perushim*'s effort to analogize the redemption from Egypt to the final redemption. In their view, just as repentance was absent as a factor in the redemption from Egypt—where the Israelites cried out not in repentance but on account of the servitude—so now, at the final redemption, great efforts to repent are unnecessary. Challenging that view, Aviezer writes: "One should not say that, after having been privileged to have reached this point, it will suffice, at the time of God's visitation, to repent only lightly, as was the case in Egypt, where they cried out only on account of the toil, and so I shall do the same, for why should I burden myself any more? But, in truth, not all times of divine visitation are the same, for repentance in connection with the future redemption (speedily and in our days) must be of the highest caliber."[43]

Revocation of the Three Oaths

No less revolutionary was the stance of the Vilna Ga'on's disciples regarding the ban on active engagement in the redemptive process, consistent with the Three Oaths by which God had bound both Israel and the nations of the world.[44] As a practical matter, the Three Oaths, during the period here at issue, implied avoidance of any efforts to press for the End or to immigrate to the Land of Israel, and this passive stance was reinforced in the aftermath of the Sabbatean debacle. In violating these "prohibitions," the Vilna Ga'on's disciples were fully aware that they were acting in a revolutionary manner. They explicitly departed from the traditional stance, confronted it, and rejected it while justifying their own posture.

We have already seen how Israel of Shklov argued, in one of his main epistles, that the Three Oaths do not bind the Jews unconditionally, but depend, rather, on the other nations' attitude toward them. God prohibited the Jews from pressing for the End or rebelling against the nations; at the same time, He forbade the nations from unduly oppressing the Jews. When the nations break their side of the bargain and persecute the Jews intolerably—as by the Russian army draft—they thereby annul the Jews' obligations as well: "And if he was somewhat angered by His people's sin, they [the nations] did much more. . . . Their yoke accentuated the harshness of the oppression, and they violated the oath by which God adjured them not to oppress the Jews excessively, so they would not hasten the End."[45]

Aviezer of Ticktin offers a different account of how the prohibition in the Three Oaths came to be annulled. In his view, the ban on pressing for the end, as referred to in the Talmud, remains in force as long as—but only as long as—times remain normal. Once the "time of divine visitation" (*'et peqidah*) arrives, as it now has, advancing the redemptive process by pressing for the End becomes not only permitted but even obligatory: "When the sages of blessed memory said . . . not to press for the End, they had in mind only the times preceding *'et peqidah*, when Israel is required to exert great efforts to repent fully and perform many good deeds, so the 'other side' [*sitra aḥra*; the evil impulse] would not overpower them. But at the time of *peqidah*, they can easily be redeemed."[46]

The oath by which God bound the Jews not to hasten the End is based on a verse from Song of Songs: "I adjured you, O daughters of Jerusalem . . . not to awaken or stir up love until it please." The verse recurs, with only minor differences, three times (2:7, 3:5, 8:4), providing the textual basis for the threefold oath. The Vilna Ga'on interpreted the oath's prohibition to apply not to *aliyah* to the Land of Israel or even to pressing for the End, but only to rebuilding the Holy Temple: "They are adjured not to go out on their own to build the Holy Temple, the highest flower, until [the Messiah] comes."[47]

The Vilna Ga'on's disciples were not alone in recognizing the revolutionary nature of their "scaling the wall"; others, too, saw their activities as audaciously contravening the Three Oaths. Solomon Hirschell (Berliner), chief judge and rabbi of the Ashkenazi community in London, points that out in condemning the contacts between the *Perushim* in Jerusalem and the London Society missionaries. He harshly criticizes that activity and sees it as tied to the essence of their *aliyah*, itself invalid: "And see, the Hasidim and *Perushim* in the Holy Land play up to them [the missionaries]. Alas for that embarrassment, and I hope to God that He will strengthen our hearts to trust and rely on Him alone. And would that our co-religionists who cannot manage to support themselves on their own in the Holy Land were still living in the Diaspora and had not stirred up love until it please[d]."[48]

Initial Awakening From Below

The abrogation of the Three Oaths by the Vilna Ga'on's disciples—that is, the revocation of the ban against human involvement in the process of redemption—opened the door to a new approach, in which such involvement was not merely permissible but was favored and even obligatory.

In their writings, the Ga'on's disciples often grounded themselves in the kabbalistic concept of "the awakening below is a precondition to the awakening on high."[49] In other words, they did not rest content simply with the belief that "the time of divine visitation" had arrived and that repentance was not a necessary condition of the anticipated redemption; they also held, as the Lurianic Kabbalah had taught, that the divine act must be preceded by multifaceted human activity. That activity, of course, includes strict observance of the Torah and its commandments, study of the meanings associated with those observances, study of Kabbalah, and a religious life suffused with fear of God. But it includes as well the act of *aliyah* and the effort to bring about the resettlement of the Land of Israel. Therein lies the second aspect of the opposition to the principles of the Three Oaths: the Ga'on's disciples did not merely object to human passivity in all matters related to *aliyah* and settlement of the Land; they adopted a diametrically opposed stance that called for human activism in the redemptive process. And while that commitment to activism followed that of Lurianic Kabbalah, it differed in an important respect: Lurianic Kabbalah taught that the *tiqqun* (repair) was to be performed in the Diaspora, by "gathering the sparks," and it was only after this that the Messiah would come. The Ga'on's disciples, in contrast, saw no positive meaning to Jewish existence in the Diaspora and insisted that the *tiqqun* should occur in the Land of Israel itself.

Israel of Shklov's Epistle to the Ten Tribes contains a one-sentence formulation of this idea: "Everything requires an initial awakening from below."[50] The Jerusalemites involved in rebuilding the *Ḥurvah* courtyard put it similarly: "The awakening below is a precondition to the awakening on high to rebuild the ruins."[51] This notion was so revolutionary that only by reliance on divine revelation, as expressed through the person of the Vilna Ga'on, could it be advocated against the traditional view.

Samuel Moltzen, relying on the Vilna Ga'on's teachings on matters of belief and providence, argues that according to the Ga'on, even the divine activity itself proceeds in a mundane rather than a miraculous manner. God's overall providence leads the world along its natural course, and His providence over individuals similarly operates through natural means, such that it is impossible to distinguish between providential and nonprovidential human activity: "And according to the Vilna Ga'on, may his memory be for a blessing, [commenting] on the beginning of the portion *Ve-Zot ha-Berakhah*, the . . . holy *shekhinah* guides the world through natural means; and even though the Creator, may He be blessed, guides and attends to all creatures individually, in accordance with His will, yet all is through natural means. And this guidance is called *elohim*."[52]

God's providence over Israel is not uniquely associated with any time or place; that is, it does not pertain to a particular period of history or to the Land of Israel alone. It operates in the Diaspora and in all historical situations, but always through natural means: "And that is what [the sages referred to when] they said that wherever Israel may be exiled to, the *shekhinah* accompanies them. It is divine providence, garbed in natural means. The meaning of the *shekhinah*'s exile is that its providence is not discernable."[53]

These concepts correspond remarkably well to the efforts of the Vilna Ga'on's disciples to immigrate to and settle the Land of Israel through natural means—or, as they put it, by "an awakening from below."

The confrontation between the miraculous and mundane views of the final redemption was considered by Judah Edel, a close associate of the Ga'on, in his book *Afiqei Yehudah*. He maintains that the model for the third and final redemption can be inferred from the nature of the second redemption, when the Second Temple was built. Given that the return to Zion at the start of the Second Temple period proceeded entirely through natural means, with no patent miracles, the third redemption a fortiori will take place through natural means: "If in Second Temple times we did not find God manifesting His might to the congregation of Israel through patent and public miracles, even though [subtler miracles did take place, for] the *tanna* attested that no man had ever been unable to find lodging in Jerusalem [during the pilgrimage festivals], how very much more so will [such miracles] not be manifest in the third redemption; rather, in the future, the event will be conducted in accord with the natural order, not a miracle."[54] Edel hopes that the future Third Temple would not share the fate of the Second, whose destruction was decreed because not all the Jews returned to the Land at that time. He is confident that during the time of the third redemption, no family or clan will turn away from God by refusing to immigrate to the Land of Israel; but if any do so, letters exhorting Jews to immigrate to the Land, settle it, and subdue it would be sent to the Diaspora. Edel sees this *aliyah* as a natural act capable of "awakening love": "If there be found among you then a family or clan whose heart turns away from the Lord our God so as not to follow Him in going up to Zion as saviors, they will send letters to the remaining exiles telling them 'O house of Jacob, come, let us go' [cf. Isa. 2:5] . . . and fill the Land and take it. Let not laziness keep you from going to the mountain of the daughter of Zion, the hill of Jerusalem. Let there not remain in our Land any empty space; and by this, they will awaken and stir up the love."[55]

The scenario described above recognizes that redemption through natural means and human action may not be as complete as it might be if it involved God's direct and miraculous intervention in history, as during the first redemption, the Exodus from Egypt. Samuel Moltzen says: "And if they merited 'I will hasten it,' the redemption would be complete, and they would go out [from exile] wealthy; but if, God forbid, they do not merit it and it takes place 'in its time' . . . there will be only a [divine] visitation, as in the Second Temple period in the time of Cyrus."[56] Moses Katzenellenbogen conveys similar ideas in the name of the Ga'on, articulating the view that redemption would occur through natural means when Israel gathers in its Land and rebuilds its ruined cities. If the nations of the world assisted the Jews in returning to the Land and building it, they would be spared the adversities prophesied for them, including the war of Gog and Magog: "I further heard from my father, may Eden be his resting place, that he had heard from the Ga'on that if the kings of the nations gather the dispersed of Israel and provide help in rebuilding the ruined cities, God will cancel all the adverse prophecies pertaining to them and the war of Gog will not take place. . . . And if the kings act in this excellent way, honoring God and glorifying His Holy Temple, which has lain in ruins for so many years, they may be assured that no evil will befall them and God's Name will be set over them . . . for God promised that after Israel's redemption, He will be called God of all the Earth."[57]

Settling the Land of Israel and Building Jerusalem

Redemption of the Land was the highest concern of the Vilna Ga'on's disciples. They saw it as the focus of human activity during the decisive first stage of the redemption and as the mechanism through which the *shekhinah* would be raised from the ashes. Settlement of the Land of Israel was not a means to promote Jewish political freedom or economic prosperity but an end in itself, so that the Third Temple might be built and all humanity brought to acknowledge the dominion of the King, King of Kings, the Holy One Blessed Be He.

An early letter from the *kolel* of the *Perushim*, signed in Safed on Friday, 16 March 1810, conveys the idea that building the Land was the principal goal of the Ga'on's disciples. It would be followed, as they envisioned it, by the ingathering of the dispersed Jews and restoration of the Temple service in Jerusalem: "Then will the ruins of the two destructions be filled with the Third Temple, which will surpass its predecessors in glory, and then the dispersed of Israel will be gathered from the four corners . . . and His Name will be exalted and sanctified over all . . . when all flesh come to bow down before Him."[58] The writers see revitalization of the Land as the important step, with the act of *aliyah* as a mechanism for awakening the Land, hitherto neglected by its children. The imagery of the no-longer-forgotten Land being awakened by the return of its children recurs in the letter in varying formulations. The writers give a human face to the Land, affording her, as a princess, the opportunity to assert her rights to be honored, as she once was, for the natural qualities she has retained despite the ravages of time: "We have come to speak of . . . and first present to you the Land's request. . . . The Land calls forth, the Land stirs itself, the Land speaks, saying, 'I remember the days when I was a mighty kingdom, crowned with God's glory, and now, too, nothing is lacking in me. Within me, the Torah is clarified, piety is ascendant, and the soul is liberated.' "[59]

But despite the natural qualities with which it was graced, the Land was cast down and abandoned by its children. Accordingly, she demands satisfaction: "Why am I blackened, demeaned, desolate, and forlorn? Am I not a desirable land, desired by heavenly and earthly alike? . . . Why am I cast down from all sanctity?"[60] The writers rise up against this unnatural state of affairs and assign it blame for the exile's continuation and the redemption's delay: "Is she not your mother, the source of your souls? Why do you not raise the ruins of Jerusalem above all your joys? Do you not remember, do you not understand the historical oath of 'If I forget you, O Jerusalem' [Ps. 137:5]? Why is she forgotten as one dead to the heart . . . ? Forgetting the Holy Land extends, God forbid, the exile. . . . The Satan inflicts indolence and causes the love of Zion and Jerusalem to be forgotten . . . [divine] overflow is diminished, affliction is unleashed, and God's enemy is humbled [i.e., God is humbled, expressed euphemistically]."[61] The writers passionately call on the Jews to take pity on Jerusalem and thereby raise the *shekhinah* from her ashes:

> Each day we wait, each year [we hope for] the awakening of great and small, who have long slept deeply, and for their concern about the suffering of the exiled *shekhinah* and the king bound in cords. But there is none who stirs to free the *shekhinah* from prison and to be fortified with Torah and piety. . . . How long will Jerusalem not be pitied, and how long will its ray of consummate beauty be cast down to earth? . . . But people sleep, and no one heeds . . . and the Throne is not complete, and the city of holiness . . . is in the hands of strangers.[62]

But, despite it all, early signs of the Land's redemption can already be perceived; the most prominent is the return of her children who engage in Torah: "Now, blessed be God who has shown mercy to the Land, and remembered me [the Land] by gathering in children prepared for all sacred activity; they dedicate themselves to me and reside in me . . . and protect it through the Torah, joining the domain [lit. "the four cubits"] of clear *halakhah* with the domain of the holy and pure Land."[63] Raising the *shekhinah* from her ashes—that is, returning her to Zion—is the goal that will be attained by redeeming the Land and settling it. And returning the *shekhinah* to Zion can be accomplished not by God, but must begin through an awakening from below, with the return of its children to Zion and their settlement of it. The view is expressed by Aviezer of Ticktin as well: "In this concealed redemption, the shekhinah cannot rise from her ashes by herself."[64]

The ideas expressed in the Ga'on's disciples' letter appear to have been very carefully formulated; they are not merely an emotional reaction to a first encounter with the Land. Their roots—literary and substantive—can be traced to the book *Hillel ben Shaḥar*, written a few years before his *aliyah* by Hillel of Kovno, one of the letter's signatories. Complaining about the exile as an illogical and unnecessary state of affairs, he blames its continuation on his generation's materialism: "We all seek material excess . . . and lose sight of [genuine] substance, diverting our attention from our Land, which lies desolate while gentile nations dance in its sanctuary. Our Holy Temple is destroyed by fire, and what has become of our oath that 'my tongue shall cleave to the roof of my mouth if I do not remember you' [Ps. 137:5]? . . . And we are unconcerned about the suffering of the Holy One Blessed Be He and His shekhinah. . . . Instead, each of us has gone his own way."[65]

The Vilna Ga'on as well, in his commentary on the Passover Hagaddah, conveys the idea that the Land's redemption and the rebuilding of Jerusalem will precede the nation's redemption. In interpreting the passage "This year we are here but next year we shall be in Jerusalem; this year we are slaves but next year we shall be free," he cites Isaiah's statement (1:27) that "Zion shall be redeemed through justice; those who return to her, through righteousness" and goes on to say: "First, Zion will be redeemed, and only later, the righteous who return. And that is why [the Hagaddah's editor] first said 'next year in Jerusalem,' referring to the redemption of Jerusalem, and only then said 'next year we shall be free,' referring to the redemption of [the nation of] Israel."[66]

Opposition to the Ga'on's Disciples' Ideas

Not all who saw themselves as students of the Vilna Ga'on endorsed his leading disciples' view that the End was a necessary, inevitable event utterly unconnected to human action such as repentance in the generally accepted sense of the term. Many scholars throughout Lithuania and Poland maintained the traditional idea of miraculous redemption preconditioned necessarily on repentance. One statement of this position appears in the introduction by Elyaqim Getzel Altschul, preacher in the Lithuanian town of Ratzki, to his father's (R. Ze'ev Wolf Altschul's) book, *Zeved Tov*.

The introduction, in my judgment, reflects the profound impression left by the Ga'on's disciples' *aliyah* on those who stayed behind, and it appears to echo the deliberations inspired by the events in the author's community and elsewhere. The message that the author sought to convey through the introduction seems to have been both controversial and urgent. The book's approbation is dated 22 Sivan 5570 (24 June 1810), showing it was published around the time of the *aliyah*. The introduction, meanwhile, bears no substantive connection to the book's subject, suggesting it was added to use the book's publication as an opportunity to express timely views on a raging controversy. It appears as well that the episode had a direct effect on the writer as an individual, since he attained the position of preacher in the Ratzki community after the previous incumbent, Hillel of Kovno (author of *Hillel ben Shaḥar*, and signatory on the letter of 16 March 1810,[67] as discussed earlier) set out for the Land of Israel with one of the first groups of the Ga'on's disciples to depart.

In his brief comments, Altschul makes the point that the present exile's duration has been revealed to no one (in contrast to the Egyptian enslavement and Babylonian exile, whose lengths were fixed at the outset). It follows that the timing of our redemption depends solely and entirely on repentance. He concludes that one should place no stock in the efforts of those who claim to know the time of the End and attempt, in reliance on that knowledge, to advance the redemption through natural means. For the first time in the polemical literature on the messianic activism of the Vilna Ga'on's disciples, he cites a rabbinic dictum discussed further below:

> King Solomon, peace be upon him, said in his wisdom, "unless God builds the house, its builders labor in vain. . . . In vain do you rise early" [Ps. 127:1–2]. . . . And God, may He be blessed, set no fixed time for this bitter exile [to be ended with] the sound of the turtledove, and it depends exclusively on repentance. . . . Therefore, it is impossible for them in any way to be redeemed before all is repaired . . . and if He, may He be blessed, did fix a time, then once the time were reached, they would necessarily be redeemed immediately. . . . But therefore He, may He be blessed, did not fix a time, and it depends exclusively on repentance.[68]

Altschul argues as well that the future redemption will take place with great fanfare—unlike the furtive efforts of the Ga'on's disciples, whose concern about the authorities' reactions required them to keep a low profile. Accordingly, the current historical reality could not be considered an awakening from below in anticipation of the full redemption:

> For it is hinted to us that the final redemption (may it occur speedily and in our days, amen) . . . will take place with great fanfare, for He will show us wonders as when we left Egypt . . . "and she shall not go forth as slaves do,"[69] as was the case the first two times, when [the departure] was at night, without fanfare; rather, it will be with great fanfare. . . . And King Solomon, peace be upon him, anticipated, through the holy spirit, that two Holy Temples were destined to be destroyed . . . and he said of it "unless God builds the house, its builders labor in vain" . . . for those who maintain a vigil for it to occur through natural means act in vain . . . meaning that in vain and for naught did you arise early to leave Egypt [i.e., Russia] without everything having first been repaired, for this final exile will endure until everything is repaired.[70]

It is almost certain that Altschul was not expressing the isolated view of an individual when he rejected the idea of a set time for the End. We have already encountered the skepticism of Menasheh of Iliya and his concerns about fictitious End-reckonings. And during the 1870s, Aryeh Leib Frumkin noted the doubts expressed in 1837 by his father, Samuel Kelmer, about whether the Vilna Ga'on really did know the time set for the End, as his other disciples believed. The document describes a conversation in Volozhin between Samuel Kelmer and a nephew of Ḥayyim of Volozhin, the kabbalist Abraham Simḥah of Amstislav. The latter wanted to convey to Kelmer three secrets, among them the Vilna Ga'on's secret of the End. Kelmer declined to receive them, professing doubt that the Ga'on himself knew that secret, for even Rabbi Akiva, a greater man than the Ga'on, had erred in that regard.[71]

5

Attempt to Renew Rabbinic Ordination in Safed

For it is a fact, widely known, . . . that before our righteous Messiah arrives, there must first be in the Land of Israel the great court of ordained judges. . . . Let there be chosen several ordained sages, who, in their mercy on the generality of God's people, will kindly come to the Land of Israel, our fathers' inheritance, and ordain some of our scholars, so that a court of ordained judges will exist in the Land of Israel, on which the beginning of the redemption is contingent.

Letter from Israel of Shklov to the Ten Tribes, 18 October 1830. In A. Yaari, *Iggerot Ereẓ Yisra'el*

The *Perushim*'s Settlement in the Galilee

The passage from theory to practice is not always smooth, for the difficulties interposed by historical reality can impede or even prevent attainment of the desired goals.

The Vilna Ga'on's disciples immigrated to and settled in the Land of Israel for the purpose of redeeming it, and they regarded the rebuilding of Jerusalem as the most direct path toward that goal. But their attempt to do so encountered numerous impediments. When they reached the Land of Israel in 1808–1812, they settled in Safed, apparently because conditions in Jerusalem precluded settlement there. For one thing, any effort on their part to settle in Jerusalem would have met with intense opposition from various quarters. Foremost in their minds was the concern that they would be required to bear financial obligations that went all the way back to the days of Judah Ḥasid's circle: Arab creditor families still had the old promissory notes,[1] and they regarded every Ashkenazi immigrant as an heir of that earlier Ashkenazi group that had come to Jerusalem early in the eighteenth century.[2]

Not only were the local Arabs a worry; other Jews were as well. The Sefardim of Jerusalem seem to have objected to the establishment of an Ashkenazi community there. They were concerned that an Ashkenazi community might request a share of the funds raised on behalf of Jerusalem and might even undertake independent collection efforts, particularly in western Europe, thereby reducing the income of the Sefardic community.[3] These groups rationalized their opposition by alleging concerns related to repaying the Arab creditors.

The newly available letters of the Clerks' Organization disclose, for the first time, an additional, and unanticipated, source of objection: the Hasidim, the survivors and heirs of the Hasidic *aliyah* of 1777. They write that "their [i.e., the *Perushim*'s] settlement in Jerusalem is not pleasing to us, for several confidential reasons."[4] The Hasidim understood that once the *Perushim* came to Jerusalem, they would seek to take control of the courtyard of the *Ḥurvah*—that is, the ruins of the Judah Ḥasid study hall—and the Hasidim objected to any such effort, claiming that the ruins had never belonged to the *Perushim* or their ancestors. The Hasidim in Safed added that they had closer ties with the original owners and that their rights to it were greater than those of the *Perushim* in possession of it.[5] Given all that, the desire to avoid intercommunal conflict contributed to the *Perushim*'s decision not to go up to Jerusalem and settle there.

Other factors as well deterred the *Perushim* from settling in Jerusalem. Security presented a challenge, for the city was remote from the seats of government in Damascus and Acre and could not be protected against raiders. Daily living was uniquely difficult: water was scarce and extremely expensive, and, in contrast to Safed, the city lacked an agricultural hinterland.[6] Safed's Jewish community, meanwhile, under the protection of the Jewish treasury officer Ḥayyim Farḥi, enjoyed low taxes[7] and a sense of security. Safed was close to the seats of government and the principal seaports in Syria, and the presence there of the consuls facilitated contact with the "old country" and the center in Vilna. Daily life was more pleasant in Safed, and the proximity of the Jewish population in some of the nearby villages further enhanced the sense of security.

Because circumstances thus prevented the Vilna Ga'on's disciples from living in Jerusalem, they could not carry out the "building of Jerusalem" aspect of "the awakening from below." But their need to reside in Safed did not cause them to compromise that kabbalistic principle, which, as the Ga'on had taught, had many aspects. One practical way in which they upheld the principle while living in Safed was through spiritual activism—discovering the Torah's light and the Kabbalah's mysteries in an effort to elevate the sparks of holiness and thereby to draw down the divine bounty and goodness and hasten redemption by the "repair" (*tiqqun*) of defects. A manuscript discovered relatively recently shows that the Ga'on's disciples living in Safed in fact attempted to hasten the redemption through higher spiritual efforts involving the revealed and the concealed. The manuscript pertains to the period preceding the great epidemic of 1813, in which many of the immigrants perished:

> At that time there were present in Safed 511 [expressed as the numerical value of the word *ashrei* (happy), the first word of the Book of Psalms] prominent Jews from among our fellow Ashkenazim, the *kolel* of the *Perushim*, and there is no doubt that by their merit, they were hastening the redemption, awakening holiness in a place where He in His anger had destroyed it, *mizmor le-Asaf* [see note]. But because of our many sins, an epidemic soon developed, may God protect us, and untold numbers of the remnant of the holy community succumbed, having been called to the upper world.[8]

Several contemporaneous sources tell of the establishment of the *Perushim*'s study hall in Safed and the special practices followed there to enhance its sanctity. A letter from the Ga'on's disciples in Safed describes the order of study:

> In our yeshiva (named for the rabbi of the Diaspora, our master, the true Ga'on, Rabbi Elijah the pious one, may Eden be his resting place, of Vilna), we study *gemara* analytically in a single group, along with *halakhah* as determined by the *Shulḥan Arukh* with the clarifying interpretations of our master the Ga'on, may Eden be his resting place. On days on which we all gather, we wear *tallit* and *tefillin* [prayer shawl and phylacteries, usually worn only during morning worship] throughout the day; blessed is the eye that has seen all this. The Torah returns to its proper home.[9]

Something else that could be done in Safed, without going up to Jerusalem, was to fulfill the commandments contingent on the Land. (As noted earlier, these are a group of commandments, related primarily to agriculture, that need be observed only in the Land of Israel.) In the context of the kabbalistic conception, the act of immigrating to the Land of Israel and settling there could be seen as a manifestation of the drive for "perfection": fulfilling the commandment to dwell in the Land and the commandments contingent on it brings a man closer to the perfection of carrying out all 613 commandments. Only when that perfection is attained does it become possible and proper to anticipate the "awakening above" as part of the process of redemption.[10] In a letter presented to Moses Montefiore on 11 June 1839, the leaders of the Ashkenazi community in Jerusalem convey that idea: "We have a tradition from our fathers that through fulfillment of the Holy Torah in the Holy Land, including all its laws and statutes regarding the commandments contingent on the Holy Land, all will be strengthened and bonded and united, and then the bounty will descend from the source of blessings. . . . And the awakening above is dependent on the awakening below; and how long will our Holy Land remain ruined and desolate and the nation of God an emblem of shame and mockery?"[11]

To enable them to fulfill the pertinent commandments, the members of the *kolel* purchased parcels of land. Ḥayyim Katz, one of the leaders of the *kolel* in Safed, speaks of that in a letter: "Concerning contributions sent for the purpose of fulfilling commandments contingent on the Land: we have already purchased real property in accordance with the view of our beloved, the true, pious, and renowned *ga'on*, our master Rabbi Ḥayyim, may his lamp burn brightly, of Volozhin, such that the seller conveyed to the purchaser here on behalf of all his participating partners. And it appears we will purchase other properties that may come along, if the time and place are proper."[12] Purchasing farmland for the purpose of fulfilling commandments contingent on the Land is mentioned as well in the letter from the Vilna Ga'on's disciples in Safed.[13] These documents suggest this activity was regarded as singularly important for the purpose of hastening the redemption.

The desire to observe these commandments extended beyond the Jews residing in the Land of Israel and was shared by their brethren in the Diaspora. The latter sent contributions earmarked for the purpose of fulfilling, on the donors' behalf, commandments contingent on the Land. The contributions were segregated from other funds and separately accounted for. Most of these funds were applied to the purchase of land, so the commandments of priestly gifts and tithes (which had to be taken from produce of the Land of Israel) could be fulfilled. In their letter, the Ga'on's disciples write with satisfaction that "we purchased real property with its produce already on it,"[14] which would enable them to fulfill those commandments in the very near future.

Yet another spiritual activity involved prostrating oneself on the graves of the righteous and praying there. Connecting thereby with the soul of the departed righteous person, parts of which may reach the highest heavens, was said to enable one to exert influence on heavenly activities by pleading before God's throne of glory. In his letters to Lehren, Israel of Shklov writes several times of such experiences: "What they did amidst a group of colleagues—rabbis, scholars, and righteous ones, may God preserve and protect them—also going to the graves of the righteous of the world and praying publicly, in a manner that could not until now be done [communally]." Lehren responds, closing with wishes that naturally flow from the description of the event: "May God augment His graciousness to His people and hasten our true salvation and complete redemption, for the time very much requires it."[15]

A letter from Joseph of Kalish, a member of the *kolel* of the Safed *Perushim*, suggests that they regarded the practice of prostrating oneself in prayer on the graves of the righteous as a powerful spiritual experience:

> Believe me, my brothers and friends, that it restores the unique soul of one who fears God in his heart, and he can take pleasure in going out with the entire group of friends for a day or two to prostrate oneself on the graves of the *tanna'im* and *amora'im*, and, while en route, they recite many prayers and words of praise. It is the greatest pleasure and contentment. I lack the ability to describe for you the sweetness and pleasure that I felt last summer, when I prostrated

> myself on the graves of the righteous on the anniversaries of their deaths. All pleasures of this world are as naught in comparison. How can physical, material pleasure be compared to the delicate pleasure felt by the soul in this activity?[16]

Aftermath of the 1813 Epidemic

Only a short while after their community organization began to function, the *Perushim* suffered a body blow to their sense that they were acting, in accordance with the Ga'on's divine directive, as God's emissaries to lead the Jewish people in the process of redemption. In 1813, a severe epidemic struck the Galilee, nearly wiping out the *Perushim* in Safed. Of the 511 members of the group, only a few dozen survived, "and the *kolel* was nearly destroyed and the remnant fled to the hills."[17] The epidemic afflicted the community mercilessly, drawing no distinctions among people. Israel of Shklov writes: "The best among us were lost; our righteous elders went to their resting places; the eyes of our community, appointed by the leaders, have for the most part been summoned to the heavenly academy; and the few who remain want to shed the burdens of community affairs."[18] The high spirits that accompanied the group as it set out on its mission of hastening redemption through spiritual perfection were a thing of the past, as the horrific epidemic called the very project into question. It may be assumed that their powerful faith in their calling gave way, in the survivors' minds, to searing doubt. Was it good and proper to immigrate to the Land? Did they not, in fact, thereby violate the Three Oaths? And might the epidemic not be the punishment imposed for violating the oaths, which was why they were left to be killed like "hinds of the field"?[19]

A religious understanding of the world sees the outbreak of such a severe epidemic as a heavenly sign of something amiss in the afflicted community's way of life. Any such community must take stock of itself to identify the flaw, uproot it, and repair it.[20] But there were intense disputes over how to proceed. Menaḥem Mendel of Shklov disagreed with Israel of Shklov, his colleague in the community leadership. The former apparently saw the epidemic as punishment for the group's not having immediately settled in Jerusalem, for its having been swayed by the difficulties of living there and choosing the easy path of settling in the Galilee. In fact, seventy-one refugees from the epidemic took up temporary residence in Jerusalem until the winter of 1813–1814,[21] proving that the impediments to settling there had been removed. The Arab creditors' antipathy had eased—"the Ishmaelites' hatred had already been forgotten"[22]—and the *Perushim*'s concern about rejection by their Sefardic brethren had likewise been proven groundless. It is almost certain that the decision to move to Jerusalem and found a community of *Perushim* there took shape in Menaḥem Mendel's mind as early as then.

The dispute between the two leaders of the *Perushim* was referred to the Nobles of Vilna for decision. The latter determined in principle that a community of *Perushim* would be established in Jerusalem, subject to the authority of the center in Safed: "For it has been firmly determined in Vilna and the entire province, as a matter of practice, that the community's hub would be in the holy mountains of Safed, may it be built and established."[23]

Despite the decision of the Nobles of Vilna, Israel of Shklov continued to have reservations about establishing a community of *Perushim* in Jerusalem. In addition to the practical concerns already noted, he appears to have had kabbalistic arguments against settling there. According to Ẓevi Hirsch Lehren (in a polemic against Rabbi Moses Sofer, who had criticized Israel of Shklov and his notion of settling in Safed), Israel's objection to settling in Jerusalem grew out of his concern that Jerusalem's intense sanctity causes the *sitra aḥra* ("the other side," that is, the evil force) to direct all its power there in order to trip up the Jewish nation. The Jews therefore lacked the ability to confront the forces of impurity situated in Jerusalem, "for on account of our many sins, the impurity of the Christians and their places of worship continue to be present in the holy city of Jerusalem, and it is known what that causes."[24] Lehren adds that a Sefardic sage had told him of a kabbalist who "had seen the 'unclean side' in some form in Jerusalem, with one foot on the Church of the Holy Sepulcher and the other on the Temple Mount or the Mount of Olives . . . and this is a true story and one may say it precludes achieving [the goal of settling in Jerusalem], and for that reason, the holy Ari likewise chose to dwell in Safed, may it be built and established speedily and in our day."[25]

To substantiate the claim that Ashkenazi settlement in Jerusalem at that time was beyond their capacity, they cited the failure of Judah Ḥasid's group in 1720 to establish themselves in the *Ḥurvah* courtyard in Jerusalem. They went so far as to argue that the places in which that group had lived bore a curse and that resettling them posed dangers.[26] But beyond all these considerations, Israel of Shklov's opposition to establishing a settlement of *Perushim* in Jerusalem seems to have been based on his fundamentally different notion of how the redemptive process would unfold, a notion in which Safed has a role preceding that of Jerusalem.

Renewal of Rabbinic Ordination Before Rebuilding Jerusalem

Two texts provide the key to understanding Israel of Shklov's concept of the stages of the redemption process. One is in the introduction to his book, *Taqlin Ḥadtin*;[27] the other is his Epistle to the Ten Tribes.[28]

Toward the end of his introduction to *Taqlin Ḥadtin*, Israel of Shklov adopts the talmudic view (as described in *Megillah* 17a–b) regarding the stages of the future redemption. He writes: "May we merit that our brethren, the entire House of Israel, will be gathered to our Holy Land. Once the dispersed of Israel are gathered, the righteous will be ascendant [lit., "the horn of the righteous will be raised"]. Once the righteous are ascendant, Jerusalem will be built, and once Jerusalem is built, the Messiah son of David will come and the Holy Temple will be built."[29] The source for that formulation is the weekday *amidah* prayer (the Eighteen Blessings) instituted by the Men of the Great Assembly;

the sequence of blessings in that prayer sets the following order of redemptive events:

1. Ingathering of exiles: "Sound the great horn of our liberation and raise the banner to gather our exiles."
2. Restoration of justice: "Restore our judges as at first, and our counselors as they were."
3. Extirpation of apostates: "May all evil instantly perish, and all Your people's enemies speedily be destroyed."
4. Reward for the righteous: "You are a support and source of security for the righteous."
5. Rebuilding Jerusalem: "Return with love to your city, Jerusalem."
6. Messiah son of David: "Speedily cause the shoot of Your servant David to sprout."
7. Prayer: "For You hear the prayer of Your people Israel."
8. Renewal of the Temple service: "Restore the service to Your Sanctuary."

It is fair to assume that Israel of Shklov saw the sequence of events in this formulation of the prayer as the plan for the future redemptive process. "Rebuilding Jerusalem" does not figure as an early element in the plan, and Israel apparently believed that any necessarily failed attempt to change the sequence of events would impede the process itself.[30]

The Vilna Ga'on's disciples held the view, as taught by the *Zohar*, that all activity related to the redemption had to begin with "awakening from below." Accordingly, they saw the very fact of *aliyah* as opening the first stage of the redemptive process: that is, the ingathering of the exiles. The next stage was not the rebuilding of Jerusalem; rather, it was the restoration of justice—in other words, establishing an authorized court of ordained sages. In taking that view, Israel of Shklov relied on Maimonides' determination that renewal of ordination[31] was a necessary precondition to the Messiah's advent. Although Maimonides ruled in his *Mishneh Torah* that we would not know the redemptive process and associated events until they actually took place,[32] in his *Commentary on the Mishnah* he refers to the existence of an ordained court as one indication of redemption: "And this [renewal of ordination] will no doubt be when the Creator, may He be blessed, prepares the hearts of men and increases their merit and their desire for God, may He be blessed, and for the Torah, and augments their wisdom before the coming of the Messiah."[33] There is no doubt that this unusual source exerted a powerful influence on Israel of Shklov's thinking.

As it turns out, talmudic and kabbalistic sources associate renewal of an ordained court more with the Galilee than with Jerusalem; and that, too, bolstered Israel of Shklov's case against attempting to rebuild Jerusalem at an early point in the process. He appears to rely on the talmudic statement that "the Sanhedrin, it was taught, was exiled from [its regular location in] the Chamber of Hewn Stone [in the Temple] to [an alternative location on the Temple Mount but outside the Temple], and from [that location] to [elsewhere in] Jerusalem, and from Jerusalem to Yavneh, and from Yavneh . . . to Sephoris, and from Sephoris to Tiberias. . . . Rabbi Yoḥanan said, from there, they will be redeemed in the future."[34] Citing this passage in his *Mishneh Torah*, Maimonides adds: "And it is a received tradition that it is to Tiberias that they will first return and from there, they will proceed to the Temple."[35] Maimonides did not intend thereby to suggest practical steps to prepare the ground for redemption; rather, he was noting the sequence of the redemptive process, in which renewal of ordination would have to precede the Messiah's coming. Ordination can be renewed, however, only by one already possessed of it, and none such now exist. Accordingly, Maimonides resolved the paradox by ruling that if all the sages in the Land of Israel could come together and choose a leader from among their number, that leader would be able to ordain others and thereby renew the chain of ordination.[36]

During the sixteenth century, Maimonides' ordinance became a means for hastening the redemption. To help realize the messianic expectations then prevailing, Jacob Berab, in 1538, initiated an effort in Safed to bring about renewal of ordination by agreement of all the sages of the Land of Israel.[37] The attempt failed because of opposition on the part of the sages of Jerusalem, led by Levi ben Ḥabib. Israel of Shklov did not attempt anew to secure the agreement of all the sages in the Land of Israel; instead, he sought a different path to his goal. Apparently relying on a suggestion by David ibn Zimri (Radbaz) in his commentary on Maimonides, Israel of Shklov finds it possible to renew ordination through ordained sages from among the Ten Tribes: "For the children of Reuben are destined to come and do battle before the advent of King Messiah, and who will tell you that they lack someone ordained by one previously ordained? Such a person will ordain others."[38] Israel of Shklov's image as a halakhist is highlighted here, for this was the first time in the history of Jewish messianism that there was an effort to assign the Ten Tribes a central role in the redemptive process through renewal of ordination. The Ten Tribes had always been taken into account, particularly during times of messianic awakening, but only insofar as it was believed they would be discovered at the end of days and might bring their military prowess to bear against the enemies of the Jews.[39] Never before had they been seen as those who would renew ordination.

The first half of the nineteenth century witnessed intensive efforts to locate the Ten Tribes. Late in 1802, the Shklov community, in which Rabbi Israel had already become a leading sage, dispatched a letter to "the children of Israel who dwell in the great land of Tartaria, on the first day of Ḥanukkah, the twenty-fifth day of the month of Kislev, the week of *Parashat Miqqeẓ*, 5563," with the goal of ascertaining "whether you know their location and can inform us of it."[40] A further reference by the *Perushim* to the Ten Tribes is noted in the journal of the missionary Joseph Wolff, who tells, in September 1821, of two Jews who met with him in Cairo and quizzed him about the location of the River Sambatyon; one was Solomon Pach of Jerusalem, and the other was an unnamed resident of Safed who had emigrated from Mogilev.[41] Late in 1823, another resident of Safed and member of its community of *Perushim*—the traveler David of the House of Hillel—set out to the Far East in search of traces of the Ten Tribes. In 1832, he reached Madras, India, where British friends persuaded him to publish some of his travel journals. In an introduction to his book, which was published in English, they wrote of his belief that he can shed light on the existence of the exiled Ten Tribes and their present condition.[42] He seems to have been preoccupied by the matter of the Ten Tribes; in his journal, he tells of a report he received in 1830 of an encounter two years earlier in Transjordan between a Jewish merchant and a Bedouin of the Tribe of Dan.[43] We have a different account of that episode by Israel of Shklov; in his version, the encounter took place not in Transjordan but in Yemen, and the Jew was not a merchant but a rabbinic emissary: "Recently, for about two years, we have had emissaries in the land of Yemen and they saw there with their own eyes a man from the Tribe of Dan named Issakhar. He told them the location of their land and its grandeur . . . and after that the man disappeared, and it was a wonder."[44]

But it was not only reports by travelers that excited Israel of Shklov's imagination. He also found in the teachings of his master, the Vilna Ga'on, a basis for his firm belief in the existence of the Ten Tribes and their role in the redemption process.[45] In his commentary on Song of Songs, the Ga'on considers the children of Moses, situated beyond the River Sambatyon, who are destined to have a central role at the time of redemption. On the verse "Turn your eyes from me, for they overcome me; your hair is like a flock of goats, descending from Gilead" (Song of Songs 6:5), the Ga'on writes: "This means that all Israel weeps over their misfortunes, and though the Holy One Blessed Be He is filled with mercy, it is impossible to redeem them before the time set for the End. . . . 'Your hair' corresponds to the sons of Moses who are beyond the Sambatyon, who are righteous and abstemious ("*perushim*"!), and they are the saviors of whom it is written 'saviors will ascend the mount of Zion' [Obad. 1:21]."[46] On the ensuing verse, "Your teeth are like a herd of ewes coming up from the washing, all of them paired and not one failing away," the Ga'on writes: "They correspond to the Ten Tribes, who are great heroes. They have a king and wage war, and they also are righteous."[47]

Mission of 1830 to the Ten Tribes

On 18 October 1830, Israel of Shklov, leader of the *Perushim* in the Land of Israel, put his signature to an extraordinary epistle. The letter was given to Barukh ben Samuel of Pinsk, then residing in Safed, who was being dispatched to locate the Ten Tribes.[48]

Israel begins the letter by telling of information he had received from rabbinic emissaries who had recently been to Yemen and claimed to have seen, with their own eyes, a man from the Tribe of Dan. According to their report, the Danite told them where the Ten Tribes resided and recounted their power, their wealth, and their righteousness.

The epistle tells us much about Israel of Shklov's messianic worldview, which was shared, at least in part, by all of the Vilna Ga'on's disciples. He rejects the prohibition, which underlies the traditional concept of the Three Oaths, against "scaling the wall" or hastening the redemption; he claims that "even if all of them [the Jews] or even most of them are not authorized to scale the wall to the Land of Israel, there is no prohibition against individuals [doing so]."[49] He likewise rejects the traditional notion that one should not recite numerous prayers in order to hasten the End. In his view, the nations of the world violated their part of the bargain by excessively tormenting the Jewish people, thereby freeing the Jews to plead for their redemption and pray for the hastening of the End: "And if He were to be angered slightly by His people's sin, they [the nations] did much worse. . . . The yoke of servitude they imposed was many times more onerous, and they violated the oath by which the Lord our God adjured them not to oppress Israel unduly, lest they hasten the end."[50]

As we have seen, the Vilna Ga'on's disciples' worldview incorporated the basic idea, borrowed from Lurianic Kabbalah, that human actions in this world have the capacity to influence God's supernal activities. And since everything requires "prior awakening from below,"[51] one cannot passively anticipate the redemption of Israel in its Land from a posture of "sit and do nothing" (a halakhic category used to describe certain offenses of omission), as the traditional approach would have it. Instead, humans must act to advance and hasten the redemption. Israel of Skhlov justifies the recourse to the Ten Tribes on that basis, and, he suggests, the accounts we now possess of the Ten Tribes' existence constitute proof that we are living in the period of Footsteps of the Messiah. As the *Zohar* puts it: "For during [the time of] the Footsteps of the Messiah, some of our brethren of the Ten Tribes will be discovered."[52] Israel of Shklov relied as well on a *midrash* in *Yalqut Tehillim*, which tells that "in the future, the exiles of Judah and Benjamin will go among them [the Ten Tribes] to bring them [back], so they can join with them in the days of the Messiah."[53] Israel simply had to follow the *midrash* to its practical conclusion: "And we hereby send an upright and conscientious messenger, the perfect sage Rabbi Barukh ben Samuel of the Holy City of the Upper Galilee, who has risked his life to wander over land, sea, and wilderness, may the Merciful One help him to come before their great throne."[54]

Israel of Shklov presents several requests to the Ten Tribes, two of them central to his notion of redemption. First, he asks that they pray abundantly in order to hasten the End: "Multiply your prayers and the tears of your pure souls and holy spirits, garb yourselves in royal garments and enter the inner court before the King, King of Kings, the Holy One Blessed Be He, in your awesome audiences in the holy sanctuaries, for we are in dire straits."[55] Another request was designed to permit carrying out the second step of the redemptive process—namely, restoration of the seat of justice by renewing ordination. Israel of Shklov here relies on Maimonides' statements, noted earlier, that before the Messiah's advent, a great court of ordained judges must convene in the Land of Israel. Since the start of the redemption is contingent on the existence of an ordained court, and since Israel of Shklov had a tradition that among the Ten Tribes were authorities whose chain of ordination goes back to Moses, he asked that they send several ordained sages to the Land of Israel to renew ordination there:

> For it is a fact, widely known from our holy sages, . . . that before our righteous Messiah arrives, there must first be in the Land of Israel the great court of ordained judges. . . . And since we have heard clearly that you have a Sanhedrin of ordained judges, . . . let there be chosen several ordained sages, who, in their mercy on the generality of God's people, will kindly come to the Land of Israel, our fathers' inheritance, and ordain some of our scholars, so that a court of ordained judges will exist in the Land of Israel, on which the beginning of the redemption is contingent.[56]

The renewal of ordination and establishment of a great ordained court will fulfill Isaiah's words (1:26): "I will restore your judges as at first and your counselors as at the beginning, after which you will be called the city of justice, a faithful town."

The third request was a more prosaic one for financial help. It, too, was based on the Ga'on's disciples' notion that redemption would be a gradual process rather than a sudden, one-time, cosmological transformation. As such, it might take longer than expected, and that concern led Israel of Shklov to ask the Ten Tribes for financial support for the *yishuv*, "lest, God forbid, the time until our redemption and salvation be long, and the birth pangs of the Messiah and associated troubles be harsh, and our lives hang in the balance—have compassion on us to provide us yearly help."[57]

Lehren received a copy of the letter, which he read before a meeting of the Clerks' Organization. He found it so moving that, as he wrote, "my eyes flowed with tears, aroused by his words of holiness,"[58] and he again cried on rereading the letter. Overcome with emotion and excitement, Lehren characterized the incident as "good news for Israel," for it is known that the Ten Tribes would not be discovered until "the time for the End" and "the time for great salvation for Israel has arrived."[59]

That said, Lehren's words nevertheless suggest that his traditionalism prevented him from buying into the letter's underlying notion that all must begin with an awakening from below. He expresses doubts about Israel of Shklov's use of the *midrash* from *Yalqut Tehillim* as a basis for his view that the initiative must come from man. The *midrash* states that "the exiles of Judah and Benjamin are destined to go to them [the Ten Tribes] and bring them [back]"; but the question is whether that will happen before or after the Messiah's coming. Under the letter's influence, however, Lehren is willing to concede that it makes no sense to pursue the Ten Tribes following the Messiah's advent, "for if the Messiah has already come, why would it be necessary . . . to burden themselves to go to them to bring them to the Land of Israel?"[60] And in his great excitement, Lehren adds his own rationales for the premise that the time of the Messiah's footsteps is, in fact, at hand: the Jewish people are downtrodden, few engage in Torah and prayer, the very basis of the faith is undermined and displaced by the poisonous weed of Reform—which Lehren terms "a scab"—

and the enemies of the Jewish people are in the ascendancy. And so, Lehren continues, if our brethren, the members of the Ten Tribes, are discovered, we will be able to rouse the nation to repentance and prove to them that salvation is at hand.[61]

That the mission itself excited Lehren cannot be doubted. He sought full, detailed reports on all aspects of it: "We await their arrival so impatiently that a day seems like a year, and how can we tarry?"[62] Lest correspondence become lost, he asks that each letter sent to him on the matter be sent in duplicate—one copy via Alexandria and one via Istanbul—so at least one will be sure to arrive.[63] And, concerned for the mission's success, he suggests that that Israel of Shklov offer a special prayer, composed by David Azulai and published in *Kaf Aḥat*, sec. 10.[64] He also expresses concern about the emissary's safety, asking why he was sent off unaccompanied; and he poses questions about the mission's details, asking how Barukh was permitted to cross the legendary River Sambatyon on the Sabbath, the only day the river was calm enough to allow passage to the Ten Tribes said to be located beyond it.[65]

Lehren's confidence in the mission was enhanced by Israel of Shklov's report that the emissary, before setting out, had visited Ḥayyim ha-Kohen, chief of the Pinsk rabbinical court, and obtained his approval and blessing. The Ga'on of Pinsk was recognized as one who had attained knowledge of mysteries "through his self-abnegation and withdrawal, such that he is seized by true dreams,"[66] and he told the emissary not to question him too much; "rather, he said the emissary should go, for the time for it has come."[67] The Ga'on of Pinsk wept as he uttered the words and added that it was his time to ascend heavenward; he died soon after. Israel of Shklov notes that from time to time he visits Rabbi Ḥayyim's grave, reminding him to intercede on high for the emissary's success, as he had promised.[68]

On 4 May 1831, Lehren enthusiastically notifies Israel of Shklov that he has decided to send the sum of 2,000 piastres to support Barukh's mission over the course of three years.[69] Later, in spring 1832, Lehren publishes Israel's letter to the Ten Tribes and disseminates it among the fundraisers in the Land of Israel and all the communities with which he maintained contact. He asks them "to add to the usual donation a gift of funds to cover that emissary's expenses . . . and how can our people not be inspired to donate for such an important matter, for if God grants the emissary success, something great will happen, with the help of God, may He be blessed, and perhaps this will bring about the salvation of Israel."[70] To enhance its importance, Lehren compares the mission to the European nations' expeditions to remote areas of the world, such as the effort to locate the origin of the Nile. The Jews likewise need to support the expedition in search of the Ten Tribes.[71]

Additional details on the emissary, Barukh ben Samuel, and on his journey can be gleaned from correspondence between Lehren and some of the great European rabbis, such as Aqiba Eger and Moses Sofer of Pressburg, who wanted to see Israel of Shklov's original letter.[72] At the same time, Lehren asks Eger to mention Barukh in his prayers, and he concludes: "In my humble opinion, if God grants him success in reaching the Ten Tribes and the children of Moses, it will be the beginning of the redemption, for we have always heard that they will not be discovered until the time of the End, may it be speedily and in our days, amen."[73]

According to later accounts by Joseph Schwartz and Jacob Sapir, the emissary, Barukh, had the qualities needed to travel a long, harsh, and unknown route. He is described as courageous and energetic, well versed in natural medicine and the qualities of grasses and herbs.[74] To cover the mission's expenses and the living costs of Barukh's family, which remained behind in Safed, Israel of Shklov advanced *kolel* funds.[75] Barukh was supplied with elegant clothes, so he could appear in royal courts, and with holy books. Israel of Shklov provided him as well with three letters. The first stated that the bearer was on a mission for the *kolel* to find husbands who had abandoned their wives and fled the Land of Israel without divorcing them, leaving them unable to remarry; that letter was signed and confirmed by a consul. The second letter was the Epistle to the Children of Moses, which the emissary was to conceal and show to no one except the Ten Tribes, once he located them.[76] In the third letter, called *Iggeret ha-Sefeqot* (The Epistle of Uncertainties),[77] Israel raises uncertainties regarding some principles of the Torah and asks the sages of the Ten Tribes' Sanhedrin to resolve them. That letter was not initially sent to Lehren, but his curiosity led him to ask Israel for a copy, promising that under no circumstances would he publicize it. He also reassures Israel that the letters would not be read by gentiles: all letters, to be sure, are opened at border crossings, but only for fumigation, to prevent the spread of infectious diseases. They are not read, and even if the border authorities wanted to, they would be unable to read all of them.[78]

According to Lehren's correspondence, he received two letters from the emissary: one, dated 16 June 1831, after he had passed by Mt. Sinai en route to Egypt; the other, sent in late summer of that year, from Suez. In the latter, Barukh tells that he had made contact with officers of the Egyptian government, who provided him recommendations and special certifications by order of the king of Egypt, calling on people to assist him wherever he may go. Barukh tells as well that he had chartered a boat sailing to Yemen and was treated well by the captain, who promised to bring him to the Rekhavites (*benei ha-rekhavim*).[79] According to an earlier letter that had arrived from the Ten Tribes, the Rekhavites lived about fifteen days' distance from them. According to Lehren, the emissary was attempting to reach the Rekhavites' encampment because he hoped they would assist him, showing him how to reach the Ten Tribes.[80] And that, in turn, was because the *Perushim* had previously heard that the Rekhavites were powerful, dominating the caravans that passed by en route to Mecca and requiring even the sultan's passing caravans to pay tax to avoid being detained.

With the passage of time, however, Lehren's enthusiasm for the mission gave way to doubt. His confidence that Barukh would succeed began to wane, and he became more and more taken by words of the Epistle of 1646 from the sons of Moses to the sages of Jerusalem: "We, the tribes of the sons of Moses, lack the ability to cross the river until the time of the End, when God will tell the prisoners to go forth and those in darkness to leave. And so, too, the four mentioned tribes are not authorized to leave their boundaries."[81] To gain a more precise and reliable understanding of that Epistle, Lehren asked Zalman Ẓoref (Salamon), who was then in Amsterdam, to provide him a copy of the original text, as recorded in the journal of the community of Reggio, in Italy.[82] The conclusion to be reached on the basis of the Epistle is that before the coming of the Messiah, "it is impossible to reach them, and that is [God's] decree in His wisdom, may His Name be blessed." Accordingly, says Lehren at the end of his letter to Israel, he is filled with worry over Barukh's fate.[83]

With his initial enthusiasm having subsided, Lehren was now open to other views regarding the mission, and we find them reflected in his letters. On first reading the Epistle to the Ten Tribes, he was struck by the absence of Sefardic signatories, and he wondered whether their failure to join in sending the emissary might betoken disagreement with Israel of Shklov and adherence to the traditional view: "Perhaps they believe that the awakening should not be initiated from our side until grace and mercy overflow from the heavens, saying 'go forth' to those who are imprisoned; and scripture says [not to awaken love] 'until it pleases' [Song of Songs 2:7]."[84] At that time, Lehren's enthusiasm clouded his thinking about the omission of Sefardic signatories, and it now became clear to him that the mission had been opposed by the Hasidim as well. A letter from the Hasid Joseph Dubner of Safed[85] shows that the Hasidim at first planned to join in the mission, but they took offense at the Epistle's content—perhaps because it failed to mention Israel Ba'al Shem Tov and other Hasidic leaders in the passage describing the chain of tradition since the Oral Torah was compiled and referred to the Vilna Ga'on as the only contemporary authority of that stature.[86]

The letters Lehren receives from the Hasidim in Safed disclose a more serious side of the matter. They report that the mission as it was carried out did not in fact enjoy the blessing of the Ga'on of Pinsk. In the deliberations that preceded the sending of the mission, the Ga'on of Pinsk demanded that Lazer Sultsk of the Hasidic community organization be included in it, but Lazer, despite having already pledged to join Barukh, declined to accompany him on the grounds he was a total boor, a consumer of nonkosher food, "acting like a gentile, with no fringes or phylacteries."[87]

Another critical fact ascertained by Lehren was that the *Perushim* in Jerusalem also appeared to oppose Barukh's mission, though they expressed that opposition only obliquely: "We had some other matters to disclose to Your Honor, but respect for God warrants concealment."[88] Lehren interprets the allusion by reference to communications from the Hasidim in Safed, who rely, in pressing their complaints, on the Jerusalem *Perushim*. It thereby became clear that the Jerusalem *Perushim* reproved Israel of Shklov for assigning so holy and fateful a mission to someone unworthy, who acts like a gentile, and for characterizing him as "the eminent, righteous rabbi, possessed of the capacity to miraculously shorten a journey"[89] and even informing him of God's ineffable Name.[90] They were concerned not only that dispatching this sort of emissary would doom the mission to failure but also that it would entail other dangerous consequences, for Lehren's publication of the Epistle and its dissemination throughout Europe would arouse messianic agitation: "And people would now abandon their affairs and attend to the voice of a false prophet [Israel of Shklov], who writes that he has already received word from [the emissary] at Mt. Sinai, and they believe that Mt. Sinai is below the mountains of darkness at the end of the world, and they now send him funds far exceeding his expenses: woe unto us."[91]

Appalled by his new findings, Lehren, during the winter of 1832–1833, turns to one of the Safed Hasidim, Jacob Ẓevi ha-Kohen of Mogilev, and to the leaders of the Jerusalem *kolel* of the *Perushim,* and requests reliable information on the origin of the mission:

> But to allay our doubt, I adjure your honors, by the power of my love for the Holy Land of Israel (may it be built and established speedily and in our day, amen) on behalf of whose poor and needy I work and strive, by the force of this oath . . . to investigate and inquire into the matter thoroughly and report to me the entire, absolute truth. For the sake of God and for the sake of the sanctity of the Land of Israel (may it be built and established speedily and in our day, amen), do not attend to rumors but examine and inquire into the truth as far as can be done, and report to me the full truth regarding the aforesaid emissary and what was said by the righteous Ga'on of Pinsk, may his memory be for a blessing.[92]

Commission letters of such momentous importance could be expected to bear the signatures of numerous community organization officials and their rabbis. Therefore, it is noteworthy that Barukh's commission letter was signed by only three individuals in addition to Israel of Shklov himself: Aryeh Ne'eman; Ḥayyim David ha-Qatan (an official of the *kolel* of Russian Hasidim in Tiberias, who had special ties to Israel of Shklov); and an individual whose identity is unknown but who certainly is not Dov Ber of Avoritsh, who immigrated to the Land of Israel in the summer or fall of 1832.[93] The absence of other signatures suggests, in my judgment, that people had reservations about dispatching Barukh.

In any event, the mission to the Ten Tribes came to a sad and unnatural end: Barukh was murdered on 12 January 1834 by the Yemeni Imam Yaḥya.[94] That setback did not daunt Israel of Shklov, who tried to send an additional emissary and even sought to enlist Lehren's help in doing so.[95] But the rebellion of the *fellahin* during the summer of 1834 and the destruction of the Jewish settlement in Safed seem to have ruled out any possibility of a renewed mission.

Israel of Shklov's project was not the only attempt made to locate the Ten Tribes. We hear of another effort, searching in a different direction, in the July 1836 report of the missionary John Nicolayson; he tells of being asked whether he knew if the Ten Tribes might be found in the area of Tibet.[96] It thus appears that the search for the Ten Tribes and the effort to hasten the redemption by renewing ordination did not come to an end.[97] It should also be stressed that

Israel of Shklov's failure to renew ordination through the mechanism of the Ten Tribes' Sanhedrin in no way diminished his confidence that, in the process of redemption, the renewal of ordination precedes the rebuilding of Jerusalem. That notion underlies his stubborn and continued opposition to rebuilding the *Ḥurvah* courtyard and to expanding the *Perushim*'s colony in Jerusalem.

6

"Raising the *Shekhinah* from the Dust" by Rebuilding Jerusalem

And now, our spirit is exalted through the Lord our God to enhance and exalt our Holy Temple and to build synagogues and study halls in the holy mountain, Jerusalem. . . . It is a good sign that it is the beginning of the redemption. . . . Be strong for the sake of our people and the city of our God to exalt the head of the Most High and raise the holy *shekhinah* so that she may find a place of respite in our study halls. . . . The awakening on high to rebuild the ruins is dependent on the awakening below.

Letter commissioning a rabbinic emissary, 1837, in P. Grajewski, *Mi-Ginzei Yerushalayim*

The *Perushim* Begin to Settle in Jerusalem

In late fall 1815, before the Safed *kolel* had recovered from the devastating impact of the long epidemic, Rabbi Menaḥem Mendel of Shklov went up to settle in Jerusalem. He left Safed even though his presence there was particularly needed at the time and even though his departure and the resulting divisions would be yet another harsh—and potentially fatal—blow to the community, already weakened in both number and quality. He went up to Jerusalem because he regarded settlement there as more important than the welfare of the *kolel*, and he was undeterred by the unfavorable prospects there. The group that accompanied him numbered fewer than ten,[1] and there was no reason to expect its numbers to grow. Indeed, the Nobles of Vilna conditioned their authorization of the move to Jerusalem on the community there remaining a satellite of the "mother community" in Safed and not developing into an independent entity.[2] The

Sefardim, meanwhile, insisted on Menaḥem's Mendel's agreement not to request any Jerusalem community funding, and they limited the number of Ashkenazi settlers, lest they establish an independent Ashkenazi community.[3]

The Hasidim likewise sought to impede the efforts of Menaḥem Mendel and his group to establish a base in Jerusalem. As already noted, the Hasidim claimed closer affinity to Judah Ḥasid's group and correspondingly greater rights to the assets of Jerusalem's Ashkenazi community—the *Ḥurvah* courtyard.[4] Missionary sources show that the *Perushim*, for their part, tried to impede further Hasidic settlement in Jerusalem and that the two groups' mutual disdain was so great that they did not even flinch from slandering each other before the government.[5] The decision of the Nobles of Vilna to establish only a symbolic outpost in Jerusalem, limited to a small number of scholars and lacking the status of a community, seems to have embodied a middle ground between the avoidance of conflict with these other groups and the establishment of a settlement of *Perushim* in Jerusalem.

But it was not to remain passive that Menaḥem Mendel of Shklov's group had taken the brazen step of settling in Jerusalem. While they tried to maintain proper relations with the venerable Sefardic *kolel*,[6] their purpose in coming to Jerusalem—renewal of the Ashkenazi settlement there—could not be achieved if they acquiesced in all the restrictions imposed on them. And so, within their first year in Jerusalem, they set aside their promises to the *kolel* in Safed. They attempted to overcome their isolation by drawing in new members, and, in an effort to consolidate their position, they requested a greater share of the funding from Vilna. Their moves to shirk their obligations can be seen, for example, in the Safed community's suspicions—fully justified—that the Jerusalemite Solomon Pach "had been sent from Jerusalem to Istanbul to sit at the crossroads and direct important people toward Jerusalem and to obtain funding from them."[7]

The Jerusalem group directed their principal efforts to rebuilding the Judah Ḥasid ruins (the *Ḥurvah*) and returning the Ashkenazim to its courtyard. The desolate *Ḥurvah* courtyard symbolized the expulsion of the Ashkenazim from Jerusalem, and only by reasserting control over the site and rebuilding it could the Ashkenazim demonstrate their intention to reestablish themselves in the city. Moreover, the rebuilding would have the kabbalistic significance of a *tiqqun*, a "repairing" of the earlier destruction; and, in accord with the doctrine of "awakening below," rebuilding one of Jerusalem's ruins would represent the first step in the rebuilding of the entire city.[8] But that required a *rebuilding*; the purpose could not be achieved by acquiring an existing, long-standing structure: "The community was not unaware of the importance the sages, of blessed memory, attached to the commandment to rebuild even one of Jerusalem's ruins. . . . And since the time our city was destroyed, throughout the days of our ancestors, their souls longed with an intense desire, wondering when they would have the opportunity."[9] To rebuild the *Ḥurvah*, as a symbolic *tiqqun* for the destruction (or, from a different point of view, as symbolically rebuilding Jerusalem itself), was the *Perushim's* greatest desire. In ranking his accomplishments since setting out to immigrate, Menaḥem Mendel of Shklov places rebuilding the *Ḥurvah* at the summit:

> And [the Vilna Ga'on's] merit and the merit of my righteous ancestors . . . served to bring me to the Holy Land and to enable me to make my residence in the holy city of Safed (may it be built and established speedily and in our day), and there, with God's help, I established study halls filled with books, for study and for prayer. But that was insufficient in His eyes, and He brought me to Jerusalem, God's holy city . . . and with God's help, I there established a study hall and a synagogue for study and prayer, and now, God has helped me to take out [of ruination] the ruin in Jerusalem, which belonged to our fellow Ashkenazim from early times and in which a synagogue was situated for more than one hundred years but which was turned over to aliens and strangers and became ruined and desolate. But now, in His great mercy and kindness, I brought it out of their hands, and I said what the sages, of blessed memory said: "One who enjoys a wedding meal . . . if he causes the bridegroom to rejoice, he merits Torah. Rabbi Naḥman bar Isaac says, it is as if he rebuilt one of Jerusalem's ruins, showing that rebuilding Jerusalem is greater [than Torah study].[10]

The *Firman* Annulling the Ashkenazi Debts in Jerusalem

It must be kept in mind that when we discuss the reconstruction of the *Ḥurvah*, we are talking about rebuilding a sizable ruined area that included dwelling houses, cisterns, ritual immersion pools, a study hall, and a large synagogue. In undertaking the project, the *Perushim* faced numerous problems. Initially, they had to deal with the Jerusalem Ashkenazi community's old debts, for which the creditors' heirs claimed the *Ḥurvah* courtyard as collateral. Once that was taken care of, they had to obtain legal recognition of their right, as heirs of the Ashkenazim, to the property. In that connection, they would need a precise and official determination of the *Ḥurvah*'s boundaries, for it was, as noted, a small-scale neighborhood. Moreover, when they sought authorization to rebuild the courtyard, they would learn that, under Muslim law, it might be permissible to rebuild ruined houses, but it was forbidden to rebuild a synagogue. Could the *Perushim* overcome this array of obstacles? Could they find legal loopholes that would permit them to rebuild the synagogue as well? Could they establish themselves in the *Ḥurvah*? Only time would tell. Meanwhile, they directed their attention to clearing the principal obstacles to reconstruction and resolving the technical problems—the matter of the debts, the legal title to the land, and the boundaries of the parcel.

At the time Menaḥem Mendel of Shklov and his band went up to Jerusalem, fear of the Arabs still prevailed among the Ashkenazim. The rumor of a government decree annulling "every debt outstanding for more than forty years"[11] did not vitiate their fear of the Arab creditors, for it proved unavailing. Because of that fear, Menaḥem Mendel "was required to disguise himself in Sefardic attire and live as a recluse."[12] But the *Perushim* could not stand by and leave matters in the control of others. That was not why they had gone up to Jerusalem. They had a goal, and they were determined to carry it out, despite the difficulties and constraints.

As early as 1816, their first year in Jerusalem, they undertook a series of steps directed to the rebuilding of the *Ḥurvah*: "In 1816, we pleaded with the powers in the city of Constantinople to obtain a royal statement (*firman*) that the Ishmaelites residing in Jerusalem would not be permitted to enforce the debts of the Ashkenazim."[13] But those efforts bore no fruit. In 1817, several leaders of the *kolel*—among them, Solomon Zalman Shapira and Solomon Pach—set out for Constantinople, to obtain the *firman*. Their efforts were time consuming, and only in autumn of 1819 did they secure the *firman* annulling the debts of the Ashkenazim. We learn of it from an explicit statement in the *a'al'am* (official document) issued by the Jerusalem *shari'a* court to Zalman Ẓoref (Solomon): "And a royal decree was issued in the year [1819], in accordance with the ruling of His Excellency Sheikh al-Islam . . . that none of the creditors may demand [payment of] the debt from these Ashkenazim, for according to the law, they are not liable."[14]

Efforts to Secure a *Firman* Authorizing Construction of the *Ḥurvah* Courtyard

Having obtained the *firman* that canceled the debts, Menaḥem Mendel of Shklov and Solomon Zalman Shapira turned to the Qadi in Jerusalem and received a legal document describing the entire *Ḥurvah* site and its contents,[15] including the courtyard, the ruined houses, and the eleven shops that had been built by the creditors' heirs on a portion of the site.

The two official documents the *Perushim* had received laid the groundwork for their efforts to secure a *firman* that would authorize construction of the courtyard and the large synagogue within it. Ẓevi Hirsch Lehren describes the situation as follows: "And now they needed another *firman* in order to build the synagogue; and that was not because of any anti-Jewish malice [on the part of the authorities], God forbid, but because of a general law that forbade the building of any house of worship or the repair of any sanctuary without a *firman* from the Sultan, and so, too, the synagogues of the Sefardi community had long been in disrepair, and they were forbidden to repair their roofs."[16] Their awareness of these legal constraints did not hinder their attempts to secure the needed *firman* from the Sultan's court in Constantinople. On 25 April 1820, a contract was signed in Jerusalem between the *kolel* of the *Perushim* and Solomon Pach, engaging the latter to obtain the *firman* in Constantinople, "so we would have the authority to build the houses and the synagogue in the aforesaid ruin."[17] But because they were cognizant of the legal constraints, they gave precedence to "building the houses," adding "and the synagogue" only afterward; and they noted that Pach's mission would be regarded as accomplished even if he secured authorization only to build the houses.[18]

But this mission of 25 April 1820 was never carried out. The Greek rebellion against the Turks and the disruption of the sea-lanes forced Pach to delay his departure. On 15 January 1821, he was asked to try again, but it appears that he was once again required to return, and this mission, too, was never carried out.[19]

Meanwhile, the renewed activity of the *Perushim* with respect to the *Ḥurvah* courtyard provoked renewed activity on the part of the Arab creditors. Israel of Shklov had feared that efforts to assert control over the courtyard would prompt the creditors to demand payment despite the *firman* canceling the old loans, and his fears were borne out. The Arabs "returned and took possession of all the shops in *dar al Ashkanaz*"[20] and demanded that the promissory notes be paid off; they even began clearing large stones from the synagogue ruins and threatening to build a mosque on the site, which they contended had been mortgaged for the loans.[21] Naturally, carrying out such a threat would dash the hopes placed by the Jerusalemites in the building of the *Ḥurvah*.[22] The *kolel* of the Jerusalem *Perushim*, which had sought to be independent, particularly with regard to fund raising, began a major effort to obtain the money needed to redeem the *Ḥurvah* from the creditors. As early as 2 September 1819, Zalman Ẓoref (Solomon) was dispatched for that purpose to Russia and western Europe.[23] In the early 1820s, Menaḥem Mendel of Shklov, the head of the *kolel*, turned directly to the rabbis of western Europe, including Solomon Hirschell of London and the rabbi of Nikolsburg,[24] asking them for special support for Jerusalem. In accord with his request, funds were raised for that purpose in 1821 in Warsaw as well and in other areas of Poland.[25] In addition, Menaḥem Mendel wanted to dedicate the proceeds from his book, *Sha'ar ha-Ẓimẓum*, "to the rebuilding of the ruins of Jerusalem."[26] He expressed his hope that "this merit will protect me, etc., and earn me the privilege of building the synagogue, which is a miniature Temple,"[27] "but his holy plan was not implemented."[28] In Jerusalem itself funds were raised for redemption of the courtyard from the Ishmaelites.

In addition to the demands of the Arab creditors for repayment of the old loans, the *Perushim* encountered unanticipated difficulties as a consequence of the Russo-Turkish War of 1821–1823. It is fair to assume that the usual arrangements for transporting correspondence and funds from Vilna were disrupted, and the developments sharpened the tension between the *Perushim* of Safed and those of Jerusalem. In these circumstances, the two communities decided in 1823 to jointly write to Solomon Pach in Constantinople, asking him to renew the connection with the center in Vilna. That connection was vital for them, and they accordingly admonished him not to disclose to the Nobles of Vilna, should he be called to appear before them, the conflicts between the groups in the Land of Israel.[29] In addition, the leaders of the Jerusalem *kolel*—Menaḥem Mendel, Isaac of Kovno, and Solomon Zalman Shapira—gave him two special assignments. First, they asked him to deter immigrants from being influenced by the Safed zealots, "whose nature it is to demean one who speaks well of the holy city of Jerusalem, may it be built and established, and of the people who dwell there,"[30] and, instead, to encourage new immigrants to accompany him on his way back to Jerusalem, for he "knows all its ways, its tranquility, and its peace."[31] Second, they gave him the "boundary document . . . in the handwriting of the Mufti Effendi," and requested that he carry out the task he had hitherto been unable to perform and secure a fully effective *firman* "to possess the land of the *Ḥurvah* . . . and rebuild the aforesaid *Ḥurvah* and the synagogue within it and the ruined houses . . . free of any protest or grumbling."[32] And since it had become clear in the interim that the occupants of the shops in the *Ḥurvah* were demanding huge sums of money in exchange for their agreement to vacate them (even though the Mufti's document on the *Ḥurvah*'s boundaries stated explicitly that the shops were included within it), Solomon Pach was instructed to request that the *firman* state explicitly that the shops as well should be returned to the Jews. His principals even transmitted through him a request that the craftsmen to be engaged in building the *Ḥurvah* be exempted from taxes and corvée. That final request suggests that the Jerusalemites saw the start of the project as within their grasp, requiring only the issuance of the *firman*.[33] But Pach's mission again did not go well; the details of his failure remain unclear.

The *Perushim* set out to achieve their goal step by step. First, they would try to secure authority to build the dwelling houses in the *Ḥurvah* courtyard, on the premise that the courtyard was property (*mulk*) of the Ashkenazim. To that end, they pursued a legal strategy: to avoid the need for a *firman* from Constantinople, they sought to rely on an old *firman* given to the Jews in 1623, which stated: "No one may object to the Jewish community in Jerusalem tearing down or *building in their quarters and their dwelling areas*."[34] Armed with that document, Menaḥem Mendel of Shklov, "representative (*waqil*) of the holy congregation of the Ashkenazim,"[35] appeared before the Qadi of Jerusalem and managed to obtain a certificate providing as follows:

a. The courtyard at issue is *mulk* of the Ashkenazi community from ancient times: "The courtyard is in the street of the Jews. It was destroyed and is of no use, and now it is a *mulk* of the *kolel* of Ashkenazi Jews."[36]
b. The courtyard's destruction was the result of the Ashkenazim having fled from Jerusalem and not of a deliberate action by the creditors: "And because the yoke of the debts burdened them, they were required to flee from these places . . . and the aforesaid courtyard was left with no residents, and that caused the destruction."[37]

It appears that this legal document, issued in March 1824, was obtained by the petitioners for a handsome price. The considerable bribes paid to the Mufti of Jerusalem, the Pasha, and the various functionaries, came to 7,311 piastres.[38] The *firman* refers as well to the eleven shops within the courtyard, whose possession by the creditors' heirs could constitute proof of their relationship to the area. Accordingly, the *firman* states: "And now it is destroyed and desolate, of no use or benefit."[39]

Taken together, these two documents—the old *firman* of 1623 and the *maḥkemah shar'iyah* ruling of 1824, which determined that the courtyard was the property of the Ashkenazi community—made it possible to rebuild the houses in the *Ḥurvah*, though not the synagogue, without a *firman* from Constantinople.[40] As a practical matter, however, difficulties of an uncertain nature prevented implementation of the plan, and the rebuilding of the houses did not get under way. The problem appears to have been connected with the *Perushim*'s inability to obtain actual dominion over the parcel of land from the Arab creditors; this conclusion is suggested by their account, to the missionary W. B. Lewis, of the local government's disregard for the documents proving their ownership of the *Ḥurvah* courtyard. They asked Lewis to intervene on their behalf with the British ambassador in Constantinople, hoping the ambassador would support their quest for a *firman* that would secure their actual dominion and their right to rebuild the ruined houses.[41]

In the summer of 1825, Solomon Zalman Shapira left on an extended mission to Europe, one of whose purposes was securing the *firman*.[42] He was requested as well to raise funds in Europe to cover the costs already incurred by the *Perushim* in trying to redeem the *Ḥurvah* courtyard.[43] His efforts to obtain the *firman* bore no fruit, neither en route from the Land of Israel nor on his passage through Constantinople on his return. Lehren states: "And Rabbi Zalman Shapira said to us [when he was in Amsterdam] that he hoped to obtain the final *firman* upon his arrival in Constantinople, but what did he achieve?"[44]

When Shapira reached Constantinople, evidently in 1828, he learned that in the wake of the Russo-Turkish war, the Turks were about to expel the Jerusalem Ashkenazim from the city as enemy aliens.[45] Securing a *firman* authorizing construction of the courtyard had to yield to obtaining a *firman* canceling the expulsion. With the intercession of the Prussian ambassador in Constantinople and the help of a bribe of 100 gold ducats, the *firman* revoking the expulsion was issued.[46] Shapira did not tarry in Constantinople and hurried back to the Land of Israel. On the eve of Rosh ha-Shanah (8 September 1828), he reached Jerusalem, enfeebled and ill.[47] He never recovered, lingering until his death early in 1829.[48]

Soon after Shapira's death, the political wheel turned again, as it did so often in the Ottoman Empire of the time. At the beginning of 1829, Rafael Farḥi, a Jew, was named head of the government in Damascus, and his appointment was accompanied by an improved governmental attitude to the Jews.[49] The missionary Joseph Wolff tells that one of the senior officials in the new government in Jerusalem was a relative of Rafael Farḥi, and that even the army commander in Jerusalem was trying to get in the Jews' good graces.[50] The leaders of the *Perushim* in Jerusalem seem to have tried to use the improved political situation to advance the *Ḥurvah* building project. On 10 September 1829, Zalman Ẓoref (Solomon) set out on another mission to Europe;

one of the purposes of his trip was to renew efforts in Constantinople. But he, too, appears to have been no more successful than his predecessors.[51]

Intensified Efforts to Rebuild the *Ḥurvah* Courtyard Under the Rule of Muhammad Ali

Muhammad Ali's conquest of the Land of Israel aroused new hopes for improvement in the Jews' situation and for the rebuilding of the *Ḥurvah* courtyard. As early as the first months of his reign in the Land of Israel, the Jews of Acre petitioned him in general terms to deal kindly with their people and to issue a *firman* that would permit the Jews of Jerusalem "to build for themselves synagogues and dwelling houses to the extent of their ability."[52]

From Aryeh Ne'eman's letters to Ẓevi Hirsch Lehren during 1833, we learn as well that the *Perushim* in Jerusalem petitioned Muhammad Ali regarding the building of the synagogue in the *Ḥurvah* courtyard.[53] Muhammad Ali adopted a generally positive stance toward the Jews; but he did not yet dare to issue such a *firman*—a measure that would be at odds with the long tradition of Muslim rule in the East and with "the Covenant of Omar,"[54] both of which prohibited the building of synagogues. Nevertheless, he did not apply the prohibition to the repair and improvement of existing synagogues that had been destroyed in the earthquake of 25 May 1834,[55] and a *firman* authorizing synagogue repairs was in fact given to the Jerusalem Sefardim on 11 October 1834. The order emphasized that it permits the repair of a synagogue but not its reconstruction: "And an order was given to them permitting the repair of the aforesaid synagogue on its pre-existing foundation. . . . Accordingly, we deliver this order into their hands and forbid all people from interfering with the repair of the aforesaid synagogue."[56]

The Jerusalem Sefardic community set to work energetically on the repairs, and they were quickly completed. The missionary John Nicolayson reports on 2 July 1835 that almost all of the structural repairs had been completed by then and that a new panel had been installed above the portal, bearing the date 5595 in numerals rather than in the more usual letters—in his view, because of concern that the corresponding letters (*t-q-ẓ-h*) spelled out the ill-omened word "will be cut off."[57]

Muhammad Ali's restoration of the authority to conduct public worship and to repair synagogues, which had been denied to the Jews in the Land of Israel throughout the Ottoman period, was seen by the Jews as signifying the beginning of the redemption.[58] In July 1835, Nicolayson writes of the influence of these changes in the area of worship. Discussing the construction of the Sefardic synagogues, he recounts that the Jews considered this revolutionary phenomenon as, in itself, a messianic development. To be sure, he says, they expect the Messiah to come in a miraculous manner; but when they compare their current situation with what preceded it, they see the change itself as proof of the Messiah's footsteps.[59]

It may be assumed that the success of the Sefardim in repairing and redecorating their synagogue prodded the *Perushim* to renew their efforts and seek new ways to obtain the *firman* authorizing rebuilding of the *Ḥurvah*. The new political situation in the region was encouraging, and realization of their goal appeared to be within their grasp. Muhammad Ali's desire for the support of the European powers was a point of vulnerability, to which pressure might be applied.

The *Firman* at Last Obtained

In spring of 1836, the Austrian consul in Alexandria, Anton Laurin, visited the Land of Israel.[60] When he reached Jerusalem, the leaders of the *Perushim* turned to him for help in obtaining the elusive *firman*. Apparently, it was agreed that Zalman Ẓoref (Solomon) would travel to Egypt, where, it was promised, the Austrian and Russian consuls would support his efforts to obtain the order.[61] He set out on behalf of the *kolel* in early summer 1836,[62] and, within less than one month, on 23 June, he obtained the long-awaited decree.[63]

It is difficult at first to see how this successful effort differed from its many failed predecessors over the preceding two decades, during part of which time the enlightened reign of Muhammad Ali was already in place. But the details that emerge from the Clerks' Organization correspondence show an entirely novel dimension to this final, successful, attempt. Ẓoref had managed to transform the authorization to build the *Ḥurvah* courtyard from a mere source of monetary gain for the consuls into a personal and political interest of Muhammad Ali. He did so by deviously invoking the prestigious name of Baron Solomon Maier Rothschild of Vienna. Spinning a tale that the baron had promised to fully fund the building of the *Ḥurvah* courtyard once the *firman* had been secured, he cajoled the Austrian consul by promising to write to Rothschild and tell him of the consul's help. Invoking the Rothschild name was likely to persuade Mohammad Ali as well: Ẓoref well understood that a favorable decision on Muhammad Ali's part might be prompted by the prospect of forging financial and political ties with the Rothschild family and thereby securing the political support of Austria and France. To flesh out the contrivance and enhance the likelihood that the Austrian consul would find it credible and lend his personal support, Ẓoref wrote to Lehren, disclosed the plan to him, and asked him to use his connections to induce Rothschild to write to the Austrian consul, thanking him for all his help in obtaining the *firman*. Lehren declined to join in the ruse,[64] fearing that when funds for the project proved inadequate, the consul would direct the Jews to Rothschild and the plot would be exposed.[65] But Ẓoref's resourcefulness, imagination, and daring—as well as his willingness even to use deceit when the ends justified it—ultimately led to success in this case.

Having received the *firman*, Ẓoref acted quickly; even before leaving Alexandria, he wrote to Lehren and tried to persuade him to apply to the *Ḥurvah* project the funds that Lehren's brother had pledged for construction of a synagogue in the Land of Israel. He no doubt had two purposes in mind: obtaining the funds from Lehren, which ought to be relatively easy now that they had the *firman*; and using the funds to bear out his assurances to the Austrian consul regarding Rothschild's "promise" to support construction of the *Ḥurvah*.

We have no text of the *firman*, but in his letter to Lehren from Alexandria, Ẓoref quotes from it and claims it reflects a greater achievement than that of the Sefardim in their day. But Lehren's treatment of the matter suggests the *firman* spoke of restoring the *Ḥurvah* courtyard to the *Perushim* but did not explicitly authorize construction of the large synagogue: "For he obtained only authorization for their synagogue to be returned to them; and adverse litigants might argue that it had been destroyed and no longer exists and that if they build it anew, they will say that this is new construction and not [restoration of] what they had."[66]

A close examination of the *a'al'am* of 1836 indeed shows that the *firman* made no explicit reference to building the synagogue, and that all it contained was a grant of "authority to the Ashkenazi Jews dwelling today in the holy city of Jerusalem to build their extant *dir* [courtyard] in the holy city of Jerusalem, known as the *dir* of the Ashkenazim in the market of the Jews, prescriptively their land . . . and the construction should be in accordance with the law, as it had been built earlier."[67] This is confirmed by a letter to Moses Montefiore, sent in the summer of 1849 by the leaders of the Jerusalem *Perushim*'s *kolel*. The letter states explicitly that Muhammad Ali's *firman* did not encompass authorization to build the synagogue. Rumor had it that Montefiore was angered by the leaders' failure to use the *firman* as an opportunity to build the great synagogue in the *Ḥurvah*; in response to those rumors, they disclose: "Accordingly, we feel an obligation to say words of truth to our lord, Sir Moses. We, too, mightily yearned to erect the synagogue before any other building, but since we lacked authorization (*firman*), the Ishmaelites did not allow us to build the aforesaid synagogue, and in order to retain possession of the area, we had to build houses along its entire perimeter."[68]

Another shortcoming of the *firman* was its failure to define the boundaries of the courtyard. Evidently recognizing this deficiency, Ẓoref took clever remedial action. On 21 August 1836, he appeared before the Jerusalem court and requested that the *firman* he had brought from Egypt be copied into the court's registry, along with a description of the boundaries of the *Ḥurvah* to which the *firman* pertains. The court sent the chief builder to measure the courtyard and, on that basis, issued an *a'al'am* setting the *Ḥurvah*'s boundaries. The *a'al'am* determined that the eleven shops held by Arabs constituted part of the *ḥurvah* courtyard and should be returned to the Ashkenazi landowners; but the occupants should be compensated in the amount of 9,750 piastres. The judge added that neither the breadth of the courtyard nor the height of the buildings should exceed what was originally there.[69] This final stage of tedious dealing with the shopkeepers and the judges went on for ten days. The Russian consul in Jaffa played a major role in it,[70] following a written directive from the Russian ambassador in Alexandria, brought back by Ẓoref, to help the *Perushim* register the *firman* and execute it.[71]

On 1 September 1836, about twenty years after having gone up to Jerusalem, the *Perushim* finally began to clear out the ruins of the *Ḥurvah* courtyard. Joseph Schwartz describes the emotional scene as follows: "With great joy, we began to remove the mounds of dust . . . and suddenly, there were revealed to our eyes the original buildings that had been there. The synagogue and ritual bath buildings peered out from the ground, along with other buildings. . . . All of them were still strong and solid. . . . Afterward, we set the cornerstone for construction of a large synagogue."[72]

According to Schwartz, in addition to the *firman*, Muhammad Ali issued a directive that the promissory notes be returned to the Jews, so that the debts could never again be raised by the Arab creditors.[73] But it appears that the creditors refused to turn over the promissory notes to the government, and, on the basis of those notes, continued to interfere with the construction of the *Ḥurvah*: "And so we began to engage in the construction work, but now we were approached by some grandchildren of the aforesaid creditors, demanding payment of the debts owed to their ancestors and producing the promissory notes."[74] With this, Ẓoref, "the Jews' administrator," was required to appear before the Jerusalem city judge on 17 September 1836 to request a ruling canceling the loans.[75] He claimed that the Ashkenazim now living in Jerusalem were not descendants or relatives of those who had borrowed the money at the start of the eighteenth century: "And so, the Ashkenazi Jews now present here in the holy city of Jerusalem are liable for no part of the aforesaid loans taken by the Ashkenazim at that earlier time."[76]

Ẓoref mentions that Sheikh al-Islam had already ruled that "none of the creditors may demand [payment of] the debt from these Ashkenazim, for according to the law, they are not liable."[77] To the creditors' argument (unsupported by documentation) that the *dir* was mortgaged for their debts, Ẓoref responds that it would have made no sense for Judah Ḥasid's circle to mortgage the *Ḥurvah* as security for their loans, for the property belonged not just to them but to all the Ashkenazim in the world.[78] The desired conclusion, of course, was that the creditors should not be permitted to interfere with the construction of the *Ḥurvah* by the Ashkenazim, and the court so ruled. Building of the study hall in the *Ḥurvah* courtyard proceeded apace and, after about four months, on 6 January 1837, the study hall was dedicated.[79] Within the community itself, however, other dramatic events were taking shape.

Lehren Family Involvement in Construction of the *Ḥurvah*

In the fall of 1832, Lehren became personally involved in supporting construction of the *Ḥurvah*. But the transaction did not go smoothly, and the preliminaries dragged on for nearly four years; thereafter, matters deteriorated into a sharp division and confrontation between Israel of Shklov on the one hand and the *kolel* of the Jerusalem *Perushim* on the other.

Ever since 1827, when the *kolel* of the Safed *Perushim* ran into financial trouble, Israel of Shklov had been in negotiations with Ẓevi Hirsch Lehren over financial support. In May or June 1827, Israel asked Lehren to take up a special collection to pay off the *kolel*'s debts.[80] Later in the negotiations, in late summer 1831, the idea arose of selling some of the *kolel*'s assets—houses or a study hall—in order to cover its debts.[81] The suggestion intrigued Akiva Lehren, Ẓevi Hirsch's brother, who around that time had pledged to build a synagogue in the Land of Israel. Ẓevi Hirsch Lehren wrote of the proposal to the Nobles of Vilna, who informed him that the *kolel* lacked the authority to sell its assets; but that the matter under consideration was dedicating the funds that would permit the synagogue to be named for him. On 29 August 1833, Ẓevi Hirsch Lehren wrote to Israel of Shklov that his brother was interested in purchasing a synagogue specifically in Jerusalem and that he hoped the new government would permit the purchase of land for that purpose.[82] Lehren thus renounced the idea of acquiring the synagogue in Safed, despite the unpleasantness that was likely to cause in his relationship with Israel of Shklov, which he had tried to cultivate. Meanwhile, reports reached Lehren about the possibility of purchasing real property in Jerusalem; and in 1833, just as Lehren was prepared to fulfill his brother's pledge to build a synagogue, Aryeh Ne'eman wrote to him of the need to establish a synagogue for the *kolel* of Jerusalem's *Perushim*. Ne'eman estimated that 600 gold ducats would be adequate to rebuild the synagogue in the *Ḥurvah*.[83] Lehren, who generally opposed using funds for purposes other than maintenance of human life,[84] struggled greatly over his involvement in the construction of a synagogue, particularly in the *Ḥurvah*. He had two reservations:

a. The Hasidim questioned the right of the *Perushim* to possess the *Ḥurvah* courtyard. Lehren was concerned that if he funded the *Ḥurvah* project, he would be seen as taking the side of the *Perushim* in their dispute with the Hasidim.
b. Lehren was determined that the synagogue built with his brother's funds be his exclusive property, and that there be no co-owners: "That it be his by outright, absolute purchase and that he rededicate it to the use of the *Perushim*'s *kolel*, may God protect it."[85]

Since funds had already been raised since 1823 for the building of the *Ḥurvah* synagogue, he was uncertain about how to treat that "partnership." Despite these reservations, Lehren recognized that the *Ḥurvah* site had been sanctified for generations and had major historical significance. If a synagogue were built there with his family's funds, it would greatly honor him and his brother.

In his earlier correspondence during 1833 with officials of the Jerusalem *kolel*, Lehren never let on that the benefactor interested in supporting establishment of a synagogue was, in fact, his brother. But from the moment he disclosed his personal interest in the matter, the negotiations descended into the vortex of his relationships with, on the one hand, the Jerusalem *Perushim*'s *kolel* and its leader, Zalman Ẓoref (Solomon), and, on the other, Israel of Shklov. In the summer of 1834, Lehren wrote to the Jerusalem *kolel* that his brother was prepared to donate 400 gold ducats, twice the amount he had initially intended to contribute to the synagogue. He tied that promise to his request that the *kolel* not negotiate with anyone else on the matter, and he said he would not seek to interest others in the project, nor would he publicize it at all until the *kolel* secured the *firman* authorizing construction.[86] At the same time, Lehren wrote to Israel of Shklov, informing him that his brother was interested in acquiring a synagogue in the *Ḥurvah* and therefore was backing off from the proposal to purchase the study hall in Safed. He asked Israel of Shklov not to interfere with his brother's effort in Jerusalem and, indeed, to help him carry it out.[87]

But the people of the Jerusalem *kolel* disapproved of Lehren's desire for exclusive patronage of the synagogue and did not heed his requests. In the spring of 1834, they turned to Solomon Hirschell (the rabbi of London), to Moses Montefiore, to Baron Rothschild, and to Asher ben Samson of London with a request to raise 2,000 gold ducats for construction of the *Ḥurvah* synagogue. By chance, their letter fell into Lehren's hands,[88] and it infuriated him. He raged that the *kolel* officials did not believe him when he said these stingy aristocrats had never made such large personal contributions and never would. Swept up by his feelings, he declared he would prevent delivery of the letters to their addressees; he then changed his mind and said, on the contrary, that they should be delivered "and let them see what their letter will accomplish."[89] He accused the *kolel* officials of intending to make construction of the *Ḥurvah* synagogue serve as a perpetual fund-raising device and of having already begun to do so in 1822, when Ẓoref went on his mission to Europe; since then, they have raised funds but built nothing. Lehren also speaks threateningly, noting his brother's wish that the synagogue be exclusively his through absolute purchase and maintaining that it accordingly makes no sense to accept construction contributions from other donors. The necessary conclusion is that he would withdraw from the entire matter, "and let the *Ḥurvah* be built by whoever wants [to build it]."[90] Lehren uses the opportunity to mention, for the first time, that Aryeh Ne'eman also wrote to him about the possibility of purchasing a "courtyard" containing a suitable structure for a pleasant synagogue. And since no one else as yet has any rights to that courtyard, he is inclined to accept this alternative.[91]

As usual, Lehren's threats gave vent to his intense feelings more than they expressed his practical intentions. His letter's inconsistent wording conveys the impression that his desire to build the *Ḥurvah* synagogue actually intensified when he learned that his "competitors" in London might accede to the request of the *kolel* leadership.[92] In fact, Lehren's interest in building the *Ḥurvah* synagogue did not weaken, and, over the ensuing year, he makes various efforts to act on it. To demonstrate that he is doing all he can to gain exclusive patronage of the project, he informs Lord Frankel of Witzenhausen, on 25 January 1835, that he cannot transfer in his name a sum of money intended for construction of a synagogue in Jerusalem because someone else had already pledged 500 gold ducats for that purpose. Lehren leaves Lord Frankel the choice of having the funds returned or of dedicating them to rebuilding the houses that had been destroyed during the revolt of the *fellahin*.[93]

As noted, the people of the Jerusalem *kolel* declined to grant exclusive rights over their synagogue; accordingly, they ignored Lehren and offered no response to his proposals. In the summer of 1835, Lehren complains to Israel of Shklov about their attitude. He is well aware, he writes, that under the new regime, it is possible to obtain outright ownership of houses in Jerusalem and that the available houses and courtyards are particularly inexpensive; the proof is that immigrants from Poland acquired houses in Jerusalem, some even outside the Jewish Quarter.[94] Lehren makes no effort to conceal from Israel of Shklov his desire to wind up the matter quickly and fulfill his brother's pledge. He gives the impression of being hurried and impatient; as soon as he threatens to direct the funds to some other *kolel*, he backtracks and acknowledges that his brother is even willing to add to his proposed contribution "out of his great desire to complete the process . . . and see his pledge fulfilled."[95] He is prepared to send the funds immediately to the Dutch consul in Beirut, Moses da Fajito, but Lehren again ties the matter to the agreement of the officials in Jerusalem and Safed "that the synagogue will be transferred . . . to him as a permanent acquisition that none may challenge. The choice is theirs, but they must build it immediately, without delay or impediment, and the artisans should be spurred on with respect to both the quality of the work and the speed with which it is performed, and we await their exalted reply as quickly as possible."[96] Since Lehren also provides notice that he has doubled the initially proposed figure and will provide, instead of 500 gold ducats, 2,000 Spanish silver duros—apparently to parallel the 2,000 gold ducats the Jerusalemites sought to obtain from the London aristocrats—he asks that "you not consider, God forbid, stinting on the *Ḥurvah* synagogue construction" and using the residual funds for other purposes.[97]

In his mind's eye, Lehren sees the *Ḥurvah* synagogue fully built; and he storms against his fellow Amsterdamer Nathan Coronel, who writes in opposition to his brother's plan to build the Jerusalem synagogue. Interestingly, Coronel uses the same arguments that Lehren himself had used in the past and would again use in the future—namely, that sustaining human beings should take priority over sinking funds into buildings: "How many souls did your fathers invest in this building?" Lehren answers that the argument pertains only to excessive adornment of a building, but where there is no synagogue that can accommodate all who worship according to the Ashkenazi liturgy, "the act [of building it] is greater than charity, especially when the recipients of the charity themselves ask for help in building their synagogue."[98]

In the fall of 1835, it again became clear to Lehren that his excitement was falling on deaf ears in Jerusalem and that the signals from there were mixed. With regard to building the *Ḥurvah* synagogue, the Jerusalemites write to him that they "do not wish to build a synagogue for an individual, for it is something the entire city should have rights to."[99] Once more, Lehren encounters an emotional morass: he again charges that the Jerusalemites' entire purpose is to make the *Ḥurvah* synagogue into a magnet for contributions, "so they will have an income . . . until the end of days,"[100] and he again recants and suggests that he would accede to a proposal to purchase the courtyard, that its renovation should cost no more than 400 to 500 gold ducats, and that he would have no objection to the building being called a study house (*beit midrash*) rather than a synagogue (*beit kenesset*). But, once again, he cannot abandon his desire that he and his brother, rather than any others, rebuild the *Ḥurvah* synagogue. At the conclusion of his long and inconsistent letter, he offers another inducement, informing Ne'eman of his willingness to pay even for the *Ḥurvah* parcel of land—"even that would be suitable for you"[101]—as long as he and his brother would be connected to the building of this prestigious synagogue.

Dispute Between Israel of Shklov and the Jerusalem *Perushim* Regarding Construction of the *Ḥurvah*

From the very start of Lehren's personal engagement with the *Ḥurvah* project, in the summer of 1834, he had involved Israel of Shklov in the affair. He asked Israel not only to refrain from impeding his brother's acquisition in Jerusalem but also "to kindly help with this [matter] and to achieve the desired goal specifically in Jerusalem, for that is the donor's wish."[102] Accordingly, Israel of Shklov was familiar with the affair's every detail, whether from Lehren's letters or from a more immediate source—Isaiah Bardaky, an official of the *kolel* of *Perushim* in Jerusalem and Israel of Shklov's son-in-law. Nevertheless, we know of no initiative on Israel's part to intervene on Lehren's behalf (or to discourage him) prior to the fall of 1835.

That Israel of Shklov did not help Lehren acquire the *Ḥurvah* can be readily understood in light of his negative attitude toward the very establishment of the *Perushim*'s Jerusalem *kolel*, his fundamental opposition to rebuilding the *Ḥurvah*, his concerns about entanglement in the *Ḥurvah*-related debts, his sensitivity regarding debt in general (as described at the start of this chapter), and the fact that Lehren himself had doubts about the acquisition because he had been denied exclusive rights. As events unfolded, Israel of Shklov was no doubt angered as well by the efforts of the Jerusalem *kolel* to take over the Lehren family funds. Those efforts, in Israel's eyes, were only part of their broader attempt to gain control of the lion's share of the funding for the *Perushim*'s *kolel* in the Land of Israel—something that greatly incensed him and sharpened the conflict between him and the Jerusalem group. It should be noted as well that Israel had a sense of personal obligation to Lehren, as is evident in their intensive correspondence, especially in later years.

Taken together, all the negative factors led Israel of Shklov, in the fall of 1835, to interject himself actively into the affair: he suggested to Lehren the acquisition of some other courtyard suitable for the erection of a synagogue.[103] Even before Lehren had agreed to the acquisition, Israel informed him that he had closed the purchase of a courtyard and synagogue. Meanwhile, Lehren instructed the consul Moses da Fajito in Beirut to turn over to the purchasers the 2,000 Spanish duros that he was holding.[104] To show his appreciation, he directed that a commission of twelve and one-half gold coins be paid to the individuals involved in the transaction.

But Lehren's delight at the purchase soon gave way to worry as he learned, from both Israel of Shklov and his opponents, how defective an acquisition it was. For one thing, the owner, who was in Egypt, had not yet authorized the sale. Lehren was disconcerted by suggestions that the substantial sum of money he had sent would prove insufficient because prices had risen and that he should, accordingly, try to enlist a partner in the acquisition. He therefore directed Consul da Fajito in Beirut to withhold payment of the funds until the purchase had been legally executed and confirmed by the consul himself.[105]

At about the same time, Lehren was taken aback by Zalman Ẓoref (Solomon)'s letter from Alexandria, advising him that the *firman* authorizing construction of the *Ḥurvah* had been issued and renewing the proposal that Lehren apply the funds to construction of the *Ḥurvah* synagogue. Once again Lehren was torn between his loyalty to Israel of Shklov and his desire to invest the funds specifically in the *Ḥurvah* project. Hastening to bring Israel into his deliberations, he writes, in summer 1836, that while he recognizes Israel's opposition to investing the money in the *Ḥurvah*, he nevertheless requests Israel to back his position on the matter. Lehren regards as exaggerated Israel's estimate that rebuilding the *Ḥurvah* would cost 500,000 piastres, and he assumes it refers to the entire project—the courtyard, as well as the synagogue itself. Ẓoref's suggestion "that he build a part of the *Ḥurvah* for the sake of the sanctuary"[106] appeals to him—"In truth, for quite a while now I, too, have been thinking that they should rebuild part of it for the synagogue"[107]—and he sees merit in the idea of gradual reconstruction: "And if God causes them to prosper, they can continue to build . . . and perhaps, bit by bit, they will build it all."[108] His desire to build the *Ḥurvah* synagogue stemmed from his sense that "the place is sanctified" but also from his concern that if he invested in building the alternative courtyard suggested by Israel of Shklov, the synagogue built there might be abandoned when the *Ḥurvah* was finally rebuilt and the great synagogue erected there: "For the place is sanctified in any event, and if they now dedicate a courtyard for the synagogue and later receive support and build the *Ḥurvah*, I am worried that they will forsake the agreement made at the time of the dedication."[109] Lehren therefore turned to Israel at the very last moment and asked him "to consider the matter thoroughly and perhaps he in his holiness [i.e., Israel of Shklov] will regard it favorably as well. For it is difficult for me to agree as a practical matter as long as his Excellency, may he live long, does not agree as well."[110]

These last comments show that Lehren felt constrained by Israel's decision and unable to freely reach a decision on his own. He thus found himself in an odd situation: all external impediments to building the *Ḥurvah* had finally been removed, and Israel of Shklov's proposed alternative faced numerous obstacles; yet at that very time Lehren hid behind Israel and asked him to decide the matter. The turn of events appears even stranger when we consider that Israel's position in the *kolel* had already been challenged because of his ongoing conflict with the other officials and that Israel had been attacked for allowing his wife to manage the *kolel* and use its funds however she wished.[111] But from the moment Lehren declares his reliance on Israel's decision, Lehren becomes progressively more passive, while Israel assumes control of the process and its development. The "*Ḥurvah* or alternate courtyard" dispute becomes not merely a personal question of where Lehren's funds are to be invested but a high-level conflict between Israel on the one hand and the *kolel* of the Jerusalem *Perushim* on the other, in which the choice between *Ḥurvah* and alternate courtyard becomes something each side can contrive to use in attacking the other. Lehren's peculiar stance does not grow out of a rational analysis of the issue; rather, it reflects his powerful emotions regarding the two personalities that he regards as representing the two sides of the argument.

The issuance of the *firman* to Ẓoref opened the way for the officials of the Jerusalem *Perushim* to seek legal validation for their effort to control the Lehren funds. In late fall 1836, we hear that they petitioned the great Sefardic court to issue an order enjoining acquisition of the alternate courtyard without explicit authorization for the transaction having been obtained from Ẓevi Hirsch Lehren and his brother Akiva.[112] The petitioners presumably presented to the court all the material they had sent to Lehren regarding the flaws in the courtyard transaction. On another front, the officials persuaded Moses da Fajito, the Dutch consul in Beirut who was serving as stakeholder, not to turn over the funds to Israel of Shklov; and Fajito writes to Lehren that he will not in fact deliver the funds until Lehren provides clear instructions on who is to receive them. Fajito offers four arguments in support of his decision:

1. The purchasers of the alternate courtyard do not have the permission of the Turkish authorities to build a synagogue at the proposed location.
2. Some Ashkenazi rabbis in Jerusalem (such as Isaiah Bardaky) favor purchase of the courtyard, while others support investing the money in the *Ḥurvah* synagogue. Since he (Fajito) has received no guidance from Lehren on what to do with the money in the event of such a dispute, he can turn it over to neither side.
3. Lehren directed him to pay in exchange for a deed of sale in accordance with the law of the Torah. The deed sent by Israel of Shklov, however, had not been issued by a rabbinic court but by a gentile one—apparently the Muslim court in Jerusalem.
4. The deed was invalid, because Turkish law forbade an alien from purchasing real estate.[113]

It appears from this that the goal of winding up the purchase of the courtyard was so important to Israel of Shklov that he dared to pursue it even by unorthodox means, such as resorting to gentile courts. And he did so even though the purchase conditions included no assurance that it would be possible to build a synagogue in the courtyard and, more surprising still, even though it was unclear whether the purchase was at all valid.

But these were not the only problems; others, as well, became known to Lehren:

1. The building in the alternate courtyard that was intended to become the synagogue was situated on land that did not belong to the owners

of the building, and the landowners were not at all interested in selling.[114]

2. The courtyard itself was pitted in seven places because of the earlier earthquake and the rains and snows of the winter of 1835–1836.[115]
3. The price of 75,000 piastres demanded for the courtyard and the building was too high, in Lehren's estimation.[116]
4. The inflated price appeared attributable to the alleged connivance of Isaiah Bardaky, Israel of Shklov's right-hand man in the transaction, with the broker, who made a profit of 10,000 piastres.[117]
5. The broker bribed the expert artisans to testify before the Sefardic Chief Rabbi, Rabbi Navon, that the parcel was, in fact, a good one.
6. The courtyard was *waqf* (subject to Muslim religious use), not *mulk* (private property), as had been thought.[118]
7. The widow of the courtyard's owner lived in the area, and the court accordingly decided that she had prescriptive rights and could not be evicted; in exchange, she would have to pay rent of 300 piastres a year.[119]
8. Above all, it became clear to Lehren that the building was too small to accommodate the entire congregation of *Perushim* in Jerusalem.[120]

Lehren's reaction to this astonishing information reveals him in all his weakness. He responded emotionally and irrationally, expressing his reaction dryly and succinctly. He appeared to rely as a practical matter entirely on Israel of Shklov and his son-in-law Isaiah Bardaky, neither of whom he had ever met face to face. He wondered: "If we are wrong here, then on whom can we rely? We know Zalman Ẓoref (Solomon) . . . and will not trust in him, for he is not upright and has never gone on a mission without taking compensation."[121]

Lehren's role had thus become totally passive; even in the legal proceedings, he was represented by Israel of Shklov and Isaiah Bardaky. The latter, meanwhile, were fighting an ideological battle, to which Lehren's personal interests were tangential. And that, of course, explains the intensity of their drive to consummate the acquisition.

Meanwhile, there were new legal developments. After the Jerusalem officials succeeded in enjoining the transfer of funds from Fajito to Israel of Shklov, the non-Jewish seller of the property sought relief from the Sefardic court in Jerusalem, asking it to require Isaiah Bardaky to consummate the purchase. The court granted the petition, allowing Bardaky thirty days to comply. Bardaky hastened to inform Israel of the situation, and the latter borrowed the sum of 2,000 duros,[122] at the high interest rate of 22 percent.[123] At the conclusion of the Fast of the Tenth of Tevet (18 December 1836),[124] Israel of Shklov set out from Safed with the requisite funds, and a few days after his arrival in Jerusalem, the transaction was completed. In its aftermath, the tensions between the two groups grew more intense. The community issued a ban on Isaiah Bardaky's Torah classes, and when he entered the synagogue, people would slip away and leave him without a prayer quorum.[125] The trustees of the Jerusalem *kolel* convened a general meeting, at which they decided to establish a special court to consider whether Bardaky should continue to serve as a trustee. The court was to comprise Eliezer Bregman, Joseph Schwartz, and Mordecai Minsker, who were regarded as neutral in the dispute. Two days later, on 3 January 1837, the trustees and other elite members of the *kolel* met to consider the matter, "and they took a secret vote and all were in the negative except one in the positive. And so, he will no longer have the title of trustee."[126] In addition, they informed Lehren that, in accordance with the court's decision, he was obligated to stop sending funds from Amsterdam in the name Israel of Shklov and his son-in-law, Isaiah Bardaky; instead, he was to send them in the name of Aryeh Ne'eman. Needless to say, Lehren declined to heed that request.[127]

Israel of Shklov spent this entire period in Jerusalem, near the center of activity. On the one hand, he was intimately affected by the humiliation of the ban against his son-in-law. On the other hand, he saw with his own eyes the intensity with which construction of the *Ḥurvah* study hall was proceeding.[128] He then heard that the dedication of the study hall was set for 5 January 1837, and, at the very last minute, he and his son-in-law petitioned the Sefardic court to issue an order enjoining the "*Ḥurvah* Trustees" from carrying out their plan to gather in the study hall for prayer and to install a Torah scroll there. They likewise sought to enjoin Solomon Pach from giving them a Torah scroll, as he had intended. They justified their request on the basis that they were, in fact, the trustees and overseers of the *kolel* of *Perushim* in Jerusalem, endowed with that authority by the powers in Vilna: "I have it in writing from the rabbis, the *ge'onim* and officials of Vilna, that we are the trustees and overseers with regard to anything that transpires in the holy city of Jerusalem."[129] In addition, they claimed, "it is known that all the land of the *Ḥurvah* belongs to our entire *kolel* in Jerusalem, and Safed, may it be built and established, also has a part in it."[130] For the same reason, Solomon Pach lacked the authority to give them a Torah scroll, for it is "a Torah scroll from our yeshiva."[131] According to the petitioners, moreover, only residential houses could be build in the *Ḥurvah* courtyard, "and a great synagogue should be built elsewhere, once funds are raised from our brethren, the House of Israel."[132] The petitioners (who included Moses ben Akiva, trustee of the Safed *kolel*, as well as Israel of Shklov and Isaiah Bardaky) asked the Sefardic court to issue its injunction immediately, for they had heard that the study hall was to be dedicated the very next day: "And we urgently request that [the judges] hurry to rule today, immediately, for we have heard that tomorrow, they wish to gather there."[133]

It may be assumed that the Sefardic court denied the petition. Two days later, on Friday, 6 January 1837, the members of the Jerusalem *kolel* of *Perushim* dedicated the study hall known as *Menaḥem Ẓiyyon* (Comforter of Zion).[134] The name appears to have multiple meanings. On the one hand, it intertwines the name of the Jerusalem *kolel*'s founder, Menaḥem Mendel of Shklov, with the idea that he hoped to embody in the redemption of the *Ḥurvah*—that is, the rebuilding of Jerusalem. On the other hand, the name bears an ideological, messianic meaning, alluding to the concluding wording of the blessing recited at the afternoon service on the fast of the Ninth of Av, which commemorates the destruction of the Jerusalem and looks forward to its rebuilding: "Blessed are You . . . who comforts Zion and builds Jerusalem," or, in the Sefardic version, "who comforts Zion through the building of Jerusalem." This idea is expressed by the builders of the *Ḥurvah* themselves: "And it was called *Menaḥem Ẓiyyon* as if to say, 'this will comfort us from the toil of our hands' [cf. Gen. 5:29] and, additionally, it will redeem us, and our Holy Temple will be built, speedily and in our days."[135]

Liturgical Changes in the Wake of the *Firman* Authorizing Construction of the *Ḥurvah*

Despite the ideological and practical row with Israel of Shklov—which intensified as the dedication of the study house approached—all the members of the community of *Perushim* in Jerusalem were seized with a powerful messianic fervor. They had begun to feel that excitement when they were granted permission to build the structures in the *Ḥurvah* courtyard: "For who had heard or who had seen such a thing said to Zion since the Land was exiled and its gates sunk into the ground—that there might be built a heavenly palace, a lesser Temple, which would have been intensely dangerous [to consider earlier] even in secret. . . . And now, our spirit is exalted through the Lord our God to enhance and exalt . . . and to build synagogues and study halls in the holy mountain, Jerusalem."[136]

Even before construction began, the *Perushim* considered receipt of the *firman* itself to be a messianic phenomenon. In the letter commissioning Abraham Meir ben Jeremiah as a rabbinic emissary to raise funds for the building of the *Ḥurvah* synagogue, they declared: "For unless God had desired us, we would not have seen all these things [happening], bringing us to tranquility and to our possession. It is a good sign of the beginning of the Redemption."[137] Aryeh Ne'eman expresses a similar attitude, but one more attentive to the Jews' newfound religious liberty. He regards the events as so overpowering as to show beyond doubt that we have already reached the stage of "awakening on high" in the redemptive process: "And we have been privileged to build the *Ḥurvah* and other buildings, last but not least the synagogue . . . and we have seen in this construction the awakening on high, and God builds Jerusalem in the present tense."[138]

In one of the rare letters from Eliezer Bregman to Ẓevi Hirsch Lehren, we find further evidence that the Jewish community in Jerusalem saw their liberty to build synagogues as confirming that the redemptive process was under way in earnest. In describing the community's reaction to the new situation, Bregman reports that in Jerusalem people are saying "the redemption has already begun."[139] He adds that the *Perushim* are not content to simply talk or think about their perception of the events; rather, they have begun to express that perception in a dramatic way, through changes in the liturgy and the traditionally accepted norms. On the premise that the redemption has in fact begun auspiciously, they changed the order of prayer and deleted, from the *Lekhah*

Dodi hymn sung to greet the Sabbath, the verse calling on Zion to rise from its dust. They likewise abandoned the recitation of dirges as part of *tiqqun ḥaẓot,* all on the premise that the *shekhinah* had already risen from the dust of exile. Reacting to this, Lehren says, "Regarding their omission of [the verse from *Lekhah Dodi*] and the dirges in *tiqqun ḥaẓot,* I would ask who introduced this innovation. If it is not a great man, one well known not to have been misled by the error of Shabbetai Ẓevi, . . . then I would be suspicious that the practice had arisen from people misled by Shabbetai Ẓevi, for *Ḥemdat Yamim* [a book likely written by a Sabbatean] also says not to recite [these passages]."[140]

We have here clear proof of just how powerfully the group believed they were in the midst of the messianic process. In daring to abandon a widely accepted custom and excise a part of the liturgy, this traditionalist, conservative, society was acting publicly and demonstratively in a way that can only be regarded as messianist.[141] This audacity is even starker when one considers that actions such as these were typical of the Sabbateans in their day. Were the Jerusalem *Perushim* willing to assume the risk of being suspected of serious heresy? Clearly, they would not have taken so revolutionary a step had they not firmly believed in what they were doing and in the proofs on which they were relying.

And so, the *Perushim* regarded the completion of construction and the splendid dedication of the study hall on 6 January 1837 as a great, heaven-sent triumph. In their view, the dispute between Safed's and Jerusalem's advocates had been resolved in favor of the latter. Four days later, they received word of another sign that appeared to be written by the "finger of God"—the terrifying report of the destruction of Safed by the earthquake of 1 January 1837.

Earthquake in the Galilee: A Further Sign of "the Messiah's Footsteps"

Each side in the controversy blamed the other for the calamity, which it regarded as punishment for its opponent's actions. In a letter to Lehren, the leaders of the Jerusalem *Perushim* attributed the destruction in the Galilee to Israel of Shklov's having come to Jerusalem to prevent construction of the *Ḥurvah* from being funded: "They again praised their building and its dedication and then wrote of Rabbi Israel's coming to complete his purchase of the [alternate] courtyard and then [follow with] a harsh vision of the Galilee's destruction, counting us as fools who would believe their idea that one followed from the other."[142] In contrast, Israel of Shklov and Lehren emphasized the former's escape from harm by reason of his having left Safed to conclude the courtyard transaction; they saw it as a sign that his position regarding building of the *Ḥurvah* was the correct one: "For the God of the Land of Israel saved me by sending me to Jerusalem to complete the purchase of the holy synagogue."[143]

In eulogizing the victims of the earthquake, Moses Sofer of Pressburg takes issue with Israel of Shklov's explanation of the event. He rejects Israel's claim that the destruction represented a punishment for the sin of baseless hatred that was prevalent among and within the various communal organizations in the Land of Israel and for the opposition of the Jerusalem *Perushim* to Israel of Shklov's conduct. In Sofer's view, the disputes in the Land of Israel should be ascribed not to baseless hatred but to poverty and suffering. Citing the Rabbis' observation that "in the time of the footsteps of the Messiah, the Galilee will be destroyed," he says: "And may this be a great consolation, for the time to act for the Lord is near."[144] What he regards as sinful is that the Ashkenazi immigrants directed their attention to the Galilee, where Rabbi Simeon bar Yoḥai and Rabbi Isaac Luria are buried, "and all the immigrants to the Land of Israel had regard only for Safed and Tiberias and Jerusalem was totally forgotten."[145] Accordingly, the destruction of Safed was on account of "Jerusalem's jealousy . . . for our God is just, and Jerusalem's jealousy caused this."[146]

Both events—the dedication of the *Menaḥem Ẓiyyon* study hall and the destruction of the Galilee—were unusual. Each represented the pinnacle of a process but also its conclusion. The two processes were opposites, one involving building and the other destruction, but both were fundamental to the messianic concept. The coincidence of two such powerful events reinforces the question that can always be asked: Which process is the desirable one? But when the pinnacle of one is success and that of the other is destruction, there does not appear to be great doubt regarding the answer.

The regrets over the two events' implications were harsh. The earthquake was a vast tragedy; about one-fourth of the Jewish population in the Land of Israel was instantly lost. Aryeh Ne'eman, who set out for Safed as soon as the bitter news came to Jerusalem, writes that "since the destruction of the Holy Temple there has not been such devastation, for the holy cities of Safed and Tiberias were destroyed to their foundations, and fourteen synagogues that had been located here in the holy city of Safed, may it be built and established speedily and in our day, were devastated and collapsed."[147] The comparison to the destruction of the Temple is not merely rhetorical; rather, it alludes to a signpost in the redemption process. Beyond the disputes over what had caused the catastrophe, everyone agreed that the event itself was a fulfillment of the Mishnah's statement at the end of tractate *Sotah* that "at [the time of] the footsteps of the Messiah, . . . the Galilee will be destroyed." Israel of Shklov, a Safed proponent, writes to that effect,[148] as does the Jerusalemite Aryeh Ne'eman; the latter prays that the blood of the earthquake's victims will be accepted before God as a burnt offering and sacrifice: "And may the destruction of the Galilee be a good omen of our redemption and the deliverance of our souls from darkness to light, and may the children return to their borders speedily; may that be the will of God, Amen."[149] There can be no doubt that the temporal proximity of the Galilee's destruction to the year 5600 fortified the messianic expectations of Jews in the Land of Israel and Diaspora Jews alike.

Aryeh Ne'eman's letter regarding the earthquake conveys a degree of optimism that the dispute will end despite the tragic turn of events. He expressly notes the change wrought by the earthquake in Israel of Shklov's position:

"And his thought now is to settle in the holy city of Jerusalem, may it be built and established, and to mend the tent so as to be united in the aforesaid holy city, may it be built and established."[150] He tells that the widows and orphans who fled the earthquake had already been sent to Jerusalem, as had the Torah scrolls and other sacred books that were rescued. The rest of the survivors were likewise prepared to go up to Jerusalem immediately.[151] Circumstances, to be sure, compelled the remainder of the Safed community of *Perushim* to move to Jerusalem, but the move reflected something else as well: their desire to finally and definitively move beyond the terrible conflict that had saddened their lives for more than two decades. From now on, Jerusalem was to be the sole center for the community of *Perushim* in the Land of Israel.[152]

Within six months after dedicating the *Menaḥem Ẓiyyon* study hall, the *Perushim* also built, in the *Ḥurvah* courtyard, a women's gallery, a bathhouse, and an immersion pool, as well as houses for Torah instructors and guests.[153] By 1841, all eleven shops and all the destroyed buildings and homes had been fully restored.[154] The *Ḥurvah* was once again the center of Ashkenazi life in Jerusalem—some twenty years after it was first reentered by a small group led by Menaḥem Mendel of Shklov, the Vilna Ga'on's greatest disciple in the study of mysticism.

7

Expanding and Solidifying Jewish Settlement in the Land of Israel

The fund would be used to purchase fields and vineyards or to rebuild the ruins of Jerusalem and rent out [the buildings] or to build workshops . . . or olive or sesame oil presses or other places where other types of work are done, or a large house containing several rental apartments or flourmills or to build shops.

Memorandum from the communal leaders in Jerusalem to the consul Elijah Fajito in Aleppo, 1837

Redemption of the Land Precedes Redemption of the Nation

According to the Vilna Ga'on's disciples, the two aspects of redemption—redemption of the Land and redemption of the nation—were not to be simultaneous; in their scheme of things, as already noted, redemption of the Land would come first. The Land, however, cannot redeem itself. Only when a significant population is firmly established on the Land, drawing its existence from it, will the Land be awakened from desolation to renewed life, signifying the start of the redemption.

In that context, the Ga'on's disciples saw themselves as emissaries of divine Providence, sent as the vanguard in the campaign to redeem the Land. Scripture speaks of the pioneering role in the redemptive process assigned to the Jews living in the far reaches of the north: "Behold, I will bring them from the north country, and gather them from the uttermost parts of the earth" (Jer. 31:8); "Awake, O north wind, and come, thou south" (Song of Songs 4:16), interpreted by the *midrash* (*Song of Songs Rabbah* 4:16) to mean "When the exiles in the north are awakened and come to camp in the south." The Ga'on's disciples saw these verses as pertaining to themselves, the Jews of Russia, dwelling in the northernmost regions of Israel's Diaspora. They had no doubt that the practical implication of such verses was to assign them a heavenly mission to serve as a vanguard, so the redemption might be hastened. Not only did they see themselves in that light; others identified them in that light as well. They are often referred to by their geographic origin: in a letter to the rabbis of Germany, the *Perushim* term the Jews of Russia "those who dwell in the land of the north."[1] In a letter to the Clerks' Organization, they call the Russian Jews "our northern brethren."[2] And a later text pertaining to the immigration of the *Perushim* states unequivocally that their *aliyah* was a fulfillment of those biblical verses: "For we see how over these last one hundred years, many faithful people have begun to love the dust of our Land and kiss its stones, and 'Awake, O north wind, and come, thou south' has been fulfilled, for the first to be awakened were the disciples of the righteous and pious one, the Ga'on Rabbi Elijah [of Vilna] (may the memory of the righteous be for a blessing) from the north, and after them [Jews] from the four corners of the earth."[3]

The Ga'on's disciples' sense of pioneering mission is conveyed in several documents. Israel of Shklov says: "Had we been created for no purpose other than this act of repair [*tiqqun*]—the settlement of our Holy Land—it would have been enough for us."[4] And, elsewhere: "So that the element of settling the Land might be realized."[5] Their sense that it is specifically they who bear the mission of advancing the redemptive process seems to have caused them to disregard the existence of the venerable Sefardic community in the Land of Israel, which they did not regard as playing an active redemptive role.[6] And that, in turn, explains why they sought to be independent, free of any dependency on the Sefardic community; any such dependency, they believed, would interfere with the establishment of the Ashkenazi community. The *Perushim* of Safed express this idea in a letter in which they seek a *firman* to authorize their separation from the Sefardic community: "Be strong, my brethren, and gain the next world and this world at the same time, for the entire settlement of our Holy Land depends on this [on an independent Ashkenazi settlement]."[7]

This powerful sense of obligation to immigrate to the Land of Israel and firmly establish a new settlement there provoked self-sacrifice on the part of its adherents. Israel of Shklov, leader of the *kolel* in Safed, was said to have "given up his life for our Holy Land, its establishment and development from the time of its founding."[8] The feeling was not confined to those who actually immigrated; it was shared by those who remained behind in Russia. They devotedly toiled on behalf of their brethren in the Land of Israel: they established a central fund-raising organization; maintained contact, by letter and emissaries, with the communities of *Perushim* in the Land; and sent new groups of immigrants to the Land. On the basis of this division of roles, the *Perushim* not only ask their brethren for funding that will permit them to survive and expand but also to send "more disciples of our rabbi, the pious Ga'on."[9]

Although the Ga'on's disciples disagreed among themselves regarding the practical implications of the term "awakening from below," they were united as to the principal goal of settling the Land. But the Clerks' Organization, led by Ẓevi Hirsch Lehren, saw things very differently. A traditionalist, Lehren saw a desecration of God's Name in the Ga'on's disciples' activist interpretation of "awakening from below." In his view, their program and activities—immigration to the Land; attempts to build the *Ḥurvah* courtyard; and efforts to acquire houses and land, engage in commerce and labor, and make it possible for the simple folk to work the land—would in no way hasten the redemption; if anything, they might delay it. He saw nothing auspicious in establishing the Ashkenazi presence in the Land; on the contrary, the commandment to dwell in the Land in order to properly determine the dates of the festivals[10] could be carried out by the old Sefardic community. In a moment of anger, he rebukes the Ashkenazim, saying their *aliyah* could easily have been forgone, since it simply augmented dissension in the Land and was likely on that account to delay the Messiah's coming: "Would that there had been only a holy congregation of Sefardim in the Land of Israel until the coming of our righteous Messiah; all this would not have happened, and there would have been no dispute."[11] And, elsewhere: "The hatred pains us, and it is likely to delay the redemption."[12]

In Lehren's understanding, there is only one legitimate form of activism that can ensure the coming of the redemption in the approaching "time of awareness": Torah study and prayer by the Jews in the Land of Israel and financial support for those Jews on the part of their Diaspora brethren. He writes: "And it is proper for us and for all Israel to provide additional charity for the Land of Israel for the stated reason; and may our righteous Messiah come speedily; and let us not disappoint or withdraw from our brethren who dwell in the Land of Israel, having cast their lives aside to dwell on the sacred ground while we rest [comfortably] on our possessions in the Diaspora."[13] In this conception, the future, third redemption will come about by miraculous means rather than through the natural means of settling the Land of Israel.

That perspective, expressed in many letters by Lehren and the leaders of the Clerks' Organization, is to be found as well in a manuscript encompassing Torah interpretations and discourses by one of the founders of the Clerks' Organization, Abraham ben Aaron Prinz. In his discourse *Yam ha-Aravah*, Prinz speaks of the distinction between *ani* and *anokhi*, the two words used in the Bible to mean "I" in connection with divine activity. He explains that *ani* signifies God's dominion and activity without any involvement of other forces, while *anokhi* signifies divine activity accompanied by natural factors. Prinz goes on to explain that in some instances God guides Israel by His might alone, while in others He integrates natural causes into his guidance: "And do not be misled into saying that at all times Israel is led by miracle alone and not by natural means. Not at all. That is why He said it is *ani* Who redeemed you from Egypt and it is *ani* Who will redeem you in the future from the fourth kingdom. He refers specifically to these redemptions, but not to the others, which are described using the terminology of *anokhi*, such as the building of the Second Temple, accomplished via an intermediary, namely, [King] Cyrus [of Persia]."[14] Prinz goes on to support his thesis on the basis of verses that speak of the redemption: " 'And yet for all that, when they are in the land of their enemies, I will not reject them, neither will I abhor them . . . for I [*ani*] am the Lord their God' [Lev. 26:44]. The wording '*ani*' refers to the final redemption, which will be under the governance of the Creator alone—and understand."[15] In contrast, he continues, the war waged by Deborah and Barak son of Avinoam involved natural factors as well and therefore is described in terms of *anokhi*: " 'I [*anokhi*], unto the Lord will I [*anokhi*] sing' [Jud. 5:3]. He means that their redemption will be through the wording *anokhi*, incorporating the forces of nature."[16] On the basis of a additional supporting verses, Prinz sums up and reiterates his view that the future redemption will be entirely an independent act by the Holy One Blessed Be He, coming by miracle and not by natural means: "And from this we learn that [it will be] when the *ani* of the Holy One Blessed Be He comes; that is, the future redemption, which God ascribed entirely to Himself, with the attribute of *ani*."[17]

Development of the Land Requires Multidimensional *Aliyah*

Neither Lehren nor any of his colleagues at the Clerks' Organization immigrated to the Land of Israel or even visited there, a fact that speaks volumes about their attitude toward *aliyah*. Lehren saw his activity on behalf of the Jews in the Land of Israel as a substitute for immigrating himself, though he acknowledged the contemporary applicability of the commandment to dwell in the Land: "I give myself no credit for my efforts on behalf of the poor of the Land of Israel, for I thereby free myself of immigrating to the Land at this time."[18] Even when he asks Israel of Shklov to fulfill on his behalf one of the commandments contingent on the Land—such as priestly gifts and tithes related to food grown there—he connects the two issues and attempts to justify himself: "And may it be [God's] will that I be privileged to go up to our Holy Land when the residents of the Land of Israel no longer need my efforts on their behalf in the Diaspora."[19] His desire to immigrate to the Land overwhelms him only once, when his messianic expectations are boosted and his sprits lifted in the wake of Barukh ben Samuel's mission to the Ten Tribes.[20] He writes to Israel of Shklov: "My dear son-in-law and friend, may he live long, pleads much with me to join him in going up to the Land of Israel, may it be built and established, and he says that all my work on behalf of the Land of Israel does not discharge my own obligation, and that I am obliged to immigrate; and I certainly yearn to do so."[21] But here, too, Lehren excuses his failure to immigrate by citing his obligation to remain in the Diaspora in order to strengthen economic support for the Land. Still, he asks Israel of Shklov to state his opinion regarding *aliyah* in accordance with the *Zohar* "and as he is directed from Heaven."[22] We may assume that Israel answered, if at all, that it would be better for Lehren to remain at home and reinforce the fundraising enterprise.

Lehren's words and deeds might lead one to conclude that he regarded *aliyah* itself as a commandment and as an important and desirable course of action. He supported the Jewish community in the Land of Israel, conveyed his distress at being unable to immigrate himself, and even expressed envy of those, like Asher ben Samson and Moses Montefiore, who visited there. But it appears that those were statements of his theoretical views and that his practical attitude toward *aliyah* was not at all positive. In his view, *aliyah* should not be permitted unless the immigrants were first assured of a proper economic base. In an argument with Nathan Neta, son of Menaḥem Mendel, and through him with the leadership of the *Perushim*, he conditions immigration on economic potential: "It is surprising to us that each year more immigrants come to the Land of Israel, from both [your] towns and from the towns of the Hasidim. And whence will come their help and their sustenance?"[23] According to his estimation, the *ḥaluqah* could sustain an individual for eight weeks only—and that with difficulty—so how could they be sustained year-round? In the absence of new immigrants, Lehren argues, the *ḥaluqah* could be augmented for those already in the Land. The extent of *aliyah*, in his view, should be commensurate with the funds flowing into the Land—and since the funds are limited, so should be the number of immigrants.[24] And that leads to the conclusion that immigration should be selective: "It is proper that the honorable nobles [of Vilna] set a limit to it, so that not just anyone who wants to immigrate can do so without their approval."[25] He is surprised that they continue to send immigrants to the Land of Israel, arguing that it would make sense to do so if funding from Russia were growing, but that since the funds being collected by the Vilna center were, in fact, declining, "Why should some thirty souls, may God preserve and protect them, be added, ruining the livelihood of those [already] dwelling in the Holy [Land]?"[26]

Lehren advises the Nobles of Vilna of his view regarding *aliyah* and of his practice of deterring those who wish to immigrate, and he announces he would be delighted if they adopted the same attitude: "But that is not our way with those who approach us about going up to the Holy [Land]. Not everyone who wishes to go up is told to go, though, with God's help, we are gathering many."[27] On another occasion, he explains his position to Abraham Reiss of Baltimore, whom he had previously deterred from immigrating: "For several years now I have kept myself from telling any person to go up [to the Land], for I know the poverty and harsh circumstances that now prevail there. And afterwards, the immigrant will rail against me."[28] Lehren rejects the contrary view of Menaḥem Mendel's son, Nathan Neta, who maintained that it was obligatory to assist anyone who wished to immigrate and fulfill the commandment to dwell in the Land, for such immigrants are highly meritorious by reason of the protection they afford to all Diaspora Jews. He likewise rejects the argument that "they have intense faith that they will make a living by their toil or miraculously," for "we do not rely on miracles, and let them make a living by their toil in the Diaspora."[29]

Distinguishing among types of *aliyah*, Lehren objects to people who immigrate for selfish reasons. He includes among them not only those who want to live off the *ḥaluqah* but also those who flee Russia to avoid either the military draft or their creditors—elements whom the *Perushim* seem to have brought to the Land of Israel: "Had he been exempt from the military without [taking] this step, he would have remained in his city and his land. This is not *aliyah* for the sake of the Land of Israel; and all the more is that so regarding one fleeing on account of debts."[30] Lehren quarrels about this with the Nobles of Vilna. He would agree to *aliyah* if the immigrants were elderly, wanting to live out their days in the Holy Land, or renowned scholars, but "youngsters lacking independent means cannot, in our view, immigrate at this time";[31] he is concerned that young immigrants will leave after encountering hardships. To effectively limit the scope of *aliyah* and make it selective, Lehren proposes to act against people who seek to immigrate without authorization. Anyone who disregards the limits imposed by the "nobles," he writes to Israel of Shklov, "will not receive *ḥaluqah* funding and will not be given loans, even in cases of risk to life."[32] Later on, Lehren adopts the Sefardic practice of limiting *ḥaluqah* funding to people having set places in yeshivas and who have ensured support for themselves. He asks that funds from Amsterdam be distributed only to scholars and God-fearing people and not to "unstable, irresponsible people . . . who should never have immigrated to the Land of Israel."[33] In justification of his position, he says that "if everyone who came to take could come and take, many poor people from surrounding lands would go up to the Land of Israel, and there would remain insufficient [resources] to support sages and those who study in the yeshivas."[34]

It thus appears that Lehren favors *aliyah* at least on the part of scholars who want to study Torah and serve God in the Land of Israel. As a practical matter, however, he differs with the *Perushim* and sees no inherent value in such *aliyah*. In spring 1839, we hear that he prevented the immigration of a young scholar from Strasbourg because he lacked financial means. Lehren bristles at the individual who directed the scholar to him, believing that Lehren would be delighted to finance his *aliyah*: "How could he think that one who lacks even the resources for the journey to the Land of Israel should immigrate there. . . . He will not be allowed to travel for free. . . . If it depends on me, I say to him he should not immigrate without funds."[35] Lehren argues: "Well and good for one who immigrates solely to fulfill the commandment of dwelling in the Land of Israel, for he will lovingly suffer everything, for he has attained his goal. But one who immigrates to study Torah will not find his mind clear if he has nothing to eat."[36] At the end of the day, Lehren writes to the fundraisers for the Land of Israel in Strasbourg, it is not enough that the person want to immigrate because his soul craves Torah, and it is not enough that he desire to fulfill the commandment to dwell in the Land; he must also tend to arranging fixed support from his town and his country. His final remarks suggest that Lehren does not support *aliyah* at all; he sums up: "Support for immigration should not be provided to just any simple man, for by his coming, he weakens the livelihood of those already there."[37]

Lehren's opposition to *aliyah* is particularly striking when contrasted with Eliezer Bregman's letters of support to potential immigrants. Though he makes no attempt to conceal the hardships that *olim* can expect to face, Bregman sees reason to immigrate despite all those hardships, and he cites his own experience as he encourages potential immigrants to make the move.[38] Lehren, for his part, adopts a skeptical and negative attitude to Bregman's letters and tries to deter potential *olim* who are inclined to rely on them. For example, Lehren tries to forestall the *aliyah* of Nathan Schnatüch of Fürth, who apparently was a widower. Lehren writes of the prohibition against living in the Land of Israel while unmarried, the hardships, the high cost of living, and the scarcity of water sources. He concludes by dismissing Bregman's letter: "As for Bregman writing to you that it would be good for you to come, would that he, too, had remained in the Diaspora."[39] He similarly writes to Abraham Wechsler of Schwabach, discrediting Bregman's observations that all is quiet and tranquil in the Land: "Would that he had stayed in business with his father-in-law, may his Rock and Redeemer protect him."[40] Lehren offers various arguments against *aliyah*, contending that it causes difficulty for the immigrant "with respect to fear of Heaven, love of Torah, and the guiding of children in God's ways and His commandments"[41] and wondering, in any event, "How could he even think of traveling with a pregnant wife?"[42] Wechsler evidently considered as well a move to America, and Lehren counsels him to go in that direction: "If you have difficulties in your town, find respite in another."[43] If he travels to America, Lehren would be prepared to help him by giving him the names of Jews in America and even supporting his journey to Amsterdam en route to the New World.[44]

Accordingly, we find a significant difference between Ẓevi Hirsch Lehren on the one hand and the *kolel* of the *Perushim* and Eliezer Bregman on the other with respect to *aliyah*, its proper scope, and its character. Bregman's description of the successful social absorption of immigrants to Jerusalem highlights the difference: "They [the Ashkenazim] do not resent the newcomers, for they say: on the contrary . . . the greater the growth in the Holy Land's population . . . the greater the [divine] bounty."[45]

Expanding the Area of Jewish Settlement in Jerusalem

As described above, the collectivist, forward-looking notions of the *Perushim*'s *kolel* favored increased immigration and continued strengthening of the Jewish settlement as a means for carrying out the commandment of settling the Land. That goal implied that the *kolel* would take responsibility for supporting all its members and establishing communal institutions, including a study hall, ritual immersion baths, children's schools, and social welfare organizations, though it saw itself involved primarily in providing housing for its members. And, despite Lehren's contrary proposals, the *kolel* applied its funds in a manner consistent with its goals. It allocated part of them to economic support and part to acquiring buildings for communal purposes or for dwellings. The *kolel* also provided its members funds for the purchase of dwellings or for investment in their businesses.[46]

Because the Jerusalem *Perushim* saw construction of the *Ḥurvah* as a symbol of the renewed Ashkenazi presence in Jerusalem, they afforded it the highest priority and the *kolel* established a separate construction fund for it. Six treasurers were assigned to the *Ḥurvah* project, three designated by the *kolel* and three others. At the start of construction in 1836, the dedicated fund borrowed 3,500 piastres from Mordecai Minsker;[47] in exchange, the lender was promised the right to live in one of the dwellings in the courtyard. The loan was to be repaid after five years, and rent payments were 30 piastres a year. The promissory note was signed by "the sages and rabbis, treasurers and officials of the reconstruction of the ruins known as the ruins of Rabbi Judah Ḥasid, may Eden be his resting place, the property of our holy *kolel* of Ashkenazim, *Perushim,* may God protect and save them, which God has given us the privilege of restoring and rebuilding in the holy mountain in Jerusalem, may it be built and established." The six treasurers were Ẓevi Hirsch ben Joseph of Dalatisch, Nathan Neta ben Menaḥem Mendel, Nathan Neta ben Sa'adyah, David ben Reuben Wolfin, Zalman Ẓoref (Solomon), and Aryeh Ne'eman.[48]

The borrowed funds proved insufficient for the job, however, and the additional obligations incurred by the *kolel* likewise were soon consumed. The *kolel* therefore took a loan in the amount of 150,000 piastres, equivalent to about 3,000 gold ducats, from Joseph Amazlag, a wealthy Sefardi. Two-thirds of that sum was used to pay off other debts, and the remaining 1,000 gold ducats were applied to construction of the courtyard. The *kolel* undertook to pay Amazlag the sum of 270 gold ducats annually, equivalent to interest at 9 percent, which was not particularly high in comparison to the going rate for loans at the time.[49] But to avoid any impression that interest was in fact being paid, it was arranged that the *Ḥurvah* courtyard would be mortgaged to Joseph Amazlag and the *kolel* would rent the buildings back from him for 270 gold ducats a year, until the loan was repaid.[50]

That the *kolel* had the resourcefulness and daring to borrow such large amounts of money demonstrates their forward-looking, collectivist drive to fulfill the vision of renewed Jewish settlement, even if it required paying a high price in the present.

In the winter of 1835–1836, before the *Perushim* had received the *firman* authorizing construction of the *Ḥurvah* courtyard, their *kolel* in Jerusalem acquired another large courtyard containing several dwellings. The purchase document contains the following, in Aryeh Ne'eman's handwriting: "Deed respecting 'the *kolel*'s courtyard,' in which is located the '*tanur*' [oven], belonging to our *kolel,* which I purchased through God's kindnesses for the benefit of the poor in the year 5596 [1835–1836] for our *kolel* of *Perushim,* may God protect and redeem them."[51] According to the site description, the courtyard had two stories:

> An upper story and a lower story, and in the upper courtyard is a large house, with five windows . . . and in that house is a small house. And also in the aforesaid upper courtyard are three additional houses . . . and on the south side are a kitchen and a respectable privy. In the lower courtyard, at the entrance, are houses and a water well, and to the west of the well is a house . . . and opposite it, to the east, is a house . . . and to the south is a house . . . and next to that house one goes into a small courtyard containing a cellar and a small dilapidated house.[52]

It appears that the structure encompassed about ten dwellings and was purchased at the low price of 1,300 piastres.

Establishing a Neighborhood in the Bab al-Ḥota Area

The period of Muhammad Ali's reign saw impressive growth in Jerusalem's Jewish population, and the waves of immigration led to overcrowding in the Jewish Quarter. Almost no dwellings in that choice area were available for purchase or lease, and the imbalance between supply and demand drastically drove up the price for the few that were to be had. The most reasonable solution to the problem was to look beyond the Jewish Quarter and purchase houses in other areas that were less desirable but therefore also less expensive. In a letter of 26 January 1835, Hillel of Shklov tells his wealthy son-in-law, Shemariah Luria, of the Jews' interest in acquiring courtyards and houses in the Bab al-Ḥota area. The only impediment at the time was the desire to have several families purchase in the area as a group, so there would be a quorum for public worship in the area: "In my opinion, it would be proper to purchase a good courtyard here, even in an area distant from the Jews' quarter . . . and there are many people who want to purchase houses and courtyards there, but each waits for the next, for as long as at least ten heads of household do not live there together, allowing for a regular *minyan* [prayer quorum], it would be difficult to live there."[53] Hillel explains not only why the Jews are interested but also why the prices there (and, correspondingly, the purchasers' bids) are low: the Arab residents of Jerusalem are under pressure to raise money to buy their way out of the military obligation imposed on them during Muhammad Ali's reign. He writes: "And now, because the gentiles need a great deal of cash to buy their way out of being soldiers, they sell cheap."[54]

Two months later, Eliezer Bregman writes to his father-in-law in Germany, Mendel Rosenbaum, that it is now possible (as it was not in the past) to purchase "houses in an outright sale,"[55] and that some Ashkenazim from Poland have already bought houses in that area: "Some Ashkenazim . . . have purchased houses for themselves in this manner, by outright sale, at one of the edges of the city, not far from one of the city gates."[56]

A halakhic discussion by Rabbi Ḥayyim Solomon Daniel Finzo, one of the city's judges (appearing in his book *Shem Ḥadash*), tells of Ashkenazim living in the Bab al-Ḥota neighborhood in 1837. At issue was an Ashkenazi couple who had undergone a betrothal ceremony in the neighborhood, after which the groom wanted to back out. According to the account, the event took place amid a group of new Ashkenazi immigrants, who were unaware of the rule in Jerusalem that, within the city walls, the wedding ceremony was to be conducted immediately after the betrothal ceremony. (The rule had been instituted to avoid the possibility of a betrothed but not-yet-married bride being left "chained" to an intended groom who for some reason did not go forward with the marriage but also did not grant the divorce she would need in order to marry someone else.)[57]

The Bab al-Ḥota housing option was not used only by individuals; the community leadership as well entered into the thick of things and acquired houses and courtyards in the neighborhood. But Israel of Shklov evidently objected to purchasing courtyards so far from the Jews' quarter, and he questioned the prudence of the investment. Writing to Lehren, he says:

> With regard to what they wrote you about from Jerusalem, that they are buying houses at cheap prices from gentiles . . . [you] should know that they are buying at a distant location among the gentiles, a distance of about three-quarters of an hour from the Jews' place, and there exists there, for the most part, danger from murderers and thieves, and the seller, too, is a weak reed. . . . And what they are hastily doing is not in accord with the will of the Sefardic sages and rabbis nor of the leaders of the Ashkenazim, may God save and protect them.[58]

The subject comes up several times in Israel of Shklov's letters to Lehren. Early in 1836, Israel again describes the acquisition of courtyards in the area. In his opinion, several purchasers have already lost their investments: "[You] should know that they are purchasing in a dangerous place distant from the city, and it is not good to live near Bab al-Ḥota, [a place of] ruins, and we warned several newcomers not to invest their money there . . . but they were unwilling to listen, and now it has come to be, that because of our many sins, several individuals have lost [their money.]"[59]

Several factors together appear to have limited the duration of the Jewish settlement in Bab al-Ḥota. First, the neighborhood's distance from the Jewish quarter created security problems for its residents. At Passover 1838, there was a blood libel. A Muslim entered Joseph of Slutsk's house, apparently to rob it, and savagely beat the owner. He claimed to have done so "because the Jew wanted to slaughter him and use his blood for Passover."[60] When the case came before the Muslim judge, he rejected the assailant's claims, "not believ[ing] that this scrawny Jew wanted to slaughter a thick, fat Ishmaelite ten times stronger than him."[61] Nevertheless, Lehren writes, the result of the case was that "the residents there were afraid to live at a distance from the Jewish neighborhood and wanted to abandon their residences and houses there."[62] A second reason for abandoning Bab al-Ḥota seems to have been the sharp decline in the Jewish population of Jerusalem following the harsh epidemic of 1838–1839 and the consequent drop in the demand for housing. Finally, the completion of housing in the Judah Ḥasid *Ḥurvah* courtyard may have contributed to Ashkenazi Jews coming back to the Jewish Quarter from Bab al-Ḥota.[63]

By the summer of 1840, the neighborhood seems to have been abandoned. In a letter of 6 July 1840 to Moses Montefiore, several Jews note the possibility of economic investments in several abandoned courtyards in Bab al-Ḥota: "And now . . . near the gate called Bab Ḥota, there are five good courtyards, with gardens and trees . . . that belong to Jews . . . and, because of our many sins, all those courtyards are desolate, with no residents."[64] It appears that those courtyards were owned by the leadership of the *kolel* of *Perushim*, and the writers ask Montefiore to establish an oil press in the area and to settle several families there, in that way shoring up the settlement of the Holy Land.[65]

Engaging in Labor and Commerce

"Settling the Land," which the *Perushim* regarded as the primary purpose of their *aliyah*, did not remain merely a matter of ideology. It gained concrete expression as the *Perushim* confronted the practical difficulties generated by their increasing numbers.

The original notion that the Jewish settlement could survive entirely on *ḥaluqah* funds proved unworkable in the long run. For one thing, the transfer of funds from the Diaspora to the Land of Israel was subject to unexpected disruptions, making the *ḥaluqah* anything but a secure source of economic support. Moreover, the realities of life in the Land of Israel forced the *kolel* leadership to look beyond theoretical questions of economic support and deal with the unanticipated problems of day-to-day life, seeking out economic and political solutions that would enable the *kolel* to survive and grow. They quickly learned to take advantage of economic opportunities such as money changing; investing in commercial ventures; lending at interest; and providing services to missionaries, consuls, and tourists. Such opportunities were seized during bad political times, as well as during the time of Muhammad Ali, whose enlightened rule opened up new possibilities for economic initiatives by the Land of Israel's residents.

As the community of *Perushim* in the Land of Israel developed and confronted the problems of day-to-day life, and as it became clear that the "beginning of redemption" would be an extended process,[66] we find the *kolel* leadership tending more and more to pursue a realistic economic basis for the community's survival, both by increasing the number of immigrants and by diversifying their occupations. This approach can be discerned primarily in the *kolel*'s willingness to lend money to its members for purposes other than bare sustenance. Lehren rails against "the fact that the *kolel* sometimes lends for the purpose of building a house or engaging in some commercial enterprise."[67] He argues that the funds were intended to sustain the life of the poor and not to be invested in businesses in the Land of Israel, and that those who lack a regular source of income outside the Land of Israel "are better off living where they are, and no one should immigrate unless he has a source of income of his own, or from relatives or friends, from which he can support himself and his family in the Land of Israel."[68] His position on this was firm, and he did not waver even in the time of Muhammad Ali, when new commercial opportunities opened up:

> One who wants to profit from commerce should remain in the Diaspora, and one who goes up to the Land of Israel should engage in Torah and prayer, each in accordance with his ability, and not waste his time with commercial involvements . . . and there is no Torah among merchants and seafarers. In any case, one who wants to be a businessman should not receive *ḥaluqah* payments; and one cannot eat one's cake and have it too—both living in the Land of Israel and supporting himself by the toil of his hands.[69]

In Lehren's view, one who attempts to engage in business in the Land of Israel will not succeed, as demonstrated by the Sefardic sages in the Land, who refrain from engaging in commerce. He can accept that the Sefardim born in the Land became involved in trade and commerce, but he objects to those who come to the Land with the intention of earning a living there.[70] One of his recurring complaints against Zalman Ẓoref (Solomon), for example, is that he immigrated in order to make the Land a source of personal wealth. Lehren therefore firmly denies Ẓoref's request to serve as on-site administrator for the funds raised in Amsterdam,[71] and even if Israel of Shklov were to agree to that appointment, Lehren would remain unwilling; "far be it from us to do so."[72] Lehren attributes his refusal to a concern about the funds going lost, saying he prefers to use the services of recognized banks. In the same context, he also criticizes wealthy immigrants who profit abundantly from differences in exchange rates when they lend funds to the *kolels*.[73]

The *Perushim* in the Land of Israel disagreed with Lehren. In a later letter to the Clerks' Organization, they declared that Ḥayyim of Volozhin had already decided, as a matter of principle, that the Diaspora Jews' charitable obligation pertained to fulfillment of the commandment to settle the Land of Israel, and that the funds that were raised should accordingly be distributed to all the Land's residents, not only to scholars:

> The question [of how to distribute the funds] was asked in the time of the rabbi, the mighty *ga'on*, the rabbi of all the Diaspora, the honored, whose glorious name is holy, our master Rabbi Ḥayyim of Volozhin, may the memory of the righteous and holy be for a blessing, and the ruling was issued that in our Holy Land it is obligatory to support everyone, not scholars alone, and the rationale he gave for this was that the charitable obligation is directed toward the com-

> mandment of settling our Holy Land, and every Jew is considered to be within the rubric of settling our Holy Land.[74]

It is apparent as well from the "*Ḥaluqah* Statutes" of the *Perushim*'s *kolel* that sustaining the community as a whole takes precedence over supporting students of Torah: "The proceeds of the donations from the Diaspora are dedicated to two areas: (a) to strengthen the standing of the community in the Land, and (b) the standing of the Torah."[75] The *kolel* accordingly determined that craftsmen would be considered members in all respects, though they would receive only a half-share in the *ḥaluqah*, since they could make up the difference through their labors: "But one pursuing a trade, even if he is a scholar . . . should be given only half of his *ḥaluqah*, because they, too, fulfill [the commandment of] settlement of the Land."[76]

Even the earliest waves of immigration included some who were not full-time scholars but, instead, engaged in various types of work in the Land of Israel in order to support themselves. Some of these craftsmen, who were also Torah students, were prominent in the community leadership. The best known were Zalman Ẓoref (Solomon), Solomon Pach, and his son, Isaac Pach. Solomon Pach, for example, would go off to Egypt or Syria every few months for business.[77] Even when he went on a mission for the *kolel*, his commission letter would expressly note that he was permitted to engage in his trade as an etcher while en route, in the cities of Syria and Turkey, and could do so even before completing his assignment from the *kolel*.[78]

Some of the wealthier immigrants brought substantial amounts of cash with them and lived off the interest on their loans to the *kolel*, to individuals, or to Christian institutions in the Land of Israel.[79] It appears that the *kolel* itself managed over the years to acquire real estate, the rental fees on which flowed into its coffers;[80] later, it tried to sell them and use the proceeds to repay debts.[81]

Although they knew Lehren's general view of trade and commerce in the Land of Israel, some of the *kolel*'s leaders approached him with a request for aid in doing business with Europe. As might be expected, Lehren declined to get involved and wrote to Aryeh Ne'eman: "As for your question regarding my brother's willingness to ship certain merchandise—we are not interested in getting into that."[82] We have no ties to merchants who ship merchandise to the Land of Israel, Lehren declares, nor can we agree to pay merchants here or to receive money up front and arrange for the shipment of goods.[83] To clarify his position, Lehren accuses the residents of the Land of Israel of downplaying their fear of Heaven and being unduly preoccupied with making profits.[84] He considers these elements to be interrelated and therefore believes it forbidden to allow involvement with trade and commerce in the Land of Israel.

The increased economic activity during Muhammad Ali's reign brought with it not only new opportunities to acquire real estate, but also an efflorescence of commerce[85] and an expanded range of potential ways to make a living. The increased economic activity also affected the attitudes of the Land's Jewish residents. The prospect of greater economic independence for the *yishuv*, of its becoming self-sufficient, now seemed more attainable. Lehren's view of the matter, of course, was rejected by the *kolel*, and the Clerks' Organization had a similar confrontation with a group of immigrants from Germany, who made common cause with the *Perushim* and became part of their *kolel*.

Bregman's View of Redemption Through Natural Processes

In the summer of 1833, Ẓevi Hirsch Lehren set out on a trip through Germany to raise funds for the purpose of discharging the debts of the *Perushim*'s *kolel*. En route, he met a group of wealthy Jews interested in immigrating to the Land of Israel. The group's leader, Eliezer Bregman, is described by Lehren as "a great scholar, involved in trade as well, a partner in a factory making iron nails, which they sell at wholesale to merchants. He asked me if there might be an opportunity to establish something similar in the Land of Israel."[86] In contrast to the two earlier immigrants from Germany—Moses Sacks and Joseph Schwartz—this group explicitly refused to benefit from *ḥaluqah* funds: "For they want to go up with the little money in their hands if they can earn their living by the toil of their hands and not by charity and gifts from other flesh and blood."[87] Moreover, in contrast to generally accepted practice, these immigrants refused as well to be supported by lending on interest, "even in a permissible manner";[88] instead, they proposed to engage in labor and trade or agriculture in the Land of Israel "only in the manner of commerce or from the produce of the Land if they purchase fields and vineyards."[89] Intending to sink roots in the Land in a manner appropriate to it, the leaders of the group issued a declaration that they had intended to immigrate since 1824, and they were now about to carry out their plan. The group sought donors willing to advance money as loans, not as charity, to cover their travel costs and, apparently, to enable them to carry out their plan of investing in commerce, labor, and agriculture. In Würzburg, the group hired accountants to administer their fundraising activities, "as a matter of credit, and on condition that they will be obligated to discharge the debt once it becomes possible for them to do so."[90]

The group's leaders included El'azar Dov Metz as well as Bregman, but it was the Bregman family that set out on its own in the summer of 1834. Bregman saw himself as a vanguard, clearing a path for the potential immigrants left behind; he therefore urged them not to be deterred from their plan by the misfortune he himself suffered en route, when he lost all his possessions at sea:[91] "Let me add that that it is not proper for anyone volunteering to join us to be cast down or deterred by what happened to my family . . . for such things routinely happen in thousands of instances, and no one considering sea travel can allow himself to be deterred by that possibility."[92]

Because Eliezer Bregman saw himself as the immigrants' vanguard, his own immigration included among its declared objectives the expansion of Jewish settlement in the Land of Israel, and he therefore wrote numerous letters encouraging his friends to immigrate. In his letters to a group of potential *olim* from Germany, he offers some practical advice. He advises them to bring particular types of coins,[93] warns "all those who follow us in good [fortune]" against paying ship captains the full price of passage in advance,[94] and counsels his friends to bring various items that cannot be purchased in the Land of Israel. In a long letter to the immigrant Abraham Mendel, he notes at length and in detail, "for the good of all who travel after us,"[95] what to bring on the journey and what not to bring in order to avoid being burdened with excess baggage: "Only metal cooking utensils should be brought, for use both on the ship and here in the Land . . . but the local pottery is not good for cooking, and my wife is still distressed, because she misses [such utensils]. . . . And, by the way . . . it is recommended, especially for families, to bring a sort of commode, please excuse the expression, to bring into the privy, even if such a device is very costly."[96] Bregman also describes the weather conditions and opportunities for making a living. He admonishes the immigrants against exchanging their European clothing for oriental garb,[97] and he asks the first immigrant to arrive to bring him a European hat and books to use in learning Arabic.[98] Nevertheless, he says, language does not pose a concern, and one can get along with European languages.

That Eliezer Bregman and his group had no intention of being supported by the *ḥaluqah* is established beyond doubt. Bregman compiled a list of the various ways in which one might earn a living through industry or commerce and offered it as practical guidance for the immigrants who followed him:

> Craftsmen and administrators are almost entirely lacking in town. . . .
> Watchmakers—There is only one, nonexpert. . . .
> Makers of musical and other instruments—Not even one between here and Cairo.
> Bakers—There are many . . . but not one of them Jewish. . . .
> Bookbinders—Not even one here, and in my opinion, a Jew could make a good livelihood at this trade. He could also be a paper merchant.
> Cobblers—Unheard of here, and a Jew in my opinion could make a living here [at that trade].
> Gold and silversmiths—There are some, but they are not expert. . . .
> Tanners—They say there are none here, and the large amount of leather needed here is brought from Damascus, so it might be worthwhile for a Jew to open a tannery here.
> Saddlers and makers of rope—There are none here, and, in my opinion, Jews could make a nice living here at these trades. . . .
> Moneychangers, bankers—I think they would be of considerable interest, given the variations in coinage even from city to city within Syria itself.
> Jewelers—They would do good business, in my opinion. . . .
> Vintners and farmers—Only a few work here . . . the fields are not properly worked, not fertilized . . . there is no doubt one could profit greatly. But one European alone could certainly not survive among them and work his field properly in his manner, but a group of ten or fifteen could easily overcome that failing, and such as already been done, I believe, in Egypt. A group such as this would certainly be well

received by Ibrahim Pasha, and would be granted preferential rights by him. . . .

Builders—There are, indeed, many, but many now are needed.

Smiths—There are none here, and experts will find a lot of business. But I believe they will have to bring their own tools.

Scribes for sacred texts—There are none between here and Safed or, perhaps all the way to Mesopotamia. . . . In my judgment, an expert will find a good living here. . . .

Physicians—None here, except for the military, and, in my judgment, even one who is only a surgeon would find a good living here, especially if he has his own pharmacy. . . .

Shoemakers—There are many, but not in the European style. A good Jewish craftsman would therefore do a good business in this trade.[99]

Bregman describes at length the business opportunities in the Land of Israel and discusses the commercial privileges of foreign citizens. Not only are Europeans exempt from paying taxes; they also enjoy the protection of the consuls for their commercial enterprises:[100] "One can do as much business here as one likes. . . . There is no need to set aside anything [for taxes], that is, on the part of resident aliens such as us. . . . When merchandise can be brought from Trieste, it is possible to make a suitable profit, and we, too, tried our hand at it."[101]

Passing through Trieste en route to the Land of Israel, Bregman takes pains to ensure his ability to do business once he reaches his destination. He arranges for his funds to be sent to Trieste, from where merchandise of equivalent value would be sent to the Land of Israel on his account.[102] He is so determined to support himself that he does not give up the idea even after all his possessions go down at sea off Jaffa and he, having already reached the Land, has to borrow money to survive. He orders and receives new merchandise: "It is possible that with the merchandise soon to arrive from Beirut, God willing, we can discharge the debts."[103] He is referring to four chests of goods, including mirrors and buttons.[104] He likewise ships barrels of the Land of Israel's soil to the Diaspora, as well as a sample of rose oil.[105]

Bregman speaks of a profit margin ranging from 40 to 100 percent on goods reaching Beirut from Trieste.[106] He says the city of Sidon is part of the Holy Land and cleaner than Beirut and that food there is cheaper, though the price is likely to rise because of the expected arrival of a two-thousand-man military force; on the other hand, that prospect can improve business generally.[107] He is happy to discover that the author of *Kaftor va-Feraḥ* also regards Sidon as part of the Holy Land, and he is prepared to live there for a few years as one living in the Land of Israel and supporting himself through business.[108] He is untroubled by the fact that some regard Sidon as outside the borders of the Holy Land, for his intention is first to establish there a community of immigrants from Germany and then to continue on to one of the cities in the Land of Israel itself.[109] When he travels south from Sidon to familiarize himself with the region, one of his principal purposes is to examine the prospects for going into business at the first opportunity, "so that when some merchandise . . . may become available . . . it will be possible to turn some profit."[110] Even when he gets to Jerusalem, he says he does not intend to settle there immediately but only to examine commercial prospects. In that connection, he reports on the crafts at which one can earn a living in Jerusalem and that are well suited to German emigrants and likely to interest them. He even asks his father-in-law to teach one of his sons the craft of shoemaking, a trade that is in demand and remunerative.[111] The list of craftsmen he enumerates includes hatters, makers of laced shoes, carpenters, hosiery knitters, builders, scribes, engravers, bookbinders, butchers, bread bakers, and pastry bakers.[112]

The revolutionary approach of Eliezer Bregman's group thus manifests itself not only in its members' determination to support themselves through labor, commerce, and agriculture but also in its support for the settling of Jews outside the four holy cities. Bregman himself, as noted, contemplated living in Sidon for a few years, but he also considered other port cities and agricultural areas in the Land of Israel and beyond: "And one can live well in all these holy cities [Beirut, Sidon, Tyre] as well as in Acre, Haifa, and Jaffa. All six of these are port cities, and Sefardim are there . . . and [there are] other places where it is possible to live well."[113]Bregman emphasizes that settlement outside of the holy cities and the six port cities is possible only when a large group of immigrants takes shape in accordance with the new political conditions, permitting the acquisition of houses wherever one wishes, as well as the purchase of rural holdings:[114] "I suggest to you and promise that it is very worthwhile to come and settle not only in Beirut, Sidon, Tyre, or Jaffa . . . but that every group of heads of household and young men that contains at least ten adults of bar miẓvah age or older, especially if they possess a Torah scroll as well, can settle in various places and regions, as they see fit, and the Land is still spacious and very good."[115]

What was Lehren's attitude toward the position advanced by Bregman and his associates? Initially, Lehren concurred in the new idea that immigrants should be people who will not become a burden on the community organizations and will not have to be taken into account in distributing *ḥaluqah*. He expresses his view of the matter in asking Israel of Shklov for information about the commercial prospects for *olim*: "And it is no trivial matter to me to settle our Holy Land, may it be built and established, with scholarly, pious people who want to benefit from the toil of their hands, for that is a sanctification of God's name before the masses . . . who say that those who immigrate to the Land do so to live [on the dole]. . . . Now they all will recognize that there are people to whom God has given wealth and who go there solely on account of the Land's sanctity and virtue."[116] But this is only Lehren's initial statement, made at a time when he did not yet fully understand the details of Bregman's plan. Moreover, it seems this attitude should be understood as a consequence of the rumors he had heard about the success of Barukh ben Samuel's mission to the Ten Tribes. They generated in him a sense that, despite everything, the *Perushim*'s activist way—the way now proposed by Eliezer Bregman—might be a legitimate way to hasten the redemption.

Soon after, while visiting Amsterdam early in 1834, Bregman had an extended conversation with Lehren. The two exchanged harsh words, and Lehren now seems to have understood the "agency" that Bregman contemplated. Not only did Lehren object to Bregman's basing his existence in the Land of Israel on commercial enterprise; he even pleaded with him not to immigrate at all.[117] Once Bregman did in fact immigrate, Lehren tried to bring him into the circle of those supported by the *ḥaluqah*, and he thought he found his opportunity when he heard that Bregman's assets had all been lost at sea off Jaffa. Bregman borrowed a substantial sum from the *Perushim*'s *kolel* in Jerusalem—some 70 gold ducats, according to Aryeh Ne'eman—and the *kolel* requested collateral, on the basis of which it would be willing to lend additional funds. Lehren, as noted, saw this as the occasion to bring Bregman into the circle supported by the *kolel*. He mentions as if in passing that Bregman could export merchandise from the Land, but he treats it inconsequentially, doubting Bregman could base his family's livelihood on it. According to Lehren, it would be more practical and productive to obtain a commitment on the part of Bregman's father-in-law and brothers-in-law to provide him a regular income. He asks Bregman's friend, Abraham Reiss, to mention to Bregman's family that he had established a factory for them, and that it therefore "was a great obligation for them to provide him sustenance out of their pockets."[118]

Bregman was of a different mind, however. Despite the difficult situation in which he found himself because of the loss of his assets and his accumulation of debts, he refused to become dependent on Lehren's kindness. He declined to receive payment for studying Torah in memory of the deceased, a common practice Lehren had recommended to him,[119] and he declined to live rent-free in a courtyard Lehren had purchased in Jerusalem;[120] instead, he strove as hard as he could to support himself by his own labors. But despite it all, it seems that at the end of the day, Bregman had no choice but to depend on *ḥaluqah* funds as well, though not before initiating an effort to direct interested Jews toward agricultural pursuits.

Against the background of these differing points of view, the animosity between Lehren and Bregman can be understood. Only recently, however, with the discovery of additional Bregman manuscripts, has it become clear beyond doubt that underlying their opposing views were starkly different concepts regarding the messianic era and the way to bring about the redemption.[121]

On the day he reached Jerusalem, 2 March 1835, Bregman writes in his journal of reflections on Torah: "If they are deserving—I will hasten it; if an individual or congregation hastens the coming of our righteous Messiah by the merit [of good deeds?], [the Messiah] will come swiftly, outside natural events. But at the time that is set for his coming by the master of all, he comes not swiftly but through natural means with events unfolding one by one, as is written (Isa. 30:15): 'In stillness and quiet will you be saved,' for it is His will, may He be blessed and praised forever, to direct His entire world according the way of nature instilled in it by the Creator of all.[122] The conception expressed here is very much at odds with the traditional messianic notion. If we consider as well that this viewpoint does not remain a theoretical matter but is, in fact, given concrete expression, we can understand its emotional force.[123]

Efforts to Establish an Agricultural Economic Base

Muhammad Ali's reign (1831–1840) presented the Jewish community in the Land of Israel with a new set of circumstances. During the regime's first three years, the population of *Perushim* quickly doubled. The need to support these immigrants and help them find housing forced the *kolel* to incur huge debts at high interest rates. The *kolel* therefore had to seek out new economic opportunities, beyond the traditional reliance on *ḥaluqah* funds.

The changes in the Land of Israel extended beyond the Jewish community. Muhammad Ali's new regime was concerned about the security of persons and property, which improved dramatically, and he was particularly interested in economic matters. A wave of agricultural development ensued under the new government's auspices, and research was undertaken on the nature of the Land's soil and the crops appropriate to it. At the end of 1836, the government resettled long-abandoned farms, and farmers were given cash incentives to prepare and work the soil. In some areas, the government cancelled the tithe tax, which in the past had consumed as much as one-fifth of the crop, and it even funded the manufacture of plows by the *fellahin* and their planting of thousands of mulberry trees, olive trees, and grape vines. In the Acre area alone, the government planted some 300,000 olive trees. Diplomatic papers from the years 1838–1836 speak of considerable growth in the agricultural yield; on backing for the manufacture of silk; on the growth of agricultural exports; on the establishment of textile mills in Shekhem, Tyre, and Acre; and on initial efforts to establish an iron-working industry, a weapons foundry, and a leather-working industry in Acre.[124] All this intense activity quickly brought about changes in the landscape.

There was also movement in the Jewish community's economic situation. Israel Baeck, a member of the Hasidic *kolel*, went up to Safed in late 1831 and there established the first modern Hebrew printing press. Thanks to the ties he had forged with Ibrahim Pasha, Baeck was granted, after the suppression of the *fellahin* rebellion of 1834, a rural holding in Kefar Jirmak, as he had requested. After the earthquake, he and more than ten other Safed Hasidim moved to Kefar Jirmak and turned it into a productive farming enterprise.[125] It may be assumed that Israel Baeck's multifaceted economic initiatives also influenced the behavior of the *Perushim*'s *kolel*, which was inspired to action, as we shall see below, by the confluence of, on the one hand, new economic opportunities and, on the other, the need to find new economic solutions that could enable the *yishuv* to stand on its own feet.

A controversial figure associated with these developments was the first immigrant from Germany, Moses Sacks.[126] His principal contribution to the chain of events was the spirit of optimism he instilled via the letters of support he sent to the Land of Israel, which reported on the Diaspora community's backing for the project. In late summer or early fall of 1834, Sacks set out from Jerusalem and went abroad.[127] His purpose appears to have been a private one—to trace his son-in-law Ẓadok ha-Levi, a rabbinic emissary of the *Perushim* who had disappeared after setting out for North Africa in 1829.[128] Moses Sacks carried references from the *Perushim*'s *kolel*, but it is unclear whether the *kolel* endorsed the plans for agricultural settlement that he presented when he arrived in Europe or whether they were his own ideas, developed before or after his departure. In the winter of 1834–1835, he visited the cities of the Maghreb, as evidenced by the accounts of the German Count Pikner[129] and the missionary Ewald, who ran into him in Tunis.[130] At that point, he had not yet begun to speak of Jewish agricultural settlement in the Land of Israel, as he was later to do in Europe. He tells Pikner and Ewald that he intends to benefit his fellow Jews in the Land of Israel by establishing a boys' school in Jerusalem,[131] and Pikner evidently thought well enough of the idea to recommend Sacks to Baron Rothschild. In his correspondence with Lehren, Sacks was similarly silent about his agricultural plans. It may be that they had not yet taken shape, but it is also possible that he was acting out of deliberate caution. In his letter, he focuses solely on a subject likely to please Lehren, telling him that he left Jerusalem to raise support for the establishment of a yeshiva in the holy city, a place "of intricate argumentation and diligent Torah study."[132] Sacks thought he could thereby influence Lehren to increase his support for German emigrants by transferring funds for the establishment of the yeshiva.

From the Maghreb, Sacks sailed to Trieste, from where he seems to have continued on to Vienna;[133] and we now hear for the first time of an agricultural settlement. En route, he meets Rabbi Yequti'el Hirschenstein, and he takes the opportunity to tell Hirschenstein that the purpose of his journey is to promote the settlement of the Land of Israel by Jews who would work the soil.[134] Rabbi Hirschenstein was impressed and suggested that Sacks approach the leaders of the German Confederation.[135] According to Hirschenstein's account, Sacks, during his first two years away from the Land of Israel, regularly visited the great cities of western Europe and preached to the Jews about the idea of an agricultural settlement in the Land of Israel.[136]

We may assume that when he met with Rabbi Moses Sofer in Pressburg[137] and with Rabbi Hamburg in Fürth, Sacks brought them up to date on the situation in the Land of Israel, where the Jews were now permitted to acquire real property, something barred to them in the past.[138]

To provide a firmer footing for his idea of agricultural settlement, Sacks asks Joseph Schwartz for updated information on the rights now enjoyed by the Jews in the Land of Israel: "to purchase and build houses and to sow and plant fields and vineyards."[139]

Sacks's plan is disclosed to Lehren indirectly. As might be expected, Lehren protests: "And now [one] comes with a new project, to buy houses and fields and vineyards to build and sow and plant. And it is all vanity and an ill wind."[140] Lehren attacks the notion from several directions. In his opinion, a Jewish agricultural settlement cannot be established in the Land of Israel before the coming of the redemption, for Providence has so decreed; as Scripture says, "those who dwell thereon shall be desolate" [a paraphrase and interpretation of Lev. 26:32; see further in the note]."[141] Moreover, the Land is unlike others, as evidenced by the fact that even under the rule of Muhammad Ali, who favors and supports settlement and allows the purchase of fields and vineyards for that purpose, the effort is unsuccessful. Lehren notes in that regard that, notwithstanding Muhammad Ali's enlightened rule, the *fellahin* revolt of 1834 was accompanied by rioting against the Jews of Safed and Hebron and after the revolt was put down, Ibrahim Pasha's soldiers also attacked the Jews of Hebron. Lehren observes that historical circumstances have religious significance, that the believer will not ascribe them to blind chance, and that "it is decreed from Heaven that there is no livelihood or settlement to be had on the basis of commerce or agriculture in the Land of Israel."[142] He continues: "And who is so foolish . . . as to seek settlement in the Land of Israel in the same manner as outside the Land"; the proof that it cannot be done is "that all he [Eliezer Bregman] possessed went down at sea between Sidon and Jaffa, including the money he had borrowed to engage in commerce in the Land of Israel."[143]

Sacks appears to have left Amsterdam for London at the end of 1836 or the beginning of 1837, around the time of Hanukkah. Lehren writes to the rabbi of London, Solomon Hirschell (Berliner), to warn him against Sacks, describing at length Sacks's journey from the Land of Israel and the project he proposed in Vienna: "that funds be given for the purchase of fields and vineyards in the Land of Israel so the Jews living in the Land could become tillers of the soil and support themselves by their toil."[144] In typical form, Lehren lambastes his opponents. He notes Sacks's contacts with missionaries in the Land of Israel, even alleging, "I do not think it unlikely that he will there [in London] join up with a sect of apostates. Let him go to hell, but let him not return to our Holy Land."[145] He audaciously asks Rabbi Hirschell to prevent Sacks from returning to the Land of Israel: "And God forbid anyone help him to return to the Land of Israel, may it be built and established speedily and in our days, amen, to defile the inner reaches of holiness."[146] He even adds, on his own initiative: "It would be an act of virtue if it were possible to extract from him a bill of divorce to his wife, Rachel, the daughter of Ẓadok ha-Levi."[147]

In his heart of hearts, Lehren certainly recognized that his insults could not foreclose the possibility of Sacks meeting with Montefiore or Rothschild and trying to enlist their help for his plan. Accordingly, he had no alternative but to write disparagingly of them as well. It mattered not to him that Montefiore would fall for Sacks's scheme, he wrote, and there was no need to warn him against it, "for he regularly donates money for idolatry."[148] Nor does he want to warn Rothschild about Sacks, for even otherwise he would see him as flawed for eating nonkosher food and desecrating the Sabbath.[149]

Evidently, Count Pikner's recommendation of Sacks to Baron Rothschild, along with Rabbi Hirschenstein's suggestion that Sacks make contact with the leaders of the German Confederation, led Sacks to approach not only Jewish communities, rabbis, and western European Jewish leaders who knew him but also non-Jewish players. In April 1836, during his stay in Vienna, Sacks, through the intervention of Archduke Johann, submitted a memorandum to the Austrian government. In it, Sacks presented his conclusion that it would be possible "to improve society in the Land of Israel by means of Jewish agriculture,"[150] and he requested the Austrian government to take the effort under its wings. The government treated his memorandum seriously and referred it to the Austrian representative in Constantinople, asking for his assessment of the proposal and its practicability.[151]

Sacks's efforts to enlist the support of governments for his ideas also are alluded to in passing in a letter from Lehren to Moses Sofer: "That miscreant complained about me before our lord the king, may he be glorified, saying he wants to remove the shiftless and idle malingerers from the markets and direct them to the Land of Israel to work the soil and that I object to doing so and confiscated his documents and writings."[152] Here we see a new theme: Moses Sacks's plan contemplates not only that Jews already in the Land of Israel are to be made into farmers, but also that unemployed Diaspora Jews would be brought to the Land of Israel to engage in useful and productive livelihoods. That sort of plan would interest not only the Jews themselves but also the rulers of the countries in which they live; it clearly entails elements of increasing productivity.

Sacks maintained contact as well with his friends in the Land of Israel, and his letters made an impression on them. The promises he claims to have been given by the House of Rothschild and other wealthy western Europeans, and the significant support he gained from Rabbis Moses Sofer of Pressburg and Wolf Hamburg of Fürth, produced a positive reaction in Jerusalem. His ideas were taken up and efforts made to carry them out. Five leaders of the *Perushim*—including Eliezer Bregman, Aryeh Ne'eman, and Sacks's father-in-law, Ẓadok ha-Levi—organized themselves as a group[153] and, in total disregard of Lehren and the Clerks' Organization, set out to find new sources of support for the *Perushim*'s economic programs. In mid-March 1837, soon after the trauma of Safed's destruction in the earthquake and the successful dedication of the *Menaḥem Ẓiyyon* study hall in Jerusalem, the group approached the consul Elijah Fajito in Aleppo with a request that monies raised in the Diaspora be centralized under his auspices and that a portion be used to establish a dedicated fund for expanding the economic opportunities of Jerusalem's Jews. The dedicated fund would be applied to the purchase of fields, vineyards, and buildings and to the building of houses for lease, factories, and flourmills. Craftsmen would even be brought from Europe to assist in the enterprise. In the words of the memo: "The fund would be used to purchase fields and vineyards or to rebuild the ruins of Jerusalem and rent out [the buildings] or to build workshops . . . or olive or sesame oil presses or other places where other types of work are done, or a large house containing several rental apartments or flourmills or to build shops or to bring artisans from the cities of the Franks with their tools to engage in crafts not found in these climes. And the profits that God may bring about would be distributed regularly to Torah scholars by faithful treasurers as they see fit."[154] The steps taken to carry out the plan bear Eliezer Bregman's mark, primarily because he had connections in

Aleppo; despite his Ashkenazi origins, he was the spiritual leader of a community of Aleppo Jews in Jerusalem. That led to the idea of persuading the consul to adopt the program, through the intervention of his former treasurer, who had come up to Jerusalem and settled there. In addition, Bregman had technical knowledge and expertise, as well as personal experience running the agricultural enterprise in the city of Zahl and establishing and running an iron nail factory of the sort he wanted to set up in the Land of Israel. Moreover, Sacks's program was consistent with Bregman's views.

As noted above, Bregman dreamed, even before his own *aliyah*, of a Jewish settlement in the Land of Israel sustained by its own labor rather than by charitable distributions—a sort of redemption through natural means. His radical viewpoint was tempered by Ne'eman, who did not favor such extreme changes; he did not foresee an end to reliance on the *ḥaluqah*, contemplating, instead, the establishment of an economic structure side by side with the *ḥaluqah*, capable of responding to new needs. It is important to emphasize that Ne'eman joined the group as a representative of the *kolel* of *Perushim* in Jerusalem, symbolizing the *kolel*'s ongoing involvement in the processes necessitated by the new circumstances in the Land. A practical step in that direction had already been taken by acquiring land and buildings in the Bab al-Ḥota area, in an effort to expand the area of Jewish settlement in Jerusalem, even beyond the Jewish Quarter.

Paralleling the presentation of the project to Elijah Fajito, Zalman Ẓoref (Solomon), "the representative of the Ashkenazi community" in Jerusalem, turned to the municipal authorities with a request to enable them to purchase property so as to engage in working the soil. The request was turned down because the *Perushim* had asked that the acquisition be in the nature of *mulk*, and real property in the Land of Israel could be acquired only as *waqf*.[155] The *kolel* of the *Perushim* was not discouraged by the negative reaction of the local authorities and, in 1838, presented its request to Muhammad Ali himself.[156] That request as well appears to have been turned down, and this initiative on their part also failed to bear fruit.

"But You, Mountains of Israel, You Shall Shoot Forth Your Branches for My People Israel—There Is No Better Revelation of the End Than This"

Two more or less simultaneous but very different sorts of events—the catastrophic destruction of Safed and the dedication of the *Menaḥem Ẓiyyon* study house in Jerusalem—were taken, each on its own but also in view of their coincidence, as signifying the beginning of the redemption. Safed's destruction was particularly traumatic for Israel of Shklov. He was the paragon of the spiritual messianic concept, who had assigned Safed priority over Jerusalem in the redemptive process and had mightily opposed concrete steps connected with the rebuilding of Jerusalem, such as construction of the *Ḥurvah* or purchasing houses outside the Jewish Quarter. Only recently had he failed in his attempt to prevent the dedication of *Menaḥem Ẓiyyon*, which the Jerusalem *kolel* saw as its crowning glory, a symbol of the city's rebuilding. Was it conceivable that all these reversals would not bring about a change in his position? Outwardly, he was unchanged, blaming the destruction of Safed on the dispute imposed on him by the Jerusalemites. Nevertheless, there are signs suggesting that his spiritual messianic conception was, in fact, modified, and that he moved in the direction of a more concrete notion. For the first time, we now hear him express the view that purchasing fields and vineyards and working the soil were an additional step in the redemptive process. In view of the new opportunities abroad in the Land, such actions should not be delayed. The very availability of those opportunities proved that the redemptive process was progressing along the path set for it by Providence, in accordance with the Talmud's dictum: "Rabbi Abba said: There is no better revelation of the end than this, as Scripture says, 'But you, mountains of Israel, you shall shoot forth your branches and yield your fruit to my people Israel' [Ezek. 36:8]."[157]

Israel of Shklov was influenced by Eliezer Bregman and, apparently, by Moses Sacks's letters describing his successes and the support he was able to enlist from kings, princes, and the wealthy, as well as from great Torah authorities such as Moses Sofer of Pressburg. He turns to Lehren, his longstanding friend and benefactor—though he knows better than anyone Lehren's negative attitude toward anything smacking of labor, commerce, or agriculture in the Land of Israel—and tells him of his intention to return to Safed and engage in the rebuilding of the city.[158] He adds that he believes it necessary to purchase fields and vineyards and provide an agricultural base for the livelihood of the Land's residents.

Israel of Shklov and Eliezer Bregman seem to have persuaded themselves that they finally could convince Lehren. But he stood firm, writing that "development through the purchase of fields and vineyards seems a matter of madness to all of us, and I am extremely surprised that your excellency, may your lamp burn brightly, has been deceived by the words of our teacher Rabbi E. Bregman, may his lamp burn brightly, to write about this."[159] It becomes clear from Lehren's letter that Israel of Shklov and Eliezer Bregman were so serious about purchasing fields and vineyards that they wanted to dispatch an emissary for that specific purpose alone. Lehren rants in response: "And he went even further with the outlandish suggestion that they should send another emissary to deal with this matter. How can I be furious at Rabbi Zalman Ẓoref, who wants to send emissaries for the building of the *Ḥurvah*, if your excellency, may your lamp burn brightly, now sides with sending an emissary for this lunatic business?"[160] Lehren's polemic continues with familiar arguments; he sees no surprise in so foolish an idea coming from Bregman, who, after all, had in the first instance "decided to immigrate to the Land of Israel in order to do business there and accordingly first settled in Sidon."[161] He also reiterates his notion "that a person cannot eat his cake and have it too. The Land of Israel is acquired only through torments, and one who wants the privilege of settling in the Land of Israel for the sake of Heaven has to lovingly accept the torments of the Land of Israel and receive human charity."[162]

Quoting talmudic statements on the importance of Torah study, Lehren goes on to discuss the historical reality in which, even under Muhammad Ali's rule, the Jews of Safed and Hebron suffered devastating raids in 1834. He asks:

> And if, at that time, the entire . . . Land of Israel had been given over to fields and vineyards, they would have burned it all, from stalk to kernel, granary and winepress. And what would the poor of the Land of Israel do? Can you conceive that the wealthy of the Diaspora would contribute replacement funds? And would it occur to your excellency, may your lamp shine brightly, to base the entire livelihood of the Land of Israel's inhabitants on working the soil? As for Moses Sacks's comment that the wealthy of Ashkenaz want to send funds for the purchase of houses and fields and vineyards . . . in truth, that refers only to the desire of the innovators and transgressors, who are unconcerned about neglecting Torah study."[163]

Those "innovators," who in any event would have neglected Torah study in the Diaspora, seized on Sacks's plan enthusiastically, for their desire was that the Jews of the Land of Israel withdraw from the study hall and instead be like all the nations—farmers, tillers of the soil, and planters of vineyards. Lehren's remarks imply that Sacks in fact succeeded in influencing some wealthy individuals, among them Anschel Rothschild, who promised to support the project once it got under way. But "we," Lehren concludes, will adamantly refuse to receive funds for this project.

There is a profound gap between the traditional view of redemption as a heavenly phenomenon, entailing radical changes in the ways of the world, and the idea of redemption as an extended natural process. The full import of that gap manifests itself in the practical dispute between Lehren on the one hand and Bregman and Israel of Shklov on the other regarding the acquisition of fields and vineyards on which to base the Jewish community's livelihood.[164]

These ideas about increased productivity find expression elsewhere in Bregman's writings as well. In his notebook of reflections on Torah, Bregman ponders the conclusion to the third of the blessings that make up *birkat hamazon*, the grace after meals—"Praised are You O Lord, Who in His mercy builds Jerusalem"—and wonders about its link to the expression of thanks earlier in text for "the good land, livelihood, and sustenance." His answer: "The principle appears to be simple, for food and livelihood depend, essentially, on the soil . . . and it is evident that the essence of livelihood, with no Jew dependent on another Jew or an outsider, depends on the building of Jerusalem, which is the purpose of coming to the Land of Israel. Then, each one will earn his own living from the portion of the Land that the Holy One Blessed Be He will assign to him. And so may it be [God's] will, speedily and in our days, Amen Selah."[165]

Moses Montefiore and Implementation of the Agricultural Project

Rumors of Montefiore's imminent arrival began to reach the Land of Israel as early as 1837. We can only speculate about whether he came with preexisting plans for agricultural settlement or whether he thought of them only upon arriving. We lack direct evidence regarding the nature of the close tie between Montefiore and the Jerusalem *Perushim*'s *kolel* from late 1835 through 1838, but we learn of the relationship's formation, in parallel to the *kolel*'s growing estrangement from Lehren, through Lehren's abundant expressions of jealousy. It is hard to imagine, therefore, that Montefiore did not hear even before his arrival in the Land, at least indirectly, of the ideas and plans for agricultural settlement. Details of this sort were brought to the attention even of the consul Elijah Fajito, and Israel of Shklov had audaciously tried to persuade Lehren regarding the matter. It seems likely, then, that the *kolel*'s leaders wrote to Montefiore of their ideas, viewpoints, and plans during this period, and it is fair to assume as well that details of the new plans became known to Montefiore through accounts of Moses Sacks's special efforts. Even if Sacks himself never reached London, Montefiore may have heard of him and his ideas from Solomon Hirschell, London's rabbi; and he also knew of him through Lehren's letters.[166] It is even possible that Montefiore heard of the plans for Jewish agricultural settlement from a direct source, just before his arrival in the Land of Israel. While en route, perhaps in Italy, Montefiore met Aaron Selig Mann, a rabbinic emissary who was traveling to Europe as "fundraiser for the *Ḥurvah* of Rabbi Judah Ḥasid," with responsibility for the entire region. It is hard to imagine that Mann did not tell Montefiore about the Jerusalem *kolel*'s efforts to acquire agricultural lands, which had been going on since the winter of 1836–1837.

When Montefiore arrived in the Land of Israel, the leaders of the Jerusalem *Perushim* presented him with several letters on the subject. The letters show their serious and very pragmatic approach with regard to working the land: they recognized the practical limitations to the program and were prepared to deal with them. The letters from Aryeh Ne'eman and Mordecai Ẓoref[167] show clearly that the *kolel* leadership had for some time been considering questions of agriculture, manufacturing, processing, and marketing. These letters expressly refer to Jews themselves engaging in agricultural work and cite, in proving the need for such an enterprise, the famine that Jerusalem suffered in 1838 and the ensuing epidemic of plague. One lesson drawn from that experience was that exclusive reliance should not be placed on funds flowing from the Diaspora and that energy should be directed to the establishment of alternative sources of sustenance by the working of agricultural lands. Aryeh Ne'eman knew well enough that the Jews were ill equipped to do all the work themselves, "for they are too weak to plow and till the soil and sow and do everything properly,"[168] and because they are not permitted to work on the Sabbath. These obstacles, though, can be overcome; first, however, Montefiore must obtain assurances that the farming settlements will be secure, so Jews can move to the farms and begin working the land. The approach to working the land appears practical, though at the outset it involves only certain types of labor and primarily a specific type of Jew—one who is unequipped or unwilling to engage solely in Torah study. One could go so far as to say that the program shows its full measure of seriousness precisely in its presentation of the practical difficulties it poses.

Mordecai Ẓoref, the son of Zalman Ẓoref (Solomon)—the builder of the *Ḥurvah*—writes to Montefiore in a similar vein. Referring to his own agricultural experience and expectations, he is pleased that Montefiore's intention "to support the holy project of settling the Holy Land by working the soil"[169] dovetails with his own plans and expectations. He himself attempted to form a partnership to lease and work a parcel of farmland where conditions were very favorable to agricultural success and to the possibility of taking up residence, "and if a person wished to plow and sow all its fields, to the length and breadth of its borders, he could employ 500 oxen to work it. Planting is also very good, as I have seen with my own eye . . . and there is good pasture for sheep and cattle . . . and this land is also good for cultivating trees and planting vineyards and olive trees, and it contains bee hives as well."[170] In addition, Mordecai Ẓoref says, there are raw materials at the site for the construction of houses. In view of the approaching sabbatical year, he advises hastening to lease the land, to have it worked by a gentile during the sabbatical year, and to acquire it for the *kolel* after that. His proposal speaks of engaging in various tasks other than planting and plowing, for those labors "could be done by Jews only later, for they require [skilled] craft."[171] The memo speaks of two groups of workers to be organized by the *kolel*. One would comprise some twenty heads of household who would move permanently to the farm and engage in oversight, supporting activities, and, of course, prayer and regular periods of Torah study. The second group would comprise scholars from the *kolel*, who would be divided into four squads: "Each squad would serve for a month and return regularly to the farm to work in whatever way was needed, for there is very much work to be done."[172] This group would continue to live in Jerusalem.

The proposal thus contemplates not only labor on the part of hired *fellahin* but also manual labor by some *kolel* members who would move permanently to the farm and others who would come from Jerusalem as part of the four-squad rotation. Ẓoref acknowledges to Montefiore that there are dissenters from his program: "Some question whether Jews could ever reside on farms, in rural conditions; others question whether Jews could ever succeed at agricultural labor; and still others say that nothing could get them to move from the holy city of Jerusalem, may it be built and established."[173] Nevertheless, Ẓoref concludes his letter on an optimistic note: "And the scholars fit to live in the aforesaid farm have already been persuaded, and even some of the scholars have already volunteered to serve on the squads rotated into the farm, as explained above."[174]

A previously unpublished letter from Ẓoref to Montefiore, written on 14 June 1839, reveals that consideration was given as well to an alternative proposal, under which the land would be purchased on behalf of individual members of the *kolel* who would settle there on their own, without the *kolel* undertaking responsibility for the venture. The alternative appears to have been proposed in the wake of opposition to the initial plan. Like the initial plan, the alternative clearly contemplated manual labor on the part of the Jewish settlers. In a brief letter, Ẓoref reviews the two plans—settlement under the *kolel*'s auspices and in reliance on its resources, and private settlement with no tie to the *kolel*:

> If it is my lord's wish that the sustenance of the entire holy congregation be treated in common—and the merit of the many is indeed great . . . I take it upon myself to present to my lord, may God protect him, a document signed by the entire community . . . and, specifically, the four squads, among whose number scholars are included, who will take upon themselves all aspects of working the land except for plowing and sowing, and signed by the ten scholars who will reside in the village to oversee each person's labor. But if my lord, may God protect him, prefers that each person should own his own property, each under his own vine and under his own fig tree, then I will present to my lord, may he be exalted, the signatures of about twenty men, most of them scholars, who undertake to work the land, except for plowing and sowing . . . and as soon as my lord, may he be exalted, leases the farm, they will happily move there, and may God assist them.[175]

A close examination of other letters in the Montefiore archives—not previously studied or reviewed—shows that additional proposals submitted to Montefiore in Jerusalem and Safed speak explicitly of manual labor by Jews. Near the beginning of a roster of the *Perushim*'s *kolel* submitted to Montefiore we find the following passage, not hitherto considered: "And most if not all of them want to support themselves with the toil of their hands, by working the land, the holy land, to eat of its fruit and be sustained by its bounty"[176] A similar note is struck in a joint letter from the officials of the Sefardic and Hasidic communities in Safed: "And they should be given some business or labor to work at, even work in the field . . . and in view of the great need, and their love of settling the Land of Israel, they will take such work upon themselves."[177] In another letter, signed only by the Sefardic rabbis of Safed, we read as follows: "And [for] the remnant, let there be found for them . . . some sort of work for each of them—field work, work in vineyards, working with animals as shepherds . . . and in this way, there will be an effective settlement; for the sages—our rabbis and their students—will diligently study Torah, and the rest of the people will engage in their respective labors."[178]

The revolutionary nature of the change in how the *yishuv*'s leadership[179] viewed economic development (in particular, the agricultural work of the *Amei ha-Araẓot* group), and the magnitude of the new concept's departure from traditional notions, are demonstrated by the intensity of Lehren's outraged reaction. In the fall of 1840, the rabbi of Pressburg refers to Lehren a person interested in purchasing real property in the Land of Israel. As usual, Lehren disparages the idea: "What can be better for a person than plowing [the field of] Torah . . . and even if this plan is actually carried out, it will be many days before they can support themselves from this."[180] Some months earlier, Lehren recounts to him, Moses Montefiore had asked that he "purchase real property for them so they could work the Land."[181] The intention was that "the scholars would be supported by the excess profits earned by the common folk (*amei ha-areẓ*)."[182] Taking a practical approach, Lehren claims the common folk will never work to support the scholars, and that even the Sefardic scholars declined to accept Montefiore's plan, seeing no prospect of a successful Jewish agricultural settlement, given concerns about security. Lehren similarly sees security as a crucial matter, for the land is replete with lawlessness, "and Ishmael consumes the progeny of Israel."[183] His comments allude as well to the unrecognized fact that small-scale efforts to engage in agriculture had been made in the past: "As we know that in the past, they planted potatoes that they had brought from Poland, and the Ishmaelites uprooted them before they had fully grown, and not even what they needed for a second planting remained."[184]

Montefiore's reaction provides a measure of the seriousness with which he took the matter. If lack of security were the sole impediment to carrying out the plan, Montefiore would be prepared to deal with the problem by sending a guard force from England to provide security for the farm settlements: "He replied to them that he would dispatch an armed force from his country."[185]

Given how little Lehren generally says about his opponents' views—if he mentions them at all—we can infer from his few words on the matter that in 1839, with Montefiore's arrival in the Land of Israel, the hopes and plans for Jewish agricultural settlement reached their peak. And only on that basis can we understand Montefiore's journey to Egypt in July 1839 and his effort to persuade Muhammad Ali to lease farmland to him.[186] It seems to me that Montefiore, to ensure against the risk of appearing the fool before Muhammad Ali if the Jews showed no interest in working the land, sought express written commitments from the leadership of the various *kolel*s that their people were prepared to engage in agriculture. The documents in our possession, I believe, are the undertakings that Montefiore brought with him on his trip to Muhammad Ali in Egypt.[187] But Montefiore's failure to gain Muhammad Ali's consent to the leasing of lands, and Muhammad Ali's removal in 1840 as ruler of the Land of Israel, left Jewish agricultural settlement in the Land of Israel as an unfulfilled quest.

To sum up: There is no doubt that in 1839, the leadership of both communities—Sefardim and *Perushim* alike—bestowed absolute legitimacy on the idea that Jews in the Land of Israel might engage in various forms of labor and even in agricultural work. In contrast to the ideology of the Jewish Enlightenment, however, whose goal was to change the economic situation of the Jewish nation through a process of making the Jews more productive, the *Perushim* saw the working of the land by Jews as a means for firmly grounding the commandment to settle the Land of Israel and rationalizing the existence of those who dwell there. They assigned priority to settling the Land, which would pave the way for the coming of the Messiah; for on their understanding of the redemptive process, the Land's redemption precedes that of the nation.[188]

And so, this entire project was envisioned not as a secular solution to the mundane difficulties faced by the *Perushim*'s Jerusalem *kolel* but as a corollary of their kabbalistic conceptions. Indeed, in the letter presented to Montefiore by the leadership of the Ashkenazi community on 11 June 1839, they base their attitude toward Jews tilling the soil in the Land of Israel on the foundations of their messianic belief.[189] According to the kabbalistic understanding of the Song of Songs, the Land's granting its yield to the people of Israel provides conclusive evidence for the arousal of the love between the Holy One Blessed Be He and His holy people, and thereby constitutes a symbol that the redemption is taking shape. Relying on that notion, they write: "Israel's eyes and hearts are with us; the holy ones anticipate and await the time when the love will be aroused and the Land will grant its yield to the holy ones [living] upon it."[190] Through their use of kabbalistic concepts, the writers of the letter imply that carrying out the commandments contingent on the Land (related primarily to agriculture), will bring about the perfection of observing all of the Torah's 613 commandments—a "perfection" that is a precondition to redemption: "We have a tradition from our fathers, that through the fulfillment of the Torah in our holy Land, including all the laws and statutes related to the commandments contingent on the Land, all will be strengthened, bonded together, and unified, and then the bounty will descend from the source of blessings."[192] So important are the commandments contingent on the Land that the Torah promises to reward those who fulfill them: "Although we are not to perform God's [other] commandments for the sake of receiving a reward, that is not the case with respect to the commandments contingent on our holy Land. Our holy Torah [the reference in fact is to the Prophets] said, 'Put me to the test [by properly tithing], said the Lord' (Mal. 3:10); and, as our sages of blessed memory said, 'Tithe so you may become wealthy' (*Shabbat* 119a)."[192] Now that there is an opportunity to carry out this commandment, we certainly must do so, for "one who comes to purify himself is given assistance." They sum up with a kabbalistic formulation: "And the awakening on high is dependent on the awakening below, and how long will our holy Land be ruined, desolate, and uninhabited, and the nation of God an emblem of shame and an object of taunting?"[193]

8

Crisis of Faith in the Wake of Unfulfilled Expectations

And now we come to resolve and explain the words of the holy *Zohar* . . . regarding why what is written there explicitly with respect to the year 5600 was not realized. . . . For [the Messiah] was supposed to come in the six hundredth year of the sixth millennium . . . and, if so—why does our Messiah delay [*boshesh*], for six [i.e., 5600] has already come [*ba shesh*]? And some people have become heretical on account of this, having seen that six has come [*ba shesh*], that is, the year 5600, and he [the Messiah] has not come, they said he never will come.

Aviezer of Ticktin, *Sha'arei Ẓedeq*

The English Mission and the *Yishuv*

Since the 1820s, the London Society for Promoting Christianity Amongst the Jews, sponsored by the Anglican Church, had been active in the Land of Israel. Why did the church send a mission specifically to work among the Jews? Why did it send that mission all the way to the Land of Israel, where there were fewer Jews than in European centers much closer to England? And why did it do so even though it recognized that the Jews in the Land of Israel were particularly steadfast in their religion, prepared on account of their faith and messianic expectations to endure a harsh existence without material comforts and, correspondingly, much less likely to be enticed by the mission's preaching?

The explanation grows out of Protestant Christianity's sharing of Judaism's belief that the Jewish people are destined to play a special role at the End of Days. Protestant eschatology contemplates the fulfillment of the prophetic vision of a return to Zion and the redemption of Israel on its Land. Protestants believe as well that the nations of the world are to have a decisive role in advancing that process and that they are divine emissaries to promote the return to Zion. The crucial distinction, of course, is that they believe the redemption of Israel on its Land is not the end of the process but only a necessary precursor to the final stage: acceptance of the Christian messianic belief, followed by the "millennium," a thousand-year period during which Jesus, having reappeared, will reign.[1] Against that background, we can understand why the missionaries concentrated their efforts on the Jews and on the Land of Israel: the redemption of the Jews is a precondition to that of the world; and the redemption of the Land of Israel and its restoration to the status it enjoyed in its golden age are necessary steps in the process of human redemption.

There are additional parallels between the Jewish and Protestant concepts of redemption. Following the Jews, Protestant eschatologists similarly set the time for Israel's redemption on its Land at the middle of the nineteenth century, and they, too, expected decisive changes in the course of human history to precede the return to Zion. In their view, the precursor to the redemption would be the defeat of the anti-Christ's forces by a Christian ruler. On that basis, they saw their historical context—the Napoleonic Wars and the ensuing political and social changes, and the disintegration of anti-Christian rule (that is, the Ottoman Empire) in the East—as signs confirming that the beginning of the return to Zion and of Israel's redemption on its Land was at hand.

When two related points of view make use of similar basic terminology, the dispute between them is focused on the crucial point—the identity of the true Messiah. Judaism sees the Messiah son of David as a charismatic, particularistic figure, who will gather Israel's Diaspora, rebuild the Temple, and restore the crown of Israel's sovereignty. Christianity, meanwhile, foresees a universalistic new age in which Jesus as Messiah will rule over the world. In the understanding of the missionary groups, Christians are required to prepare for the fulfillment of the imminent process of the return to Zion. That requires forging close relationships with the Jews so that all will be harnessed to the advancement of that process. Following that, they must prepare the Jews to recognize Jesus as the Messiah.

When the first missionaries reached the Land of Israel in the 1820s, there still remained two decades before the anticipated time of Israel's redemption. In the meantime, the first order of business was to become a presence in the Land, to disseminate the mission's goals among the Jews in writing and orally, and to help the Jews establish themselves in the Land.

How did the Jews of the Land of Israel receive the missionaries? Were they willing to talk with them, to receive the Scriptures they published and printed, to look at their publicity materials, and to accept their economic and medical support and their intervention with the authorities in defense of Jewish interests? Did they engage with them in theological discussions over matters of faith?

As we have seen, the leaders of the *Perushim* maintained an understanding of redemption that differed from the traditional one, and their view of the missionaries' activities could likewise be expected to differ. The Sefardic sages, almost to a man, saw only the negative side of the missionary activity. This was their first encounter with missionaries, and their response, in my judgment, was decisively shaped by their historical memory of their experiences with the Christianity of the Iberian Peninsula. They feared that the missionaries' economic resources might enable them to sway the Sefardic poor, and they accordingly imposed a strict ban on any contact with the missionary Wolff.[2]

The leaders of the Jerusalem *Perushim* took a different tack. As foreign citizens, they stood to gain more from the missionaries than could the Sefardim, who were Ottoman subjects. From their first encounter with the missionaries in the 1820s, the *Perushim* recognized the potential usefulness of maintaining contact with them.[3] The state of war at that time between Turkey and Russia complicated their lives, and they hoped the missionaries would intercede to help them secure the protection of the British consul in Beirut.

During the 1820s and 1830s, missionary activity in the Land of Israel concentrated on distributing sacred texts and tracts, providing material and medical support, and offering substantive defense against governmental scheming. The Ashkenazim were in such dire straits at that time that rejecting those forms of assistance would have been suicidal. Few voices of protest were raised against their willingness to receive the missionaries' help; that may have been because of the missionaries' failure during that time to achieve any of their religious goals. Even Lehren (unlike Solomon Hirschell of London) was prepared to understand the *Perushim*'s motives.[4]

But while the economic assistance provided by the missionaries helped secure the position of the Ashkenazim in the Land of Israel, the leadership of the *Perushim* saw more to it than that alone. In their view, the involvement of Christian missionaries in efforts on behalf of the Jewish community represented the fulfillment of the prophetic promise that gentiles would help promote the return to Zion: "And strangers will build your walls" (Isa. 60:10). Consistent with that understanding, the leaders of the *Perushim* saw the church's emissaries not as missionaries but as representatives of "the princes sitting at the head of the Kingdom of England, noblemen, etc."[5] Recounting the hardships imposed on the Jews by the scheming of the Greeks and Armenians, Solomon Zalman Shapira relies on Joseph Wolff's statements that the British want to see the Jews living tranquilly and securely in Jerusalem and therefore requests their assistance. Interestingly, when he writes to the Missionary Society in London, he refers to Wolff not by his current name but by his original Jewish name: "And having heard from Joseph Ze'ev that the princes of England and its rulers have taken counsel together to speak well of the Jews and treat them liberally, I therefore informed you of our plight."[6] When ties are strengthened between the missionary Lewis and the leadership of the *Perushim*, they ask for his help, via the British ambassador in Constantinople, in securing the *firman* that authorizes them to rebuild the *Ḥurvah*. And in a letter to Lewis dated 23 February 1824, they explicitly state their belief that the representatives of the Protestant church are divine emissaries sent as part of the redemptive process: "There is no doubt that divine Providence sent you, the prince among us, inspiring you to come and protect us."[7]

The missionaries' honest desire to help the Jews, sometimes at their own risk, surprised the *Perushim*'s leadership, for it represented a new departure in Jewish-Christian relations. Previously, Christians had regarded the Jews as dispersed individuals, lacking any homeland, abandoned by God, and severely persecuted. All that suddenly changed: the Jews were no longer seen as a people persecuted for their failure to recognize Jesus as Messiah but as a nation with a divine destiny—a nation bearing the seeds of eschatological hopes, whose return to Zion and national resurgence would open a new period in world history. Without doubt, the radical change represented by these strange Christians, and their avowed and demonstrated desire to assist in the return to Zion, were seen by the *Perushim* as a sign of the approaching redemption.

Beyond that, the *Perushim* saw in the contemporary historical situation a revolutionary shift of messianic and theological significance. Two parallel processes were at work: the decline of the Ottoman Empire and, with it, of Islam's sway; and the growing strength of Christian western Europe, sympathetic to the return to Zion, as shown by the encounters of the *Perushim* with missionaries from England, Ireland, Scotland, Germany, Switzerland, and America, all of them working for the London Society. The *Perushim* saw these two developments as confirming that the redemptive process was being realized, for midrashic and kabbalistic sources told that the Edomites (i.e., the Christians) would triumph over the Ishmaelites (the Muslims) and help the Jewish nation realize its revival on its Land.[8] In general, they viewed Protestant Christianity as much closer to Judaism than the extremist and obscurantist Slavic Christianity that they knew from Russia, and as closer than the Catholic or Greek Orthodox Christianity that they encountered in the Land of Israel.

But it was not always possible to maintain equanimity toward the missionaries' efforts to proselytize and, in particular, toward their attacks on the Oral Torah. It seems likely that the leaders of the *Perushim* allowed only a narrow group—in effect, only the leadership itself—to be in close contact with the missionaries. During the 1820s, most of the dealings with the missionaries were conducted by Menaḥem Mendel of Shklov and Solomon Zalman Shapira; the meetings took place in the rabbis' own homes. One by one, others were forbidden to meet with the missionaries or enter into theological discussions with them. The 1820s also were a time when Jews needed the missionaries' support, but when their circumstances began to improve, with the appointment in 1829 of Rafael Farḥi as head of the government in Damascus,[9] the ban against the missionaries began to gain strength. The missionary Wolff reports that the local authorities were even trying to curry favor with the Jews, and, in the wake of the Jews' improved circumstances, the ban they had imposed on him was more perceptible. He expresses regret that the rabbis of Jerusalem—including Menaḥem Mendel of Shklov, Solomon Zalman Shapira, Isaac Abolafia, Moses Zakkut, and Rabbenu Meyuḥas—are no longer alive. Wolff attributes the changed Jewish attitude toward the missionaries to the departure of "the enlightened leadership," failing to recognize that the change is also attributable in large part to the simple fact that the Jews no longer needed the missionaries' protection.[10]

With Muhammad Ali's conquest of the Land and the granting of equal rights to the Christian and Jewish communities, the missionaries increased their activity. At the same time, the Jews drew further away from them, and Sefardim and Ashkenazim alike intensified the ban imposed on people who had any contact with them. The Jews' interest in forging ties with the missionaries in order to maintain contact with the European consuls in the coastal towns of Syria steadily diminished as Muhammad Ali consolidated his rule over the Land of Israel. In 1834, the missionary John Nicolayson took up residence in Jerusalem; and from that point on, missionary activity intensified, as did the conflicts between the missionaries and the Jewish community. The presence among the missionaries of the apostate physicians A. Gerstmann and M. P. Bergheim, who had worked devotedly during the harsh epidemic of 1838–1839, generated a deep divide within the *Perushim* over the attitude to be maintained toward them.[11] During the epidemic, Israel of Shklov declined to pronounce a ban against the two physicians, whose medical efforts were indispensable. The physicians tell that when the plague was rampant in Jerusalem, in November 1839, they cared for some fifty Jews a day; and when the apostate Bergheim himself took ill, the Jews prayed at the Western Wall for his recovery.[12]

During Muhammad Ali's reign, the relationships between the Jewish community of Jerusalem and the missionary delegation grew more complex. The role of the missionaries as "emissaries of England," assisting in the redemptive process, was largely preempted by the enlightened, "Christian" rule of Muhammad Ali. All eyes were fixed on the approaching year of 5600 (9 September 1839 to 27 September 1840); and the belief in that year as the beginning of the redemption was reinforced by the enlightened government, its religious liberalism, and its direct and indirect support for the growth of Jewish settlement in the Land of Israel. Over the course of the period, each side grew more confident of its position. While the missionaries by no means abandoned their efforts to draw the Jews into theological debates, one senses among them, as well, a tense anticipation of the fateful year. It was clear to them that as long as the year 5600 was approaching, no Jew would dare cross the lines, even Jews who were part of the group that, for reasons unknown to us, continued as late as 1839 to maintain close relations with the missionaries.

Tensely Anticipating the End of the Year 5600

As the year 5600 drew closer, the Jews' anticipation of the Messiah's arrival grew stronger, both in the Land of Israel and in the Diaspora. The journal of the Prussian ambassador to Italy states that in wide reaches of Germany and Poland, one sensed the expectation of an imminent event that would bring about the return of the Jews to the Land of Israel. This report is confirmed by other sources discerning a similar expectation amidst the Jews of the Near East and Asia.[13] Missionaries working in the vicinity of Lublin, Poland, similarly report, early in 1840, that a local group of Hasidim believed that year, corresponding to the year 5600 in the Jewish calendar, would see the coming of the Messiah.[14] Another source attributes similar expectations to the Jews of the Land of Israel: "Among the Jews of the Land of Israel, there exists a genuine expectation of the Messiah's arrival, and that belief is growing stronger and stronger."[15]

We have already seen that the strength of the *aliyah* movement provides a practical measure of the seriousness of the Jews' messianic expectations. According to missionary reports, the Jews immigrating to the Land say their purpose is to be there to await the anticipated Messiah. Echoes of an immigration movement in anticipation of 5600 can be heard in the official account of the British priest T. S. Grimshawe, who set out in the winter of 1839 on a tour of Izmir, Constantinople, Egypt, Syria, and the Land of Israel, where he remained until the spring of 1840. In his view, the very universality of the belief proves its derivation from the word of God; the belief gains strength as the year approaches; and it encompasses all Jews. The Jews' return to their land in the context of the belief in 5600 as the year of redemption seemed so realistic to him that he wanted to speak with Muhammad Ali about the practical problems likely to result, as if the return were already taking shape and could go forward immediately.[16] When he reached Cairo, Father Grimshawe, through the intervention of the British Consul General in Egypt, Colonel P. Campbell, sought an audience with Muhammad Ali. In the ensuing meeting, Grimshawe discussed the Jews' deep-seated desire to return to the Holy Land. Noting that many Jews had already immigrated, Grimshawe asked for clarification of Muhammad Ali's attitude toward them and whether he, as the highest authority in the Land of Israel at the time, would impede or facilitate the Jews' return. Muhammad Ali replied that he would treat the Jews' return to their Land on the practical rather than the speculative plane; on that basis, he would interpose no obstacle in their path, help them in every way, and provide them full protection, both for lives and for property.[17] Father Grimshawe asked as well whether Muhammad Ali would be willing, in view of the poor economic condition of many Jews, to grant them property in the Land of Israel, on the premise that he would then be able to collect taxes from them. Muhammad Ali responded that he had no properties in the Land of Israel that could be used in this manner; while he had dominion over everything, he had no personal right to any of the properties, which belonged to their owners. But, he added, if property owners were prepared to sell and Jews were prepared to buy, he would afford legal protection to the transactions and assure the Jews of all their rights to the purchased property.[18] Grimshawe adds that, in his presence, the Jews acknowledged that if the Messiah failed to arrive during 1840, it would prove that he had already appeared in the form of Jesus of Nazareth. In that regard, Grimshawe states: "One of the rabbis told him that at present, Jews could not come to the mission house or read the New Testament or even whisper the name of Jesus, but that if the Jewish Messiah did not appear in 1840, hundreds or thousands of Jews would become Christian."[19]

The belief that the coming of the Messiah was set to take place in 5600 is referred to in one of Ẓevi Hirsch Lehren's letters. On 25 October 1838, he writes to his confidant, Israel of Shklov, and inquires as to the exact date in 5600 on which the Messiah is to come:

> While I am speaking with him [i.e., you, using third person as a sign of respect], let me ask him, for he is erudite and knows the secrets of the pious Ga'on, may the memory of the righteous and holy endure to the life of the world to come, and it is not concealed that he wrote it . . . in *Sefer Sifra de-Ẓeni'uta* with his commentary, and adjured one who knows it not to disclose his secret, I thought his way in sanctity that the time was 5600 or thereafter, and knowing that many anticipated it would be the year 5600, he did not want to weaken their hope and ordered it be hidden; but your Torah Excellency knows to which part of the year he alluded.[20]

As the time approached, the spiritual tension associated with the expectation grew, and Lehren, unable any longer to contain himself, sought to learn from the last of the Vilna Ga'on's disciples what the exact time would be. The expectation of the Messiah's imminent arrival affected the personal aspirations of the believers. Lehren, for example, considered his present problems in the context of the future situation, in which the Messiah will resolve all interpersonal difficulties.

As a practical matter, anticipation of the Messiah's coming was the dominant motive for Lehren's intensely devoted activity on behalf of the Clerks' Organization, for it was not a sense of immediate personal fulfillment that led him to devote his life to working in that organization. His letters convey no such sense of fulfillment; on the contrary, they are replete with bitterness over the ingratitude of the *kolel*s in the Land of Israel, the attitude of disdain shown by the Nobles of Vilna toward his philanthropic efforts, and the reservations of the prominent European rabbis regarding his battle against building the *Ḥurvah*. Especially troubling to him was the baseless accusation leveled against him by Aaron Zelig Mann regarding financial irregularities and allegedly improper distribution of funds.[21] Confronted with such ingratitude for accomplishments so productive, any other person would have given up the role, but Lehren, though sometimes considering it, never carried out his threat to do so. Despite all the humiliation and torment he endured, he retained his firm belief in the Messiah's imminent arrival, in the year 5600, and in his own ensuing vindication. Evidently, Lehren drew the fortitude to continue at his job from his belief that the Messiah himself, in all his glory, would soon intervene in the dispute and raise him from indignity. On 7 December 1838, he writes to Israel of Shklov about his dispute with Solomon Hirschell: "Although I am unworthy to approach the King Messiah, I nevertheless am confident that regarding the Land of Israel, I am more in the right than the rabbi of London, may the Merciful One protect and bless him; and our righteous Messiah will neither favor persons nor suppress the truth, which now is lacking."[22] His reward from the Messiah for his endeavors on behalf of the Land of Israel serves as a principal impetus for his devotion to his task.

This aspiration is expressed primarily through Lehren's feelings of jealousy toward Montefiore. In a letter in which he disparages Montefiore's work on behalf of the Land of Israel in comparison with his own, Lehren makes no effort to conceal his jealousy, crying out: "And how can he presume to inscribe [the name] 'Jerusalem' on his seal! And when our righteous Messiah comes, speedily in our days, we will then see whom he allows to carry the flag of Jerusalem."[23] He is envious even of Montefiore's work on behalf of the Land of Israel, lest it entitle him to the reward from the Messiah that Lehren himself craves. When he rebukes Montefiore for "seeming to raise himself to rule and be a king of Jerusalem,"[24] he says, "I await God each day, and may our righteous Messiah come speedily and in our days, amen, so they will not need any of his [Montefiore's] beneficence."[25] Lehren says he will do more good than Montefiore, "and God will grant me the privilege of immigrating to the Land of Israel may it be built and established speedily and in our days."[26] Lehren claims he does not envy Montefiore's glory but only "that he went up to the Land of Israel."[27] At the end of 1836 or early in 1837, when he heard a rumor that Montefiore planned to travel to the Land of Israel for a period of two years, Lehren became concerned that this regal, pompous figure would upstage him and seize his rightful place of honor, by the Messiah's side. Claiming that Montefiore is driven solely by an appetite for honor and that his only goal is to be called "Prince of the Land of Israel" or "Prince of Jerusalem," Lehren writes: "Having already arrogantly made himself a princely seal, which contains the image of a lion holding a flag on which is inscribed 'Jerusalem,' he therefore decided to tarry [in the Land of Israel] for so long [two years] . . . and I cannot understand why, if his intentions are only for the sake of Heaven, to walk four cubits in the Land of Israel, and even if his intention pertains as well to the coming of the Messiah, speedily, amen, why he needs two years."[28] No doubt, it is Montefiore's plan to remain in the Land of Israel during the course of the year 5600 that arouses Lehren's envy. Not only did he himself believe in the Messiah's coming in 5600; he must have been certain as well that even Montefiore, whom he regarded as removed from proper Judaism and whom he termed "a boor," likewise awaited the Messiah's arrival in 5600. Lehren wanted to be at the scene of the action when the Messiah came, something expected to happen upon the departure of the sabbatical year—that is, at the festival of Sukkot.[29] At the start of 5600, Lehren wrote to Rabbi Moses Sofer of Pressburg: "And my eyes look heavenward; may this year be a year of redemption and salvation, and we will go up to Zion in song, and there we will serve God in unison, and we peruse His Torah day and night, and in His service we shall always rejoice, and at the festival of ingathering [Sukkot] there will be gathered to Him joy and delight."[30]

It is easy to picture the feelings of anticipation and spiritual tension that bore on Lehren during the course of the year 5600. As the "departure of the sabbatical year" of 5600 approached, he ceased to do his usual work. The copy file of letters contains not a single entry between 17 September and 22 October 1840, a gap unparalleled in all the volumes of the Clerks' Organization correspondence.[31] This silence provides evidence for the powerful emotional tension to which Lehren was subject during those fateful days. It is fair to assume that Lehren, and perhaps his colleagues as well, were engaged in final preparations for greeting the Messiah: self-mortification, prayer, and study of Torah and Kabbalah.

We have no other personal descriptions of how the tense messianic expectations affected the many believers during the course of the year 5600. Accordingly, Lehren's personal beliefs and emotions, which make a statement unique in the original literature of the period, can serve as a model for many others. It may also be assumed that in the Land of Israel, the arena in which the expected events were to be played out, the tense feelings of anticipation were even more powerful than in the Diaspora.

The Damascus Blood Libel

With the harsh epidemics having ended, it appeared that the Jewish community would be able to disengage from the missionary presence in the Land of Israel, for it no longer had any need for the missionaries' medical assistance or for their intervention or protection. But right in the middle of the year 5600, on 3 March 1840, the Damascus blood libel burst forth on the scene. The Jerusalem *yishuv* was dumbstruck. The atmosphere of a pogrom overtook the city, and the Jews of Jerusalem feared to go out, lest they be attacked by the Greek Christians or the Muslims.[32] During this difficult time, the Jews drew help and encouragement from their only true friends—the men of the mission led by Nicolayson. On 16–17 March, the leadership of the Jerusalem *yishuv* approached Nicolayson and G. W. Pieritz, a missionary convert from Judaism, and it was decided that Pieritz would travel to Damascus with one of the rabbis in order to refute the claims that Jews use Christian blood for ritual purposes on Passover.[33]

On 18 March, Pieritz set out for Damascus. Several rabbis wanted to accompany him to the city line, but Nicolayson, concerned about attracting attention, advised against it.[34] Pieritz spent several months in Damascus, and his defense of the Jews was published in the local press.[35] In addition to Pieritz's assignment, it was decided as well that Isaac, the son of Solomon Pach, would set out for Alexandria bearing a letter of recommendation from Nicolayson, in which the missionary conclusively refuted the libel.[36] It appears that Isaac Pach was accompanied by Isaiah Bardacky and Ḥayyim Nissim Abolafia.[37]

In the aftermath of the Damascus libel, the tie between the London Society's mission and the leadership of the Jewish community grew stronger. Confirmation of that development can be found in Nicolayson's account of a meeting between the missionaries and the leadership of the *yishuv* to consider how to react to the libel: at the meeting, the seat next to his was occupied by Rafael Navon, who had only recently threatened him that the Jews would destroy the Christian church that had been under construction for a month.[38] In another report, Nicolayson tells of the changed attitude of Jerusalem's Sefardic rabbis toward the missionaries. He writes that the Sefardic rabbis of Jerusalem criticized their colleagues in Tiberias for having expelled the Jewish apostate Simḥon from their city, and in the course of their complaint, they directed them to annul the ban that had been decreed against the missionaries who had "stepped into the breach" during the trying times of the Damascus libel. The statement is a not-very-veiled allusion to the defense mounted by Pieritz in Damascus.[39] Nicolayson adds, however, that while Isaiah Bardacky was likewise angered by what the rabbis of Tiberias had done, he nevertheless declined to add his signature to the letter from the Sefardic chief rabbi, Jonah Navon, and Rafael Navon, lest his adversaries in the Jerusalem *yishuv* turn that to their advantage.[40]

What led the Jews to once again accept help from the missionaries, from whom they had only recently tried to disengage themselves? It appears that by taking the initiative to defend the Jews against a libel couched in religious terms, the missionaries renewed the Jews' perception of their unique quality as facilitators of the *yishuv*'s continued existence. The missionaries themselves were no doubt happy to take advantage of the opportunity they had been given to renew their relations with the Jews and revive the dialogue between them, though there is no basis for questioning their sincerity in rising to the Jews' defense.

Mission Preparations for the End of the Year 5600

From the London Society's viewpoint, the Jews' return to their Land in the context of their belief in 5600 provided a rare opportunity to convert them right in the Holy Land. The missionaries saw the Jews' disengagement from them as only temporary and tried to prepare for the coming events.

In that spirit, Nicolayson carried on energetically. As early as the start of 1835, he concluded that Jerusalem needed a church in which Jews could pray without concern about idolatrous overtones, such as those associated with Catholic statuary. In addition, he wanted to attract Jews by conducting worship services in Hebrew. On 12 April 1836, Nicolayson was called to London to consider plans for building such a church. The mission asked the British government to involve its embassy in Egypt in an effort to secure from Muhammad Ali a *firman* authorizing acquisition of a parcel of land for the church and its construction.[41] In August 1837, en route back to the Land of Israel, Nicolayson stopped in Alexandria to deal with the technical aspects of the project;[42] and on 22 July 1838, daily prayer in Hebrew was instituted for the first time in one of the structures Nicolayson had build on the parcel of land he had acquired.[43] On 10 February 1840, the cornerstone was set for the English church to be built on the site.[44] In the meantime, paralleling the efforts to build the church (which encountered numerous obstacles), the missionary delegation in Jerusalem was reinforced in response to Nicolayson's special request. By 1838, it included four converts from Judaism: Levi, Pieritz, and the physicians A. Gerstmann and M. P. Bergheim.[45]

Christians affiliated with the Anglican Church also felt increasing tension as the year 5600 approached. We learn of it from a London Society report on an extraordinary event: on Yom Kippur in the year 5600 (18 September 1839), several hundred Anglican Christians gathered in Liverpool for a special prayer service whose principle feature was the invocation of God's mercy on His people the Jews. The press described that Yom Kippur as a unique day, unparalleled since the Jews had been exiled from their Land—a day on which Christians joined with Jews in anticipating the coming of the Messiah. But the reports also quoted statements by Jews that if their Messiah did not come during 5600, they would recognize Jesus as the Messiah.[46]

The passing of the year 5600 marked a historic turning point in the annals of the Land of Israel. At the end of 1840, Muhammad Ali was removed from his post, and his enlightened reign, seen by many Jews as evidence for the approaching redemption, came to an end. In November 1841, at discussions held in England by the European powers regarding the future of the Land of Israel, it was suggested that the Jewish convert Michael Solomon Alexander be sent to Jerusalem as Anglican bishop. The proposal was no doubt a political move, with the purpose of intensifying Anglo-Prussian involvement in all the affairs of the Ottoman Empire. But the appointment as bishop specifically of someone with Jewish origins had missionary purposes as well, in view of the renewed prospects for success in missionary work among the Jews.[47]

The British foreign minister, Lord Palmerston, negotiated with the Prussian government and king about the prospect of sending a joint Anglo-Prussian religious mission to the Land of Israel; it would be centered in Jerusalem and have jurisdiction over nearby lands as well, such as Egypt and Syria. To ensure a proper reception in Jerusalem, the British contacted the Turkish sultan, hoping to clear the way for establishment of the Protestant church on Mount Zion that Nicolayson had begun working toward during Muhammad Ali's reign. On 7 November 1841, Michael Solomon Alexander, professor of Hebrew literature at Kings College, London, was appointed bishop of the English and Irish church in Jerusalem.[48] In attendance at his investiture were the leaders of the Anglican Church, representatives of the king of Prussia, the British ambassador to Constantinople, Lord Ashley, and William Gladstone. Queen Victoria issued a special royal decree allowing the Anglican Church to appoint a bishop whose see would be beyond the borders of England,[49] and the British government put a large warship at the disposal of the entourage escorting Bishop Alexander to Jaffa.[50] On 21 January 1842, the group reached Jerusalem and the bishop was solemnly received by the city's governor and Protestant community.[51]

There are different versions of the Jews' reaction to Bishop Alexander's arrival. Nicolayson writes in his journal that the Jews were pleased that one of their number had attained so high a rank in the English church. But his comments suggest as well that the Jews did not regard his coming to Jerusalem favorably.[52]

The mission placed very high hopes in the establishment of the Jerusalem bishopric. One priest, Father Parmental, explained that a bishopric was being established in a place where there were no believers because Jerusalem is nonetheless a place of immense importance. And while Jerusalem has only five thousand Jews, he continued, it could be expected that a bishop of Jewish origin would exercise great influence on the Jews dispersed throughout the world for seventeen hundred years. In the image of a bishop of Jewish origin, Parmental suggested, the Jewish people would again find a symbol of national revival, while the church would find itself returning to the source of its life. He saw this extraordinary event as a concrete expression of the prophecy of the return to Zion and as fulfillment of the prophetic promise that "kings shall be your foster-fathers" [Isa. 49:23].[53]

At the investiture, the clergy expressed the view that appointing a Christian of Jewish origin to serve as the shepherd of Israel is an event unparalleled since the destruction of Jerusalem and will initiate a new era in the history of the Jewish people and the Christian church. Their hopes and expectations for the appointment can be summed up as follows: The friends of the Jewish people hope, pray, and are prepared to work to ensure that Bishop Alexander's mission results not merely in the conversion of isolated Jews but in the revival of the Jewish nation and of "the Jewish Church"; they likewise express the hope that the event will unite the hearts of the western Christian church with those of its eastern sister.[54]

On 23 November 1841, a farewell gathering for Bishop Alexander was held in London. One of the speakers at the occasion declared that the appointment proved the truth of Scripture, for Jerusalem rather than Rome was the focus of Christian faith and the western Church was not destined to be the center of Christianity. Before our very eyes, he continued, we see the fulfillment of the verse "you shall arise and have mercy on Zion" [Ps. 102:14]; and we are confident that God's house of prayer in Jerusalem will be a house of prayer for all nations.[55] In his response, Bishop Alexander said his appointment was indeed the most important appointment in the history of the Christian church and that he was fortunate to return to the land of his ancestors.[56]

Given such assessments of the situation, the English clergy were united in the view that they had to be prepared for the coming events so that the opportunity would not be lost. They believed Divine Providence had brought about a historic revolution by inclining the hearts of kings and statesmen to support the important work of restoring the nation of Israel to the bosom of the Christian faith. God had not called out to his believers in this way since the Persian King Cyrus permitted his people to provide gold and silver to assist the Jews returning to Jerusalem from the Babylonian Exile.[57] In assessing the event's importance, they noted the unusual fact that the sovereigns of England and Prussia had joined forces in returning a Jewish bishop to the land of his ancestors. This one-time chance given by God, they said, must not be lost. God must be thanked for the opportunity and believers must redouble their efforts to act as partners; apathy or rejection would be considered ingratitude to the Creator of all. The sovereigns have done their part of the job, they added, and now it is up to the English public to play its part in supporting the effort.[58]

Crisis of Faith Within the Jewish Community

As long as the year 5600 had not yet ended, the Jews maintained their faith in it as the year of the Messiah's coming. They debated with the missionaries self-confidently, from what they sensed to be a position of strength, and that stance accounts as well for their leadership's accommodationist attitude toward the missionaries. But when reality slapped the Jews in the face—the year 5600 ended without the Messiah's appearance—they lost their principal argument, their faith's defensive weaponry, and they were left vulnerable to the missionaries' attacks and arguments. Moreover, feelings of disappointment, frustration, and remorse began to fill the vacuum left in their hearts by the loss of hope and anticipation. Not everyone, of course, had agreed that the Messiah would come in 5600, and some viewed the redemption as a gradual, on-going process; but even they expected an event that would clearly herald the start of the time of redemption. With the passing of 5600, the ending of Muhammad Ali's enlightened reign, and the dismal memory of the Damascus blood libel a continuing presence, it became clear that this expected year of divine visitation would be as much of a disappointment as had been the earlier ones of 4856 (1096) and 5408 (1648). Many could not withstand the disheartening situation and continue in the old ways of life; and one Christian traveler appears to have accurately portrayed the Jews' spiritual perplexity, as their sincere wish to return to the land of their fathers and their belief that the time of their redemption was near gave way to a sense of having erred. Several rabbis did not hesitate to so declare, he noted, and many have recently converted.[59] In this situation, the English missionary presence posed a real threat to the Jews, and it is not surprising that from this point out, their attitude toward the mission became hardened and uncompromising. Indeed, it is clear from post-1840 reports by the missionary Ewald that the Messiah's failure to appear became a central argument in the missionaries' debates with the Jews. The missionaries used it to prove that the talmudic statements and kabbalistic traditions on which the Jews had relied were not reliable, and they succeeded in winning over several dozen members of Jerusalem's Jewish community.[60] In 1841, the missionary press tells of the agitation and sense of crisis afflicting the Jews in various lands in the wake of the dashed messianic expectations. In the writers' judgment, the disappointment experienced by the Jews could affect them in one of two ways: it could lead them to cling even more firmly to traditional Jewish beliefs and reject Christianity even more forcefully, or it could lead them to embrace the Christian alternative. By approaching the Jews in a suitable manner at this time of crisis, the writers say, the church can influence the choice they make. Reports such as these come from St. Petersburg, Constantinople, Izmir, and Persia.[61]

As noted, the London Society focused its attention specifically on Jerusalem. From their perspective, the conversion of the Jews in Jerusalem would be more than an isolated event; it would be an important symbol. Some 1800 years earlier, the Jews of Jerusalem had rejected Jesus as Messiah, and there could be no greater success now than bringing about the Jews' reversal of that decision, and their acknowledgement of Jesus as Messiah, within Jerusalem itself. In fact, two sages of the Jerusalem *Perushim* actually converted in 1843.

That story begins as early as 1839, when we hear of progressively stronger ties between the missionaries and three sages of the *Perushim*: Eliezer Luria (a second cousin of David Luria—a leading Lithuanian rabbi—and a third cousin of Shemariah Luria, the son-in-law of Hillel of Shklov); Benjamin Goldberg; and Abraham Nisan Walfin (the brother of David Walfin, a trustee of the *kolel* of the *Perushim* and son-in-law of Menaḥem Mendel of Shklov.)[62] The missionaries swooped down on the three as on the most precious of spoils.

The events leading up to the conversions are recounted in very dramatic terms, with every detail recorded in the missionaries' journals. The three rabbis did not reach their decision overnight; their inner struggle went on for more than three years, and, in the end, one of them, Abraham Nisan Walfin, backed out at the last minute. It is fair to assume that they were influenced by the difficult times that preceded 5600 and that the suffering wreaked by the plagues and famine in Jerusalem during 1838 and 1839 could have sown doubt and thoughts of conversion in their minds. Nor can one disregard the possibility that the missionaries' dedication and self-sacrifice during the epidemics had a profound effect on them; it may even be that the three rabbis themselves were saved during the epidemic by the missionary medical people. But there can be no doubt that their decision to take the fateful step was made against the background of the final crisis in the wake of the Messiah's failure to appear in 5600.[63] Support for firming-up that decision came from the missionary delegation headed by the convert Bishop Alexander, who reached Jerusalem at the start of 1842. A principal goal of that delegation was to justify the hopes that had been placed in it by bringing about the conversion of these three rabbis at any price.

Few Jewish sources tell of conversions to Christianity resulting from the crisis of 5600; the reasons for that silence are natural and easily understandable. Publicizing the phenomenon could lead the weak or those already so inclined to take a similar step; concealing it, in contrast, would help make it less likely that others would be encouraged to do so. Nevertheless, some rabbis were determined to grapple with the question of faith in the Messiah and the time of divine visitation, and they dared to note in their publications, by implication, that they were writing in order to prevent additional conversions and to bolster faith in redemption by means of a new understanding of the subject and of the End-time. We have seen that Moses Turgeman in his essay *Pi Mosheh* sought to ward off conversions to Christianity.[64] In his book *Oholei Yehudah*, published in Jerusalem in 1843, R. Judah ben R. Solomon ha-Kohen similarly argued that people had erred in betting everything on 5600 being the fateful year of the Messiah's coming. They simply misunderstood the statements attributed to Rabbi Simeon bar Yoḥai in the *Zohar*, and their faulty understanding was their downfall, leading to apostasy:

> And behold, I have seen fit to teach understanding to the people, who have gone astray in [their understanding of] the words of the divine *tanna*, that is, the holy Rabbi Simeon bar Yoḥai, may his merit protect us, amen. . . . They have sought to reveal [the time of] the End . . . and some of our people erred in the vision . . . and they trusted, in accord with their limited understanding, in the year 600, wandering as blind men in the streets [cf. Lam. 4:14], saying God does not see and, God forbid, that there is no Messiah for Israel. . . . But they erred in thinking the statement referred to the coming of the Messiah and now that they see the time has passed, by reason of our many sins, some of them have apostatized.[65]

We hear of a causal relationship between the crisis of faith and the conversions in an account by Aviezer of Ticktin:

> And now we come to resolve and explain the words of the holy *Zohar, Vayeira* 117 . . . regarding why what is written there explicitly with respect to the year 5600 was not realized . . . for his meaning is explicit, that [the Messiah] was supposed to come in the six hundredth year of the sixth millennium . . . and, if so—why does our Messiah delay [*boshesh*], for six [i.e., 5600] has already come [*ba shesh*]? And some people have become heretical on account of this, having seen that six has come [*ba shesh*], that is, the year 5600, and he [the Messiah] has not come, they said he never will come.[66]

Attempting to play down the severity of the conversion problem, Aviezer claims that the people who converted were descendants of the "mixed multitude" who left Egypt with the Israelites and were responsible for making the golden calf in the desert. Using a homiletical method that treats everything written in the Torah as open to contemporary explication, he goes on to interpret the verses: " 'The people saw that Moses delayed [*boshesh*] in descending from the mountain' [Exod. 32:1]—the mixed multitude said that since six hours have already come [*ba shesh*] and he [Moses] has not come, he never will come. And therefore they said to Aaron, 'Arise, make us a god' [ibid.] and the holy Torah certainly means to allude to those people of this current generation who speak arrogantly, disparaging and reviling with regard to six [5600]."[67]

A further account in a Jewish source that leaves no doubt regarding the tragic events appears in the "Sick Visitation Register" (*Pinqas Biqqur Ḥolim*) of the *Perushim*'s *kolel*, in which the earliest entry dates from 1837. In the register, which is written on parchment and contains several listings of the society's members, the names of the two converts are blotted out; next to them appears an abbreviation for the phrase "may his name and memory be erased; he is subject to a ban."[68] Benjamin Goldberg's name is blotted out by a simple pen stroke, and it can be easily read; but the name of Eliezer Luria "the wayward" seems to have been furiously scratched out—silent testimony to the tumultuous events that followed on the crisis of faith.

9

Retreat from the Idea of "Redemption Through Return to Zion"

The believers in the redemption of Israel will believe with perfect faith, in accordance with our trustworthy tradition, that it will take place in a miraculous and wondrous manner and that He will show us wonders as when we went out from Egypt and [it will be brought about] by means of Torah, repentance, and charity. . . . "Unless the Lord builds the house, its builders labor on it in vain" [Ps. 127:1]; in vain do you rise early, before sunrise to eat unripe fruit, before the time when God will hasten.

Jacob Sapir, *Ha-Levanon*

Struggle Against the Mission

The Messiah's failure to appear in 5600 did more than frustrate an intense hope. For many, it aroused disbelief in one of Judaism's thirteen principles of faith, and it was poised to weaken faith in Judaism in general. Rabbis, leaders, and ordinary Jews were compelled to confront pressing questions: Had the idea of the Messiah's coming in 5600 been a false belief all along? If not, why did the son of David delay his coming? Could there have been a calculation error, such that the indicated year was something other than 5600? Or, perhaps, were all efforts to reckon the End fundamentally flawed?

To prevent the missionaries from taking advantage of the spreading crisis of faith—or, at least, to limit as far as possible their ability to do so—the Jewish leadership hardened its stance regarding all of the missionaries' activities. To curtail contact with them, the Jewish leadership in some places imposed a ban on any Jew who dared to maintain ties with the missionaries or accept any help whatsoever from them.

In their reports, the missionaries include their success stories side by side with accounts of the hardened Jewish position. A report submitted on 29 April 1841 tells of a ban imposed by the *Ḥakham Bashi* (Chief Rabbi) of Constantinople against anyone who sent his children to the local missionary school or who accepted medical treatment from the missionary physicians in that city.[1] In Izmir as well, the Jewish leadership threatened prohibition and ban against Jews who maintained contact with the missionaries.[2] The communal leaders complained to the Ottoman authorities that the missionaries were promising British passports to anyone who would convert to Christianity, thereby impairing the welfare of the local community.[3] Similar reports on rabbinic bans and hard-line positions against anyone maintaining contact with the missionaries come from Galicia.[4]

But bans alone could not prevail against the mission's dangerous influence. It was necessary as well to reinforce the basic beliefs of the Jews who were so devastated by the debacle of 5600 as to be at risk of being impelled by it to embrace Christianity. The communal rabbis presumably worked hard at it, preaching to strengthen the weak and raise their spirits and explaining why the Messiah did not make his anticipated appearance. At the same time, withdrawal from contact and debate with missionaries did not obviate efforts to refute the substantive claims they were pressing on the basis of the Messiah's failure to appear when expected, which they cited to challenge the fundamentals of Jewish belief and try to steer it toward accepting Jesus as Messiah. It was clear that the longer people had to wait for acceptable explanations of the confusing turn of events, the more intense their crisis of faith was likely to become. The needs of the hour gave rise, therefore, to several works on the subject, some seeking to bolster belief in the fundamentals of Judaism, some explaining the Messiah's failure to appear, some holding out further hope for redemption in the near future, and some providing guidance to Jews in their dealings with the missionaries. The very composition of books like these, and the reprinting of older works on such subjects, attest to the need for outward-looking defense against the missionaries and for inward-looking reinforcement of belief.

One such reprinted book is *Ḥizzuq Emunah* (Strengthening Belief), by the Karaite Isaac ben Abraham of Troki. The book was originally written in 1681 and reprinted in 1717; thereafter, 128 years elapsed before its new printing in 1845 in Jerusalem at the Israel Baeck press, after a rare manuscript was rushed to the Land of Israel by Moses Montefiore to be available to contest the missionaries' claims on ideological grounds.[5] Thereafter, the book was repeatedly reprinted, in 1846, 1850, 1856, 1865, and 1873; evidently, the great demand for it, which had been renewed by the crisis of 5600, did not quickly subside, and the post-1840 crisis of faith continued for several long years.

A similar purpose underlay the 1847 publication in Metz of the manuscript *Kur Miẓraf ha-Emunot u-Mar'eh ha-Emet* (The Crucible That Refines Beliefs and Shows the Truth).[6] The work, written in 1695 by Isaac Lopes, similarly came to be printed only in the wake of the crisis of 5600 and the threat by the missionaries. The publisher writes as follows:

> And since only recently troubles increased for our brethren in distant lands, especially those dwelling in the land of delight [the Land of Israel], the cities of the East, as is known from the letters that have come from the Land of Israel. . . . But this did not sufficiently demean them to satisfy the enemies of our faith . . . for they added torments of the spirit to torments of the body, and the emissaries called "missionaries" who were sent from various nations come to these lands to capture our brethren in their nets, which they set to ensnare their feet. . . . And when they learned of this pressure [our brethren] were under, they thought to turn them away from the faith of their fathers.[7]

Also printed in Jerusalem during this time was *Mishmeret ha-Berit* (Preservation of the Covenant),[8] one of the most practical of these books. Its author, Aviezer of Ticktin, set out to guide the Jewish masses in steering clear of the missionaries' nets. On the one hand, he tried to frame for the masses, simply and logically, a set of winning arguments with which they could refute the claims of their opponents; on the other hand, he set rules for halakhic behavior in the new environment. In the author's words, the purpose of the book is implied in its name: "And I have called this book . . . *Mishmeret ha-Berit* because in accordance with what it says, the words of the Torah covenant are preserved from those who slander it and say that God regretted the covenant of his Torah and gave a new covenant."[9]

Since one of the missionaries' techniques for challenging the truth of Judaism was to cast aspersions on the reliability of the Oral Torah, Aviezer of Ticktin attempts to refute that line of argument. He presents the Oral Torah as a matter of pure reason and uses simple language to prove its superiority. Those caught up in heresy, he claims, are the unlearned, who are ill-equipped to confront the missionaries' arguments. In order to make sense to everyone, he avoids reliance on Kabbalah, wordplay, or numerology: "I took care not to cite any statements by our sages of blessed memory that are not straightforward . . . so my statements will not resemble the statements of those who go astray. . . . Rather, I began by setting things out in accordance with logic and reason, and only after did I cite the words of the *gemara*."[10] He disputes those who argue that the Written Torah is not from Heaven, that the sages invented the Oral Torah themselves, and that the words of the Torah should be understood in accord with their simple meaning and are not laden with the allusions the sages found in them.

In our harsh times, Aviezer believes, every Jew must know and understand all the passages in the Torah that the missionaries rely on to prove the truth of Christianity; he must be persuaded in his innermost being of the malice of their interpretations; and he will thereby be able to stand his ground in debating with them. He warns against the missionaries who claim that they intend only to show the Jews the true religion, seeing that claim as a satanic effort to drive a wedge between the Jewish nation and the Holy One Blessed Be He.[11] Acting cautiously, the missionaries do not attack Judaism's firmly established foundations; such an attack would naturally enough arouse strong opposition among the Jews. Instead, they slice away at supposedly "minor" matters, such as the rabbinically imposed obligations related to covering the head. Aviezer is concerned that such attacks could have a severe effect, for they could lead to challenges to other established elements of Judaism; he therefore sets out to defend the commandment to cover one's head, finding that it is derived from the Torah itself.[12]

Because the era is that of the Messiah's footsteps, the trial the nation is enduring is particularly harsh: "Be strong and fortify your pure hearts to accept the yoke of the Torah's glory. And this period is a time of increased testing associated with the days when, because of our many sins, the crown of our glory has fallen from the heavenly heights to the depths of the earth . . . when all mock its laws and its sages, and the esteem for our position is reduced . . . and not only that, but the kings and princes in whose shadow we sit regard us and our Torah as foul-smelling."[13] In his view, the mission concentrates its efforts on Jerusalem precisely because of the city's special sanctity: "And let no person wonder why impurity and even malignant *ẓara'at* [biblical "leprosy"; an emblem of impurity] reside and are to be found in Israel, the holy nation, more than in all the other nations. Know, that in the place of holiness, there the impurity is to be found. For the husks are drawn to the holiness to draw succor from them, for it is their principal source of vitality, just as Jerusalem the holy city is more sanctified than all other lands."[14] Relying on the sages' enactments against the sectarians of their day, he says: "And if they issued such enactments in earlier times, how much more so is it proper to take counsel and act resourcefully under the pressure of these difficult times . . . when their [the missionaries'] barking flares and burns, scorching people residing near them who do not know the precious worth of the Torah."[15]

The very writing of a book on this unique subject, and its printing and dissemination, were extraordinary steps, intended to serve as a barricade against Jews being caught in the missionaries' net. But Aviezer of Ticktin sensed as well a need to set explicit rules of conduct. At the end of his book, in a section entitled "The Ways of the Heretics," he sets rules of conduct to guide the Jews of Jerusalem in the threatening new environment—an environment that did not exist before the missionaries began their efforts in Jerusalem in the early 1830s and intensified them in the mid-1840s. The rules, based primarily on the talmudic tractate of *Avodah Zarah* (which deals with issues of idolatry), reflect the actual circumstances of the time the book was written and the struggles of the *yishuv* in Jerusalem. In Rule (*Halakhah*) 11, for example, Aviezer determines that it is forbidden to accept charity from the missionaries, "but if he is needy, it is possible to accept in private, and likewise [when] he has nothing with which to sustain his life [it is permitted] . . . but one who guards his soul will distance himself from them even in time of need for the preservation of life."[16] So, too, Rule 12, which forbids accepting medical treatment from the missionaries, "but in private, where there is no possibility of being served by a Jewish physician, it is permitted."[17]

Bolstering Faith by Adjusting the End-Date

But books such as the foregoing could not by themselves fully dispel the widespread bewilderment over the dashed messianic expectations. It was necessary to respond as well to the many people whose reactions were not so extreme as to entail the prospect of conversion but who nevertheless were profoundly despondent because their hopes had been deferred to the distant future. Another timely book by Aviezer of Ticktin, titled *Sha'arei Ẓedeq le-Zera Yiẓḥaq* (Gates of Righteousness),[18] written before his *Mishmeret ha-Berit*, represents an effort to defer the belief in 5600 to the year 5606 or some later time. The book is addressed primarily to the scholarly class:

> From the fiery sparks of the flame of God, there burned within me love and comfort for the children of Israel, Zion, and Jerusalem; and in order to raise the *shekhinah* from the dust, they impelled me to bring my thoughts to light. . . .[19] And for this I took my life in my hands to determine a specific estimate [of the End-date] . . . to speak of matters pertaining to the subject of our future redemption, speedily and in our days, and I had no fear that people might say, "See, this is something new, never before done, for from the day Israel was exiled from its Land, there has not been a person confident enough to issue from his heart to his mouth words related to eternal mysteries."[20]

Because of his concern that the crisis of 5600 could seriously injure Judaism, Aviezer of Ticktin determined to locate the center of the fire raging primarily within the Jerusalem community and to extinguish it. He was not certain that he could bring about the return and repentance of those who already had been ensnared by the missionaries, but he hoped his essay could prevent others from joining them. To that end, it was necessary to raise their spirits and bolster their Jewish faith, and he therefore defended the authenticity of the *Zohar*: "In order to show the meaning of the teachings of Rabbi Simeon bar Yoḥai, so that the words he wrote with regard to the year 5600 will be faithfully on our lips, as proper and true."[21] He tried both to prove that the belief in 5600 was justified and to strengthen the faith of those in despair over its failure to materialize. Assembling an elaborate array of proofs to confirm that the belief in 5600 had been warranted, he finds a single error: 5600 was the year in which the process of redemption would begin, but it would not be completed until 5606. The five intervening years were to be years of testing and could therefore be expected to be difficult for Israel. He bases his analysis on elemental ideas of Lurianic Kabbalah and on numerous wordplays and numerologies; and when he finds a numerology thought to allude to the year 5600 written with the thousands figure (represented by the letters *h-t-r*), he reinterprets it as alluding to the year 5605, written without the thousands figure (represented by the same letters rearranged as *t-r-h*).

Deferring the date of redemption is a clear reaction to the Messiah's failure to appear in 5600 and a transparent ploy to overcome the disappointment, maintain the sense of anticipation, and head off the unfolding crisis at all costs. A striking example is the treatment of the passages in Song of Songs that the Vilna Ga'on's school had read as the song of the future redemption. On the verse "The flowers appear on the earth; the time of singing has come and the voice of the turtledove is heard in our land" (Song of Songs 2:12) Aviezer of Ticktin says: "This was only on high, but it has not yet come about below. . . . 'The flowers appear on the earth' refers to the start of the budding, but the flowering still waits in the upper regions, and human beings know nothing of it. But 'the voice of the turtledove [*ha-tor*, spelled *h-t-w-r*] is heard in our land' means that when the year *h-t-w-r* [5606], that is, five thousand [*h*]and 606 [*t-w-r*], [arrives], then it will be heard in this our land as well."[22]

Aviezer of Ticktin explicitly states that all the earlier times of visitation referred to in the *Zohar* were fundamentally true, but the people of the generation failed to repent and therefore did not merit the scheduled redemption. He endorses efforts by sages to determine the End and abrogates any prohibitions on End-reckonings, for even the early authorities knew well that it sometimes is necessary to raise the nation's spirits and avoid allowing it to despair of the redemption: "rather, they should see the time of redemption as near."[23] Accordingly, the path he takes is absolutely legitimate, for its immediate goal is reviving the nation's spirit. The anticipation of 5600 involved human error, and its frustration should not be tied, God forbid, to a breakdown of God's world order. Aviezer even hints at the end of his book that the redemption might come not in 5606 but in 5612, "corresponding to the 612th of the 613 commandments, the commandment of *haqhel* [gathering the nation every seven years to hear the Torah read]"[24]; or in the year 5613—"in the year [5]613 a person will cast away his idols of silver and gold . . . and engage in God's Torah"[25]—or in [5]620 [*t-r-k*], "which is [an anagram of] the word "crown" [*k-t-r*], and that is the secret of the verse "and he placed a royal crown on her head" [Esth. 2:17]."[26]

A report by the missionary Ewald conveys echoes of the effort to set up "signposts of hope" for a distressed nation. In depicting a debate with a rabbi—a rare event during this period—Ewald recounts that the rabbi argued that the *Zohar* had indeed set 5600 as the year in which the Messiah would arrive, but that is not the exclusive time of visitation; in each generation, the great sages of Israel identified times at which the Messiah was destined to come, and his failure to meet the expectation was not seen as impugning in any way the basics of their belief. The nation's leaders, that rabbi went on to explain, had to sustain the people with hope that the Messiah's coming was imminent and would take place during their very lifetimes; without such hope, the Jews could not withstand the terrible suffering of the Exile and might abandon the Jewish religion. But, the rabbi stressed, no man in fact knows for sure the time of the Messiah's coming.[27] Ewald tells of another explanation of the Messiah's failure to come that he heard from four Hebron rabbis, whom he met in the Jerusalem home of Joseph Amazlag. They argued that the Messiah was in fact meant to come at the anticipated time, but the nation's sins delayed his coming. The most prominent of the four added that we now do not know when the Messiah will come, for God has revealed that mystery to no one.[28]

Critique of the Activist Approach

The Messiah's failure to arrive at the expected time reignited the old disputes over the mechanics of redemption. One emergent group within the *kolel* began to retreat from the accepted notion of hastening the redemption through construction and other action. This group found its voice in Aviezer of Ticktin, who incisively presented the position in his book *Sha'arei Ẓedeq le-Zera Yiẓḥaq*. But the apologetic chord he struck in the first half of the book—the year 5600 had indeed been a "time of visitation," and though it failed, other times of grace lay in the future—was insufficiently stirring. There remained a need to identify the reasons for the Messiah's failure to appear in 5600 and to repair the situation, lest future times of visitation likewise fail.

Searching out reasons for failure—or locating scapegoats—fulfilled a psychological need, but it also exposed differences of opinion that had lurked beneath the surface of the emotional messianic turmoil that preceded 5600, during which all eyes were fixed on the indications that the Messiah was indeed about to come. Aviezer of Ticktin uses an examination of earlier events to mount a trenchant critique of the *kolel* leadership: "And I have set my mind to investigate and to know the reasons for the delay in the time of our redemption, and why the son of Jesse has not come."[29] In his view, the Messiah's failure to arrive in 5600 was not a free-standing event; rather, it was preceded by three other misfortunes afflicting the *yishuv*: the "sword" that attacked Safed and Hebron in 1834 during the revolt of the *fellahin*, the "earthquake" that hit Safed in 1837, and the "plague" that came upon Jerusalem during 1837–1839. Aviezer sees all three as punishments for the sins of the generation, primarily their challenges to the leadership and leadership style of Israel of Shklov, and, accordingly, the Messiah's failure to appear in 5600 was a natural sequel to these tragic events. Consistent with the prevalent view in the Vilna Ga'on's school that everything in the Torah had significance in every age, Aviezer understood the rebellion of Korah and his assembly (Num. 16–17) to be more than a one-time event. It provides a model for possible future episodes and closely parallels contemporary experience: "And certainly it was because of the dissension, as we find in the case of Korah, where because of his dissension, the opening of the earth [i.e., the earthquake] was accompanied by two other woes, namely, plague and conflagration."[30]

This theological understanding of the events' significance was not at all unique to Aviezer. We have two other accounts in which great Torah sages living far from the scene explained the developments in a manner calculated to support their views regarding the path to redemption and the possibility of achieving it. In June 1837, Moses Teitelbaum writes as follows: "And it seems clear to me from the troubles that have come over the holy city year after year—including its being despoiled and its women being defiled and so, too, Torah scrolls in the sanctuary [1834], and this year, because of our many sins, thousands being killed in the earthquake—that the will of the Lord, may He be blessed, is that we not go to the Land of Israel on our own initiative; rather, we should wait for our righteous Messiah to lead us to our Land."[31] Joseph bar Judah Edel likewise sees the earthquake as a sign that the settlement of Jews in the Land of Israel is not yet desired by God, for the redemption is to come by miraculous, not natural, means and we are forbidden to press for the End:

> It can be seen from this [the earthquake] that the animosity is still preserved with the Holy One Blessed Be He on account of the satan that prances among us to this day . . . to the point that the Land cannot tolerate us. . . . For we perceive with our senses that we are not yet worthy of existing in the Holy Land, for even these worthy people did not merit existing there. And the sign for this is that the Land abandoned us. And it cast us out . . . and that earth tremor only affected the cities in which Jews dwell, and the gentiles who dwell there were not thrown [out]."[32]

Remarks such as these call to mind the controversy between the *Ḥurvah* group and Israel of Shklov over who was responsible for the earthquake, and Aviezer of Ticktin makes no effort to conceal whose side he takes. In 1843, he expresses the view that the root of all the troubles is the fundamentally invalid approach that regards the building of Jerusalem as a key act of "awakening below" and that correspondingly downplays spiritual activity. He skillfully deploys kabbalistic terminology, wordplay, and numerology in a lament for those who fell in the rebellion of 1834, the earthquake of 1837, and the epidemic of 1837–1839. Blaming the *Ḥurvah* group for having caused their deaths through the controversy they spawned, he reaches his peroration, comparing the deaths of these righteous individuals to the destruction of the Temple. He maintains as well that the *Ḥurvah* advocates who sink large sums into the building of a synagogue thereby seriously worsen the economic situation of righteous people who study Torah. They assign priority to building the synagogue because of their belief that they are thereby somehow rebuilding the Temple itself. But aside from the questionable merit of that notion, their order of priorities is fundamentally distorted, for the existence of righteous people is even more important than the existence of the Temple: "Let us search their ways and return [cf. Lam. 3:40] to examine and explain the merit of righteous people engaged in Torah study, which exceeds even [that of] restoring the Temple; for it is impossible for the Temple to exist without righteous people, but Israel can exist without the Temple. Moreover, it is impossible for the world to exist without the Torah and righteous people."[33] He continues:

> And let us return and examine the principal purpose for which the Temple is built. It cannot be for the building itself, for there is no sanctity in wood and stones. Rather, one must say willy-nilly that it is built to house something holy, that is, the Ark, in which the Torah was placed. If so, the principal sanctity of the Temple derives from the Ark that contained the tablets. . . . Moreover, the *shekhinah* dwells in this world primarily for the sake of the Holy Torah and not for the sake of the Temple.[34]

Aviezer of Ticktin elevates the spiritual concept of the redemptive process, unceremoniously burying the activist concept of producing and building. He begins by casting doubt on the purity of the activists' intentions, accusing them of base motives. Having earlier compared them to Korah and his assembly, he now compares them to the builders of the Tower of Babel [Gen. 11]: "And despite their being for the most part heads of yeshivas and honorable judges of worldwide renown, in their actions they resemble the generation of the dispersion [of nations and languages], who built a tower with its top in the heavens, and their principal reason for doing so was, as Scripture says, 'That we may make a name for ourselves' [Gen. 11: 4]."[35] The *Zohar*'s comments on this episode constitute "an important source and basis for our subject."[36] According to the *Zohar*, the people of the generation of the dispersion were likewise great in Torah, "men of renown," but they became corrupted because they only wanted to glorify their name through construction projects: " 'Let us build ourselves a city and make a name for ourselves,' and building synagogues and study houses and placing a Torah scroll inside with a crown on it, not for the sake of God but in order to make a name for themselves . . . and the evil impulse overcomes Israel."[37]

The targets of Aviezer's arrows are not in doubt, though he does not dare to mention them by name. He portrays the members of the *Ḥurvah* group, like the men of the Babel generation, as materialists spending their time on earthly matters instead of engaging in the study of Torah: "There are men who build cities and whose names are spoken throughout the world in order that they not be forgotten. And in this regard, Ecclesiastes spoke of the great error made by those involved in physical, earthly matters . . . while those involved in God's work and His holy Torah will endure and exist forever and ever."[38]

Lehren's Reaction to the Crisis of 5600

Ever loyal to the traditional conception of the redemption and the Messiah's coming, Ẓevi Hirsch Lehren similarly ascribed the Messiah's failure to appear to the people's wrongdoing: the establishment of the Reform movement, the sin of baseless hatred that pervaded the *yishuv*, and the preoccupation with various construction projects in the Land of Israel at the expense of Torah study. The people did not repent, so the redemption did not come about and the

Messiah did not appear. Even before the year 5600 had run its course, on 3 April 1840, Lehren expressed his concern that the disputes in the Land of Israel and in Jerusalem might cause the redemption to be delayed, for groundless hatred had been responsible for the Second Temple's destruction, and there could be no hope of building the Third Temple while it endured. He summed up: "We anticipated salvation in the year 5600, and it may yet come this year. But on account of our many sins, we have not yet seen the banner waving to announce salvation."[39]

Of particular interest is Lehren's evolving attitude toward the Damascus blood libel of 1840. With the arrival of the first reports, he saw the libel in the context of the pending messianic expectations. In his view, the libel represented the finger of God, the birth pangs of the Messiah, whose purpose was to arouse the people to repent.[40] But one can sense as well an incipient doubt that the results of the libel would be as he had hoped, for only a few believed, as he did, that these were birth pangs of the Messiah, intended to provoke Israel's repentance.[41] He writes: "And if the suffering and anguish had made the desired impression, perhaps God would have announced the liberation of His people during this year of visitation. To my sorrow, however, we see no sign of that and we hear of no awakening of repentance in the world."[42]

Toward the end of 5600 (late summer 1840), Lehren's attitude toward the Damascus libel undergoes a change. He now believes that while the libel was initially intended to provoke repentance, it has become clear that it will not do so and that, accordingly, salvation will not grow out of it. He regards the libel, after the fact, as punishment, not only for the reformers' efforts to conform Jewish ritual to a Christian model and abolish all the practices that create social barriers between Jews and Christians but, even more, for their attempts to eliminate from Jewish liturgy and practice any references to the return to Zion and the coming of the Messiah, which they regarded as indications of political disloyalty—all as the price of achieving civil and political equality. He objects to regarding the libel as an event void of theological significance, for Providence functions actively in human history, and its operation is laden with meanings and messages: "For not by natural means did that libel come to pass, for it has already been clear for several hundred years that it is a lie and a calumny that we, the Children of Israel, would defile our souls with human blood, God forbid . . . and now the libel has been renewed by an evil emissary of the French Kingdom, though they were the first to grant liberty to our fellow Jews and to say that they would be subject to the same laws as others in the kingdom."[43]

What is strange is that it was specifically the French, who raised the banner of granting equal rights to all human beings, including the Jews, who were involved in the libel and who proclaimed its truth: "And we never could have thought that there could be such a libel in our time and that it would be in France, where they say they are enlightened, wise, and intelligent, that the people would believe the libel . . . and even the leader of the cabinet ministers defends the evil enemy Ratti-Menton."[44] Lehren sees France's involvement in the libel as intended not only to belie the hopes of the reformers and slap them in the face but also to indicate the reason for the libel—the sin of imitating the gentiles: "As I said, it is the finger of God."[45]

Lehren's understanding of the theological meaning of the Damascus libel effectively changed his attitude toward the reformers, for he now blamed them for the Messiah's failure to come in 5600. Until now, Lehren had believed that the messianic era would bring about a new world order and that many problems would automatically be solved. And as long as he believed the Messiah would come in 5600, he believed as well that the evil of the Reform would be resolved in that context, and he therefore did not wage a war of excommunication against them. His principal interest during the period of anticipation was directed toward the existence of the Jewish settlement in the Land of Israel, rather than toward removing obstacles from the Messiah's path, and his conciliatory approach to the reformers can be seen primarily in his willingness to accept their charitable contributions for the Land of Israel. To justify doing so, he argued that he saw his actions as sanctifying God's Name. Not only was the goal holy and capable of sanctifying the receipt of contributions from the reformers; there was hope as well that doing so would lead them eventually to repent: "From on high a spirit of repentance will alight on His nation the Children of Israel and those who stray will return to Him."[46] Even when Moses Sacks protests that he "accepts charity for the Land of Israel from the wicked who deny the Messiah and the Torah of Moses,"[47] Lehren justifies his approach with the claim that "they [the sages] did not forbid accepting [charity] from the wicked but only from an apostate, and Scripture clearly contemplates their repenting; perhaps by the merit of the charity they will return to God."[48]

In the wake of the Damascus libel, however, Lehren began to attack the Reform movement much more sharply than before. Moreover, until now his objection to the *Perushim*'s activism in the Land of Israel had grown out of his different view of the nature of the messianic era and the process of redemption. In the aftermath of the crisis of 5600, however, Lehren began to regard the innovative activism of the *yishuv* as having reformist overtones, especially after individuals within the Reform movement became involved in founding hospitals and schools in the years following 5600.

Influence of the Crisis on the Leadership of the *Perushim*

We have already seen how the *Perushim*, the disciples of the Vilna Ga'on, deviated from the traditional view in their understanding of the process that would herald the redemption in the years leading up to 5600. Their attitude toward the year 5600 itself was likewise distinct. As described above, they conceived of the redemption as a gradual process rather than as a sudden change that would take place within a defined time. They expected 5600 to see the start of a new age of "the beginning of the redemption," and they anticipated the occurrence of events clearly showing that a substantive change in Jewish history was under way. But a concept of that sort, which does not tie the entire redemption to an initially defined period of time, lacks any standard against which its reliability can be measured.[49] Accordingly, a final determination that the concept was erroneous cannot be reached when the critical time has come and gone but only long after, and, even then, the significance of retreating from the idea is not unambiguous. This permits us to understand why the crisis of 5600, which influenced the various groups of Jews awaiting the Messiah in varied ways and to varied degrees, had such little outward effect on the narrow leadership cadre of the *kolel* of *Perushim*—Nathan Neta ben Menaḥem Mendel, Nathan Neta ben Sa'adyah, Aryeh Ne'eman, Zalman Ẓoref (Solomon), and Moses Maggid. In their understanding, one must work within the process of "beginning of redemption" in order to advance it. Accordingly, even in the years that followed 5600, they continued their activity in all the areas in which they had worked before, despite the new difficulties they had to face with the restoration of the Ottoman government and the battle against the missionaries.

And so, they continued to work energetically to complete the building of the *Ḥurvah* courtyard. Soon after the "ending of the sabbatical year" of 5600, they sought the sultan's renewed authorization to build the synagogue in the *Ḥurvah*. On 1 January 1841, Lehren sends on to Montefiore, who was then in Frankfurt-am-Main, a letter transmitted to him by Maggid, in which the leaders of the *Perushim*'s *kolel* ask that he take care of obtaining the *firman* from the sultan.[50] Later that year, the *kolel* sends the rabbinic emissary Gershon Ze'ev to Constantinople to further the effort.[51] Fund-raising for the building of the *Ḥurvah* also continued; during 1841, the *kolel* augmented those efforts through the work of the rabbinic emissary Aaron Zelig Mann, who was then in western Europe, and in 1844, the *kolel* sent an additional emissary, Me'ir ben-Yehudah.[52] In 1847, Ẓoref himself set out for eastern and western Europe as an emissary of the *Ḥurvah*.[53] The following year, Mann again set out on a mission, this time to the United States,[54] and Samuel of Salant went to Russia for the same purpose.[55]

Nevertheless, several developments during the 1840s, taken together, prompted questioning of the *Perushim*'s basic positions and led to the ascendancy of the spiritual concept of the redemption. As already noted, the end of 5600 saw the termination of Muhammad Ali's reign, which only recently had been seen as one of the important signs on the road to Israel's redemption. The restoration of Ottoman rule set back the messianic hopes that the Jews had placed in Muhammad Ali's administration.

Moreover, the Jews' lot in Russia, the *Perushim*'s country of origin, did not improve. Beginning in 1843, the decrees of Czar Nikolai I aimed at "remedying" the condition of the Jews became more frequent. Edicts were issued against wearing Jewish garb and against Jewish autonomy and the traditional education system, more Jews were drafted into the military for the express purpose of being converted, and many Jews' freedom of movement was limited. In these circumstances, with the Russian Jewish leadership directing all its financial energies toward countermanding these decrees, neither serious financial support nor even moral support could be expected in the aftermath of the debacles in the Land of Israel. The strong sense that the *yishuv* constituted simply an additional, hopeless burden weakened the hands of those involved in building it. The conversion of Eliezer Luria and Benjamin Goldberg, along with the battle against the inclination of others to convert, made life for the *Perushim* during those years even more difficult. In Lithuania and Russia, where the year 5600 had been intensely anticipated, the Messiah's failure to appear seems to have generated a spiritual crisis as well. The study of the laws related to the sacrificial cult and the order of worship in the Holy Temple, which had been undertaken in study groups in Vilna in 1832, was discontinued.[56] Similarly, the termination of the study of Kabbalah at the Volozhin yeshiva can also be tied, in my judgment, to the disappointment caused by the Messiah's failure to appear in 1840.[57]

With the approach of 5606, it became apparent that the efforts to move the time of redemption from 5600 to 5606 had failed miserably. The year 5606 (2 October 1845 to 20 September 1846) was one of the warmest of the nineteenth century, a year of harsh famine that led to the disintegration of the *yishuv* and even to the flight from the Land of Israel of some of the *kolel* leaders, who could no longer bear the burden of meeting their constituents' needs.[58] From that point on, the *Perushim* leaders suffered blow after blow. The second generation of the Vilna Ga'on's disciples—Nathan Neta ben Menaḥem Mendel, Nathan Neta ben Sa'adyah, and Moses Maggid ben Hillel, the leaders of the *kolel*—died off.[59] The senior leadership group, which had overseen the *kolel*'s affairs since the 1830s, gave way to a newer group led by Isaiah Bardacky, Joseph Zundel of Salant, David Berliner, Naḥman Solomon ha-Levi (chief judge of Zamoscz), Asher Lemel (chief judge of Galin), and his brother, Naḥum (chief judge of Shadik). The last three of these immigrated to the Land of Israel only in the late 1840s and had no connection to the *kolel*'s early history.

The proponents of the messianic activism within the *kolel* of the *Perushim*, led by Zalman Ẓoref (Solomon), who spent the late 1840s outside the Land of Israel, could not muster the strength to oppose the new ideas. Ẓoref died on 16 September 1851,[60] and, thereafter, the group's construction and production efforts noticeably lacked the messianic drive that had characterized them in days past.[61]

Renewal of *Tiqqun Ḥaẓot*: Reversion to the Traditional Construct

In addition to the intramural accusations and assignments of blame for the Messiah's failure to come, we see as well from this point on a marked withdrawal from the *Perushim*'s understanding of "awakening below" as referring to the building of Jerusalem. Instead, we hear again the traditional argument that redemption depends on repentance and that it was a failure to repent that had undercut the potential of the year 5600 to be the year of divine visitation.

We hear again the cry to abandon messianic activism and instead cling to the Torah and the commandments, engage in the study of Torah and Kabbalah, and rest content with passively anticipating the divinely initiated redemption.

As early as 1843, Aviezer of Ticktin issued such a plea in his book *Sha'arei Ẓedeq*. He emphasized to all the importance of studying Torah and Kabbalah as mechanisms for "repair [*tiqqun*] of the *shekhinah*": "That is, a person must study the mysteries of the Torah, for such study raises the *shekhinah* from her dust . . . and on account of such study, Israel will be redeemed from the Exile."[62] In his view, the *shekhinah* can direct its bounty to us only through Israel's awakening from below—"that is, by their observing the commandments for their own sake and yielding themselves to the sanctification of the Name."[63] There are those, he says, who question "why this great effort to cry out and pray to God, for we are powerless and God will certainly bring about our redemption even without our awakening, for God knows everything, and the final end will come on its own."[64] But Aviezer assails that view, continuing that "Israel therefore needs first to produce an awakening below, through prayer and good deeds so they will be prepared to receive the good bounty of the Holy One Blessed Be He, and it thereafter will flow to them."[65] He issues a cry for repentance centered on love of one's fellow (gratuitous love, in opposition to the gratuitous hatred that brought about the destruction of the Temple), punctilious observance of the Sabbath (consistent with the rabbinic dictum that if Israel properly observed two successive Sabbaths, they would immediately be redeemed), and observance of the kabbalistic custom of reciting *tiqqun ḥaẓot*: "And so for this, our brethren the children of Israel, take to yourselves counsel . . . and arise and act to observe these three principal commandments. . . . And the third is to awaken at midnight to grieve and keen over the *shekhinah*'s exile . . . and the destruction of the house of our God."[66] This call to renew the kabbalistic practice of *tiqqun ḥaẓot*, and its elevation to the status of the two other commandments that are mentioned, both of them biblical in origin, signify, as a practical matter, a call to step back not only from the *Perushim*'s abandonment of *tiqqun ḥaẓot* (a step they had taken after obtaining the *firman* authorizing construction of the *ḥurvah*), but also from the messianic conception underlying that step: the idea that building Jerusalem, and the step taken in the *Ḥurvah* courtyard, had already brought about the raising of the *shekhinah* from her dust.

In the spring of 1847, after the hopes for 1846 had been dashed and after the veteran leaders had passed on, the "remnant" gathered the courage to take a symbolic step indicating the profound change in their ideology. They met, and a sizable number of them signed a communiqué calling for renewed recitation of *tiqqun ḥaẓot* in their center at the *Menaḥem Ẓiyyon* study hall in *Ḥurvah* courtyard: "The princes of nations gathered and we took counsel regarding what to do about the termination of the daily sacrifice in the House of our God . . . and from the day it was destroyed, the Holy One Blessed Be He has in His world only the four cubits of *halakhah*, and all that is left to us is this Torah."[67] To repair the situation, according to the communiqué, groups should be established to study Torah at night and recite *tiqqun ḥaẓot*: "And many other great and wondrous statements of our sages, may their memory be for a blessing, . . . highlight studying Torah and grieving over the destruction of the Temple during the nighttime, [activities] on which the upper and lower [realms] depend and are based; they are among the matters that stand at the pinnacle of the world, on which the entire House of Israel rely."[68] The justifications and rationalizations included in the communiqué show that the step was not taken lightly, that not everyone shared the implicit view that the Vilna Ga'on's early disciples had acted entirely in vain, and that their settling in Jerusalem was not the high road to the redemption. The communiqué was signed by only thirty-two men; those who did not sign included Zalman Ẓoref (Solomon), who was outside the Land of Israel at that time, Aryeh Ne'eman, Samuel of Salant, and Eliezer Bregman.

It should be stressed that the change at the outset was primarily ideological, not yet bearing much on practice. An example is provided by an 1849 petition to Moses Montefiore, read in comparison with some earlier petitions addressed to him. In sharp contrast to the requests presented to Montefiore during his 1839 visit,[69] the 1849 petition lacks any trace of kabbalistic motifs that tie the economic development of the Land of Israel to the concept of redemption. It is oriented solely to the continued existence and growth of the *yishuv* and to meeting its economic needs:

> And so, this is the counsel that was taken. . . . The preferable work is industrial work, as in the lands of Europe, particularly the spinning and weaving of cotton. And with the help of God, may He be blessed, many people will be able to support themselves thereby, for much cotton grows in this land. . . . May [your] kindness be manifested in the establishment of factories here as we have requested. And may each boy whom God wills [to do so] succeed in Torah and worship. May he be raised to Torah . . . but one who does not succeed in studying Torah properly should go to work in the factory, and so, too, the poor and the women should engage in spinning and weaving in order to support themselves, and by this means, relief and deliverance will come to the Jews and the settlement of our holy land will increase.[70]

A letter written in 1850 provides the first indication of nascent changes in practice,[71] recounting the objection of some of the *kolel*'s officers to teaching young men to do manual labor.[72] The writer contrasts those *Perushim* leaders to the Sefardim and Hasidim, who are more open to change and modernization, and characterizes them as narrow and "struck blind."[73] He is the first to tell of *Perushim* making the argument that the earlier building and expansion efforts had been hopeless and to observe that the ideology of work, construction, and expansion was being displaced by an opposite viewpoint grounded on the verse "Unless the Lord builds the house, its builders labor on it in vain" (Ps. 127:1). In all the polemics of the early 1840s over the building of a hospital in Jerusalem, this verse had never been cited, even by Ẓevi Hirsch Lehren. Lehren's opposition to building the hospital was based on his concern that the modernization associated with running a hospital would be a bad influence and that Jewish physicians would instill in the *yishuv* a sprit of heresy and apostasy. In contrast, the new slogan reported on by the letter writer implies a ban on all economically productive work:

> And they [the people from Poland] repudiated the favors of the Rothschild noblemen, may God save and protect them, and constantly utter "unless the Lord builds the house . . ." But the eight thousand Sefardim and their sages do not rely on this verse that was pronounced by King David, peace be upon him, and they are pleased and request and hope that some improvement will come through Sir Moses Montefiore, may God save and protect him, or through another.[74]

The *Yishuv*'s New Focus on the Immediate and the Particular

The new outlook, expressed in the verse "Unless the Lord builds the house," encompassed more than a religious faith that imposed sole responsibility for the future on the Holy One Blessed Be He. During the first half of the nineteenth century, the dominant perception of the role of the *Perushim*'s leadership reflected a forward-looking, universalist, orientation. It called for investment in and construction of an infrastructure to serve a Jewish settlement growing through a nonselective rise in immigration, thereby firmly grounding the economic survival of the *yishuv*. The new concept, in contrast, was guided by an orientation of particularity and immediacy, and the leadership's attitude toward the needs of the community correspondingly changed. Concern about the *yishuv*'s future was cast aside, and attention was confined to meeting immediate needs: that is, simply sustaining life. This orientation was reflected as a practical matter first and foremost in the splitting of the *kolel*s—those of the *Perushim*, the Hasidim, and the Sefardim—into a large number of sub-*kolel*s, based on their members' towns or lands of origin. The groups that broke off did so primarily to care for the needs of emigrants from a particular town, without taking account of the attendant inequality or the lack of response to general communal needs.

The development is exemplified by events within the *kolel*s of the *Perushim* and the Hasidim. In 1848, the Warsaw *Kolel* was founded; it broke the existing paradigm by including both Hasidim and *Perushim* from that city. In 1851, a *kolel* was founded for emigrants from the Grodno region; in 1852, emigrants from Austria broke away from the *kolel* of Volhynian Hasidim; and later, in 1858, emigrants from Hungary broke away from the *kolel* of the Hasidim and established the *Shomerei ha-Ḥomot* (Guardians of the Walls) *kolel*.[75] Each *kolel*'s fundraiser attempted to obtain as much money as possible to sustain his *kolel*'s own members. In these circumstances, there was a weakening of the communal leadership's obligation to consider the overall needs of the entire community, particularly the need for long-range policy making. This tendency gained strength over the course of the second half of the nineteenth century, reaching its extreme expression in an unyielding opposition to making the *yishuv* more productive and even in voices crying out against Jewish immigration to the Land of Israel.[76] The harsh circumstances that afflicted the *yishuv* at the time were cited in support of this attitude and helped to sustain it.

The Crimean War period (1853–1856) saw circumstances even harsher than those previously experienced by the Jewish settlement in the Land of Israel, accustomed though it was to travail. In 1854, hunger afflicted every Jewish family in the Land. Thousands of people could not obtain even a simple piece of bread. Death by starvation became a regular occurrence, and some were in such dire straits that they sold their children to Muslims for a piece of bread or to save them from starvation.[77] The Crimean War sharply curtailed the transmission of funds to the Jews in the Land of Israel. Funds from the Turkish territories could not reach the Sefardic *kolel*s, and the Ashkenzim could no longer receive support from their brethren in Russia and Poland, because Czar Nikolai I had strictly prohibited the transfer of funds to the Land of Israel.[78] In these harsh economic conditions, for the first time in the history of the *yishuv*, the Sefardic chief rabbi himself, Isaac Kubo, left the Land of Israel to raise funds to sustain the Sefardic community. Kubo was eighty-four years old at the time, and his venturing out from the Land of Israel embodies the seriousness of the economic straits of the *yishuv* in general and, in particular, of the Jerusalem Sefardic *kolel*, which had accumulated many debts.[79] The cries of desperation sent to western Europe by the Ashkenazi *kolel*s are almost unparalleled in the history of the *yishuv*.[80]

The western European Jews tried to sustain the *yishuv* economically through increased productivity, but the idea proved controversial within the *kolel* leadership, whose reaction to it was ambivalent. The difficulties of sustaining life in the present were so severe and so numerous as to preclude paying any considered attention to the needs of the future. The *yishuv*'s leaders graciously received Baron Rothschild's emissary, Dr. Albert Kohen, who arrived early in the fall of 1854,[81] as well as Moses Montefiore, who came in 1855.[82] But that reception did not imply full agreement with their point of view; the *yishuv*'s principal leaders wanted only to maximize the support provided for immediate sustenance. To that end, they agreed to any activity that could be understood as serving that purpose, such as establishing a hospital and even schools.[83] But the ideology of meeting immediate needs only, which had been the view of the Clerks' Organization in its time, was now taking root within a portion of the *yishuv*'s leadership. As noted, its influence did not come to an end with the conclusion of the Crimean War; it continued to grow in the ensuing years as well.

The leadership's exclusive interest in meeting immediate requirements did not stop some individuals from trying to act with an eye toward future needs. The conflict between the two groups can be seen in Joshua Yellin's account of the leadership's reaction to the request by several young *kolel* members to acquire large parcels of land outside the walls. The land, available for purchase at reduced prices, would be used for the construction of Jewish homes and neighborhoods. The young group argued that it made sense to allocate a small portion of the *ḥaluqah* funds to the purchase of land and the building of neighborhoods, for the funds would in any event be used for housing, applied to the rental of housing within the walls. The leadership's disappointing answer was "life in the short term is [of] greater [concern] than the life in the long term."[84]

In this way, the ideology of "unless the Lord builds the house" generated a new orientation, which limited the leadership's responsibility to meeting the population's immediate need for sustenance. A corollary notion, reflecting the easing of messianic tensions, is that the settlement of the Land—which the Vilna Ga'on's disciples had seen as a decisive factor in the redemptive process—does not in fact serve that purpose. That stance gains expression during the 1860s in a letter from Meir Auerbuch, one of the foremost Jerusalem rabbis, to Rabbi Ẓevi Hirsch Kalisher. Objecting to Kalisher's position that settlement of the Land of Israel is a means for advancing the redemption, Auerbuch draws conclusions from the failure of the Vilna Ga'on's disciples' earlier efforts to do so: "But this is not the way to attain our desired goal, and let us not be, God forbid, the objects of derision, like certain ones who came before, who thought [so] and erred, even though they, too, had pleasant intentions, and they fell into the pits, and many with them[85] and it enfeebles and weakens, God forbid, the belief in the true redeemer."[86]

In an open letter to Rabbi Judah Ḥai Alcalay, Jacob Sapir, another of the *kolel*'s young leaders, rejects as a practical matter the view that settling the Land of Israel partakes of redemption through natural means. He criticizes the earlier generation for its reliance on numerology and wordplay in bringing people to the Land of Israel and concentrating on production and development of the Land:

> For these interpretations are of no use in this matter. For the believers in the redemption of Israel will believe with perfect faith, in accordance with our trustworthy tradition, that it will take place in a miraculous and wondrous manner and that He will show us wonders as when we went out from Egypt, and [it will be brought about] by means of Torah, repentance, and charity . . . "Unless the Lord builds the house, its builders labor on it in vain" [Ps. 127:1]; in vain do you rise early, before sunrise to eat unripe fruit, before the time when God will hasten . . . to fulfill . . . "I the Lord have built the ruins, planted the desolate places" [Ezek. 36:36].[87]

This new outlook can be seen as well in Sapir's evaluation of the failure of Barukh ben Samuel's mission to the Ten Tribes. Even though he is speaking of events that took place in 1834, Sapir's view of the matter seems to have taken shape around the time it was written, during the 1860s: "And God had it turn out that his [Barukh's] effort was frustrated, so as to fulfill the words of the vision (Isa. 27:13)—'and on that day a great horn will be sounded'— . . . such that that vision, of bringing out the lost and gathering the dispersed, will occur only on the day the great horn is sounded at the time of the End, and in vain they labor before its time comes."[88]

It appears that only a few prominent individuals in the *kolel* and its leadership—among them, the descendants of the Vilna Ga'on's disciples who were the original immigrants—remained devoted to the idea that the settlement of the Land of Israel was the legitimate way to bring about the redemption. Important data on this appear in a letter written in 1865 by Naḥman Nathan Koronel, a leader of the Dutch-German *kolel*; he notes that those advocating settlement of the Land are a minority within the *yishuv*, that he and others see no prospect for settling the Land through natural processes as long as Ottoman rule continues, and that the settlement of the Land of Israel has nothing to do with the redemption unless it is brought about by miraculous rather than natural means: "And though he [Isaac Rosenthal of the Dutch-German *kolel*] is one of the faction advocating settlement of the Land of Israel, in my opinion such settlement would be a great disaster as long as the conduct of the Muslim kingdom has not changed and unless God, may He be blessed, consents, [as is written,] 'unless God builds . . . ' "[89]

The 1860s saw the building of neighborhoods outside Jerusalem's city walls. The construction was undertaken at the initiative of individuals, led by Joseph Rivlin and Joel Moses Solomon. They were the grandsons, respectively, of Moses Maggid ben Hillel and Zalman Ẓoref (Solomon), the builders of the *Ḥurvah* courtyard and part of the original *kolel* of *Perushim* in Jerusalem. Without doubt, the fathers' spirit inspired the sons, but unlike their predecessors, who expressed themselves openly, they were prevented by historical circumstances from doing so. Moreover, they were a minority—the leadership of the *Perushim* as such did not stand behind their construction efforts, and they carried them out only through personal sacrifice and initiative.

The ideology implicit in the verse "Unless God builds the house, its builders labor on it in vain" became progressively more entrenched. It underlay the opposition of the *Perushim* leadership to proposals to modernize the *yishuv* and make it more productive. The opposition was compounded by concerns about Enlightenment cultural influences, infiltration by the Reform movement, and weakening of the *ḥaluqah* system; by conservatism for its own sake; and by problems associated with fulfilling the commandments contingent on the Land. The ideological position of the leaders of *Perushim* had become one of denying that building the Land had anything at all to do with bringing about the redemption, and that the only legitimate position within traditional Judaism was the belief in miraculous redemption.[90]

Concerned that the settlement movement of the 1880s might rely on the ideology that accompanied the *aliyah* of the Vilna Ga'on's disciples, the leadership of the *Perushim* made every effort to conceal the entire episode, even deliberately avoiding any mention of the immigrants' names.[91] They sought to draw a heavy curtain over the messianic expectations for 5600 and, especially, over the extraordinary phenomena associated with it, such as the liturgical changes and the abandonment of *tiqqun ḥaẓot*, the conversion of some members of the community, and the messianic crisis. They tried as well to erase from historical consciousness any trace of the founders' audacious revocation of the traditional prohibition on hastening the End and of the "misguided" attempt to "raise the *shekhinah* from her dust" by the novel means of rebuilding Jerusalem's ruins. And to avoid any future surprises, they fortified themselves with the old idea, certain and reliable, of passively anticipating the miraculous redemption.

Epilogue

Emergence of a Jewish Majority in Jerusalem

Two historic phenomena, both of them expressions of renewed interest in the destiny of the Land of Israel, marked the beginning of the modern period in the history of Jewish settlement in the Land. One, an external factor, was the new involvement of European powers in the region; the other was the changed attitude of the Jews themselves toward their homeland.

European interest in the area—the earlier of the phenomena—began in 1798, when a French military force commanded by Napoleon Bonaparte set out from Egypt toward the Land of Israel in an effort to wrest it from the Turks. According to contemporary sources, Napoleon declared that the purpose of his campaign was to support the political restoration of the Jews in their historical homeland. Although the effort failed militarily, it conveyed the European nations' new interest in what had transpired in the region since the Middle Ages. Over the course of the ensuing century, that interest would grow, intensify, and reach the point of active involvement in the affairs of the Land of Israel, as the powers competed for spheres of influence in the area. It would reach a political resolution with the area's military conquest from the Ottomans and the Balfour Declaration of British support for the establishment of a Jewish national home in the Land of Israel.

Within the Jewish world as well, the nineteenth century saw a dramatic shift in outlook on the Land of Israel. Unusually large numbers of Jews from the various reaches of the Diaspora immigrated there, motivated primarily by the expectation that the Messiah would arrive in A.M. 5600 (1840). While most of the immigrants came to the Land of Israel to await the Messiah's coming, the disciples of R. Elijah of Vilna (the Ga'on of Vilna) were caught up in a messianic ideology holding that passive waiting was not adequate and that the process of redemption should be actively advanced by settling the Land of Israel and rebuilding Jerusalem. This ideology until now has escaped the attention of most Jewish historians, who, lacking important archival materials unearthed only during the last thirty years, mistakenly thought that the Ga'on of Vilna and his disciples, in sharp contrast to the Hasidim, were rationalists far removed from involvement in mysticism and messianism.

Along with the Vilna Ga'on's disciples, whose *aliyah* to the Land of Israel was clearly messianist in its inspiration, came other immigrants from places where life was harsh; they understood the persecution they were suffering as "tribulations of the Messiah," harbingers of the coming redemption. They included refugees from Jewish communities attacked during the 1822 Greek rebellion against the Turks; immigrants who abandoned various areas of the Ottoman Empire on account of the economic and social crisis attendant on the abolition of the Janissary forces in 1826; Jewish families who fled Russia on account of the mandatory military draft that began in 1827; and Jews who fled the persecutions in Algiers in 1830. The new immigrants imposed additional burdens on the old *yishuv*, a situation that caught the notice of many devoted Jews around the world and moved them to act on behalf of the *yishuv* as it began to renew itself. In eastern and western Europe and in the Ottoman Empire, Jews stepped forward to sustain the physical and economic existence of the Jewish community in the Land of Israel. In Vilna and in Amsterdam, and even earlier in Constantinople, aid organizations were established. For decades, these supracommunal organizations gathered large sums of money to support the developing *yishuv*. In so doing, they increased the interest and involvement of Diaspora Jews in the lives of their brethren living in the Land of Israel.

Paralleling the Jews' messianic hopes for the year 5600 were messianic expectations in the Protestant world that Jesus' second coming would be in 1840, the year roughly overlapping with the year 5600 on the Hebrew calendar. Major figures in Christian millenarian groups, who enjoyed political influence in Great Britain, believed that their government bore a responsibility to help the Jews return to their historical homeland and reestablish the Kingdom of Israel in the spirit of the prophetic promises. Believing that the "return to Zion" would culminate in the Jews' acceptance of Jesus as Messiah and begin the redemption of mankind, a group of Christians in 1809 established the London Society for Promoting Christianity Amongst the Jews. The group dispatched representatives throughout the Jewish world to keep close tabs on the messianic awakening among the Jews and their movement to immigrate to the Land of Israel. In 1822, the convert-missionary Joseph Wolff came to Jerusalem as the London Society's representative. Despite the concern that he would be shunned by them, he managed to forge close ties with the Jews of the Land of Israel, particularly the leader of the Jerusalem *Perushim*, the Ga'on of Vilna's disciple, R. Menaḥem Mendel of Shklov. Their collaboration played out against the background of the prophet Isaiah's vision that the nations of the world were destined to have a central role in the process of Israel's redemption. The

Perushim saw Great Britain and its representatives as agents sent by divine providence to help them in the "return to Zion"; the London Society's emissaries saw their role as defending the Jews of Jerusalem against harassment and oppression by the Ottoman government and enlisting England's political support for returning the Jews to their historical homeland.

In 1831, the Egyptian ruler Muhammad Ali conquered the Land of Israel, and that, too, was seen by believers as another real-world step toward redemption. Wanting to gain legitimacy in the eyes of the European powers, the new ruler granted formal equal rights to the Christian and Jewish communities in the Land of Israel and thereby brought about an immediate improvement in their situation and in the Land's image. Under his patronage, Jerusalem was revitalized as a political center. For the first time in hundreds of years, the ruler granted Jews permission to renovate their synagogues and to build community buildings within the city. Security was significantly improved under his protection, economic and agricultural development moved ahead energetically, transportation routes were developed, and ties between the Land of Israel and the outside world were improved with the introduction of steamships into the postal service and ocean-going commerce. These improvements led to the *aliyah* of wealthy, not just impoverished, Jews; in addition, the Land was visited by thousands of Christian pilgrims, tourists, travelers, merchants, archaeologists, writers, artists, missionaries, and consular agents. They infused wealth into the Land, contributed to its economic prosperity, and rejuvenated it, ending its desolation and preparing it for a new life.

In an instance of tragic irony, the improvement in Jerusalem's condition came in the wake of the destruction of Safed and Tiberias in the earthquake of 1837, which prompted an increased flow of Jewish immigrants to Jerusalem. The growing Jewish population in Jerusalem began to overflow from the Jewish Quarter of the city toward the Muslim Quarter, where the *kolel*s and wealthier immigrants began to purchase houses. Jerusalem was poised for a wave of development. With the growth of the *yishuv* and its increased needs, the various *kolel*s undertook economic development programs that included the opening of shops, workshops, and olive presses for the manufacture of oil and soap. Hopes for further development were high, and when Moses Montefiore visited the Land of Israel for the second time, in 1839, he asked Muhammad Ali for permission to purchase some 100,000 dunams of agricultural land on which Jews might be settled, consistent with his program for enhancing the *yishuv*'s productivity and the agreement of its leaders to participate in his plans for Jewish settlement.

The new vibrancy in the Land of Israel raised the western powers' interest in this part of the disintegrating Ottoman Empire. The first signs of Jerusalem's boom made it appear to be a place of great future potential, and the western powers' efforts to gain a foothold there led to active involvement in its destiny. At the highest governmental echelons, attention began to be directed to the Land of Israel's political future. Some suggested plans for leaving the Land under Muhammad Ali's rule or, alternatively, for internationalizing Jerusalem. The British, in contrast, developed plans to bring the Land under British control by removing Muhammad Ali and restoring a weakened Turkish sultan to power, dependant on British protection. This political involvement in the Land of Israel was helped along by the Anglican mission, eager to advance the Jews' return to Zion. The Land of Israel in general and Jerusalem in particular became objects of competition among the European powers. The consular protection of Jews, some of whom were considered foreign citizens, provided cover for the powers' intervention in the Land; as a clear indication of that, between 1838 and 1849, consulates were opened by Great Britain, Prussia, France, Sardinia, the United States, and Austria. Russia remained content with its representatives in the port cites of Egypt and Syria and a general consul in Jaffa.

Although the Messiah's failure to appear as expected in 1840 was a harsh and disappointing blow to the Jews of the Land of Israel, it did not cause the *yishuv*'s spirit to flag. Nor was the *yishuv*'s strength undermined by the Damascus blood libel of that same year. Most of the community survived the crisis of faith and stood firm even in the face of the weakening position of the established aid agencies during the years 1840–1856. The messianic motivations that had influenced much pre-1840 *aliyah* grew weaker over the years but did not entirely disappear; and new reasons for *aliyah* were added. With a background of religious and spiritual oppression in western and eastern Europe, the number of immigrants continued to grow. Even the reduced economic support by the established aid organizations did not leave the *yishuv* abandoned; along with the reduction came the development of new sources of support. As the European powers and western European Jews became more interested in the Land of Israel, doors were opened to broader and more varied sources of support. Philanthropists and Jewish charitable organizations in western Europe who had been asked to help the Jews in the Land of Israel in the wake of the Crimean War (1853–1856) took the opportunity to set a higher-order goal for themselves and to change the form taken by their support. Instead of simply helping individuals survive, as had the aid organizations, they directed funding to the establishment of modest economic projects that would provide employment to Jews instead of leaving them exclusively reliant on charitable allocations. Under the influence of western ideas on the importance of modernizing and becoming productive, various proposals were made to improve the *yishuv*'s way of life and its health, cultural, and social condition through the establishment of modern medical, educational, and vocational educational institutions. Over a period of only three years, this revolutionary concept of the *yishuv* became solidified and the influence of western Jews became firmly established through the successful efforts of the House of Rothschild and its representative Albert Cohen in 1854, of Moses Montefiore in 1855, and of the Jews of Vienna acting through Ludwig Frankel in 1856.

As far as the *Perushim*, the descendants of the Ga'on of Vilna's disciples, were concerned, this western philanthropic activity represented a continued implementation of the messianic ideology of Menaḥem Mendel of Shklov. In his day, Menaḥem Mendel had accepted support for his program of "rebuilding Jerusalem" from, among others, Christians and missionaries; later on, the leaders of the *kolel* of the *Perushim* cast their fate with England's diplomatic representatives. Following the 1840 watershed, a major portion of Jerusalem's Ashkenazim backed off from the idea of redeeming the Land through human activity, but a small minority of the *Perushim* continued to believe that advancing the redemptive process depended first and foremost on human actions, especially the development and rebuilding of Jerusalem. To attain these goals, they were willing to cooperate with western Jews to promote modernization and improved productivity, even though they did not share their outlook on education and culture. In contrast, most of Jerusalem's Sefardim and their leaders wanted to advance the growth of their community through reliance on western philanthropy. With the choice of Rabbi Isaac Kubo as *Rishon le-Ẓiyyon* (chief rabbi of the Sefardim) at the end of 1848, the position of the Sefardim underwent a radical change: radical opposition to all innovation (as in the days of his predecessor, *Ḥakham Bashi* Abraham Ḥayyim Ganin) gave way to a readiness to come to terms with the processes of modernization. Rabbi Kubo's successors as *Rishon le-Ẓiyyon*, Rabbi Ḥayyim Nissim Abolafia and Rabbi Ḥayyim David Ḥazzan, continued in his path and solidified the community's favorable attitude toward modernization.

The overall Ashkenazi community in Jerusalem also showed surprising changes in its attitude toward the new trends. The spirit of extremism that characterized the Ashkenazi *yishuv* in Jerusalem during the second half of the nineteenth century was not shared by all the *Perushim* or by the Jerusalem Hasidim, and certainly not by the Jews from Germany. It was, rather, the province of a group of highly conservative rabbis who had only recently immigrated from Poland. In order to freely promote their viewpoint, they converted the Ashkenazi court on which they served into a religious-spiritual power base. In 1848, the leaders of the group, known as "the righteous rabbis," and their circle established a separate, independent "Warsaw *kolel*" and made it the focus of extremism in Jerusalem—all this long before the arrival of the Hungarian immigrants who founded the *Shomerei ha-Ḥomot* (Guardians of the Walls) *kolel* and the immigration in 1877 of Rabbi Moses Joshua Leib Diskin of Brisk.

The Ashkenazi extremists' aggressive battle against all changes in the traditional structure of life and against the establishment of modern schools worked, in a dialectical way, to the advantage of Jerusalem's development and growth. It led to increased awareness of the Land of Israel's potential as a "land of refuge" from spiritual influences prevalent elsewhere that were inimical to Judaism—a consideration that complemented the ideas of fulfilling the commandment to reside in the Land of Israel (a commandment said by some to be equal in weight to the entire remainder of the Torah) and of anticipating the coming of the Messiah. Accordingly, life in the Land of Israel, in which the structures and social program of traditional Judaism can be carried out undisturbed, came to be understood as preferable to life in foreign lands, and *aliyah* came to be seen as an appropriate step. The fight against modernization in Jerusalem thus echoed widely and led to increased *aliyah* on the part of ultraorthodox Jews in central and eastern Europe who were concerned about the influence of Reform, modernity, and secular education in their lands of origin. The social make-up of the group was varied; it encompassed many young and mature families, along with elderly men and widows who wanted to experience, in their last years, a religious life in the shelter of the Land's sanctity. Their immigration was accompanied by a corresponding increase in economic and financial resources provided by their supporters—family members, relatives, and townsfolk.

The rapid growth of the Ashkenazi *yishuv* in Jerusalem and, in particular, the strengthening of its extremist element pushed to one side the old disputes that had previously preoccupied the community. The usual disputes over sources of funding gave way to a principal main area of dispute now centered on the shaping of the *yishuv*'s image and way of life. On one side of the line were the "old-timers," descendants of the Ga'on of Vilna's disciples, who continued to promote messianic activism and wanted to be integrated, like the Sefardim, into the modernization and productivity processes proposed by the western Jews. Arrayed against them were the "newcomers," eager to defend against modernization and the educational values of the western world and to preserve all the values of the traditional, pre-messianist society.

Against this background, two centers of political power took shape in the Ashkenazi community. The first was focused on the political administration of the *kolels* and on organizational and economic questions, particularly securing the continuation of the *ḥaluqah* (the system of charitable distributions) and the effort to obtain the financial support of western Jews for development programs in Jerusalem. The second power center included the members of the Ashkenazi community's rabbinic court, who sought to deny to the officers of the *kolels* any spiritual leadership role in the community and who opposed any initiatives proposed by the leaders of the *kolels* or by western Jews on their advice, such as the establishment of modern schools. This dual leadership led to conflict and endless ideological battles within Jerusalem's Ashkenazi community.

Surprisingly enough, however, the conflicts over organization and values strengthened and steeled the *yishuv* more than they weakened it. Despite their differences in language, cultural background, and communal-social allegiances and their varied stances on questions of culture and values, all those involved in the dispute—from Turkey and the Balkans, North Africa, Lithuania, Poland, and central Europe—succeeded in maintaining their distinctive ways of life in Jerusalem, together with a shared way of life, common to all the communities. The competition among the factions seems to have made both old-line aid organizations, now divided by place of origin, and western philanthropic groups more acutely aware of the need for more intense efforts to provide economic support to the *yishuv*.

Jewish settlement in Jerusalem continued to grow even after the crisis of 1840, accelerating to the point of creating a housing shortage within the city's walls. Under these circumstances, the Jews had no choice but to overflow into in the expanses outside the walls. Paralleling the plans by immigrants from Germany to establish, in 1857, the Batei Maḥseh neighborhood within the walls, the first neighborhood outside the wall, Mishkenot Sha'ananim, was built during 1855–1860 on the initiative of Moses Montefiore. It was followed by additional Jewish neighborhoods, built in 1869–1881 on the initiative of

Joseph (Josha) Rivlin, Joseph Joel Solomon, and a group of young men, marking the beginning of what is now known as West Jerusalem. In that period, Jews already constituted a majority of Jerusalem's residents, exceeding the combined number of Muslims and Christians. Following the establishment of clinics and hospitals by the Anglican missionary society, the *kolels*, Moses Montefiore, and the Rothschild family, the quality of life and public sanitation improved immeasurably; then, following the improvement of transportation within the Land, the introduction of the telegraph in 1865, and the opening of the Suez Canal in 1869, commerce and finance developed even more. Cultural and religious activities were also renewed. Synagogues, study halls and yeshivas were established, along with modern schools. The print shops that were opened in Jerusalem likewise contributed to economic and cultural development and were followed by the appearance of the first Hebrew newspapers in the Land of Israel.

The Jerusalem *yishuv* thus underwent a remarkable transformation over the course of the nineteenth century, from oppressed ethnic minority, existing in filthy, almost unbearable conditions, to a majority in the city living in significantly improved and improving circumstances. The change took place despite the many factors that would have led a realist to regard it as unlikely: the sharp differences of ideology and values among the various strata that made up the nineteenth-century *yishuv*; the harsh, sometimes unresolved, internal battles within the *yishuv* itself, taking place against a background of communal, class, economic, political, cultural, and religious distinctions; the existence within the *yishuv* of two parallel streams, one favoring modernization, increased productivity, and education, and one devoted to continuing the old *ḥaluqah* system, on the premise that the Jews residing in the Land of Israel should occupy themselves exclusively in Torah study; and the moral flaws and social decay that developed around the *yishuv*.

The processes of change within the *yishuv*, and the important part played by the *ḥaluqah*—initially something positive that physically sustained the *yishuv*—have been perceptively assessed by the scholar Jacob Goldman. Goldman concludes that without the *ḥaluqah* system, Jews would never have developed an awareness of the real existence of the Land of Israel. He claims that it was only the Diaspora Jews' financial support of the aid organizations during the nineteenth century that made possible the *yishuv*'s existence and development. Moreover, it was only thanks to the existence of a Jewish *yishuv* in the Land of Israel during the first half of the nineteenth century that masses of Jews in the Diaspora, as well as the nations of the world, began to be aware of the reality of the Land of Israel as a place in which the Jewish nation could settle in the future.

Glossary

Admor (pl. *admorim*): acronym for the Hebrew honorific "our lord, teacher, and rabbi"; usually (though not exclusively) used to refer to a Hasidic *rebbe*.

A'al'am: official document issued by a Turkish court.

Aliyah (pl. *aliyot*): immigration to the Land of Israel; refers as well to a cycle or wave of immigration; see also *Oleh*.

Ari: "the Lion," acronym for "the divine Rabbi Isaac" and soubriquet for R. Isaac Luria (1534–1572), an important kabbalist; see also *Lurianic Kabbalah*.

Awakening from below (*it'aruta de-le-tata*): as taught by the *Zohar*, all activity related to the redemption had to begin with this; the awakening from below is a precondition to the awakening on high.

Birth pangs (tribulations) of the Messiah (*ḥevlei mashiaḥ*): difficult times believed to precede the coming of the Messiah.

Clerks' Organization: organization of *Peqidim* and *Amarkalim* [clerks and administrators] in Amsterdam, established in 1809 and engaged for many years in the raising of funds for the Jews of the Land of Israel.

Commandments contingent on the Land of Israel: various provisions of Jewish law, related primarily to agriculture and agricultural produce, that are in effect only in the Land of Israel and need not or may not be fulfilled elsewhere.

Footsteps of the Messiah (*iqveta de-meshiḥa*): the period of history immediately preceding the coming of the Messiah, marked by portentous events.

Firman: a royal decree in the Ottoman Empire.

Gematria (pl. *gematriot*): an interpretive method based on the numerical value of words, each letter bearing a designated numerical value, or a specific application of the method.

Gilgul meḥillot: "underground rolling," the rabbinic concept that when the dead are resurrected, Jews who died and were buried outside the Land of Israel would return to the Land by rolling through underground tunnels, a difficult process; see, e.g., *Yalqut Shim'oni*, Isaiah, *Remez* 431.

Halakhah: Jewish law, both ritual and civil.

Ḥaluqah: "distribution"; charitable distributions of funds raised in Diaspora communities for the support of Jews residing in the Land of Israel.

Haskalah: enlightenment movement.

Ḥurvah: the ruins of the synagogue, study hall, and surrounding courtyard built in Jerusalem by R. Judah Ḥasid and his circle; rebuilding those ruins became an important goal of the *Perushim* in Jerusalem.

Judah Ḥasid: eastern European rabbi, leader of a group of Ashkenazi Jews who settled in Jerusalem in 1700.

Kolel (pl. *kolelim*): one of several community and welfare organizations of groups of Jews in the Land of Israel; the various *kolelim* tended to comprise Jews of common ideological or geographic background.

London Society: the London Society for Promoting Christianity Amongst the Jews, a Christian missionary organization established in London in 1809 and active in the Land of Israel during the period studied here.

Lurianic Kabbalah: the kabbalistic doctrines developed by and taught in the name of R. Isaac Luria.

Messiah son of Joseph: a figure believed to be a precursor of the Messiah son of David; destined to die in battle against the enemies of God and Israel.

Mulk: a type of private property interest under law in the Ottoman Empire.

Nobles of Vilna (*Roznei Vilna*): a group of dignitaries in Vilna who supported *aliyah* by the Ga'on of Vilna's followers; see also *Perushim*.

Oleh (fem. *olah*; pl. *olim*): immigrant to the Land of Israel.

Peqidah (*et peqidah*): time of divine visitation, the End-time.

Perushim: literally, "those who withdrew," followers of the Ga'on of Vilna in the Land of Israel, so termed after their dissociation from the Hasidim there.

River Sambatyon: legendary river beyond which the exiled Ten Tribes are located; it flows so violently on weekdays that it cannot be traversed, becoming calm only on the Sabbath, when traversing it is forbidden.

Scaling the wall: metaphor connoting en masse return of Jews to the Land of Israel, with the intention of reestablishing Jewish dominion there; see also *Three Oaths*.

Shekhinah: the presence of God; God in His immanence (as distinguished from His transcendence); sometimes interpreted, especially in Kabbalah, as God's feminine aspect.

Tanna'im (sing. *tanna*): rabbinic sages in the Land of Israel during the mishnaic period, roughly the first and second centuries C.E.; their teachings are recorded primarily in the Mishnah.

Ten Tribes: the Israelite tribes who renounced the unified Davidic monarchy after the death of King Solomon and separated as the kingdom of Israel, leaving only the tribes of Judah and Benjamin (and Levi) in the Davidic kingdom of Judah; the kingdom of Israel was destroyed by the Assyrians in 722 B.C.E., and the Ten Tribes were sent into exile in parts unknown; legends regarding their fate abound, and various efforts have been made to locate them.

Three Oaths: three oaths, according to a *midrash*, that God imposed on Israel and the nations of the world: "What are these three oaths? One, that Israel would not scale the wall [i.e., would not prematurely attempt to restore Jewish dominion in the Land of Israel]; one, that God adjured Israel not to rebel against the nations of the world; and one, that God adjured the heathen not to subjugate Israel excessively" (see., e.g., *Ketubbot* 111a).

Tiqqun: "repair"; used in Lurianic Kabbalah in a mystical sense to refer to remedying cosmic flaws through human acts.

Tiqqun Ḥaẓot: a mystical ritual of mourning for the destruction of Jerusalem, conducted in the middle of the night.

Waqf: property subject to Muslim religious ownership.

Yishuv: the Jewish presence in the Land of Israel, referring to both individuals and their community structures.

Ẓaddiq (pl. *ẓaddiqim*): literally, "a righteous one'; usually refers to a *rebbe*, the leader of a Hasidic group.

Notes

CHAPTER 1

1. Several studies have treated messianism during this period. They include B. Z. Dinur, "The Question of Redemption and Its Ways During the Early Enlightenment and the First Controversy Over Emancipation" (Hebrew), in his book *Mifneh ha-Dorot* (Jerusalem, 1972), pp. 231–354; J. Katz, "The Historical Figure of R. Ẓevi Hirsch Kalisher" (Hebrew), *Shivat Ẓiyyon* 2–3 (1951), pp. 26–41; idem., "Messianism and Nationalism in the Teaching of R. Alcalay" (Hebrew), *Shivat Ẓiyyon* 4 (1956), pp. 9–41; M. Vereté, "The Restoration of the Jews in English Protestant Thought 1790–1840," *Middle Eastern Studies* 8 (1972), pp. 3–50 (Hebrew original in *Zion* 32 [1968], 145–179); B. Mevorakh, "The Messianic Question in the Polemics Regarding Emancipation and Reform 1781–1819" (Hebrew), Ph.D. dissertation, Hebrew University of Jerusalem, 1966; idem., "Belief in the Messiah in Early Polemics Over Reform" (Hebrew), *Zion* 34 (1969), pp. 189–218.

2. "R. El'azar bar Avina said: If you see kingdoms inciting one another, anticipate the footsteps of the Messiah" (*Genesis Rabbah* 42).

"R. Yoḥanan said: The generation in which the [Messiah] son of David arrives [will be one in which] scholars become few and others watch helplessly in anguish. Numerous afflictions and harsh persecutions will be renewed; by the time one passes, another will hasten to arrive." (*Sanhedrin* 97a.)

3. "What are these three oaths? One, that Israel would not ascend the wall [i.e., would not prematurely attempt to restore Jewish dominion in the Land of Israel]; one, that God adjured Israel not to rebel against the nations of the world; and one, that God adjured the heathen not to subjugate Israel excessively" (*Ketubbot* 111a).

4. Applications of the "Three Oaths" during the period in question include the following: "The hoped-for return to Palestine . . . has absolutely no influence on our conduct as citizens. Experience has always taught as much in all places where the Jews have been tolerated, down to today. In a sense,

that fact is consistent with human nature, for a person normally does not daydream, but loves the land on which it is well for him. But it may also be attributed to our Sages, who foresaw the future and often in the Talmud taught us the prohibition against even contemplating the use of force to return. . . . They forbade us from taking even the simplest step toward scaling the wall and reestablishing the nation in the absence of the great miracles and supernatural signs promised by Scripture." Moses Mendelssohn, quoted in *Sefer ha-Ẓiyyonut: Mevaserei ha-Ẓiyyonut*, ed. Ben-Zion Dinberg (Jerusalem, 1944), p. 183.

"We are not permitted to extend a hand and help ourselves. . . . We must remain quiet and calm, not contravening the commands of our ruler in each city and province. Until each and every nation, every ruler and prince, through his own good will and great love inspired by God becomes excited about this nation . . . and himself sends or brings it . . . to the House of the God of Jacob. . . . In this way, we hope only that they will send us to Jerusalem our holy city of their own will . . . and if they do not wish to do so of their own good will, then even if it appears to us that we are able to go up to Jerusalem by our own mighty force, we are not permitted to do anything on our own, so as not to violate the oath by which the God of our fathers adjured us." *Ẓeror ha-Ḥayyim*, R. Abraham Lowenstam (Amsterdam, 1820), p. 76a.

On the Reform movement's various approaches to the question of messianism, see W. Gunther Plaut, *The Rise of Reform Judaism* (New York, 1963); Michael A. Meyer, *Response to Modernity: A History of the Reform Movement in Judaism* (New York, 1988).

5. "I believe with perfect faith in the coming of the Messiah, and even if he tarry, I nevertheless daily await his arrival" (Maimonides' Thirteen Principles of Faith, Principle 12).

6. *Sanhedrin* 97a.

7. The Fürth community formed the arena for a sharp conflict between reformers and traditionalists. In the 1820s, the reformers gained ascendance; in 1830, Wolf Hamburg was removed as head of the yeshiva and was replaced as rabbi by the reformer Dr. Isaac Levy. The local yeshiva was closed, and its students were expelled from the city by the government.

8. In describing the appearance of the Reform movement in his city, Hamburg uses terms borrowed from the Talmud's definitions of the generation of the Redemption: "But the people of our generation even on the Sabbath study only non-canonical books. And in that respect, the face of the generation is like the face of a dog. For it is written, 'And the dogs are brazen of spirit, not knowing satiation' (Isa. 56:11), that is, they fail to recognize the virtue of the Torah. . . . And it may also be said that the face of the generation is a new sect . . . whose face is turned only toward food and sustenance and this-worldly matters, pursuing physical desires, just as the face of a dog." *Qol Bokhim*, R. Wolf Hamburg (Fürth, 1820), p. 44a.

9. Ibid., pp. 31a–32a. Hamburg elsewhere returns to his desired conclusion that the Messiah's advent will be in a generation that is entirely culpable: "What follows from this is that even if we are not eligible and worthy of being redeemed, there nevertheless is hope, as the prophet [Micah 7:15] said, 'as in the days when you left the Land of Egypt' . . . and just as they were redeemed then at the [designated] time though unworthy, so will it be at the final redemption, to be redeemed though unworthy and even though we are intermingled with the nations of the world and have learned from their deeds, those of the wicked of our generation." *Misped ha-Mishneh*, R. Wolf Hamburg (Fürth, 1823), p. 1a.

10. *Simlat Binyamin*, part 2, R. Wolf Hamburg (Fürth, 1841), p. 62b. A similar

attitude can be found in a eulogy for Rabbi Moses Sofer of Pressburg: "Given what our rabbis and sages of blessed memory informed us and determined—that the Torah will in the future be forgotten in Israel—see, we are genuinely living in [fulfillment of] their words. For they knew, through their spirit of understanding; and a spirit from on high alighted on them and they prophesied and knew what was before and after. . . . And, behold, they see us, who, in our great sins, have destroyed truth, for we have descended ten degrees . . . and there is no doubt *that this is the time of the divine right hand,* for a reason hidden with the Creator. . . . And so we hope for him, to quickly see his magnificent might, and see the light he will bring to Zion." *Evel Mosheh,* Eliezer Lipman of Solish (Offen, 1840). (Emphasis supplied, here and below.)

11. *Iggerot ha-Peqidim ve-ha-Armarkalim mei-Amsterdam* (1826–1870) ("Letters of the *Peqidim* and *Amarkalim* [Clerks and Administrators] in Amsterdam"; referred to as the "Letters of the Clerks"), 15 vols, Yad Ben-Zvi Library, Jerusalem, vol. 8, p. 168a.

12. "It is an act of Satan in each and every city and province, not just among the lay leaders but even among the rabbis. The holy congregation of Fürth will demonstrate it: Who sits at its head? A member of the Neologist [the term used in Hungary for Reform] sect [Dr. Levy], who does not believe in the giving of the Torah and its commandments orally . . . And they did not remove him; rather, they admonished him to conduct himself properly and to attend synagogue services on the weekdays. In Frankfurt-am-Main, the God-fearing ones thought they had prevailed, but nine were selected, all of them innovators. All of this shows that we are close to the set time for redemption, and salvation is near." *Iggerot ha-Peqidim* (Letters of the Clerks), vol. 8, p. 161a (letter of 18 June 1839).

13. "Emancipation" refers to the recognition of the civil, legal, and political equality of Jews as citizens of the state, particularly in the wake of the French Revolution and its Declaration of the Rights of Man.

14. *Binah le-Ittim,* R. Elyaqim ben Abraham (London, 1795), p. 26b.

15. *Hilkhot Yemot ha-Mashiaḥ,* Eliezer Sinai Kirschbaum (Berlin [?], 1822).

16. *Shivat Ẓiyyon,* part 2, A. J. Slutsky (Warsaw, 1892), p. 49. Even though this source is late, one may regard it as representing a concept expressed in Kalisher's letter of 25 August 1836 to Anschel Rothschild. J. Klausner, ed., *The Zionist Writings of Rabbi Ẓevi Kalisher* (Jerusalem, 1947), pp. 1–14 (Hebrew).

17. *Megillah* 17b. So, too, in the *midrash*: "At the hour of the King Messiah's revelation, all the kings of the nations will be fighting one another . . . and Israel will be agitated and terrified, saying, 'where shall we turn?' . . . and he will say to them . . . 'Fear not; the time of your redemption has come.' " *Yalqut Shim'oni,* Isaiah, sec. 497.

18. *Sefer ha-Zikkaron,* R. Moses Sofer of Pressburg (Jerusalem, 1957), p. 38.

19. Ibid., p. 53. It may be inferred that Moses Sofer sought to avoid praying for the end of the war, lest the time of messianic potential go by. It is recounted that during World War I, in reliance on this passage, several *admorim* (Hasidic *rebbes*; sing. *admor*—an acronym for the Hebrew honorific "our lord, teacher, and rabbi") wanted to declare a communal fast, "but the *admor* of Munkacz declined to pray for the peace of the nations, for in his view, war, too, was the beginning of the redemption." *Yemot ha-Mashiaḥ,* an anthology of the sayings of Ḥayyim El'azar Shapira, the *admor* of Munkacz (Jerusalem, 1970), p. 57a. It is told of Rafael ha-Kohen, the rabbi of Altona and Hamburg and the first teacher of Ḥayyim of Volozhin, that he aspired all his life to emigrate to the Land of Israel and was never able to, but in the wake of the wars of 1803, "he discoursed much on contemporary world events, in case they bear an opening of hope or will allow, once the sound of war is quieted, an opportu-

nity to journey to his destination." Rafael ha-Kohen never succeeded in fulfilling his hopes, and he died on 11 November 1803. *Zekher Ẓaddiq*, R. Eliezer Katzenellenbogen (Vilna, 1879), p. 21a.

Writing from Jerusalem in 1816, a Christian traveler, James Buckingham, described the attitude of the Jews toward the French Revolutionary Wars: "They still faithfully hope for the coming of the Messiah, and they are convinced that the recent wars served as preparation for his coming." *Mas'ei Noẓrim le-Erez Yisra'el*, ed. M. Ish-Shalom (Tel-Aviv, 1966), p. 419.

20. *Divrei Yemei Yisra'el, Dorot Aḥahronim*, R. Mahler, part 1, vol. 1, p. 129.

21. R. Mahler, *History of the Jews: Modern Times*, Part I, Vol. 1 (Merḥaviah, 1952), p. 129 (Hebrew).

22. Ibid.

23. Some of Napoleon's early campaigns, in which the Jews were rescued from the rage of the local Christian populace, aroused messianic excitement: "It must be recognized that the French love for the Jews is unqualified. This is proven by [their treatment of the Jews] in all the cities and lands they have conquered, for if Jews are present, they augment and elevate them and subdue the children of Edom [a euphemism for oppressive Rome and, later, Christianity—***translator***]. And it appears to me that the prophet Obadiah alluded to this when he said [1:1] "a representative [*ẓir*] has been sent among the nations." *Ẓir* [spelled *ẓ-y-r*] is an acronym for *ẓorfatim yashpilu romiyim* (the French will subdue the Romans) and over all is their great general, known as "the good portion," that is, *Buene Parto*. "We must know that everything that happened to us this week, and the intentions of these Christians against us, had been revealed by God to this loyal general, for God makes everything a vehicle of his agency." *Ma'aseh Nisim (Chronicle from Ancona of the Days of Napoleon's First Italian Campaign)*, in Mevorakh, *Napoleon and His Time*, pp. 28–29; see also pp. 42, 53–54, 57, 85–86.

24. *Divrei Yemei Yisra'el*, part 1, vol. 1, p. 290.

25. E.g., *Sefer ha-Zohar, Peirush ha-Sulam, Parashat Va'eira*, par. 13; *Leviticus Rabbah, Seder Shemini*, end of chap. 13.

26. The question was examined at the Second World Congress of Jewish Studies in Jerusalem in 1957. Prof. M. Vereté contended that no such a decree was ever issued, and he continued to adhere to that view, as I conclude from a discussion we had. In contrast, others say that Napoleon did issue a decree to the Jews; see Franz Kobler, *Napoleon and the Jews* (Jerusalem, 1975), and N. M. Gelber, "Napoleon I and the Land of Israel," in *Sefer Dinberg*, ed. Yiẓḥaq Baer, Yehoshu'a Guttman, and Mosheh Sova (Jerusalem, 1949) (Hebrew), pp. 263–288.

27. *Qorot ha-Ittim le-Yeshurun be-Ereẓ Yisra'el*, R. Menaḥem Mendel of Kamenetz (Vilna, 1840), p. 22.

28. Mevorakh, "The Messianic Question," p. 22.

29. Ibid., p. 50. English millenarian literature treats Napoleon's "messianic" mission at length. One book devotes hundreds of pages to examining every event in Napoleon's life and finding its basis in Scripture. In the writer's opinion, Napoleon's eastern expedition was motivated by his intense hatred for England and his great appetite for conquest and destruction, but God subjugated these motivations to the fulfillment of the divine mission with respect to the nation of Israel. The writer was convinced that Napoleon would proclaim himself the Jews' Messiah and return some of them to Zion. James Holty, *A Combined View of the Prophecies of Daniel, Esdros and St. John* (London, 1815), pp. 387, 466.

30. Mevorakh, "The Messianic Question," p. 51. See also the study by Abraham

G. Duker, "The 'Tarniks,' " in *Joshua Starr Memorial Volume* (New York, 1953), p. 196. The Scottish missionary McCaul tells that that when he visited the Warsaw suburb of Praga, he was received by the rabbi of the Hasidim, who told him he had long thought of Napoleon as the Messiah, a belief disproven by Napolenon's death. Nevertheless, the Hasid continued, one who returns the nation of Israel to its land will be recognized by the Jews as the Messiah. *Jewish Expositor* (London, 1821) (hereafter: *J. E.*), pp. 466–467.

31. M. Vereté, "The Concept of Israel's Return in English Protestant Thought, 1790–1840" (Hebrew), *Zion* 33, pp. 176–178. An English Christian theologian wrote in 1818 that Great Britain's destiny as a tool of Providence for bringing about the return to Zion is alluded to in Isa. 60:9: "For the isles await me, and the ships of Tarshish are in the lead, to bring your children from afar." *J. E.* (1818), p. 73.

32. Mevorakh, "The Messianic Question," p. 140. On the Jews' messianic expectations in the wake of Napoleon's military victories in 1806–1807, see A. Shischa, "Epistle of the Rabbinic Emissary Ḥayyim Barukh of Miastro" (Hebrew), in M. Benayahu, ed., *Sefer Zikkaron le-Rav Yiẓḥaq Nissim*, part 4 (Jerusalem, 1985), p. 330.

33. Despite Napoleon's failure, he continued to be regarded as having plans to restore the Jews to the Land of Israel. His purposes in establishing a Sanhedrin in 1806–1808 were examined in that light, and Metternich likewise assumed that Napoleon's purpose was to harness the Jews of Europe to his cause so they would assist him in his conquests. A note from that period states: "The Jews are beginning almost to believe in Bonaparte as the Messiah." Mevorakh, "The Messianic Question," pp. 88–91.

34. Thousands of Jews perished in the European cholera epidemic of 1831–1832. Those of a messianist bent saw the phenomenon as a positive omen. For example: "Although my soul is terrified and my spirit still has not calmed down within me after the sorrows and tribulations that have come over us . . . do not fear . . . for according to my reasoning, and what has been verified to me and my confidants regarding the force of the decree that has been issued on account of our many sins to augment the torments for our good, *to bring near the set time for our redemption, may it be speedy*." Remarks of the *Admor* of Munkacz, Ḥayyim El'azar Shapira, to his *ḥasidim* on the eve of the festival of Sukkot, 1831, *Yemot ha-Mashiaḥ*, pp. 76–77.

Judah Ḥai Alcalay asserts that the ten years between 5590 (1830) and 5600 (1840) were a sort of "ten days of penitence" and that the woes afflicting Israel were designed to rouse them to repentance in anticipation of the End-year: "In 1831, there occurred the first cholera [epidemic], which destroyed many families and embittered many mothers." *Kitvei ha-Rav Yehudah Alqal'ai*, Yiẓḥaq Refael, ed., vol. 1 (Jerusalem, 1975), p. 75.

One eulogist brackets the earthquake in Safed with the second outbreak of the epidemic in Europe in 1836: "[In] which, on account of our many sins, great communities in Safed and Hebron were destroyed, houses collapsed, and several hundred were killed. . . . A plague and epidemic, the illness of cholera, God protect us, spread throughout almost all the cities of Europe and claimed many victims." The eulogist associates the cholera epidemic with the decline of the Torah's status following Akiva Eiger's death in 1838: "It is said at the end of [tractate] *Sotah* [49b], 'in the [time of] the Footsteps of the Messiah, brazenness will prevail, etc., and those who fear sin will be despised and truth will be absent . . . until the fulfillment of their statement that the son of David will not come until a fish is sought for one who is ill and will not be found,' for it is known that a sage is compared to a fish." *Qol Bokhim*, R. Israel ben Leivush of Krotchin ([Breslau], 1838).

That said, it should be noted as well that other eulogists tied the events solely to the sins of the generation, assigning to them no messianic quality.

35. *Iggerot ha-Peqidim* (Letters of the Clerks), vol. 4, p. 48b.

36. Ibid., p. 102b.

37. Ibid., p. 116b.

38. This is the only occasion on which Lehren manifests an understanding of the priority of local needs over funding for the Jews in the Land of Israel.

39. *Iggerot ha-Peqidim* (Letters of the Clerks), vol. 5, p. 66b.

40. Ibid., p. 78a. These modes of thought appear as well in English millenarian literature. In an essay printed apparently in the 1830s, one finds the view that the Napoleonic Wars and the success of the Greeks in gaining their independence from the Turkish yoke are signs heralding the return of Israel to its land. E. Irving, *The Signs of Time* (London, 1810), pp. 10–14. Opposition to the view that there is a link between this-worldly wars and the approaching arrival of the Messiah can be found in *Sefer ha-Zikhronot* by Mordecai Samuel Girondi: "I heard the sound of a great tumult . . . the masses of many nations endeavoring to throw off the fear of their kings and princes who rule over them. With many sounds and full-voiced cheering, these cities and provinces, with no knowledge and no understanding, plan to destroy the peace of the world, and this brings fear and trembling to the hearts of those who fear God and love peace. . . . But I have come to tell you that you are a delight in my eye and your heart should not believe the words of the sage R. Solomon Samuel of Ancona, a teacher in the *talmud Torah* study house in your holy encampment, who heralds and says publicly that these sounds and cheering are signs of our righteous Messiah, for they are all dreams and vanities that have passed through his deceiving mind for several years." Samuel Mordecai Girondi, *Sefer ha-Zikhronot*, sec. 230 (1848), ms. Montefiore no. 58 in Jews' College Library, London.

41. S. Ettinger, "The Statute of 1804," *He-Avar* 22 (1977), pp. 87–110 (Tel-Aviv) (Hebrew).

42. Y. ha-Levi Lifschitz, *Zikhron Ya'aqov*, part 1 (Kovno-Slobodka, 1924), photocopied edition (Israel, 1968), pp. 203–208. Of these measures' profoundly disturbing effects Lifschitz writes: "No pen is powerful enough, and no writer's hand enduring enough, to describe and depict the shocking images, the cries of despair and howling of the mothers, fathers, and family of the pitiful soul snatched by the kidnappers. . . . The kidnappers would burst into the house accompanied by armed soldiers and forcibly snatch the child away from his parents, carrying him in their arms to the guardhouse. . . . The parents would run after the kidnappers, screaming bitterly. The mothers and the wives would beat their breasts and pull the hair from their heads . . . even hearts as hard as flint would melt and become springs of water upon hearing the wails and keening of the mothers: 'My son, my son, would that I had miscarried before you were born; woe, woe is me, would that you were now given over to be a slave to slaves, to trample your flesh so you are not defiled by eating non-kosher meat; I would rather you were brought to the grave now, for then you would be dancing in the circle of God and I would rejoice, for you would be buried in a Jewish grave. Woe, woe is me, for your bones will fall into a grave of cruel gentiles, from numerous torments and murderous beatings by the wicked. People! . . . Why are you silent about my poor son being murdered?' . . . Such [mournful] sounds are now heard in the streets . . . but [after a short while] they will fall silent . . . for can it be that they will cancel the edict?" Ibid., p. 114.

The author goes on to recount the harsh fate that befell those who were taken: "Many of those who were seized at first did not put any food in their mouths, because of their great anguish. And some continued [to refuse food], contriving thereby to choose death and thereby be saved from a more bitter death, that is, service in Nikolai's army, which was regarded as a double death—a death of cruel torment, and a spiritual death of apostasy and conversion. But nature takes its course, and when hunger bore down on them, and they smelled the aroma of the food placed before them, slowly they were persuaded to eat." Ibid., p. 115. And see, more recently, M. F. Stanislawski, *Tsar Nicholas I and the Jews: The Transformation of Jewish Society in Russia 1825–1855* (Philadelphia, 1983).

43. Over the course of the nineteenth century, about 70,000 Jewish soldiers converted. Lifschitz, *Zikhron Ya'aqov*, p. 211.

44. Ibid., p. 213.

45. Ibid., pp. 210, 213.

46. *Hillel ben Shaḥar*, R. Hillel of Kovno (Warsaw, 1804), p. 23a.

47. Ibid., p. 24a.

48. Ibid., p. 25a.

49. *Sanhedrin* 97b.

50. *Hillel ben Shaḥar*, p. 8a.

51. Ibid., p. 25a.

52. Ibid., p. 42a.

53. J. J. and B. Rivlin, *Iggerot ha-Peqidim ve-ha-Armarkalim mei-Amsterdam* (Letters of the *Peqidim* and *Amarkalim* of Amsterdam), vol. 1 (Jerusalem, 1970) (Hebrew) (hereafter: Rivlin and Rivlin, *Letters of the Clerks*), pp. 10, 11, 14, 25, 127–133.

54. "And now, in this recent generation, when troubles come frequently, there is no source of livelihood; and this people of God are at a low point—for on that account we fall and plead before our Master, have mercy, have mercy upon us! . . . Help us as we pray! . . . And if He is a bit angry over the sins of His people, they [the gentiles] have augmented their harsh yoke many times more than warranted . . . and they have violated the oath imposed on them by the Lord our God not to subjugate Israel too harshly so they will not press for the End." *Iggerot Ereẓ Yisra'el* (*Letters of the Land of Israel*), ed. A. Yaari (Tel-Aviv, 1943), p. 352.

55. The spread of the belief in the existence and possible discovery of the Ten Lost Tribes of Israel during the period under consideration is noteworthy. To cite some of the evidence: "So they are not mislead by vanity, we should go and make them wings so they may return to the land of our ancestors, as many went sixty years ago on hearing rumors of the Messiah son of Joseph and the Ten Tribes proudly returning, cited by journalists as a basis for mocking Israel and withdrawing support for their activities." *Ha-Levanon*, no. 32 (20 March 1873). The author was Ẓevi Hirsch ha-Levi Lifschitz of Anikast, reacting to rumors, reported in the newspaper *Ha-Maggid*, that the Turkish sultan intended to sell the Land of Israel to the Jews. This evidence is supported by the reprintings of Menasheh ben Israel's book about the Ten Tribes in Shklov in 1797 and in Vilna in 1836 and 1837. The Shklov 1797 edition contains the following remarks by the printer: "And so, we have found that this book is nearly unavailable in our region, so we have taken the initiative to bring it to press so the Children of Israel may find some respite for their souls in our present exile." He continues: "For a long time now I have wondered why nothing has been heard from our brethren, the Ten Tribes. . . . For why should not our brethren the children of Israel in the lands of Germany, Holland, England, and Italy—whom God has endowed with a scientific mind and with high standing in the hearts of the nations and their princes—investigate this important matter? . . . Accordingly, I said that since this is a time of good news . . . and our brethren the Children of Israel in this bitter exile have an op-

portunity to rest from their sorrow and sadness and stop the fools of the nation from going astray by denying the existence of the Kingdom of the Jews." *Miqveh Yisra'el,* Menasheh ben Israel (Shklov, 1797). The same wording appears in the Vilna editions of 1836 and 1837. I believe the concluding words of the quotation to be directed against rationalist circles that battled against the belief in the existence of the Ten Tribes and the prevalent sense of the approaching End-time. That rationalist view, it seems to me, was expressed in the publication of *Sippur Ḥalomot Qeẓ ha-Pela'ot* or *Me'ora'ot Ẓevi,* a collection of letters written against Shabbetai Ẓevi and his disciples and published in six editions during the years 1804–1840. The introduction to that book states: "And now we have brought [it] to print, to stir the congregation of the children of Israel and fortify it so as not to budge the least bit from our commandments . . . and not to heed words of falsehood that contradict our holy Torah."

Further evidence of the belief in the Ten Tribes is provided by Jacob Safir: "The persecutions in the Diaspora in the year [1830] aroused many of the leading authorities among our brethren the Children of Israel in Lithuania to ask the *ga'on,* the splendor of Israel, may his memory be blessed [R. Israel of Shklov] to select wise men to search after our brethren the tribes of Jeshurun and sons of Moses, for it is told that in previous years there was a time of trouble for Israel, and those lost ones came and saved them from their woes." Jacob Safir, *Masa Teiman* [1858], ed. A. Yaari (Jerusalem, 1951), p. 154. See further discussion in chapter 5 of this volume.

56. Yaari, *Iggerot Ereẓ Yisra'el,* p. 353.

57. Ibid., pp. 347–348.

58. Ibid., p. 348.

59. "And all sources of livelihood and sustenance will be diminished, and Israel will become greatly impoverished. The poor and deprived will seek bread and there will be none; other harsh decrees will beset [them]; and children will come to the point of birth but the strength to bear them will be lacking. It will be a time of trouble for Jacob, but from it, he will be saved." Ibid., p. 351.

60. [*Tanna'im* (sing., *tanna*) are the rabbis of the mishnaic period.—***translator***]

61. Yaari, *Iggerot Ereẓ Yisra'el,* p. 348.

62. *Sefer ha-Zohar, Peirush ha-Sulam, Parashat Va'eira,* par. 13.

63. *Lev. Rabbah, Seder Shemini,* end of chap. 3. [The *midrash* make this point through wordplays on Lev. 11:7, which mentions the swine as an example of an animal that may not be eaten. One wordplay is noted in the text; the other is based on the multiple meanings of the Hebrew verb stem *g-r-r,* including "grind"—as in "chew the cud"—and "follow upon." As already noted, Edom (or Esau), is rabbinic code for Rome and, later, Christian Europe.—***translator***]

64. In addition to granting equal rights to the Christian minority, Muhammad Ali also arranged and outfitted his troops in the European manner.

65. *Iggerot ha-Peqidim* (Letters of the Clerks), vol. 5, p. 86a. Elsewhere Lehren says: "May it be [God's] will that this king or ruler remain in power, but if, God forbid, the government returns to what it was under his predecessor, then let the Protector of Israel protect the remnant of His nation. Ibid., vol. 8, p. 7a.

66. Ibid., vol. 5, p. 113b.

67. *Jewish Intelligence* (London, 1836) (hereafter: *J. I.*), p. 203.

68. *Yis'u Harim Shalom,* Sila and Eliezer Bregman, ed. A Bartura (Jerusalem, 1968), p. 76.

69. Ibid. p. 99.

CHAPTER 2

1. "R. Qatina said, the world will exist for six thousand years . . . just as the sabbatical year sets the land aside for one year out of seven, so the world is set aside for one thousand out of seven thousand years. . . . It was taught in the academy of Elijah, the world will exist for six thousand years." *Sanhedrin* 97a.

2. *Zohar, Peirush ha-Sulam, Genesis, Parashat Veyeira,* part 1, sec.117. One of the most widely recognized interpreters of the *Zohar,* Shalom Buzaglo, writes in his *Miqdash Melekh* on the *Zohar* that "if Israel were but worthy, they would be redeemed during the first sixty years of the sixth millennium, and so during every succeeding sixty-year period; but if they do not merit it, the limiting point of the End would be six hundred years [of the sixth millennium]." *Miqdash Melekh,* part 1 (on the Book of Genesis), p. 148b–149a (Amsterdam 1750).

3. *Kitvei ha-Rav Yehudah Alqal'ai,* p. 78.

4. Ibid., p. 73. [The text reads "600," equivalent, as noted, to 5600. The distinction will not be drawn unless pertinent.—***translator***]

5. Ibid., p. 106.

6. Ibid., p. 147.

7. Ibid., p. 275.

8. Jacob Katz, "Messianism and Nationalism in the Teaching of Rabbi Alcalay," *Shivat Ẓiyyom* 4 (1956), p. 12 (Hebrew).

9. See his letter to Baron Anschel Rothschild, 12 Elul 5596 (1836), in Klausner, *Rabbi Kalisher's Zionist Writings,* pp. 1–14.

10. *Qol Mevasser* (A Voice Brings Tidings), R. Mattityahu ha-Kohen Mizraḥi (Matthias ben Samuel ha-Kohen), San Francisco, Sutro Library, 136; Jerusalem, Yad Ben-Zvi Library, 2672 (microfilm).

11. Ibid., p. 53b.

12. Ibid., p. 17a.

13. Ibid.; similarly, pp. 37b, 93b, 114a.

14. Ibid., p. 57b. [*Tiqqun ḥaẓot* is a mystical ritual of mourning for the destruction of Jerusalem, conducted at the middle of the night.—***translator***]

15. Ibid., p. 94b.

16. Ibid., p. 93a. [A leap year is created by intercalating a thirteenth month when needed to keep the 354-day lunar year synchronized with the 365¼-day solar year. The Hebrew term for the process is *ibbur ha-shanim,* literally, "making the years pregnant."—***translator***]

17. Ibid., p. 104a.

18. Ibid., p. 97b.

19. Ibid., p. 93a.

20. "This teaches that Israel will be gathered in the Upper Galilee and Messiah son of Joseph will anticipate them from the Galilee and they will go up from there, with all Israel joining him, to Jerusalem." *Pesiqta Zutreta, Balaq, Midrash Leqqet Tov* on the verse "I see it but not now . . ." (Num. 24:17). Similarly, Maimonides ruled: "At first, when the Temple was built, the great court sat in the chamber of hewn stone. . . . But when things went awry, they were exiled from place to place, to ten different places, ultimately sitting in Tiberias. . . . And there is a tradition that from Tiberias they will begin to return, and from there, they will be moved to the Temple." Maimonides, *Mishneh Torah, Hilkhot Sanhedrin* 14:12. Evidence that the Jews of northern Persia adhered to this notion as a practical matter is provided by the missionary Jo-

seph Wolff, who notes that many Jews believe the Messiah will appear in Safed. Joseph Wolff, *Researches and Missionary Labours* (London, 1835), p. 55.

21. *Qol Mevasser*, p. 81a.

22. Ibid., p. 60a.

23. Ibid., p. 81a.

24. Ibid., p. 56b. [According to Gen. 7:6, the flood came when Noah was six hundred years old.—***translator***]

25. Ibid., p. 104 a; see also p. 53b.

26. Ibid., p. 73b. This vision is reported to have been on Thursday night, 18 Sivan 5576 (1816) in the city of Kozbin. It is noteworthy that most of his visions occurred on Thursday night, the time for reciting *tiqqun ḥaẓot.*

27. Ibid., p. 97b. The name Jacob (*Ya'aqov*) is sometimes spelled *y-'-q-w-b* rather than the more usual *y-'-q-b;* the extra *waw,* the letter having the numerical value six, is taken as alluding to the six hundredth year of the sixth millennium.

28. Gen. 32:23 et seq.

29. *Qol Mevasser*, p. 10a; see also p. 73b. The numerical value of Yabboq (*y-b-q*) is 112, the Jubilee cycle comprises 50 years, and 112 × 50 = 5,600.

30. Ibid., 51a.

31. Ibid. 94b. [The quoted verse is not biblical; it appears in the liturgy for Rosh ha-Shanah and is based on Jer. 20:17, understood as "her womb was pregnant with the world."—***translator***]

32. Ibid., p. 57a. (The numerical value of the highlighted letters is 600.)

33. Ibid., p. 75b.

34. Ibid., p. 4a.

35. Ibid., p. 39a.

36. Ibid. This verse had also been used as support for the messianic revelation of Shabbetai Zevi in 5426 (1666).

37. Ibid., p. 37b.

38. Ibid., p. 3b.

39. Ibid., p. 10a. [The allusion is in the numerical value—590—of the boldface letters in the phrase "beginning of the End," ***teḥillat ha-qeẓ,—translator***]

40. 5590 is 410 years before 6000. A different calculation based on the *gematria* of the trebled word *qadosh* (in Isa. 6:3) can be found in an account of the meeting between the convert Joseph Wolff and the rabbinic emissary Me'ir ben Isaiah of Safed. Wolff claims he met the rabbinic emissary on 12 December 1831, while touring Teheran, and the latter argued that the Messiah would arrive within nine years. He relied on the argument that the duration of the three Temples would be equivalent to the value of *qadosh qadosh qadosh.* Since the First Temple stood for 420 years and the Second Temple for 410 years, it follows that the future Third Temple will stand for 400 years, until the end of the sixth millennium—that is, from the year 5600. Wolff, *Researches*, pp. 55–56.

As the Hebrew edition of this book was going to press, Dr. Joseph Tovey advised me—and I thank him for doing so—that M. Brinner had presented a paper on the manuscript of *Qol Mevasser* at the Fifth World Congress of Jewish Studies; his remarks are printed as W. M. Brinner, "A Nineteenth-Century 'Messiah' From Azerbaizn," in *Proceedings of the Fifth World Congress of Jewish Studies*, vol. 2 (Jerusalem, 1972), pp. 6–12. Brinner surmises that A. Sutro purchased the manuscript from the convert Shapiro, who lived in Jerusalem; in his view, Shapiro obtained the manuscript after Matthias ben Samuel immigrated to the Land of Israel. It is surprising that Brinner failed to note the frequent references in the manuscript to the year 5600 and was taken only by the reference to the year 5590, even though it was merely the passageway to the complete redemption in 5600.

41. *Ḥishuvei Qeẓ*, R. Mattityahu ha-Kohen Mizraḥi (Matthias ben Samuel ha-Kohen), Israel National Library, Manuscript Institute, 4°1065.

42. *Qol Mevasser*, p. 110b.

43. Ibid., p. 75b. In discussing the mission of two messianic brothers, the author appears to be using a messianic passage in *Pirqei de-Rabbi Eli'ezer*: "R. Ishmael says, The Ishmaelites are destined to do fifteen things in the world at the End of Days . . . and two brothers will stand over them at the end as princes, and in their days, the scion of David will arise." *Pirqei de-Rabbi Eli'ezer* (Eshkol edition) (Jerusalem, 1973), pp. 102–103.

44. *Qol Mevasser*, p. 70b; see also p. 111a.

45. Ibid., p. 72b.

46. Ibid.

47. Ibid., p. 93a–b.

48. Ibid., p. 86b.

49. Ibid., p. 106a.

50. Ibid., p. 72a.

51. Ibid., p. 75b.

52. Ibid., p. 105a.

53. Ibid., pp. 110a, 111a.

54. Ibid., pp. 58b, 87a.

55. Ibid., pp. 81a, 87a.

56. David of the House of Hillel from the community of *Perushim* in Safed spent the years 1824 to 1832 in Syria, Mesopotamia, the Persian Gulf coast, and India. Among other things, he sought traces of the Ten Tribes. Abraham Yaari, "The Travels of David Beit Hillel" (Hebrew), *Sinai* 4 (1939), pp. 24–53; H.R.Y. Fischel, "Journey to Kurdistan, Persia, and Babylonia" (Hebrew), *Sinai* 5 (1939), pp. 240–247. The apostate and missionary Joseph Wolff lived in that area at the start of 1831; he had the same purpose in mind. Wolff's quest took him as far as Kashmir and China in order to establish that some descendants of the Ten Tribes could be found there. Wolff, *Researches*, pp. 56, 194.

57. *Qol Mevasser*, pp. 97b–98a.

58. Ibid.

59. "*Shemu'ah al Ma'aseh bi-Yerushalayim* 1835," London, ms. Sassoon, 672; Israel National Library, Manuscript Photocopy Insitute, 8959. The manuscript bears the date of 14 Tishri 5595 (17 October 1834).

60. Ibid., p. 8a.

61. Ibid., p. 9a.

62. *J. I.* (1836), p. 255.

63. Y. D. Bet ha-Levi, *History of the Jews of Kalish* (Hebrew) (Tel-Aviv, 1965), pp. 327–328.

64. *Yis'u Harim Shalom*, p. 101.

65. *Jerusalem: A. M. Lunz Memorial Volume* (Hebrew), ed. E. L. Sukenik and Y. Peres (Jerusalem, 1928), pp. 170–171.

66. S. N. Spyridon, *Annals of Palestine, 1821–1841, Journal of the Palestine Oriental Society* 18, nos. 1–2 (1938), p. 123.

67. *J.I.* (1835), p. 199.

68. *Pi Mosheh* (The Mouth of Moses), R. Moses Turgeman, Israel National Library, Manuscript Institute, 8°4424.. This important source may shed light on the fig-

ure of Moses Turgeman. It seems to me that the manuscript's author was the Moses Turgeman mentioned twice in the *Mifqad Montefiori be-5599* (Montefiore Census of 1839)—first in *Luaḥ Shemot Benei Yisra'el ha-Sefaradim ha-Yoshevim be-Ir ha-Qodesh Ẓefat t'v'b'b'* (Listing of the Names of the Sefardic Jews Residing in the Holy City of Safed") and again in *Eileh Shemot Ḥakhamei ve-Rabbanei ha-Nimẓa'im Poh Ir ha-Qodesh Ẓefat t'v* (These Are the Names of the Sages and Rabbis Here in the Holy City of Safed"). According to these entries, R. Moses emigrated to the Land of Israel from Tuscany in 1834. Evidence that he was an acknowledged sage appears in a listing compiled in the community of Fez: "When the perfect sage, the honorable rabbi R. Maimon ben Petshitsha came on a mission for the Mughrabi sages and poor people in Jerusalem (may it be built and established speedily and in our day) and recounted all the events . . . especially of the Mughrabi rabbi, the perfect sage, whose treasure was fear of God, the honorable rabbi R. Moses Aturgeman, may God protect and bless him. . . . In the days of his youth, he lived here in Fez (may God protect it) [contrary to the view that R. Moses Turgeman was born in Tiberias] and all who know him speak his praises. *Fez ve-Ḥakhamehah* (*Fez and Its Sages*), ed. Ovadiah David, vol. 2 (Jerusalem, 1979), p. 318. It seems to me that R. Moses Turgeman moved from Safed to Jerusalem in anticipation of the year 5600 ["The mouth of the speaker and compiler, a fellow of the study house of Shem *within Jerusalem*, the youngster Moses son of the honorable rabbi Aturgeman (may his end be good)," in *Pi Mosheh*, p. 2a], where he later led an open battle against the leadership of the local Sefardic community. The details regarding Turgeman and the battle of the Mughrabi community against the Sefardic establishment in Jerusalem remain to be clarified through further research. See the sources mentioned in Y. Barnai, "The 'Mughrabi' Community in Jerusalem in the Nineteenth Century," in *Chapters in the History of the Jewish Community in Jerusalem: Jerusalem in the Early Ottoman Period, Jerusalem in the Modern Period*, ed. Aharon Kedar and Ben-Zion Yehoshua (Hebrew) (Jerusalem, 1976), vol. 1, pp. 132–135.

69. *Pi Mosheh*, part 2, p. 38b.

70. Ibid., p. 40a.

71. Ibid., p. 1a.

72. Ibid., p. 38b.

73. Ibid.

74. Ibid., p. 11a.

75. Ibid., p. 38a–b.

76. Ibid., p. 14a.

77. Ibid., p. 7a.

78. Ibid., p. 40a.

79. *Ḥibbur al Shenat 5600* (Essay on the Year 5600), Moses Turgeman, Jewish Theological Seminary of America (New York, 1982); Israel National Library, Manuscript Photocopy Institute, 11080. The two manuscripts read almost identically. *Pi Mosheh* antedates *Ḥibbur al Shenat 5600*. On p. 2b of *Ḥibbur al Shenat 5600*, Turgeman refers to *Pi Mosheh*. On the manuscript's first page, he writes: "The completion of this portion on the Eve of Rosh ha-Shanah 5601 [1840]."

80. Menasheh of Ilya's grandson writes: "The Ga'on R. Menasheh journeyed several times to the provincial capital Mogilev . . . to seek out his friend, the rabbi, sage, and renowned nobleman, R. Shemariah Luria." *Alfei Menasheh*, part 2, R. Menasheh ben R. Joseph of Ilya (Vilna, 1822), p. 8.

81. Ibid., pp. 51–52.

82. Ibid. p. 52.

83. Ibid. pp. 53–54.

84. Menasheh of Ilya died on 14 July 1831. Ibid., p. 13.

85. "And know that all these days allude to six thousand years . . . and all the details of these six days [of creation] pertain to the six thousand [years], each one at its day and hour. Know, accordingly, that the time of redemption is at hand . . . but I adjure the reader, by the Lord God of Israel, not to reveal this. . . ." *Sifra de-Ẓeni'uta* (Commentary of R. Elijah ben Solomon Zalman) (Vilna, 1820), p. 54b.

86. Benjamin Bary, *Zeitgemesse Gedanken über die Emancipation des Menschen,* (Königsberg, 1843), p. 205. My thanks to Dr. Saul Stampfer and Prof. Jacob Katz for telling me of this source and providing me a photocopy of the only extant copy, located in the Harvard University Library.

87. According to the *Mifqad Montefiori be-5599* (Montefiore Census of 1839).

88. *Sha'arei Ẓedeq le-Zera Yiẓḥaq,* R. Aviezer ben Isaac of Ticktin (Jerusalem, 1843), p. 56a.

89. [In *h-t-r*, the letter *h*, with a numerical value of 5, represents 5,000; *t-r* represents 600. The thousands column is usually omitted in the representation of dates, however, so *r-t-h* (= 605) represents 5605.—***translator***]

90. Ibid., p. 60b.

91. Judah Yudel Rosenberg, *Tif'eret Maharal* (Pyetrikov, 1912), sec. 30.

92. Ibid. The *Ẓaddiq* Aryeh Leib of Shpola died on 24 September 1811.

93. Jacob Ẓevi Yellish (of Dynow), *Qehalot Ya'aqov* (Lemberg, 1870), introduction. Jacob Ẓevi Yellish died on 28 March 1825.

94. Ibid.

95. Joshua Mondshain, ed., *Migdal Oz* (Jerusalem, 1980), p. 490.

96. Yiẓḥak Alfasi, *Gur, the Founder; the Author of* Ḥiddushei ha-Rim (Hebrew) (Tel-Aviv, 1954), pp. 89–90. My thanks to Dr. Alfasi for directing my attention to the matters treated in his book.

97. *Yemot ha-Mashiaḥ,* p. 52.

98. In his study of "The Tarniks" (above, n. 30) Prof. Abraham Duker published similar literary traditions. He even pointed to an interesting connection between the messianic movement among Polish Jews and a similar, contemporaneous movement among Christian mystics in Europe generally and Poland in particular. Nathan of Nemerov, a disciple of Naḥman of Bratslav, tells of the messianic hopes for 5600: "Just as many erred with respect to that year, the year 5600, saying that the End would take place that year, and many were ruined by that, for it caused several apostasies and profanations of God, as is known." See Mendel Piekarz, *Polish Hasidism* (Jerusalem, 1990) (Hebrew), p. 261; Mendel Piekarz, *Hasidic Conduct* (Jerusalem 1999) (Hebrew), p. 360. See also the historian Rafael Mahler, *Hasidism and Enlightenment* (Israel, 1961) (Hebrew), p. 321: "Masses of the people in eastern Europe, as well as Hasidic leaders and great Torah-scholars, were caught up in that belief [in the year 5600]."

99. R. Jacob Emden, *Torat ha-Qana'ut* (Amsterdam 5512 [1752]), p. 68b, cited in Judah Liebes, "The Messianism of R. Jacob Emden and Its Relationship to Sabbateanism," (Hebrew) *Tarbiẓ* 49 (1980), pp. 122–165. R. El'azar Rokeiaḥ, a leader of the renowned *kloyz* in Brody, likewise determined, in his Torah commentary *Ma'aseh Rokeiaḥ,* "that the time of the future redemption will be no later than 600 [years] into the sixth millennium." *Ma'aseh Rokeiaḥ* (on the Torah), R. El'azar Rokeiaḥ (Lvov, 1850), p. 10b, cited in Y. Ḥisdai, "Early Settlement of 'Hasidim' and 'Mitnaggedim' in the Land of Israel: Immigration of '*Miẓvah*' and of 'Mission' " (Hebrew) *Shalem* 4,

(1984), p. 266 n. 151. Rokeiaḥ served as rabbi of Amsterdam from 1736 to 1740; he emigrated to the Land of Israel and died in Safed in 1742. It can be assumed that these ideas were current in scholarly and kabbalistic circles throughout Poland.

100. *Binah le-Ittim*, p. 23b.

101. *Ahavat David*, R. El'azar ben David [Plekelsh] (Prague 1800), author's introduction.

102. Ibid.

103. Ibid., p. 21b.

104. In contrast to the Jews of eastern Europe, who generally feared committing their hopes for redemption to writing, Lehren had no qualms about freely expressing himself on matters of messianism and redemption.

105. *Iggerot ha-Peqidim* (Letters of the Clerks), vol. 4, p. 96b. Letter of 2 May 1831.

106. Ibid., vol. 5, p. 118a. That the year 5600 was to be a sabbatical year buttressed the belief that it was the year in which the Messiah would come, for it fit the Talmud's statement that "at the departure of the sabbatical year, the son of David will come." *Sanhedrin* 97a.

107. *Iggerot ha-Peqidim* (Letters of the Clerks), vol. 5, p. 140a, letter of 28 August 1833. ["Omitting the thousands figure" (lit. "in the small enumeration") is a standard way of describing a date represented by Hebrew letters; it is sometimes expressed and always understood. As already noted, for example, the year 5600 is usually represented by the letters *t-r*, equivalent to six hundred.—***translator***]

108. Quoted in Jacob Katz, "On the Year 5600 as a Messianic Year and Its Influence on the Efforts of the *Perushim* to Hasten the Redemption" (Hebrew), *Cathedra* 24 (1982), p. 73.

109. *Simlat Binyamin*, p. 57a.

110. Joseph Crooll, *The Restoration of Israel* (London 1814), p. 48.

111. Joseph Crooll, *The Fifth Empire* (London, 1829), pp. 6–8.

112. Ibid., pp. 73–74.

113. Joseph Crooll, *The Last Generation* (Cambridge, 1829), p. 16.

114. Ibid., p. 18.

115. Ibid.

116. Ibid., p. 20.

117. Ibid., p. 23.

118. *J. E.* (1828), p. 157.

119. *Monthly Intelligence* (hereafter: *M. I.*) (1831), p. 103.

120. *M. I.* (1834), p. 22.

121. *Ibid.*, p. 133.

122. A. E. Bonar and R. McCheyne, *Narrative of a Mission of Inquiry to the Jews from the Church of Scotland in 1839* (Edinburgh, 1841) 3rd ed., p. 321.

123. *M. I.* (1832), p. 103.

124. Bonar and McShane, *Narrative of a Mission of Inquiry*, p. 352.

125. Ibid., pp. 378–379.

126. Ibid., p. 402.

127. *J. E.* (1827), p. 52.

128. *J. I.* (1840), p. 73.

129. Bonar and McShane, *Narrative of a Mission of Inquiry*, p. 429.

130. Ibid.

131. *J. I.* (1836), p. 294.

132. Ibid.

133. *J. E.* (1823), p. 426.
134. Ibid.
135. Ibid.
136. *M. I.* (1830), p. 91.
137. *J. I.* (1836), p. 5.
138. Ibid.
139. Ibid., p. 188.
140. *J. I.* (1841), p. 226.
141. *J. I.* (1839), p. 131.
142. *J. I.* (1841), pp. 16–17.
143. *J. I.* (1842), p. 233–234.

CHAPTER 3

1. Joshua Ben-Arieh, *A City Reflected in Its Times: Jerusalem in the Nineteenth Century*, Vol. 1: *The Old City* (Jerusalem, 1977), p. 318 (Hebrew).

2. *Iggerot Ereẓ Yisra'el*, p. 339.

3. Ben-Arieh, *City Reflected in Its Times*, pp. 100–121.

4. "For at this time we could do such a thing [immigrate to the Land of Israel] only in poverty and hardship, and we would be likely to return to live outside the Land. As we have heard so have we seen daily in practice." *Qol David*, R. David Joseph Ayash (Leghorn, 1821), p. 26b.

5. "And thank God, many of the holy nation are coming to settle in God's territory . . ." (written in 1832). *Ḥibbat Yerushalayim*, R. Ḥayyim Horwitz (Jerusalem, 1844), p. 39a.

6. M. Solomon, *Three Generations in the Yishuv, 1812–1913* (Jerusalem, 1951), p. 18 (Hebrew); M. Benayahu, "A Response to R. Benjamin Mordecai Navon," *Sinai* 24 (1949), p. 206 (Hebrew); Aryeh Leib Frumkin, "The Beginnings of the Settlement of the Ashkenazim Called *Perushim: Ha-Emet mei-Ereẓ Tiẓmaḥ* (Hebrew) in *Me'asef Ẓiyyon* [Zion anthology], 6 volumes (Jerusalem, 1926–1934), vol. 2, p. 132; *Yis'u Harim Shalom*, pp. 60–61; *J. E.* (1827), p. 72; and many others.

7. T. H. Rivlin, *The Vision of Zion: Shklov to Jerusalem* (Tel-Aviv, 1947), p. 43. This is one of several versions of the account of the beginning of the *aliyah* by the Vilna Ga'on's disciples.

8. *Amud ha-Yemini*, R. Abraham ben Asher Anschel (Minsk, 1811), author's introduction.

9. Ibid.

10. Ibid.

11. Ibid.

12. *Pinqas Qehillat Brod* (Brody Journal), 5568–5572 [1808–1812], Ms. 76004, Jewish Theological Seminary, New York; Israel National Library, Manuscript Photocopy Institute, 29842, p. 89.

13. A bill of sale signed by the leaders of the community of *Perushim* in Safed, 8 November 1812, to "the venerable Rabbi Joseph Jacob Yakovka Frenkel ben Asher Anschel of Breslava"; *Ha-Emet mei-Ereẓ Tiẓmaḥ*, p. 143.

14. ["Commandments contingent on the Land" are various provisions of Jewish law, related primarily to agricultural matters, that apply only within the Land of Israel.—***translator***]

15. *Sha'arei Ẓedeq*, R. Abraham Danzig (Vilna, 1812), author's introduction.

16. Ibid., p. 11a.

17. In 5571 (1811), Abraham Danzig was sent to Germany to arrange for regular subventions to the *kolel* of the *Perushim*. In the letter given him by the Nobles of Vilna, addressed to the leaders of the Berlin community and dated to 21 March 1811, they wrote: "For in those days and at this time, several esteemed and leading members of our community will be journeying to our holy land . . . and, perhaps, the aforementioned rabbi as well." *Sheluḥei Ereẓ Yisra'el*, ed. Abraham Yaari (Jerusalem, 1951), pp. 759–760.

18. *Sha'arei Ẓedeq* (Danzig), p. 12a.

19. Ibid.

20. Ibid.

21. Ibid., Introduction. It appears that the requests for passports were justified on the basis of a desire to visit "ancestral graves." *Qorot ha-Ittim*, part 2, p. 17.

22. *Sha'arei Ẓedeq* (Danzig), p. 12a.

23. P. Grajewski, *Jerusalem Journal* (Jerusalem, 5704 [1944]), p. 2 (Hebrew). The figure of 461 *olim* referred to by Israel of Shklov apparently refers to the period preceding the epidemic or perhaps to an even earlier date in the calculations of R. Aryeh Ne'eman; *Ha-Emet mei-Ereẓ Tiẓmaḥ*, p. 135. In the year 1816, the *Perushim* numbered only 188; the decline was due to the large number that had succumbed to the epidemic. Rivlin and Rivlin, *Letters of the Clerks*, vol. 1, p. 218. According to a recently discovered manuscript by Menaḥem Mendel of Shklov, the number of Lithuanian *olim* circa 1812 was 417. *Kitvei ha-Ga'on R. Menaḥem Mendel* (Jerusalem, 2001), vol. 1, p. 9.

24. The individuals were Naḥum of Zamot; Isaac, the preacher of Dvaranoy; and Jeremiah of Vilna. *Ha-Emet mei-Ereẓ Tiẓmaḥ*, p. 130. The missionary Joseph Wolff reports that in Jerusalem, on 27 March 1822, he met the young Abraham ben Jeremiah, whom he estimated to have been born in 1806. Because he had been born in Jerusalem, the *Perushim* referred to him as a "holy child." It appears that this Abraham was the son of Jeremiah of Vilna, implying that the latter was already in the Land of Israel at that time and even attempted to settle in Jerusalem. The *Mifqad Montefiori be-5599* (Montefiore Census of 1839) likewise reports that Abraham son of Jeremiah (rabbinic emissary of the *Ḥurvah*) was born in Jerusalem in 5568 (1808) (?).

25. *Ha-Emet mei-Ereẓ Tiẓmaḥ*, p. 132. On the number of immigrants in 1810, R. Ḥayyim Katz says: "In that year, the arrivals in the holy land outnumbered the Sefardim, and many came from all lands and settled here [in Safed]." *Iggerot Ereẓ Yisra'el*, p. 338.

26. *Sheluhei Ereẓ Yisra'el*, p. 760.

27. Solomon, *Three Generations in the Yishuv*, p. 18.

28. Elijah Bialystoker signed, on behalf of the *Perushim*, the settlement agreement reached with the Hasidim in Warsaw on 24 February 1818.

29. *Iggerot mi-Yerushalayim*, Central Archive for the History of the Jewish People, Jerusalem Unit, sec. J/26.

30. *Sefer Dor Yesharim* [including the genealogy of the Harkavy family] (New York, 1903), p. 12.

31. Rivlin and Rivlin, *Letters of the Clerks*, vol. 2, p. 26.

32. Phinehas ben Zevi Grajewski, *Ẓiyyun le-Qever Raḥel Immenu: Mi-Ginzei Yerushalayim* (Monument to the Tomb of the Matriarch Rachel: Secrets of Jerusalem) (Jerusalem, 1932), 17, p. 10.

33. N. M. Gelber, "The Emigration of Jews from Bohemia and Galicia to the Land of Israel, 1811–1869," in [*Sefer Peres*], ed. Michael Ish-Shalom, Me'ir Benayahu, and Azriel Schochet (Jerusalem, 1953), pp. 244–245 (Hebrew).

34. Rivlin and Rivlin, *Letters of the Clerks*, vol. 1, pp. 10, 20, and *passim*.

35. Gelber, "Emigration of Jews from Bohemia," p. 245.

36. Ibid., p. 246. Ḥayyim ha-Levi Horowitz described his own *aliyah*: "And my plan was agreed to by our lord, master, and teacher, the great rabbi, the holy luminary . . . our master the rabbi R. Mordecai, may his memory endure to the life of the world to come, of the holy community of Kremenitz, whom I served as scribe. And on 17 Sivan 5577 [1 June 1817], my family and I set out and departed via Wallachia and on 17 Tammuz [1 July], we reached the city of Galacz . . . and on the day preceding the New Moon of Elul [29 Av; 11 August] we arrived near Acre." *Ḥibbat Yerushalayim*, author's introduction.

37. Rivlin and Rivlin, *Letters of the Clerks*, vol. 1, p. 91; see also pp. 95, 125. A text dated 5570 (1810) describing a substantial immigration at that time likewise portrays the immigrants as poor people seeking to be supported by the *ḥaluqah*: "And even worse is the immigration to this goodly hill-country [the Land of Israel; cf. Deut. 3:25] from foreign places of wretched Jews; every man and woman who has a creditor and is fed up with laboring says to himself, I will go to Safed in order to live off the dole . . . and His land was filled with the poor, Sefardim and Ashkenazim alike." Excerpted from a letter by the Sefardic rabbinic emissary from Safed to Abraham ben Ḥason, in Abraham Isaac Katz, "Three Emissaries from Safed in Italy," *Sefunot* 7 (5724 [1964]), p. 237 (Hebrew).

38. *The Jewish Repository*, London, 1813, p. 247.

39. Ibid., p. 248.

40. Ibid.

41. Ibid.

42. *Seventh Report of the Committee of the London Society for Promoting Christianity Amongst the Jews* (London, 1815), p. 33.

43. *J. E.* (1821), p. 32. [*Gilgul meḥillot* refers to the rabbinic concept that when the dead are resurrected, Jews who died and were buried outside the Land of Israel would return by rolling through underground tunnels, a difficult process. See, e.g., *Yalqut Shim'oni*, Isaiah, *Remez* 431.—***translator***]

44. *J. E.* (1821), p. 74.

45. Benayahu, "Response to R. Benjamin Mordecai Navon," p. 206.

46. *J. E.* (1821), p. 32.

47. *J. E.*, (1825), p. 14.

48. *Ninth Report of the Committee of the London Society for Promoting Christianity Amongst the Jews* (London, 1817), Appendix, p. 42.

49. Ish-Shalom, *Mas'ei Noẓrim le-Ereẓ Yisra'el*, p. 413.

50. *J. E.* (1829), p. 111.

51. *M. I.* (1830), p. 13.

52. *M. I.* (1832), p. 103.

53. *Meḥqarim u-Meqorot*, ed. Yitẓḥaq Ben-Ẓevi (Jerusalem, 1969), pp. 125–126.

54. *Iggerot ha-Peqidim* (Letters of the Clerks), vol. 5, p. 66b.

55. Ibid., p. 92b. The episode is discussed as well in the book by Mendel of Kamenetz, *Qorot ha-Ittim*, p. 18.

56. *Iggerot ha-Peqidim* (Letters of the Clerks), vol. 5, p. 46a; E. Rivlin, "Letter from R. Hillel Rivlin to His Son-in-Law R. Shemariah Luria," *Me'asef Ẓiyyon* 5 (1933), pp. 141–147 (Hebrew); A. M. Lunz, *Jerusalem Yearbook for the Diffusion of an Accurate Knowledge of Ancient and Modern Palestine*, 17 vols. (Jerusalem, 1882–1919), vol. 5 (1901), p. 230 (Hebrew).

57. *Sheluḥei Ereẓ Yisra'el*, p. 691.

58. *Zikkaron la-Ḥovevim ha-Rishonim,* P. Grajewski (Jerusalem 1928), no. 9, p. 3.

59. *Qorot ha-Ittim,* p. 17.

60. *Iggerot ha-Peqidim* (Letters of the Clerks), vol. 6, p. 38b.

61. Ibid., vol. 5, p. 115a.

62. "*Qol mei-Heikhal: Qeri'ah le-Hafsaqat ha-Aliyyah le-Ereẓ Yisra'el*" (A Voice From the Sanctuary: A Call for Pause in the Immigration to the Land of Israel), in Benjamin Kluger, ed., *Min ha-Maqor* (Jerusalem, 1978), vol. 1, p. 45.

63. Ibid.

64. *Iggerot ha-Peqidim* (Letters of the Clerks), vol. 6, p. 56a. R. Me'ir, grandson of the Vilna Ga'on's brother R. Abraham, tells of his desire to emigrate: "May I be privileged to go from here and come to there in peace, and with a soul eager to serve Him there wholeheartedly; and may He who created His world with mercy lead me on still waters and grant me courage and strength to arrive at my desired goal and lead me to the Holy Land . . . and not to come there in vain with respect to material matters and, certainly, with respect to spiritual matters." *Naḥalat Avot,* R. Me'ir ben Elijah (Vilna, 1836), author's introduction.

65. *Yis'u Harim Shalom,* p. 99.

66. *M. I.* (1833), p. 180. The following source, dated in 1831, contains a call to support an immigrant from Arbat, R. Elisha ben R. Joseph Berdugo: "The spirit of the Lord impelled him to go up to the Land and appear before the Lord, he together with his family, in the city of our God, in the Land of Israel (may it be built and established speedily and in our days). He sold all his chattel and furnishings. . . . Be a help to him wherever he goes." *Iggerot Shederim* (Rabbinic Emissaries), Israel National Library, Manuscript Institute, 4°199 (188).

An account of the arrival in 1832 of more than two hundred North African Jewish families appears in a letter of 29 November 1854 from the rabbis of Tiberias to the Chief Rabbi of France: "For it is a fact that in the holy cities of Safed and Tiberias and Jaffa (may they be built and established speedily and in our days), there are to be found more than two hundred families (may the Lord grant them life and protect them) from the city of Orgil and its environs (may God protect it), and they are under the wing of the mighty and gracious Kingdom of France, may its majesty be exalted; and for twenty-two years now they have not been lorded over by the kingdom of Ishmael, may its majesty be exalted." Simeon Schwartzfuchs, "The Jews of Algeria in the North of the Land of Israel and French Protection," *Shalem* 3 (1981), p. 337 (Hebrew).

67. *M. I.* (1833), p. 180.

68. *M. I.* (1834), pp. 27, 63.

69. *M. I.* (1833), p. 180.

70. Ibid.

71. Wolff, *Researches,* p. 187.

72. *J. I.* (1835), p. 122.

73. *Iggerot ha-Peqidim* (Letters of the Clerks), vol. 6, p. 73b.

74. Ibid.

75. *Yis'u Harim Shalom,* p. 60.

76. Ibid., p. 62.

77. Ibid., p. 70.

78. Ibid., p. 72.

79. Ibid., p. 116; also *J. I.* (1843), p. 256.

80. *Iggerot ha-Peqidim* (Letters of the Clerks), vol. 6, p. 225a.

81. Wolff, *Researches,* p. 318.

82. *J. I.* (1838), p. 153.

83. Bet ha-Levi, *History of the Jews of Kalish*, p. 312.

84. *Iggerot ha-Peqidim* (Letters of the Clerks), vol. 8 p. 139a. The *aliyah* of R. Mordecai Minsker, R. Me'ir Shalom of Karelitz, and R. Joseph Zundel of Salant is worthy of separate consideration.

85. Bonar and McShane, *Narrative of a Mission of Inquiry*, pp. 164–165.

86. Ibid.

87. *J. I.* (1839), p. 205.

88. R. Joseph Mesas, *Collected Letters*, part 1 (Jerusalem, 1969), p. 14 (Hebrew).

89. *J. I.* (1839), p. 267.

90. Ibid., p. 226.

91. Bonar and McShane, *Narrative of a Mission of Inquiry*, p. 246.

92. *J. I.* (1839), p. 8.

93. *Ha-Emet mei-Ereẓ Tiẓmaḥ*, p. 135; P. Grajewski, *Jerusalem Journal*, pp. 1–3.

94. *Pe'at ha-Shulḥan*, R. Israel of Shklov (Safed, 1836), author's introduction.

95. *J. E.* (1829), p. 152.

96. Rivlin and Rivlin, *Letters of the Clerks*, vol. 2, p. 63.

97. Ibid., pp. 62–63.

98. *Ha-Emet mei-Ereẓ Tiẓmaḥ*, p. 138.

99. Rivlin and Rivlin, *Letters of the Clerks*, vol. 2, p. 52.

100. *J. E.* (1829), pp. 33, 75, 278.

101. Rivlin and Rivlin, *Letters of the Clerks*, vol. 3, p. 19.

102. List of the deceased maintained by the burial society "Crown of the Young and Eternal Ways," in *Ateret Baḥurim ve-Hilkhot Olam*, Rosenthaliana Library, Amsterdam, MS-Ros-54.

103. *J. I.* (1832), p. 130.

104. Ibid.

105. *Iggerot ha-Peqidim* (Letters of the Clerks), vol. 5, pp. 26a, 66b.

106. *Qorot ha-Ittim*, p. 20.

107. *Iggerot ha-Peqidim* (Letters of the Clerks), vol.8, p. 59b.

108. *Toledot Ḥakhmei Yerushalayim* (*History of the Sages of Jerusalem*) R. A. L. Frumkin and A. Rivlin (Jerusalem, 1929), vol. 3, p. 175 (Hebrew).

109. *J. I.* (1839), p. 62.

110. *Iggerot ha-Peqidim* (Letters of the Clerks), vol. 8, p. 125b.

111. *J. I.* (1839), p. 199; *Iggerot ha-Peqidim* (Letters of the Clerks), vol. 8, pp. 154a, 171b.

112. Ish-Shalom, *Mas'ei Noẓrim le-Erez Yisra'el*, p. 492.

113. Ibid., p. 478.

114. Ibid., pp. 494–495.

115. *Iggerot Ereẓ Yisra'el*, pp. 364–365.

116. Ibid., pp. 365–366.

117. Ish-Shalom, *Mas'ei Noẓrim le-Erez Yisra'el*, p. 495.

118. *Iggerot Ereẓ Yisra'el*, p. 361.

119. *Iggerot Soferim*, Shelomoh Sofer (Vienna–Budapest, 1929) Letter 62, pp. 56–62.

120. Ish-Shalom, *Mas'ei Noẓrim le-Erez Yisra'el*, p. 495.

121. P. Grajewski, *Jerusalem Journal*, pp. 1–3, quoting Ne'eman's letter.

122. *Qol David*, p. 26b.

123. *Meḥqarim u-Meqorot*, p. 125.

124. *Ha-Emet mei-Ereẓ Tiẓmaḥ*, p. 136.

125. Spyridon, *Annals of Palestine*, pp. 66–73.

126. *J. E.* (1825), p. 109; *J. E.* (1824), p. 460.

127. Rivlin and Rivlin, *Letters of the Clerks*, vol. 1, p. 174; Spyridon, *Annals of Palestine*, p. 80.

128. Spyridon, *Annals of Palestine*, p. 80; *J. E.*, (1826), p. 232.

129. Spyridon, *Annals of Palestine*, p. 80.

130. *J. E.* (1829), p. 115.

131. *Toledot Ḥakhmei Yerushalayim*, vol. 3, p. 163; Lunz, *Jerusalem Yearbook*, vol. 17 (1919), p. 235 (Hebrew).

132. *J. E.* (1828), p. 238.

133. Rivlin and Rivlin, *Letters of the Clerks*, vol. 2, pp. 197, 207; vol. 3, p. 201.

134. *M. I.* (1830), p. 13.

135. For more extensive treatment, see *Qorot ha-Ittim*. See, as well, M. Abir, "The Rebellion Against Egyptian Rule in the Land of Israel in 1834 and Its Context," master's thesis, Hebrew University, 1961 (Hebrew).

136. *J.I.* (1836), p. 282. In the attacks by the Arabs against the Jewish populace in 1834, five Jews were killed in Hebron and five in Safed, and several more, their number unknown, died of fear. *Iggerot ha-Peqidim* (Letters of the Clerks), vol. 6, p. 98a.

137. *J.I.* (1836), p. 283.

138. Ibid.

139. Ibid., p. 282.

140. *Iggerot ha-Peqidim* (Letters of the Clerks), vol. 8, p. 4a.

141. Rivlin, "Letter from R. Hillel Rivlin," p. 143. Back in Russia, R. Shemariah Luria continued to work on behalf of the Jewish settlement in the Land of Israel. His son-in-law, R. Yeḥiel Mikhel Pines, later immigrated there.

142. Rivlin and Rivlin, *Letters of the Clerks*, vol. 1, p. 125.

143. J. Meisel, "The 1839 Register of Jews in Safed and Its Environs," *Sefunot* 6 (5722 [1962]), pp. 427–473 (Hebrew).

144. Ibid., p. 427.

145. Ibid.

146. Ibid., p. 445.

147. See U. O. Schmelz, "Demographic Trends in Jerusalem Jewry During the Nineteenth Century," *Topics in the History of the Jewish Settlement in Jerusalem* (Jerusalem, 1976), pp. 68–72 (Hebrew). (The article appeared in English as "Some Demographic Peculiarities of the Jews of Jerusalem during the Nineteenth Century," in M. Maoz, ed., *Studies on Palestine during the Ottoman Period* [Jerusalem, 1975], pp. 119–142.)

148. Meisel, "Register of Jews in Safed," p. 434.

CHAPTER 4

1. For a bibliography on the Vilna Ga'on, see Israel Jacob Dienstag, "Rabbenu Elijah of Vilna," *Talpiyot* 4, 1–2 (1949), pp. 269–356; 3–4 (1949), pp. 409–413; 5 (1950), pp. 861–862 (Hebrew). See also the study by Ḥayyim Hillel Ben-Sasson, "The Personality and Historical Influence of the Vilna Ga'on," *Zion* 31 (1966), 1–2, pp. 39–86; 3–4, pp. 197–216 (Hebrew); A. Nadler, *The Faith of the Mithnagdim: Rabbinic Responses to Hasidic Rapture* (Baltimore, 1997); *The Gaon of Vilnius and the Annals of Jewish Culture: Materials of the International Scientific Conference, Vilnius, September 10–12, 1997*, Izraelis Lempertis, compiler (Vilnius, 1998); A. Morgenstern, *Mysticism and Messianism: From Luzzatto to the Vilna Ga'on* (Hebrew) (Jerusalem, 1999);. I. Etkes,

The Gaon of Vilna: The Man and His Image, trans. Jeffrey M. Green (Berkeley, 2002); M. Halamish, Y. Rivlin, and R. Shuchat, eds, *The Vilna Ga'on and His Disciples* (Hebrew) (Ramat-Gan, 2003); Y. Vinograd, *Bibliography of the Vilna Ga'on* (Hebrew) (Jerusalem, 2003); and A. Morgenstern, "Between Sons and Disciples: The Struggle Over the Vilna Ga'on's Heritage and Over the Ideological Issue of Torah Versus the Land of Israel" (Hebrew), *Da'at* 53 (2004), pp. 83–124.

2. It was said his soul was the soul of Hai Ga'on. *Emunah ve-Hashgaḥah*, R. Samuel ben Abraham of Slutsk [Moltzen] (Slutsk, 1864), introduction.

3. *Pe'at ha-Shulḥan*, author's introduction.

4. A letter from the 1840s, in *Yad Eliyahu*, R. Elijah Rogoler (Warsaw, 1900), p. 34.

5. *Sifra de-Ẓeni'uta*, introduction by Ḥayyim Volozhin.

6. *Iggerot Ereẓ Yisra'el*, p. 351.

7. *Alfei Menasheh*, part 1, p. 73b.

8. *Toledot Ḥakhmei Yerushalayim*, vol. 3, p. 158.

9. *Statutes and Documents of the "Eliyahu" Study Hall in memory of the Ga'on Rabbi Elijah, may the memory of the righteous and holy be for a blessing, established in the year "Aderet Eliyahu" ["Elijah's cloak"; the letters of the Hebrew term have the numerical value 657, indicating the year 5657 (1897)] in Jerusalem, the one-hundredth year since Elijah's ascent heavenward.* The expression "had not Elijah his chosen one stood in the breach" evokes a comparison to Moses, who is described in similar terms in Ps. 106: 23: "Had not Moses His chosen one stood before Him in the breach to bring about the withdrawal of His destructive anger . . ."

Isaac Ḥaver, a student of Menaḥem Mendel of Shklov, refers at several points in his writings to the figure of the Vilna Ga'on as he heard of it from his teachers: "And it is not surprising that in recent times it was revealed to him what was not revealed to some generations that preceded him, for who [except the Ga'on] stood within God's secret council? And He, may He be blessed, anticipated and foresaw all generations in advance, doing all in a manner proper to its time, for we had declined by ten levels, and the time was right to illumine the world, in order to raise the flag of holiness and repair the world. And so, with our own eyes we saw, in our own times, we were privileged to have the great light of our teacher, the Ga'on Rabbi Elijah, like whom there had been none for several generations before, and there were revealed to him awesome matters that had not been revealed to any person, and he was privileged to have great and wondrous revelations and privileged that [the prophet] Elijah, may his memory be for a blessing, taught him. . . . And [Ḥayyim of Volozhin] said of him that he experienced an ascent of the soul every night, and revelations from the heavenly academy." *Magen ve-Ẓinah*, Isaac Ḥaver (Amsterdam, no date), p. 54b.

10. *Toledot Ḥakhmei Yerushalayim*, vol. 3, p. 158.

11. *Sifra di-Ẓeni'uta*, p. 55a.

12. *Pe'at ha-Shulḥan*, author's introduction.

13. *Emunah ve-Hashgaḥah*, p. 43b.

14. Rivlin, *Vision of Zion*, p. 34.

15. *Alim li-Terufah* (Minsk, 1836).

16. *Pe'at ha-Shulḥan*, author's introduction.

17. *Aliyyot Eliyahu*, R. Joshua Heschel Levin (Vilna, 1856), p. 39b.

18. Rivlin, *Vision of Zion*, p. 33. See also the comments there of Rabbi Y. M. Charlap, ibid., Appendix (*Mosdei ḥa-Areẓ*), p. 8.

19. *Iggerot ha-Peqidim* (Letters of the Clerks), vol. 8, p. 27a.

20. *Iggerot mi-Yerushalayim*, sec. J26.

21. *Emunah ve-Hashgaḥah,* p. 43b.

22. *Peirushei Nakh le-ha-Ga'on mi-Vilna,* National Library, Department of Hebrew Manuscripts, No. 8°3426, p. 21a. (The ms. was written during Ḥayyim of Volozhin's lifetime, that is to say, before 1821.)

23. *Iggerot Ereẓ Yisra'el,* p. 337.

24. *Hillel ben Shaḥar,* p. 21a.

25. Ibid., p. 7b.

26. *Emunah ve-Hashgaḥah,* p. 29a.

27. *Alfei Menasheh,* part 1, p. 73a–b.

28. *Sifra di-Ẓeni'uta,* p. 54b.

29. *Ma'ayanei ha-Yeshu'ah,* R. Moses Katzenellenbogen (Frankfurt, 1859), p. 11.

30. *Sanhedrin* 97a.

31. Maimonides rules: "All of the prophets commanded repentance, and Israel is redeemed only through repentance. And the Torah has already promised that Israel will ultimately repent at the end of their exile and be immediately redeemed." Maimonides, *Mishneh Torah, Hilkhot Teshuvah* 7:5. It appears that the Vilna Ga'on does not accept this ruling, agreeing, instead, with Nachmanides' statement in his commentary on a passage in Deuteronomy: "This song [*Ha'azinu;* chapter 32 of Deuteronomy] refers to the present, and to the past, and to the future; it refers to this world and to the world to come. . . . [It] is an explicit promise of the future redemption. . . . The song refers to no condition of repentance and worship . . . [declaring that] God, may He be blessed, will subject us to His wrath but not wipe us out, and will forgive our sins for His Name's sake" (Commentary on Deut. 32:40). My thanks to Dr. Moshe Ḥalamish for this observation.

32. *Sanhedrin* 98a.

33. *Sifra di-Ẓeni'uta,* p. 54b on *Sanhedrin* 98a.

34. *Even Shelomoh,* R. Solomon ben Abraham Moltzen (Vilna, 1873) p. 33b.

35. *Ma'ayanei ha-Yeshu'ah,* p. 14.

36. *Margaliyot ha-Torah,* R. Ẓevi Hirsch of Samyatitsch (Parisk, 1788), p. 17.

37. *Derekh ha-Melekh, commentary on Song of Songs by Rabbi. Pinḥas, son of our master the Rabbi Judah, preacher in Palitsk* (Grodno, 1804), on the verse "Hark, my beloved comes, skipping over the mountains, jumping on the hills" (Song of Songs 2:8).

38. In the Rosenthaliana Library in Amsterdam, in a ledger of "Nineteenth-Century Discourses" (*Derashot min-ha-Me'ah ha-19*) HS-Ros-445, I found loose pages in a handwriting identical to that in the ledger. One of them contained the following passage: "Beloved of God, though my heart is too small to encompass going there to burden one as great as he [?] I have heard of his great goodness and modesty. . . . I said I will [go and] seek with the book, and may my words be desired before my soul's beloved, so that he chooses for me a time to go before him. Thank God, I grew up on the knees of great men, mighty in Torah and wisdom and fear of God, namely the ga'on, the rabbi known to the ends of the earth, Rabbi Ḥayyim of Volozhin and his son, who took his father's place, and the geniuses of Vilna, as we find in several writings. The preciousness of his testimony, and I have trust [?] in his great goodness, the good and doer of good . . . the seeker of his love brought me to a land whose language I am not familiar with and where I know no one, and to which of the holy ones shall I turn [?] One who dwells here in Hamburg [?]."

39. Ibid., on a loose page within the ledger.

40. Ibid.

41. *Sha'arei Ẓedeq le-Zera Yiẓḥaq* (Aviezer), p. 24a.

42. Ibid., p. 28a.

43. Ibid., p. 26b. Ideas such as these can be found as well *Oẓar Binah,* a book of discourses by a sage of the Land of Israel, Aaron Ẓevi ben Moses Judah Ashkenazi: " 'Stay the night, and, when morning comes, if he redeems you, good, let him redeem; but if he does not wish to redeem you, then I myself will redeem you, as the Lord lives' [Ruth 3:13] . . . 'If he does not wish to redeem you'—[this means] if you lack the time to repent and do good deeds as are required . . . with respect to that, it is said 'I myself will redeem you,' for the sake of My Name . . . if You wish to await my repentance, there is no power to repent in this bitter exile; rather, act for Your own sake and not for ours." *Oẓar Binah,* R. Aaron Ẓevi Ashkenazi (Izmir, 1841), sec. 217.

The Scottish missionaries A. Bonar and R. McCheyne report in September 1839 (*Narrative of a Mission of Inquiry,* p. 403) that Polish Jews are denying any need to repent before the Messiah's coming, for he would come as well in a totally guilty generation.

44. *Ketubbot* 111a. For an early-nineteenth-century statement of the traditional concept, which forbade human efforts to press for the End, see *Ẓeror he-Ḥayyim* by Abraham Lowenstam: "Since we are commanded not to involve ourselves in any way or at any time in hastening our redemption through any action on our part . . . as is said in Ketubbot." According to the traditional concept, the redemption will be miraculous, with no human involvement whatsoever. Lowenstam continued: "Would not sound reasoning tell us that if the first redemptions transpired with no help or support on our part . . . how much more so will that be the case with respect to the final redemption that we await, speedily and in our days, as promised by all of God's prophets. . . . Not by rebellion and not by treachery will Judah be raised high; not by strength and not by might will the yoke be broken and the reins released. Not by bloodshed or by the moaning of the wounded will Israel do well; but only He Who alone works great wonders . . . He alone, with all his miracles and wonders that will take place at the end of days." *Ẓeror he-Ḥayyim,* pp. 61b–62a.

45. *Iggerot Ereẓ Yisra'el,* p. 352.

46. *Sha'arei Ẓedeq le-Zera Yiẓḥaq,* p. 26a.

47. *Siddur ha-GRA (Prayer-Book of the Vilna Ga'on)* (Jerusalem, 1891), "Collected Comments on the Hidden Meaning of the Song of Songs," p. 48a.

48. *Mikhtevei R. Shelomoh Hershel Berliner mi-London,* Jewish Theological Seminary of America, New York, 528; Israel National Library, Manuscript Photocopy Institute, 29424, p. 152a. It appears that Hirschell inadvertently included the Hasidim with the *Perushim,* for his anger was directed at the contacts of Menaḥem Mendel of Shklov and Solomon Zalman Shapiro with the English missionaries in Jerusalem.

49. *Zohar, Va'eira* 196b.

50. *Iggerot Ereẓ Yisra'el,* p. 348.

51. Grajewski, *Mi-Ginzei Yerushalayim,* 2, pp. 2–3 (a rabbinic emissary's appointment document, dated to the spring of 1837, telling that the rebuilding of the *Ḥurvah* courtyard had begun).

52. *Emunah ve-Hashgaḥah,* p. 7a.

53. Ibid., p. 12b.

54. *Afiqei Yehudah,* R. Judah ha-Levi Edel (Zolkow, 1803), p. 109a.

55. Ibid.

56. *Even Shelomoh,* p. 33b.

57. *Ma'ayanei ha-Yeshu'ah.*

58. *Iggerot Ereẓ Yisra'el,* p. 329.

59. Ibid. The Hebrew takes the form of rhymed verse.
60. Ibid., pp. 329–330.
61. Ibid., p. 332.
62. Ibid., pp. 332–333.
63. Ibid., p. 330.
64. *Sha'arei Ẓedeq le-Zera Yiẓḥaq*, p. 64a.
65. *Hillel ben Shaḥar*, p. 81b.
66. *Seder Eiliyahu*, Commentary of the Vilna Ga'on on the Passover Hagaddah (Prague, 1813), p. 5b.
67. *Iggerot Ereẓ Yisra'el*, p. 337.
68. *Zeved Tov*, R. Ze'ev Wolf Altschul (Warsaw, 1814), introduction by the author's son, Elyaqim Getzel Altschul.
69. [Cf. Exod. 21:7; in context, the verse distinguishes the freeing of a maidservant from that of a male slave.—***translator***]
70. *Zeved Tov*, introduction.
71. "My father, may his memory be for a blessing, told that when he was in Volozhin in 1824 and again in 1836, the ga'on Rabbi Abraham Simḥah of Amstislav wanted to teach him the hidden wisdom. In 1836, the ga'on met him as he was taking a walk outside the city and said 'see, I have grown old and I am concerned lest my death also be the death of some secret wisdom I learned from my teachers, and I want to transmit them to none of my students other than your honor, who I am confident is righteous and God-fearing.' And when my father asked him what they were, he replied 'the Ga'on of Vilna's secret of the End, and an amulet for a woman suffering a miscarriage, and prostrating oneself [on the graves of the righteous?].' And my father replied, 'I can accept none of these. As for the End of days, I do not believe the Ga'on himself knew when it would be, for one greater than he, namely Rabbi Akiva, erred [in that regard]. As for the remedy for miscarriage, I do not deal in amulets and I am not a bearer of the Name (*ba'al shem*). And as for prostrating, I fear that if I knew it, I might do it.' " *Even Shemu'el.* Rabbi Aryeh Leib Frumkin, Israel National Library, Manuscript Institute, 4°32, p. 257.

CHAPTER 5

1. *Mi-Ginzei Qedem: Documents and Sources From the Writings of Pinḥas Ben Ẓevi Grajewski*, ed. Isaac Beck (Jerusalem, 1977), p. 74.
2. Ibid.
3. It appears that two or more disciples of *Ḥatam Sofer* settled in Jerusalem in 1803, and the attitude of the Sefardim toward them can be gleaned from the following text: "On last Simḥat Torah [1803], I received a letter from one of my students living in Jerusalem, the holy city. The letter had been written on . . . 3 August 1803 and told of the great hardships suffered there by the Ashkenazim and of the great and palpable hatred of the Sefardim toward them. It told as well that the rabbi with whom we are involved was scorned there, and but for the help of the aforementioned student, no one would have him into his house. He concludes that it is proper to declare that one should not journey there without a purse filled with money." *Sefer Ḥatam Sofer, Resp. Even ha-Ezer*, part 1 (Pressburg, 1858), Responsum 132, p. 84b.
4. Rivlin and Rivlin, *Letters of the Clerks*, vol. 1, p. 219.
5. *Iggerot ha-Peqidim* (Letters of the Clerks), vol. 6, p. 56a; vol. 8, p. 56a.
6. P. Friedman, "Letters From the Land of Israel, 1814–1822" (Hebrew), *Zion* 3 (1938), pp. 267–274.

7. *Meḥqarim u-Meqorot*, p. 125.

8. *Iggerot mi-Yerushalayim*, sec. J/26. The manuscript itself was written in 1875; its text speaks in the name of Aryeh Ne'eman. *Mizmor le-Asaf* appears to allude to Psalm 79, which bears that caption and reads, in part: "O God, heathen nations have entered Your estate . . . and turned Jerusalem into ruins. . . . How long, O Lord, will you be angry. . . . Do not hold the sins of our ancestors against us. . . . Forgive our sins for the sake of Your name." The chapter contains a series of ideas paralleling the Ga'on's disciples' concept of redemption, the most important of which is the redemption of Israel in order to sanctify God's Name in the world. See chapter 4 in this volume, n. 20.

9. *Iggerot Ereẓ Yisra'el*, p. 330. The journal of the Sefardic court in Safed for 1811–1813 refers to "the *Perushim*'s study hall," whose owners sought to place windows over the roof of their neighbor, Shalom. Jacob Moses Toledano, "Journal of the Court in Safed", manuscript of Ḥayyim Amram, in *Jerusalem: Studies in the Land of Israel*, ed. M. Ish-Shalom, M. Benayahu, Y. Peres, and E. Shochet (Jerusalem, 1955), p. 234 (Hebrew). ["Blessed is the eye that has seen all this" is borrowed from the liturgy of the Day of Atonement, where the phrase is used to describe people fortunate enough to have witnessed the service in the Jerusalem Temple before its destruction.—***translator***]

10. *Sanhedrin* 98a. The commandments' ties to the Land of Israel have the power to awaken the Land's fertility, which reflects the awakening above associated with the revealed End. As the Talmud says: "And Rabbi Abba said: There is no better revelation of the End, as Scripture says, 'And you, O mountains of Israel, shall send forth your branches and provide your fruit to My people Israel" (Ezek. 36:8).

11. Salo Baron, "Aspects of the History of the Jewish Settlement in Jerusalem" (Hebrew), in *Sefer Klausner*, ed. N. H. Torczyner, A.A. Kabak, A. Tcherikover, and B. Shochetman (Jerusalem, 1937), p. 304, n. 2.

12. *Iggerot Ereẓ Yisra'el*, p. 341.

13. Ibid., p. 336. The journal of the Safed court has an entry, dated 24 January 1811, regarding a parcel of land running "from north to south, to the parcel purchased by the Ashkenazim." Toledano, "Journal of the Court in Safed," p. 235.

14. Ibid. Mendel of Kaminitz recounts the observance in Safed, in accordance with Ẓevi Hirsch Lehren's request, of the commandments related to the first shearing and to the redemption of the first born of an unclean animal. *Qorot ha-Ittim*, p. 24. His account is confirmed by the letters of the Clerks' Organization, which speak of additional commandments, such as priestly gifts and tithes: "If it is possible to purchase a small field and plant it so as to produce [crops subject to] priestly gifts and tithes, I would ask his excellency to kindly inform me how much I would have to pay to do so . . . and, moreover, . . . to direct that a lamb be purchased on my behalf and slaughtered and the [prescribed] gifts presented to the priest." *Iggerot ha-Peqidim* (Letters of the Clerks), vol. 4, p. 168b. The letters also contain reports on observing the commandment of first shearing and using the wool to prepare *ẓiẓit* (fringes prescribed for four-cornered garments). Ibid., vol. 5, p. 113b.

15. Ibid. We hear in Lehren's letter of Israel of Shklov's arrival in Tiberias: "When he arrived with his group at the resting place of the *tanna* Rabbi Me'ir *Ba'al ha-Nes*, may his merit protect us, Amen." Ibid., vol. 4, p. 127a.

16. Bet ha-Levi, *History of the Jews of Kalish*, p. 322.

17. *Tevu'ot ha-Areẓ*, R. Jehosef, ed. A. M. Lunz (Jerusalem, 1900), p. 471. In 1816, the community numbered 118 souls, including those who arrived after the epidemic had subsided in the winter of 1813–1814.

18. *Ha-Emet mei-Ereẓ Tiẓmaḥ*, p. 134.

19. "What are the three oaths that the Holy One Blessed Be He imposed in the Song of Songs? One was that he adjured Israel not to reveal the End, and one was that they not hasten the End, and one was that they not rebel against the nations. The Holy One Blessed Be He said to Israel: If you carry out the oaths, well and good; if not, I permit [consumption of] your flesh like that of gazelles and hinds of the field [cf. Song of Songs 2:7], for which no one is held to account. So will I not hold [spillers of] your blood to account." *Midrash Tanḥuma* (Eshkol edition), *Parashat Devarim*, 848–849.

20. "My teacher, may his memory be for a blessing [Rabbi Isaac Luria], told me of another mechanism for unification when a plague strikes, as follows. I have already told you that all the souls of human beings are derived from what is clarified from the seven Edomite kings . . . and when the clarified substance contains some dross that had not been removed, this dross becomes a mortal poison that kills people during an epidemic. . . . And the husks that are in the clarified substance, as mentioned, assail and harm a person during an epidemic and cannot be separated from him and always cling to him." *Sefer Sha'ar ha-Kavvanot*, Part 1, *Sha'ar* 6, R. Ḥayyim Vital (Tel-Aviv, 1962), p. 89.

21. Grajewski, *Mi-Ginzei Yerushalayim*, 3, p. 35. Elsewhere, Grajewski reports a tradition he heard from the people of Jerusalem: "The leaders of the community perceived the hand of God in the epidemic, commanding them to go up to Jerusalem, may it be built and established, and to settle it anew." *Tevunah*, year 1, number 17 (3 August 1932).

22. *Tevu'ot ha-Areẓ*, p. 471.

23. Grajewski, *Mi-Ginzei Yerushalayim*, 17, p. 10.

24. *Iggerot ha-Peqidim* (Letters of the Clerks), vol. 4, p. 155a.

25. Ibid., p. 155a.

26. Lehren attributes the deaths of Eliezer Bregman's family members to their places of residence; he writes that they lived where the members of Judah Ḥasid's group had dwelt before: "For it is known that those houses built in the ruins where the synagogues had previously stood, equivalent to the numerical value of the word *mileiti* ['I am full'; the numerical value is 481] are dangerous places in which to dwell." Ibid., vol. 8, p. 34a. Elsewhere, Lehren tells that Bregman "left his home in the middle of its lease term because he was ill the whole time he had lived there, and the previous summer, his mother and his eldest daughter had died. . . . He surmised that the fate of the house had brought that about, for they had a tradition that houses built on the ruins where there earlier had stood one of those 481, . . . numbering *mileiti*, were dangerous." In both letters, Lehren uses the word *mileiti*, having the numerical value of 481, alluding to the year [5]481 (1720–1721), when the members of Judah Ḥasid's group fled Jerusalem. For the use of the word *mileiti* to connote trouble and sorrow, see Jer. 31:25 and Zech. 9:13. On the other hand, Lehren elsewhere mentions that in 1837, after the destruction of Safed, Israel of Shklov visited the *Menaḥem Ẓiyyon* study hall in the *Ḥurvah* court (which he had not previously done) and thus could not be regarded as still believing that the " 'unclean side' dwells there." *Iggerot ha-Peqidim* (Letters of the Clerks), vol. 8, p. 157b.

27. *Taqlin Ḥadtin*, R. Israel ben Samuel (Minsk, 5572 [1812]), author's introduction.

28. *Iggerot Ereẓ Yisra'el*, pp. 344–359.

29. *Taqlin Ḥadtin*, author's introduction.

30. He relies on the Talmud's statement that "once the exiles are restored, the

wicked will be judged." Rashi there observes, "before they settle in Jerusalem"—that is, Jerusalem will be settled only after the wicked are judged. *Megillah* 17b.

31. [Classical "ordination" (*semikhah*), required before a rabbi may participate in ruling on certain matters and regarded by tradition as representing a chain of transmission all the way back to Moses, had lapsed in late antiquity or early medieval times.—***translator***]

32. "And [regarding] all these matters . . . no man will know how they will occur until they do occur." Maimonides, *Mishneh Torah, Hilkhot Melakhim* 12:2.

33. Maimonides, *Commentary on the Mishnah, Sanhedrin* 1:3. According to one tradition, the effort of the Vilna Ga'on himself to immigrate to the Land of Israel was connected to the idea of renewing ordination. Y. L. ha-Kohen Maimon, "Prominent Jerusalemites on Renewing the Sanhedrin," *Sinai* 32 (1953), p. 134 (Hebrew).

34. *Rosh ha-Shanah* 31a–b.

35. Maimonides, *Mishneh Torah, Hilkhot Sanhedrin* 14:12.

36. "It seems reasonable to me that if all the sages in the Land of Israel agree to appoint judges and ordain them, they are considered ordained." Ibid., 4:11.

37. See Jacob Katz's study, "The Ordination Dispute Between Rabbi Jacob Berab and Ralbaḥ [Rabbi Levi ben Ḥabib]," *Zion* 16 (1951), pp. 28–45 (Hebrew). See also Katz, "On the Year 5600 as a Messianic Year."

38. *Commentary of Radbaz on Maimonides, Yad Ḥazaqah, Hilkhot Sanhedrin* 4:11. My thanks to my brother, Nisan Morgenstern, for bringing this reference to my attention.

39. See the reports that circulated around 1666 regarding the conquest of Mecca by the armies of the Ten Tribes. Gershom Scholem, *Shabbetai Ẓevi*, vol. 2 (Tel-Aviv, 1963), p. 461 (Hebrew).

40. *Derishat Ẓiyyon* (Frankfurt-am-Oder, 5566 [1806]).

41. *J. E.* (1822), p. 160.

42. Yaari, "Travels of David Beit Hillel," p. 25.

43. A. Yaari, *Journeys in the Land of Israel* (Tel-Aviv, 1946) (Hebrew).

44. *Iggerot Ereẓ Yisra'el* p. 348.

45. *Sefer Shir ha-Shirim, Peirush ha-Ga'on he-Ḥasid Eliyahu mi-Vilna,* R. Elijah of Vilna (Warsaw, 1842).

46. Ibid., on 6:5.

47. Ibid., on 6:6.

48. *Iggerot Ereẓ Yisra'el,* pp. 344–359.

49. Ibid., pp. 354–355.

50. Ibid., p. 352. It is almost certain that the first outcries from Russia over the cantonist decree, issued on 22 September 1827, strengthened that position.

51. Ibid., p. 348.

52. Ibid.

53. Ibid.

54. Ibid.

55. Ibid., p. 353.

56. Ibid., pp. 353–354. To be sure, the idea of renewing ordination in this manner is halakhically problematic. According to Maimonides, there can be no "ordination" outside the Land of Israel (*Mishneh Torah, Hilkhot Sanhedrin* 4:6), and it is hard to understand how there could have been ordained rabbis among the Ten Tribes.

57. Ibid., p. 356.

58. *Iggerot ha-Peqidim* (Letters of the Clerks), vol. 4, p. 168b.

59. Ibid., p. 98b.
60. Ibid., vol. 4, p. 99a.
61. Ibid.
62. Ibid., p. 98b.
63. Ibid., vol. 5., p. 20b.
64. Ibid., vol. 4, p. 98b.
65. Ibid., vol. 5, p. 20b.
66. Ibid., vol. 4, p. 160a.
67. Ibid.
68. Ibid.
69. Ibid., vol. 4, p. 98b.
70. Ibid., vol. 5, p. 13b.
71. Ibid., p. 14b.
72. Ibid., vol. 4, pp. 111b, 160a; vol. 5, p. 1b.
73. Ibid., vol. 4, p. 160a.
74. J. Schwartz, *Das Heilige Land* (Frankfurt-am-Main, 1852), pp. 416–418; Jacob Sapir, *Yemenite Journey*, ed. A. Yaari (Jerusalem, 1951), pp. 154–163.
75. *Iggerot ha-Peqidim* (Letters of the Clerks), vol. 5, p. 114b.
76. Ibid., vol. 5, p. 11a.
77. The letter is unknown except through Lehren's reference to it.
78. Ibid., vol. 4, p. 168b.
79. Ibid., p. 160a.
80. Ibid., vol. 5, p. 12b. In his article "Emissaries From the Land of Israel to the Ten Tribes," *Sinai* 6 (1940) (Hebrew), A. Yaari claims to have seen a certificate of appointment as a rabbinic emissary, dated 24 August 1830, issued to Barukh ben Samuel; signed by the Ashkenazi community organizations in Jerusalem, Hebron, and Safed; and addressed to the Jews of Yemen, India, Dagistan, Gorgestan, and Kurdistan—the lands the rabbinic emissary expected to traverse en route to the Ten Tribes. On the basis of that letter, Yaari attacks the view of Joseph Schwartz, who writes, in *Das Heilige Land* (p. 416) that Barukh made his way to Yemen via Alexandria, Cairo, and San'a. Yaari accepts Jacob Sapir's version, "that his journey began in Damascus, Aleppo, etc." Sapir, *Yemenite Journey*, p. 155. But the material in the Clerks' Organization letters supports Schwartz's view and suggests that Sapir and Yaari erred.
81. *Sefer Ma'aseh Nissim* (Amsterdam, 1818), pp. 9–10.
82. *Iggerot ha-Peqidim* (Letters of the Clerks), vol. 6, p. 89b.
83. Ibid., vol. 5, p. 67b.
84. Ibid., vol. 4, p. 98b.
85. Ibid., vol. 5, p. 76a.
86. *Iggerot Ereẓ Yisra'el*, p. 350.
87. *Iggerot ha-Peqidim* (Letters of the Clerks), vol. 5, p. 76a.
88. Ibid., vol. 5, p. 78a.
89. Ibid., p. 76a.
90. Ibid., p. 118a.
91. Ibid., p. 76a.
92. Ibid.
93. Frumkin writes (*Toledot Ḥakhmei Yerushalayim*, part 3, p. 174) that Dov Ber immigrated in 5592 (1831–1832). Rivlin writes (ibid., p. 175 n.) that "his signature appears on the epistle to the Ten Tribes from the year 5591 [1830–1831]," but that cannot be. It seems to me that Dov Ber set out for the Land of Israel in the summer of 5592 (1832) and arrived around Rosh ha-Shanah or soon after, at the beginning of 5593.

According to the *Mifqad Montefiori be-5599* (Montefiore Census of 1839—the "Listing of the Jews of Safed," the most reliable source for this matter), Dov Ber immigrated, together with a group of his family members, in 5593. See J. Maisel, "The 1839 Register of Jews in Safed and Its Environs," *Sefunot* 6 (1962), pp. 459–461.

94. Sapir, *Yemenite Journey*, p. 160.

95. *Iggerot ha-Peqidim* (Letters of the Clerks), vol. 6, p. 62a.

96. *J. I.* (1836), pp. 195–196.

97. When asked by his brother about the mission to the Ten Tribes, Joseph ben Shabbetai of Kalish responded that "I will write you a separate letter on this important matter and will describe what I heard from several of our sages." Bet ha-Levi, *History of the Jews of Kalish*, p. 329. Mendel Rosenbaum, the father-in-law of A. Bregman, likewise took an interest in the mission's fate. *Yis'u Harim Shalom*, p. 118. On 12 March 1861, Joseph Zundel of Salant responded to an inquiry regarding the truth of the belief in the Ten Tribes; he based his response on sources in the *Zohar*, the *midrashim*, and the writings of the Vilna Ga'on. Eliezer Rivlin, *The Pious One, Rabbi Joseph Zundel of Salant, and His Teachers* (Hebrew) (Jerusalem, 1927), p. 147.

CHAPTER 6

1. *Ha-Emet mei-Ereẓ Tiẓmaḥ*, pp. 135, 145.

2. "For it has been firmly determined in Vilna and the entire province, as a matter of practice, that the community's hub would be in the holy mountains of Safed, may it be built and established." Grajewski, *Mi-Ginzei Yerushalayim*, 17, p. 10.

3. "The number of people should be small; the people should be high-minded, God-fearing, and faithful; and they should have no leadership structure at all." Ibid.

4. *Iggerot ha-Peqidim* (Letters of the Clerks), vol. 8, p. 56a; vol. 10, p. 376.

5. *J. E.* (1822), p. 507.

6. *Mikhtavim mei-Izvono shel R. Shelomoh Paḥ*, Israel National Library, Manuscript Institute, 4°1468 (12).

7. Grajewski, *Mi-Ginzei Yerushalayim* 17, p. 10.

8. *Toledot Ḥakhmei Yerushalayim*, vol. 3, p. 158.

9. Grajewski, *Mi-Ginzei Yerushalayim*, 2, p. 3.

10. *Toledot Ḥakhmei Yerushalayim*, vol. 3, p. 158. In a recently discovered 1820 letter, Menaḥem Mendel of Shklov writes of the rebuilding of the *Ḥurvah*: "For, God be praised, in this way the beginning of redemption took place in our day." The letter, now in the collection of Dr. Manfred Lehmann in New York, will be printed as an appendix to my forthcoming Hebrew book *Ha-Shivah li-Yerushalayim* (The Return to Jerusalem), to be published in 2006.

11. *Ha-Emet mei-Ereẓ Tiẓmaḥ*, p. 145. The annulment of loans outstanding for more than forty years has always struck me as a strange business, for that is a fairly short interval, and the matter became no clearer to me after I consulted with experts in Ottoman law. Still, the issue is twice mentioned in some detail in the letters of the Clerks' Organization, though the interval mentioned is one hundred years rather than forty. Lehren writes as follows: "For over one hundred years earlier, a large community of Ashkenazim were on the site, but one by one, they incurred great debts to the local powers, and they sank into debt over their heads. . . . Eventually, they were required to flee and hide. . . . They left their portion and their homes in the holy city of Jerusalem. . . . And since then, no Ashkenazi was seen there (unless disguised in Sefardic clothes), until one hundred years had elapsed since those events, for under the laws of the Ishmaelites, every debt outstanding for that long is automatically canceled

and is no longer to be enforced." *Iggerot ha-Peqidim* (Letters of the Clerks), vol. 3, p. 171b.

12. *Ha-Emet mei-Ereẓ Tiẓmaḥ*, p. 145.

13. *Tevu'ot ha-Areẓ*, p. 472.

14. *Mi-Ginzei Qedem*, p. 74.

15. Ibid., p. 138.

16. *Iggerot ha-Peqidim* (Letters of the Clerks), vol. 8, p. 213a.

17. *Mikhtavim mei-Izvono shel R. Shelomoh Paḥ*, 4°1468 (1).

18. Ibid.

19. In September 1821, the missionary Joseph Wolff ran into Solomon Pach in Alexandria; he was making his living at the time as an engraver. *J. E.* (1822), p. 156.

20. *Ha-Emet mei-Ereẓ Tiẓmaḥ*, p. 145.

21. *J. E.* (1824), p. 382.

22. Ibid. We may find an expression of this in the pronouncement issued by Samuel Bernstein of Amsterdam on 22 February 1822: "If the fixed-term debts are not paid off, they will retain the property forever and the Ishmaelites will take pride in building there a castle for their prince." M. Eliav, "The Jews of Holland And the Jewish Settlement in the Land of Israel During the Nineteenth Century," in *Studies in the History of the Jews in Holland*, vol. 2 (Jerusalem, 1979), p. 145 (Hebrew).

23. M. Solomon, *Three Generations in the Yishuv, 1812–1913* (Jerusalem, 1951), p. 30 (Hebrew).

24. Rivlin and Rivlin, *Letters of the Clerks*, vol. 1, p. 218.

25. S. Askenazy, *"Pierwszy 'Syonista' Polsky,"* in *Dwa Stulecia*, II (Warsaw, 1910), pp. 421–441. The approach by Menaḥem Mendel Burukhowitz (son of Barukh), referred to as "rabbi of the Ashkenazi Jewish community in Jerusalem," was made through the intervention of a Warsaw Jew named Solomon Polonsky, from the city of Polonsk, who visited Jerusalem in 1819. He wrote to his father-in-law in Warsaw, transmitting Menaḥem Mendel's request to raise funds for the synagogue. The letter states that they had already received the Sultan's authorization to build the synagogue and expresses the hope that the rebuilding of all Jerusalem will follow.

26. *Toledot Ḥakhmei Yerushalayim*, vol. 3, p. 158.

27. Ibid., p. 159.

28. Ibid., p. 161.

29. Grajewski, *Mi-Ginzei Yerushalayim*, 17, pp. 5–6.

30. Ibid., 16, p. 1.

31. Ibid.

32. *Mikhtavim mei-Izvono shel R. Shelomoh Paḥ*, 4°1468 (4), and, with minor differences, in P. Grajewski, *Zikkaron la-Ḥovevim ha-Rishonim*, 11 (1928).

33. Grajewski, *Mi-Ginzei Yerushalayim*, 17, pp. 7–8.

34. *Mi-Ginzei Qedem*, p. 68.

35. *Ha-Emet mei-Ereẓ Tiẓmaḥ*, p. 146.

36. Ibid.

37. Ibid. The lack of any reference in this source to the burning of the synagogue in 1720 is surprising, and the surprise grows when we consider that the episode likewise goes entirely unmentioned in two long, detailed letters by Ẓevi Hirsch Lehren concerning the *Ḥurvah* courtyard. According to Lehren, the destruction of the courtyard was the result of its having been abandoned after the Ashkenazi debtors fled from it. On 1 December 1829, he writes: "They could not manage to pay the creditors the sum needed to redeem [the property] and they found it necessary to flee surreptitiously and were dispersed throughout the three other holy cities, may they be

built and established, and they abandoned their portions and their homes in the holy city of Jerusalem, and the synagogue and the study hall and a very large courtyard . . . out of fear that they would be caught in bonds of iron and imprisoned in fetters for repayment of their debts." *Iggerot ha-Peqidim* (Letters of the Clerks), vol. 3, p. 171b. On 4 May 1840, he returns to the subject: "And a demand for payment had already been pressed against them, and a deadline for payment had been set . . . and when salvation was delayed, they all fled surreptitiously and settled in the other holy cities, may they be built and established speedily and in our days, and they left the entire courtyard, including the synagogue and the study hall and several small dwelling houses, to be looted and trampled by the creditors. And when [the creditors] saw [the Ashkenazim] had fled and were not returning, they retained possession of the courtyard that had been mortgaged to them." Ibid., vol. 8, p. 213a. M. Benayahu cites several sources dealing with the events of the period, but only some of them tell of the fire. M. Benayahu, "The Ashkenazi Experience in Jerusalem," *Sefunot* 2 (1958), pp. 151–153 (Hebrew).

38. *Ha-Emet mei-Ereẓ Tiẓmaḥ*, p.146. The missionary W. B. Lewis likewise mentions that the Jews had to pay about 7,000 piastres to obtain the *firman*. *J. E.* (1824), p. 109.

39. *Ha-Emet mei-Ereẓ Tiẓmaḥ*, p. 146.

40. Ibid., pp. 145–146.

41. *J. E.* (1825), p. 109.

42. *J. E.* (1826), p. 179.

43. Rivlin and Rivlin, *Letters of the Clerks*, vol. 1, p. 197.

44. *Iggerot ha-Peqidim* (Letters of the Clerks), vol. 4, p. 169a.

45. Rivlin and Rivlin, *Letters of the Clerks*, vol. 2, p. 175.

46. Ibid.

47. I. Rivkind, "Separate Pages (Documents on the History of the Jewish Settlement in the Land of Israel in the Eighteenth and Nineteenth Centuries)," in *Jerusalem (A. M. Lunz Memorial Volume)* (Jerusalem, 1929), pp. 147–149 (Hebrew).

48. The letters by community officials cited in the reference in the preceding note do not permit an unambiguous determination of the date of Solomon Zalman Shapira's death. But one important account is that of Joseph Wolff, whose journal states that when he arrived in Jerusalem on 7 January 1829, Solomon Zalman had already passed on. *J. E.* (1829), p. 319. Frumkin writes that "the date of his death is unknown." *Toledot Ḥakhmei Yerushalayim*, vol. 3, p. 117.

49. *M. I.* (1830), p. 13.

50. Ibid.

51. M Solomon, *Three Generations in the Yishuv*, p. 45.

52. *Mi-Ginzei Qedem*, p. 89.

53. *Iggerot ha-Peqidim* (Letters of the Clerks), vol. 5, p. 56a.

54. The Covenant (or Pact) of Omar refers to a series of discriminatory regulations applied in Muslim lands against protected Christians and Jews.

55. Rivkind, "Separate Pages," p. 170.

56. *Mi-Ginzei Qedem*, p. 69.

57. *J. I.* (1836), p. 203. Nicolayson adds that he expects the interior improvements to be completed within a month. His reliability is evident in this instance as well. At the entry to the Istanbuli synagogue in Jerusalem, the following inscription appears on a marble panel: "This is the gateway of the Lord / God will save Zion / He will build the cities of Judah / His people, the sheep of His flock / will enter His gates in gratitude / 5595." Eliyahu Elyashar cites this inscription in his article "Syna-

gogues Named for Rabban Yoḥanan ben Zakkai," in J. ben-Porat, A. Kedar, et al., eds., *Aspects of the History of the Jewish Yishuv in Jerusalem*, vol. 1 (Jerusalem, 1977), p. 70 (Hebrew). He erred, however, and listed 5596 instead of 5595 as the date in the inscription. On the building of the Sefardic synagogues, see A. Morgenstern, "The Construction of the Courtyard of 'the *Ḥurvah* of R. Judah Ḥasid' in Jerusalem," *Shalem* 4 (1984), pp. 290–293 (Hebrew).

58. *Iggerot ha-Peqidim* (Letters of the Clerks), vol. 5, p. 113b.

59. *J. I.* (1836), p. 203.

60. *Iggerot ha-Peqidim* (Letters of the Clerks), vol. 8, p. 113b.

61. Ibid. Ẓoref set out equipped with recommendations from Joseph Schwartz. *Tevu'ot ha-Areẓ*, p. 471.

62. *Mi-Ginzei Qedem*, p. 90.

63. Ibid., p. 70. Also *Ha-Emet mei-Ereẓ Tiẓmaḥ*, p. 147.

64. *Iggerot ha-Peqidim* (Letters of the Clerks), vol. 8, p. 141b.

65. Ibid., vol. 6, p. 228b. Lehren writes: "I have no idea how any reasonable person could imagine that I would intervene to support and validate a lie . . . in addition to which, I believe Rothschild would not listen to me and would not write even for the sake of rebuilding all of the Land of Israel, much less the *Ḥurvah* in Jerusalem." Ibid.

66. Ibid., vol. 8, p. 5b.

67. *Mi-Ginzei Qedem*, p. 70.

68. Ms. Montefiore 577(2). Israel National Library, Manuscript Photocopy Institute, no. 6193.

69. *Ha-Emet mei-Ereẓ Tiẓmaḥ*, p. 147; *Mi-Ginzei Qedem*, pp. 70–72. At p. 72, Grajewski cites Ẓoref's name as "Zalman Marpo," but that is an error; it should be "Marco" (father of Mordecai). Rivlin noted this in *Toledot Ḥakhmei Yerushalayim*, vol. 3, p. 181. I also found the name Marco in Ẓoref's travel document in the archive of the Jerusalem municipality.

70. Report of Zalman Ẓoref (Solomon) to Moses Montefiore, 1 February 1843, printed in the appendix to issue 17 of the journal *Der Orient*, 1843, p. 273.

71. A similar account appears in a letter from Joseph Schwartz to his brother. The Hebrew translation appears to be corrupt, however, and it is difficult to understand the connections between Muhammad Ali, the "advisors," and the "official" in Jaffa. *Mi-Ginzei Qedem*, p. 91.

72. Ibid. A similar account appears in Ẓoref's letter to Montefiore.

73. *Mi-Ginzei Qedem*, p. 91.

74. Ibid., p. 74.

75. Ibid.

76. Ibid.

77. Ibid.

78. Ibid.

79. *Ha-Emet mei-Ereẓ Tiẓmaḥ*, p. 147. Note that the editor of *Mi-Ginzei Qedem* erred in his precise identification of some of the documents on pp. 69 and 76.

80. Rivlin and Rivlin, *Letters of the Clerks*, vol. 2, p. 107.

81. *Iggerot ha-Peqidim* (Letters of the Clerks), vol. 4., p. 168a.

82. Ibid., vol. 5, p. 141a.

83. Ibid., vol. 8, p. 56a.

84. On 6 March 1834, he wrote as follows to the Ḥabad Hasidim in Hebron, who had requested support for the building of a synagogue: "Regarding [your] request that we seek your welfare and help you to acquire a new synagogue, we cannot help

you at all. . . . It is not good in our eyes, as is said in the [*Talmud*] *Yerushalmi* that shekels [able to support] several souls are sunk in this building." *Iggerot ha-Peqidim* (Letters of the Clerks), vol. 6. p. 29b.

85. Ibid., vol. 6, p. 56a.

86. Ibid.

87. Ibid., vol. 6, p. 59a.

88. Ibid., p. 61a.

89. Ibid.

90. Ibid.

91. Ibid., p. 170b.

92. Ibid.

93. Ibid., p. 88b.

94. Ibid., pp. 140a, 146b.

95. Ibid., p. 146b.

96. Ibid., p. 147a.

97. Ibid. Lehren's pledge was a matter of public knowledge. See the letter of Rabbi Joseph, who immigrated to the Land of Israel from Kalish, regarding a donation of 925 ducats. Bet ha-Levi, *History of the Jews of Kalish*, p. 327.

98. *Iggerot ha-Peqidim* (Letters of the Clerks), vol. 6, p. 147a.

99. Ibid., p. 170b.

100. Ibid.

101. Ibid.

102. Ibid., p. 59a.

103. Ibid., p. 205b. It is not clear whether he was referring to the "courtyard" mentioned earlier by Aryeh Ne'eman or to some other "courtyard." According to Aaron Moses of the family of Ẓevi, the leader of the Jerusalem Hasidim, Israel of Shklov said "the *Ḥurvah* is a place in which the 'other side' [the evil impulse] dwells." Ibid., vol. 8, p. 156b; the letter dates from 4 June 1839.

104. Ibid., vol. 6, p. 157a.

105. Ibid., p. 228b.

106. Ibid.

107. Ibid.

108. Ibid.

109. Ibid.

110. Ibid.

111. Ibid., vol. 8, p. 4b: "Our souls are cast down and our hearts ill, for we have seen such as we never expected to see and we are covered by shame." Ibid.

112. Ibid., p. 7b.

113. Ibid., p. 18b.

114. Ibid., p. 7b.

115. Ibid.

116. Ibid., p. 14a.

117. Ibid.

118. Ibid., p. 21b.

119. Ibid.

120. Ibid., p. 14a.

121. Ibid. "And of all the officials, none are left who are faithful to their mission except the *ga'on* Rabbi Israel and his son-in-law Rabbi Isaiah. Ibid., vol. 10, p. 377.

122. Ibid., vol. 8, p. 56a.

123. Ibid., p. 55b.

124. Ibid., vol. 10, p. 377.

125. Ibid., vol. 8, p. 22b.

126. Ibid., p. 40a. Lehren claims that the ban was issued on the day of the earthquake in the Galilee, that is, 1 January 1837, but that after the Jerusalem *Perushim* heard of that coincidence, they changed the date of the ban to 3 January.

127. Ibid.

128. On Israel of Shklov's shaky position within the *kolel* of the Jerusalem *Perushim,* see A. Morgenstern, "The Organizational Unity of the *Perushim Kolel* in the Land of Israel" (Hebrew), *Zion* 47, 3 (1982), pp. 293–310.

129. Y. Alfasi, "Documents About the History of the Old Settlement," *Bar-Ilan Yearbook* 3 (1965), p. 219 (Hebrew).

130. Ibid.

131. Ibid.

132. Ibid.

133. Ibid.

134. *Ha-Emet mei-Ereẓ Tiẓmaḥ*, p. 147; *Tevu'ot ha-Areẓ*, p. 471. The marble tablet affixed above the entry to the study hall suggests construction was supposed to have been completed earlier, on 8 Kislev 5597: "This is the house of the Lord; the righteous shall enter into it, awesome praises to God, 8 Kislev 5797. P. Grajewski, *Avnei Zikkaron* 1 (1928), p. 3.

135. Grajewski, *Mi-Ginzei Yerushalayim*, 2, p. 2.

136. Ibid., p. 1.

137. Ibid., p. 2. Some of these key ideas appear as well in a letter endorsing the rabbinic emissary Aaron Zelig Mann, published in (1838) by Israel Kunian of Padua; they include the idea that receipt of the *firman* signifies the start of redemption: "We are obliged to praise the one who loves the gates of Zion, for He has inclined the heart of the king who rules over Egypt and the holy cities to all that He wishes, to grant the request related to our city and show concern for it in mercy and grant their request to see the building of the land, including the great synagogue and great study hall, which have been in ruins these many days and subjected to the rule of strangers, and this sort of thing is the beginning of redemption. *Qol Qore le-Ezrat Bonei ha-Ḥurvah*, ms. Sasson, Jerusalem, Yad Ben-Zvi Library, file no. 285.

138. P. Grajewski, *Pinqas Yerushalayim*, p. 2.

139. *Iggerot ha-Peqidim* (Letters of the Clerks), vol. 8, p. 7a. The date of Lehren's response—20 November 1836—suggests that Bregman's letter was sent in late summer 1836, perhaps right after 1 September 1836, when they began removing the mounds of dust and trash from the *Ḥurvah* courtyard. *Mi-Ginzei Qedem*, p. 91.

140. *Iggerot ha-Peqidim* (Letters of the Clerks), vol. 8, p. 7a.

141. I. Tishby, "Immigration to the Land of Israel for the Purpose of Raising the *Shekhinah*," *Cathedra* 24 (1982), p. 75 (Hebrew). How the Sefardim regarded the messianist phenomena is a multifaceted question requiring inquiry on its own. But we have sources showing not only the liturgical changes already noted but also the excision of a passage in the longer form of the *Taḥanun* (petitionary prayers) recited on Mondays and Thursdays that begins "He Who opens His hand to repentance" and laments "How long will Your might be imprisoned and Your glory be in the enemy's hands?" According to the account of the Sefardic rabbinic emissary Moses Israel Ḥazzan, who stayed in Amsterdam during the year 1846, the Sefardim stopped reciting that passage because they believed "the *shekhinah* has already risen from her dust." In the wake of that report, Lehren writes to the *Rishon le-Ẓiyyon* (the Sefardic Chief Rabbi in the Land of Israel), Abraham Ḥayyim Ganin, expressing surprise at the litur-

gical changes and asking whether they are indeed the result of the novel ideas expressed by Moses Israel Ḥazzan: "And now, may our teacher the rabbi, may God protect and bless him, allow me to raise another matter with him, [regarding] what I heard from his excellency our friend Rabbi Moses Israel Ḥazzan, may God protect and bless him, that in the Holy City, may it be built and established, they do not say 'how long will Your might be imprisoned and Your glory be in the enemy's hands' because the *shekhinah* has already risen from her dust." *Iggerot ha-Peqidim* (Letters of the Clerks), vol. 11, p. 122. Lehren strives to find another reason for the custom, for it makes no sense to him to delete sentences whose excision compromises the mystical balance of the number of words and letters in a liturgical text. He stresses his unwillingness, under any circumstances, to accept the rationale Ḥazzan referred to: "But that reason is novel in our eyes and its purity is questionable, for that prayer is laden with [mystical] meanings." Ibid. Rabbi Ganin responds that, in fact, there is another reason for the deletion, one that Lehren finds delightful: "A thousand thanks for his holy response regarding "He Who opens His hand to repentance," and his words are as clear as dawn. . . . Not so the words of our teacher Rabbi Moses Ḥazzan, who failed to consider the intentions earlier included in that prayer and, instead, [treated it] as if it had arisen only in our time; and that was totally unacceptable to me. Ibid., p. 177. See also A. Morgenstern, "Historical Reality or Wishful Thinking in Research on the 'Old *Yishuv*,' " *Cathedra* 31 (1984), p. 177 (Hebrew).

142. *Iggerot ha-Peqidim* (Letters of the Clerks), vol. 8, p. 40a.

143. *Iggerot Soferim*, Letter 62, p. 62.

144. *Sefer Torat Mosheh*, R. Moses Sofer of Pressburg (Vienna, 1906), end of *Parashat Emor*.

145. Ibid.

146. Ibid.

147. Lunz, *Jerusalem Yearbook*, vol. 9 (1911), p. 155 (Hebrew).

148. *Iggerot Soferim*, Letter 62, p. 56.

149. Lunz, *Jerusalem Yearbook*, vol. 9 (1911), p. 156 (Hebrew).

150. *Iggerot Ereẓ Yisra'el*, p. 366.

151. Ibid.

152. *Meḥqarim u-Meqorot*, p. 130. Specifically, when seven families of the *Perushim* in Safed declined to move to Jerusalem, the *kolel* disavowed responsibility for them and refused to distribute *ḥaluqah* funds to them.

153. Lunz, *Jerusalem Yearbook*, vol. 9 (1911), pp. 381–384 (Hebrew).

154. *Tevu'ot ha-Areẓ*, p. 471.

CHAPTER 7

1. *Shomer Ẓiyyon ha-Ne'eman* (Altona), no. 180 (23 June 1854), p. 359a.

2. *Iggerot ha-Peqidim* (Letters of the Clerks), vol. 13, p. 278.

3. *Ateret Yosef*, "brought to press in Jerusalem in the year 5659 [1899], introduction by him who brought it to press, Rabbi Ḥayyim son of our master Rabbi Aaron ha-Levi." In light of these sources, it appears to me that the tradition of Vilna Ga'on's descendants on this point is reliable. Rivlin, *Vision of Zion*, pp. 21–22.

4. I. Werfel (Rafael), "The History of the Ashkenazi Community in the Land of Israel," Sinai 5 (1939), p. 95 (Hebrew).

5. *Mikhtavim mei-Izvono shel R. Shelomoh Paḥ*, Israel National Library, Manuscript Institute, 4°1468 (9).

6. There is a need to reexamine, in light of the newly available material, the rela-

tionships among the various *kolels* in the Land of Israel after the immigration of the *Perushim*.

7. Werfel (Rafael), "History of the Ashkenazi Community," p. 102.

8. Grajewski, *Mi-Ginzei Yerushalayim*, 17, p. 10.

9. *Ha-Emet mei-Ereẓ Tiẓmaḥ*, p. 131.

10. Maimonides, *Sefer ha-Miẓvot*, Comm. 153. And so, too, Moses Sofer (*Ḥatam Sofer*): "For if, God forbid, no Jew were left in the Land of Israel . . . it would be the demise of the nation, God forbid, for we lack ordained authorities who can determine the [beginnings of] months and declare leap years" (*Yoreh De'ah*, sec. 234).

11. *Iggerot ha-Peqidim* (Letters of the Clerks), vol. 8, p. 103a.

12. Ibid., vol. 4, p. 114b,

13. Ibid. p. 113a.

14. *Derashot R. Abraham Prinẓ* (1769–1851), Rosenthaliana Library, Amsterdam; Israel National Library, Manuscript Photocopy Institute, 3818: Discourse *Yam ha-Aravah* (no pagination and no date). The sole date in the ms. is Passover Eve 5589 (17 April 1829).

15. Ibid.

16. Ibid.

17. Ibid.

18. *Iggerot ha-Peqidim* (Letters of the Clerks), vol. 8, p. 103a.

19. Ibid., p. 168b.

20. Ibid., vol. 5, pp. 43a, 46a.

21. Ibid., p. 115a.

22. Ibid.

23. Ibid., vol. 8, p. 10b.

24. Ibid.

25. Ibid. During the 1830s, concerns were raised, in Russia and the Land of Israel alike, that the growing waves of immigration would cause difficulties. Despite these concerns, the influx of immigrants did not stop, and the nonselective policy of the *Perushim*'s *kolel* did not change. See further in chapter 3 in this volume.

26. *Iggerot ha-Peqidim* (Letters of the Clerks), vol. 8, p. 139a. Lehren does not shy away from expressing, in late summer or early fall of 1845, open anger at Eliezer Bregman's bringing a new wife to the Land of Israel, following the death of his first wife, along with her father and brothers, "without concern about increasing the number of people from Holland and Germany." Ibid., vol. 11, p. 76. In contrast to Lehren, Bregman believed fundamentally that hastening the redemption required fulfilling the biological potential of the Jewish people. Bregman accordingly tended toward leniency in halakhic decisions related to the possible abrogation of the medieval Ashkenazi ban on polygamy, for the biological growth of the Jewish people could help bring about the redemption. *Be-Har Yeira'eh*, R. Eliezer Bregman (Jerusalem, 1977), pp. 42, 47. Bregman based his view on such rabbinic statements as "They said: The King Messiah will not come until all the souls that were intended to be created have been created." *Genesis Rabbah* 24.

27. *Iggerot ha-Peqidim* (Letters of the Clerks), vol. 8, p. 139a.

28. Ibid., vol. 11, p. 188.

29. Ibid., vol. 8, p. 26a.

30. Ibid.

31. Ibid., p. 139a.

32. Ibid., p. 4a.

33. Ibid., p. 175a.

34. Ibid.
35. Ibid., p. 148a.
36. Ibid.
37. Ibid.
38. *Yis'u Harim Shalom*, pp. 64, 68, 76, 93, 91, 99.
39. *Iggerot ha-Peqidim* (Letters of the Clerks), vol. 8, p. 11b.
40. Ibid.
41. Ibid., p. 17b.
42. Ibid., p. 11b.
43. Ibid.
44. Ibid.
45. *Yis'u Harim Shalom*, p. 99.
46. *Iggerot ha-Peqidim* (Letters of the Clerks), vol. 8, p. 10b.
47. *Zikkaron la-Ḥovevim ha-Rishonim*, P. Grajewski, pamphlet 10 (Jerusalem, 1928), p. 11.
48. Ibid.
49. *Zikhronot Qedumim*, ed. P. Grajewski, pamphlet 1 (Jerusalem, 1928), pp. 3–4.
50. Ibid.
51. *Zikkaron la-Ḥovevim ha-Rishonim*, pamphlet 10, p. 19.
52. Ibid., p. 17.
53. Rivlin, "Letter from R. Hillel Rivlin," p. 146.
54. Ibid.
55. *Yis'u Harim Shalom*, p. 93.
56. Ibid.
57. "And in this year of 5597 [1836–1837], a case occurred within the city, in the market of Bab Ḥota, where several Ashkenazim dwell, and a *minyan* of ten gathered there, and a young man betrothed a young maid, and they recited the betrothal blessings, but after several months they wanted to separate." *Shem Ḥadash*, R. Ḥayyim Solomon Daniel Finzo (Jerusalem, 1843), introduction.
58. *Iggerot ha-Peqidim* (Letters of the Clerks), vol. 6, p. 233b.
59. Ibid.
60. Ibid., vol. 8, p. 127a.
61. Ibid.
62. Ibid.
63. Ibid.
64. Israel Bartal, "Settlement Proposals During Montefiore's Second Visit to the Land of Israel, 1839," *Shalem* 2 (1977), p. 287 (Hebrew).
65. Ibid., p. 288.
66. *Iggerot Ereẓ Yisra'el*, p. 356.
67. *Iggerot ha-Peqidim* (Letters of the Clerks), vol. 8., p. 10b.
68. Ibid.
69. Ibid., p. 26b.
70. Ibid.
71. Ibid., vol. 6, p. 5b.
72. Ibid.
73. Ibid.
74. Ibid., vol. 13, p. 278.
75. *Ha-Emet mei-Ereẓ Tiẓmaḥ*, p. 141.
76. Ibid.
77. *J. E.* (1822), p. 156.

78. *Mikhtavim mei-Izvono shel R. Shelomoh Paḥ*, Israel National Library, (1). In an 1838 letter from the Nobles of Vilna to the Jerusalem *kolel*, we hear of the attitude toward training orphans as artisans: "It was agreed amongst us to increase funding for orphans, and since we lack the ability to know who has the capacity to become a trained artisan . . . we left their *ḥaluqah* distribution in the general list and added 60 ducats. A. B. Malachi, "History of the *Ḥaluqah* in Jerusalem," in *Aspects of the History of the Old Yishuv* (Tel-Aviv, 1971), p. 100 (Hebrew).

79. A. Rivlin, "The Statute of *Azvonot*," in Y. L. Fishman, *Azkarah* 5 (Jerusalem, 1937), p. 607; Rivlin, "Letter from R. Hillel Rivlin," pp. 141–143; Bet ha-Levi, *History of the Jews of Kalish*, p. 312; *Iggerot ha-Peqidim* (Letters of the Clerks), vol. 4, p. 168a.

80. *Iggerot Ereẓ Yisra'el*, p. 336.

81. *Iggerot ha-Peqidim* (Letters of the Clerks), vol. 4, p. 168a.

82. Ibid., p. 14a.

83. Lehren's response that the funds for all the *kolels* should continue to be sent via the Rothschild Bank in Paris shows clearly that this was a project of the *kolel* rather than a private request.

84. Ibid. As early as fall 1844, Lehren takes the trouble to write to the *kolel* regarding the matter: "And their contributing to craftsmen certainly makes no sense. A craftsman can go someplace in the Diaspora and earn his living there, and the funds for the Land of Israel were founded only for the sake of those who study Torah in the Land of Israel." Ibid., vol. 11, p. 13.

85. Y. Hofman, "Muhammad Ali's Activity in Syria" (Ph.D. dissertation, Hebrew University of Jerusalem, 1963), pp. 218–272 (Hebrew).

86. *Iggerot ha-Peqidim* (Letters of the Clerks), vol. 5, p. 141a.

87. Ibid., p. 133b.

88. Ibid., p. 141a.

89. Ibid.

90. *Yis'u Harim Shalom*, p. 24.

91. Ibid., p. 99.

92. Ibid., p. 107.

93. Ibid., p. 43.

94. Ibid., p. 60.

95. Ibid., p. 62.

96. Ibid., p. 63.

97. Ibid., p. 107.

98. Ibid.

99. Ibid., pp. 66–70.

100. Ibid., p. 65.

101. Ibid., p. 58.

102. Ibid., pp. 76, 97.

103. Ibid., p. 114.

104. Ibid., pp. 110, 115.

105. Ibid., pp. 111, 114, 125.

106. Ibid., p. 64.

107. Ibid.

108. Ibid., p. 84.

109. Ibid., p. 71.

110. Ibid., p. 81.

111. Ibid., p. 91.

112. Ibid.

113. Ibid., p. 97.

114. Ibid.

115. Ibid., p. 93.

116. *Iggerot ha-Peqidim* (Letters of the Clerks), vol. 5, p. 141a.

117. Ibid., vol. 6, p. 226a and following. Lehren writes to Bregman: "And I'm not concerned about what [your wife] writes about me, that I am wrong and that she knows better . . . and it would be better if they did not immigrate to the Land of Israel." Ibid., vol. 8, p. 31b. And he writes to Rabbi Hamburg of Fürth that "Eliezer did not heed my advice and acted entirely on his own, with regard to the journey itself . . . and with regard to other things as well." Ibid., p. 34a.

118. Ibid., vol. 6, p. 175a.

119. Ibid., vol. 8, p. 20.

120. Ibid., p. 71a.

121. Lehren writes to Abraham Reiss: "I know the man and his talk, from his having been in my home and from the provocative and deprecatory words he wrote to me from his home . . . *and he broke through to go up*." Ibid., p. 118a. The highlighted turn of phrase originally appears in the admonition at Sinai that "the priests and the people shall not break through to go up to God" (Exod. 19:24). Its usage, however, is connected with the attempt of the Israelites to go up to the Land of Israel despite the decree that the generation of the Exodus perish in the wilderness: "So I spoke to you but you hearkened not, but you rebelled against the Lord's commandment and were presumptuous and went up to the hill-country. And the Amorites . . . [attacked you] and beat you down in Seir, all the way to Ḥormah." (Deut. 1:43–44.) Midrashic literature attributes the rebellious effort to go up to the tribe of Ephraim, which sought to hasten the End by the act of going up: "For the tribe of Ephraim erred and left Egypt before the End had come, and thirty thousand of them were killed" (*Exodus Rabbah* 20:11).

122. *Be-Har Yeira'eh*, introduction, p. vii; p. 3.

123. A. Bartura, *With a Listening Heart: The Life of Eliezer Bregman of Jerusalem* (Jerusalem, 1983) (Hebrew).

124. "Muhammad Ali's Activity in Syria", pp. 218–241.

125. *Zikhronot Ereẓ Yisra'el*, ed. A. Yaari, part 1 (Tel-Aviv, 1947), pp. 144–145.

126. *Iggerot ha-Peqidim* (Letters of the Clerks), vol. 5, p. 92b.

127. Bregman, who reached Jerusalem in late winter or early spring of 1835, makes no mention of Sacks.

128. *Sheluḥei Ereẓ Yisra'el*, p. 773.

129. D. Stock, "On the Origins of R. Moses Sacks's Fame," *Sinai* 2 (1938), p. 331 (Hebrew).

130. *J. I.* (1836), p. 100.

131. "The welfare of my own nation is my heart's desire. I wish I could establish schools at Jerusalem for the Jewish children there, who are much neglected." Ibid.

132. *Iggerot ha-Peqidim* (Letters of the Clerks), vol. 6, p. 172b. Lehren, of course, ridicules Sacks's plans, suspecting that Bregman sent him, and raging against Rabbi Moses Sofer of Pressburg, who supports him: "And who will come after the king, who has already been declared righteous and perfect." Ibid., p. 217a. According to Lehren, Sacks "never derived any benefit from sitting in the various yeshivas in which he studied and never found the good, that is, a woman [cf. Prov. 18:22], and he therefore went up to the sacred [place]." Ibid.

133. N. M. Gelber, "Moshe Sacks," *Sinai* 1 (1938), p. 569 (Hebrew).

134. Ibid.

135. Ibid., p. 570.

136. Ibid., p. 673.

137. *Iggerot ha-Peqidim* (Letters of the Clerks), vol. 6, p. 230a.

138. "And the words with which he wanted to entice them, related to the freedom of the Jews in the Land of Israel, are all vanity and ill wind, vanities that can be peddled in these lands but not in the Land of Israel. I, too, knew that now the Jews are permitted to purchase houses and courtyards in Jerusalem, may it be built and established, which was not the case previously." Lehren to the Rabbi of Fürth, 22 August 1836, ibid., p. 231a.

139. Ibid., vol. 6, p. 232a. Lehren opened and read Sacks's letters to the Land of Israel, which were routed through him by Rabbi Hamburg of Fürth.

140. Ibid., p. 232b.

141. Lehren does not take account of the reality or even the ideology of a change in the status of the Land of Israel once the Jews begin returning to it. He stands by the established notion that sees the desolation of the Land while it is ruled over by Israel's enemies as something good, consistent with Nachmanides' interpretation of the verse "and I will make the Land desolate and your enemies who dwell in it will be astonished at it" (Lev. 26:32). Nachmanides says: "It is good tidings . . . for our land does not accept our enemies, and it is also a great proof and promise to us, for there is not to be found any other good and broad land once settled but now desolate. It received no [other] nation or tongue, and they all try to settle it, but to no avail."

142. *Iggerot ha-Peqidim* (Letters of the Clerks), vol. 6, p. 233b.

143. Ibid.

144. Ibid., vol. 8, p. 11a.

145. Ibid.

146. Ibid.

147. Ibid., p. 11b.

148. Ibid.

149. Ibid. Lehren claims to have been told this by a Jew who was traveling with Sacks on a ferryboat.

150. Gelber, "Moshe Sacks," p. 570.

151. Ibid., p. 569.

152. *Iggerot ha-Peqidim* (Letters of the Clerks), vol. 8, p. 22b.

153. *Sheluḥei Ereẓ Yisra'el*, p. 777.

154. Y. Barnai, "Changes in Nineteenth-Century Jerusalem," *Sinai* 81 (1977), p. 154 (Hebrew).

155. A. N. Falk, *History of Real Property Relationships in Egypt, Syria, and the Land of Israel in Late Medieval and Modern Times* (Jerusalem, 1940), p. 73 (Hebrew).

156. Ruth Krok, "Lands and Plans to Work Them in the Time of Montefiore's Second Visit to the Land of Israel, 1839," *Cathedra* 33 (1984), p. 71 n. 68 (Hebrew).

157. *Sanhedrin* 98a.

158. *Iggerot ha-Peqidim* (Letters of the Clerks), vol. 8, p. 45a.

159. Ibid., p. 46a.

160. Ibid.

161. Ibid.

162. Ibid.

163. Ibid., p. 46b.

164. One can detect in Bregman clear indications of a positive attitude toward enhancing productivity in the spirit of the Enlightenment.

165. *Be-Har Yeira'eh*, p. 6.

166. *Iggerot ha-Peqidim* (Letters of the Clerks), vol. 8, p. 11b.

167. *Yoman Masa ve-Iggerot*, Yad Izhak Ben-Zvi (Jerusalem, 1974), pp. 247–270; similarly, Mordecai Solomon Ẓoref's original ms., as it appears in Bartal, *Settlement Proposals*, pp. 288–296.

168. *Yoman Masa ve-Iggerot*, p. 265.

169. Bartal, *Settlement Proposals*, p. 291.

170. Ibid.

171. Ibid., p. 295.

172. Ibid.

173. Ibid., p. 294.

174. Ibid., p. 296.

175. *Iggerot Yehudim mei-Ereẓ Yisra'el le-Mosheh Montefiori*, London, Montefiore Archive, ms. 574; Israel National Library, Manuscript Photocopy Institute, 6190, p. 71B.

176. *Mifqad Montefiori be-5599* (Montefiore Census of 1839), London, Montefiore Archive, ms. 528; Israel National Library, Manuscript Photocopy Institute, 35115.

177. *Iggerot Yehudim mei-Ereẓ Yisra'el*, 6190, p. 29A.

178. Ibid.

179. A joint letter from the *Perushim* leadership and the heads of the Sefardic community advocates agricultural work by Jews: "And Moses [Montefiore] saw the severity of their straits, and his mercies were called forth, and his pure heart volunteered to establish pillars and foundations on which the House of Israel might rely . . . lending them a hand in the holy land, the Land of Israel, so they might plow, sow, and harvest in joy. And so that each person might devote himself in tranquility and security to the Torah and to labor, under his vine and his fig tree, each in accordance with his own actions. The God-fearing and those who invoke His Name will take up their posts of both Torah and labor, and the rest of the people, the common folk, will work the holy soil, and the Land will yield them its produce . . . and all of us as one take this upon ourselves with love . . . anticipating and hoping for God's salvation, through Moses, his faithful one, saying when will this start of redemption begin. . . . To this end, may our counsel be pleasing before our noble lord, may his glory be exalted, and let Moses hasten to endeavor with all his might to gain a declaration from the king of Egypt, may his glory be exalted, with all the force and might needed for this matter, gaining his attention with words in writing . . . an Ashkenazi lion, may God save and protect him. And after this statement, the other kings of Europe will strengthen and fortify him [Muhammad Ali?] . . . particularly because next year is the sabbatical year, and we will have to teach them what to do. . . .

[signed:] Jonah Moses Navon, Judah Navon, Isaac Kovo, Nathan Neta ben R. Menaḥem Mendel, Aryeh Ne'eman, Isaiah Bardaky

Iggerot Yehudim mei-Ereẓ Yisra'el, Ms. Montefiore 574, 6190, p. 79.

180. *Iggerot ha-Peqidim* (Letters of the Clerks), vol. 10, p. 30b.

181. Ibid.

182. Ibid., p. 31a.

183. Ibid.

184. Ibid., p. 30b.

185. Ibid., p. 31a.

186. *Yoman Masa ve-Iggerot*, p. 216.

187. See, for example, the document cited in note 176 above and other documents in the Montefiore Archive.

188. In his study "Settlement Proposals During Montefiore's Second Visit to the

Land of Israel, 1839," Bartal analyzed some of the sources related to this episode. In my view as well, there is no Enlightenment-related link between the *Perushim*'s proposals for working the land and the central ideas of the productivity advocates. Nevertheless, one can detect in the *Perushim*'s proposals a desire to foster a creative society that will support the process of settling the Land of Israel. Bartal's error was in his finding that "the fundamental thrust of the Ashkenazi settlement in the Land of Israel was study [of Torah] and service of God" (p. 282). As we have seen, that was the interest of the Clerks' Organization, with Ẓevi Hirsch Lehren at its head; but Lehren therefore found himself constantly at odds with the *kolel* of the *Perushim*. The interest of the *Perushim*, as here demonstrated, was the redemption of the Land through its settlement and development in every manner possible. That said, it is only natural that one of the central characteristics of a traditional scholarly society would be study of Torah and service of God.

189. Baron, "Aspects of the History of the Jewish Settlement," p. 304 n. 2.

190. Ibid.

191. Ibid.

192. Ibid. ["Tithe so you may become wealthy" is a midrashic interpretation of Deut. 14:22; it plays on the meanings of the similar stems *'-s-r* (ten) and *'-sh-r* (wealth).—***translator***]

193. Ibid.

CHAPTER 8

1. On Protestant eschatology and its connection to the redemption of Israel, see Meir Werte, "The Idea of Israel's Return in English Protestant Thought, 1790–1840," *Zion* 33 (1968), pp. 145–179 (Hebrew); Menaḥem Kedem, "Mid-Nineteenth-Century Anglican Eschatology on the Redemption of Israel," *Cathedra* 19 (1981), pp. 55–72 (Hebrew). On the mission, see Saul Sapir, "Sources on the Anglican Missionary Societies Active in Jerusalem and the Land of Israel in the Nineteenth Century to the First World War," *Cathedra* 19 (1981), pp. 155–170 (Hebrew). See also the English missionary press throughout the nineteenth century.

2. *J. E.* (1822), pp. 424, 419.

3. In a letter to Ẓevi Hirsch Lehren, Solomon Zalman Shapira explains their attitude toward the missionaries: "Similar to the fact that in the Diaspora, we relied, for the needs of the community on noblewomen, priests, and apostates." Rivlin and Rivlin, *Letters of the Clerks*, vol. 1, p. 203.

4. Ibid., p. 234. One interesting episode epitomizes the differing perspectives of Ashkenazim and Sefardim toward the missionaries. In April 1823, the Sefardic leadership requested the Muslim ruler of Jerusalem to expel the apostate-missionary Joseph Wolff. Their accusations against him included a charge that because Wolff remained a Jew under Jewish law, his residence in the city violated the "Bachelors' Statute" of 1749 ("no unmarried Jew is permitted to live here in the holy city of Jerusalem, may it be built and established, without a wife . . . and the community, the officials of Jerusalem, may it be built and established, are authorized to expel from the land anyone who violates these words, pursuing him all the way to Ḥormah" [i.e., defeating him thoroughly ; cf. Num. 14:45]). M. D. Gaon, *Oriental Jews in the Land of Israel, Past and Present*, vol. 1 (Jerusalem, 1928), pp. 112–113 (Hebrew). According to Wolff, Menaḥem Mendel of Shklov rose to his defense, helping him move and settle

in the Armenian Quarter, near Mount Zion. *J. E.* (1822), p. 419; *J. E.* (1824), pp. 101–102.

5. *Mikhtevei R. Shelomoh Hershel Berliner*, ms. Jewish Theological Seminary of America, New York, 3619; Israel National Library, Manuscript Photocopy Institute, 29424, p. 151b.

6. Ibid., p. 150b.

7. Ibid. The passage is quoted as well in a letter by Ẓevi Hirsch Lehren. Rivlin and Rivlin, *Letters of the Clerks*, vol. 1, p. 203.

8. See chapter 1, nn. 62, 63.

9. *M. I.* (1830), p. 13.

10. Ibid., pp. 13–14.

11. *J. I.* (1842), p. 271; *J. I.* (1839), p. 97.

12. *J. I.* (1840), p. 37.

13. *J. I.* (1839), p. 131.

14. *J. I.* (1840), p. 141.

15. *J. I.* (1839), p. 266.

16. *J. I.* (1841), pp. 16–17. The travel journal of Lady Frances Egerton discusses Father Grimshawe's impressions of the Jews' expectations for the year 5600. In her account, she sensed no messianic expectations during her visit to the Land of Israel; on the contrary, she claims to have discerned a movement on the part of Jewish families to leave the Land of Israel for the Diaspora. Frances Egerton, *Journal of a Tour in the Holy Land in May and June 1840* (London, 1841), pp. 21–22. It should be noted that Lady Egerton formed an accurate impression of the depressed mood within the *yishuv* at the time of her arrival, which followed the publicizing of the Damascus blood libel. A sense of deep fear over the libel's consequences dominated the community, and the Jews avoided unnecessary circulation in the streets and markets. The fear was accompanied by a sense that the blood libel constituted proof that "the year of divine visitation" had been deferred from 5600, as it had been from 4856 (1096) and 5408 (1648); each of those years had turned out to be one of tribulation rather than redemption.

17. *J. I.* (1841), pp. 16–17.

18. Ibid., pp. 169–170.

19. Ibid., p. 136.

20. *Iggerot ha-Peqidim* (Letters of the Clerks), vol. 8, p. 113a.

21. Ibid., p. 206a.

22. Ibid., p. 117a.

23. Ibid., vol. 6, p. 41a.

24. Ibid., vol. 8, p. 35a.

25. Ibid.

26. Ibid.

27. Ibid.

28. Ibid., p. 117b.

29. In accordance with the Talmudic dictum: "At the departure of the sabbatical year—the son of David comes." *Sanhedrin* 97a. At issue is the festival of Sukkot that occurs shortly after the start of the following year, 5601. That year, Sukkot (and the immediately following festival of Shemini Aẓeret) extended from 12 October to 20 October 1840.

30. *Iggerot ha-Peqidim* (Letters of the Clerks), vol. 8, p. 172a.

31. Between 1826 and 1854, while Lehren was alive, there is no other such

gap. Lehren wrote letters even while he was traveling and would then transcribe them into the copy books. He did not refrain from dictating letters even during the intermediate days of festivals (when certain types of work, even though not forbidden as they are on festival days, are nevertheless often avoided).

32. *J. I.* (1849), p. 167. See also Lehren's account: "In Jerusalem, they are practically afraid to go out to the market, for the Christians and Muslims together beat and disparage them." *Iggerot ha-Peqidim* (Letters of the Clerks), vol. 8, p. 215a.

33. *J. I.* (1840), p. 165.

34. Ibid., pp. 166–167.

35. Ibid., p. 294.

36. Ibid., p. 167.

37. *Iggerot ha-Peqidim* (Letters of the Clerks), vol. 8, p. 210b.

38. *J. I.* (1840), p. 167.

39. Ibid.

40. Ibid., p. 295.

41. W. T. Gidney, *The History of the L.S.P.C.* (London, 1905), p. 179.

42. Ibid.

43. *J. I.* (1840), p. 37.

44. *J. I.* (1841), p. 36.

45. Ibid.

46. *J. I.* (1840), p. 136.

47. N. M. Gelber, "The Question of the Land of Israel, 1840–1842," *Zion* 4 (1930), pp. 56–64 (Hebrew).

48. Gidney, *History of the L.S.P.C.*, p. 209.

49. *J. I.* (1842), pp. 36–37.

50. Ibid., p. 442.

51. Ibid.

52. Ibid.

53. *J. I.* (1843), p. 207.

54. Ibid.

55. *J. I.* (1841), p. 442.

56. Ibid., p. 423.

57. Ibid., p. 384.

58. Ibid.

59. *J. I.* (1842), pp. 60–63. Reports of missionaries in Poland tell that in 1842, the number of Jews converting to Christianity increased substantially, even in centers of Hasidism, in contrast to the limited effects of missionary efforts in Poland over the preceding twenty years. There were three missionary outposts in Poland—in Warsaw, Lublin, and Kalish—as well as a special institute for the training of converts. Ibid., pp. 118–121, 151–157. One report in the missionary press states that "the present is the most important crisis in the history of Israel." Ibid., p. 223.

60. Ibid., pp. 166–167, 405–406. At *J. I.* (1843), p. 59, the missionaries mention thirty-six candidates for conversion in Jerusalem.

61. *J. I.* (1841), pp. 227–228, 233–234.

62. The three are mentioned in the missionaries' journals and in other sources as well; see, e.g., A. M. Hyamson, *The British Consulate in Jerusalem, 1838–1914* (London, 1939), pp. 56–63. They are likewise referred to in an appointment letter sent by Moses Montefiore with Dr. Simeon Frenkel: "And when I heard that the saboteurs of the Lord of Hosts' vineyard had attacked you and that three men had fallen into the net they had cast for them . . ." [this was written before the actual conversions], *Cathe-*

dra 27 (1983), p. 123 (Hebrew). My thanks to the Jerusalem genealogist, the pious rabbi Samuel Goor, who helped me identify exactly who was involved in the episode. The conversion took place on 21 May 1843, when Luria, Goldberg, and three rank-and-file Jews were baptized. *J. I.* (1843), p. 280.

63. Eliezer Luria, who later became a missionary himself and served in Egypt, tells of the episode in a letter dated 5 December 1846. The details of his story parallel the missionaries' reports, and they should be seen as a single source. But his account is important primarily because he tells that his final decision to become a Christian took shape at the end of 1840, that is, the start of 5601. He does not explain why he converted, however. *J. I.* (1847), p. 92.

64. *Pi Mosheh*, part 2, p. 38a.

65. *Oholei Yehudah*, R. Judah ben R. Solomon ha-Kohen, (Jerusalem, 1843), author's introduction.

66. *Sha'areiẒedeq le-Zera Yiẓḥaq* (Aviezer), p. 56a.

67. Ibid., p. 56b.

68. *Pinqas BiqqurḤolim Perushim* 5597, Israel National Library, Manuscript Institute, 4°764, pp. 2–3. My thanks to Israel Freiden for directing my attention to this manuscript.

CHAPTER 9

1. *J. I.*, 1841, pp. 238–239. Bans were imposed in Jerusalem against anyone making use of the missionary hospital, which opened on 12 December 1844. The struggle between the Jewish *yishuv* in the Land of Israel and the English mission during the 1840s warrants a separate study; see A. Morgenstern, "The First Jewish Hospital in Jerusalem," *Cathedra* 33 (1984), pp. 107–124 (Hebrew).

2. *J. I.*, 1841, pp. 238–239.

3. Ibid., pp. 404–405.

4. Ibid., pp. 243–244. On 24 April 1841, two admonitions against contact with the missionaries were cited in the journal *J. I.* (1841), pp. 243–244. The first was issued on the Sabbath of Penitence (i.e., the Sabbath between Rosh ha-Shanah and Yom Kippur) in 1840 and the second a few Sabbaths later. Both are written in a pastiche of Hebrew and Yiddish; in the translation that follows, the Hebrew and the Yiddish passages are not distinguished.

> (A) Jewish Believers! Inasmuch as it has been heard that some fools among the Jews are going to the missionary sect and engaging with them in matters of religion, and it is known to all that the tendency of that sect is to promote heresy, God forbid, and mislead our Jewish brethren into converting, God forbid. It is their way to enter into discussions of various matters with Jewish children, but their principal intention is to ensnare Jews in the trap of heresy and conversion, God forbid; and therefore, the court, may their rock and redeemer protect them, has declared: attend and listen O Israel, God forbid, God forbid that any God-fearing person speak with that sect regarding any matters of religion at all, for their only purpose is to trap Jewish souls in their nets, God forbid. Therefore, one is obligated to distance oneself from them, as King Solomon, peace be upon him, has already warned us [in saying]: "Do not approach the entry to her house" [Prov. 5:8], and our Sages of blessed memory said this refers to heresy. Accordingly, an obligation is cast on

every one of our Jewish brethren to warn one another to distance oneself from that sect and one who attends to that will be agreeable, and good blessings will come upon him.

(B) Gather and listen, O children of Israel! Inasmuch as it was proclaimed on the recent Sabbath of Penitence that one should distance himself from the missionary sect, whose entire purpose is to overturn the words of the living God with their vanities and lies, and now in the House of Israel it appears that the tragedy of the desecration of God's name has become greater, on account of our many sins; woe to us on account of that shame, all who hear of it will weep and take pains that one admonish those people who go out to insult the hosts of Israel with their lies and vanities and ill spirits. And aimless and frivolous people come to them to eat and drink and engage with them in religious issues, people who do not know their left from their right, as well as people presumed to be of good standing. . . . Accordingly, we ask the community to take well to heart the need to avoid having the desecration of God's name grow greater, and to that end, one should distance oneself from those people, who speak meaningless vanities, and those who do not do so should be publicly shamed and cast out from us. And by that merit, plundering and destruction will no longer be heard in our streets and the voice of the herald will soon be heard in our land, and all the peoples of the world will see that the name of God is upon us, amen.

5. *Ḥizzuq Emunah,* Isaac ben Abraham of Troki (Altdorf, 1681; reprinted Jerusalem, 1845).

6. *Kur Miẓraf ha-Emunot u-Mar'eh ha-Emet,* R. Isaac Lopes (Metz, 1847).

7. Ibid., publisher's introduction.

8. *Mishmeret ha-Berit,* R. Aviezer ben Isaac of Ticktin (Jerusalem, 1846).

9. Ibid., p. 2b.

10. Ibid., p. 2a.

11. Ibid.

12. Ibid., p. 5a.

13. Ibid.

14. Ibid., p. 22b.

15. Ibid., p. 2b.

16. Ibid., p. 37b.

17. Ibid., p. 38a.

18. *Sha'arei Ẓedeq le-Zera Yiẓḥaq.*

19. Ibid., p. 47a.

20. Ibid., p. 46a.

21. Ibid., p. 47b.

22. Ibid., p. 60b. Aviezer of Ticktin bases his understanding of 5600–5606 on the verse "All the souls belonging to Jacob coming to Egypt . . . [numbered] sixty-six" (Gen. 46:26) and on the ties between Jacob and Joseph; he determines that the essence of Jacob's life is epitomized in Joseph's personality and that Jacob is only a determinative stage in the emergence of the nation of Israel: "For at the time of six hundred years, which is the conclusion of the six of Jacob, his awakening will not take place, but only on high [will there be awakening], for at that time, the gates of wisdom will begin to open only in the heavens above, and what he wrote about the time of six hundred years refers only to what is written that the gates of wisdom on high

will be opened but it does not refer to the time at which the wisdom will descend below, for that depends on the awakening of the small [letter] *vav* of *yesod*, which is a different time" (p. 60a). In kabbalistic terminology: Jacob's personality represents the quality of *tif'eret* while Joseph's represents that of *yesod*. The concept of *malkhut*—the redemption—cannot be articulated until after the completion of the *yesod* process, whose time is at the conclusion of six years following completion of the six hundred of *tif'eret*. As he puts it: "The bounty of light cannot come to *malkhut*, which is in the mystery of the earth, until after the conclusion of the small [letter] *vav* [representing "six"] in the year [5]606, which will complete the awakening of the two *vavs* of Jacob and Joseph but without the awakening of the small *vav* of Joseph, the earth, which is within the mystery of the holy *shekhinah*'s *malkhut*, cannot be saved" (59a). For the purpose of his theory, Aviezer takes account of the cycle of the lunar years, about which he says: "In that very year [5605], lunar cycle 295 will be concluded, and in 5606 lunar cycle 296 will begin. . . . For cycle 295 [*r-ẓ-h*] was a time of trouble [*ẓarah*; *ẓ-r-h*] for Jacob, but . . . after cycle 295 . . . cycle 296 will begin, which is the numerical value of the word "the land" [*ha-areẓ*; in the verse (Lev. 26:42) "I will remember the Land"] . . . and then will come to pass "for your servants take pleasure [*raẓu*; *r-ẓ-w*, with a numerical value of 296] in her stones" [Ps. 102:16] . . . for the Land is within the mystery of the *shekhinah* . . . that is, all the great sorrows that will afflict Israel at the end of the exile . . . will only be during lunar cycle 295, from which they will be saved . . . and His hand is outstretched to magnify the troubles mightily during the last five years of cycle 295, which began in 5600" (p. 54a–b).

To bolster the veracity of the notion that 5606 was to be the year of redemption, Aviezer cites numerous numerologies and acronyms. For example, Isa. 61:10 contains the clause "I will greatly rejoice [*sos asis*; *sos* is spelled *s-w-s*, with a numerical value of 606]; Aviezer states "this comes to allude to the time of rejoicing, which begins in the year *sos*" (p. 55a). On the verse [Num. 23:21] "And the shouting [or trumpeting] for the king [*teru'at melekh*] is among them," he writes: "This comes to allude to the time at which the shofar of King Messiah will be heard and the *shekhinah* will inspire, for that is *teru'at melekh*, inasmuch as *teru'at* [spelled *t-r-w-'-t*] is an anagram of "the time of 606" [*'-t t-r-w*]" (p. 61a). On the verse "Moses took the bones of Joseph [*'aẓmot yosef*] with him" [Exod. 13:19], he writes: "This comes to allude to the time of his coming, which is 606, the numerical value of *'aẓmot* [spelled *'-ẓ-m-w-t*] of Joseph, for then will be seen the might [*'oẓem*, in a play on words] of His hand and the power of Joseph, whose flame will be ignited and burn the straw of Esau. (p. 59b).

23. Ibid., p. 47b. See *Pi Mosheh* for parallel remarks by Moses Turgeman. See also chapter 2 in this volume.

24. *Sha'arei Ẓedeq le-Zera Yiẓḥaq* (Aviezer), p. 67b.

25. Ibid.

26. Ibid.

27. *J. I.*, 1842, pp. 405–406.

28. Ibid., pp. 166–167.

29. *Sha'arei Ẓedeq le-Zera Yiẓḥaq*, p. 39b.

30. Ibid., p. 19a.

31. *Yismaḥ Mosheh*, part 1, R. Moses Teitelbaum (Lvov, 1848; reprinted [with different arrangement and pagination] New York, 1947), end of the book (in the 1947 edition). Rabbi Teitelbaum's approach is based on his underlying notion that Israel's final redemption will be entirely miraculous, with no human involvement at all: "For the coming redemption will be by the Holy One Blessed Be He, Himself and in His glory, may He be blessed. And it appears to me that this is in accordance with the

words of the *midrash*: In the past, you were saved by people. In Egypt, by Moses, Aaron, and Miriam. In Babylonia, by Ḥananiah and his associates. But just as they do not endure forever, neither is their redemption eternal. But in the future, you will be redeemed solely by Me and My glory, and just as I endure for ever and all eternity, so, too, [My] redemption. And that is as it is said [Isa. 45:17], 'Israel is saved by the Lord with an everlasting salvation.'

And that itself is the reason why it will not be by a human being but by the Holy One Blessed Be He, so it will be an everlasting and eternal redemption.

The coming future redemption will be marked with God's Name to confirm that it is the conclusion and end to all our troubles. . . . For the first three redemptions began from below, with human activity to assist God on high, but one will be reversed, that is, the future, fourth, redemption will be from on high, by the Holy One Blessed Be He, Himself . . . and just as He lives and endures forever, so our redemption will be eternal and endure forever, speedily and in our days, amen." *Yismaḥ Mosheh* (1848 edition), preface, p. 2b.

32. *Darkhei Yosef*, part 2, by R. Joseph Eliezer Leib ha-Levi Edel, preacher in the holy congregation of Slonim (Johannesburg, 1861), p. 144.

33. *Sha'arei Ẓedeq le-Zera Yiẓḥaq*, p. 14a.

34. Ibid., 15a.

35. Ibid., p. 40a. The expression "who build a tower with its top in the heavens" may imply that even then there were ideas and perhaps even actual plans for building the synagogue with a disproportionately high dome, as was later done in the "House of Jacob" synagogue in the *Ḥurvah*.

36. Ibid.

37. Ibid.

38. Ibid., p. 20a–b. It appears that after so open a criticism of the leadership of the Jerusalem *Perushim*, Aviezer of Ticktin could not continue to live in the city. In the summer of 1850, he left the Land of Israel, and a year later in Lemberg he published his book *Meqor ha-Berakhah*. In 1852, he died in Lvov. The approbations for *Meqor ha-Berakhah* offer, in my judgment, a glimpse of the hostility that prevailed between him and the leadership of the *Perushim*, for not one of the *Perushim* sages approved the book. Those who did write approbations were the Sefardic chief rabbi, Isaac Kubo; Ḥayyim Nissim Abolafia; Mordecai Benjamin Navon; and, in their wake, Ḥayyim Falaji of Izmir. Of the Jerusalem Ashkenazim, only two less important sages wrote approbations, and they said they had done so only after numerous requests by the author and the prior approval of the Sefardic sages.

39. *Iggerot ha-Peqidim* (Letters of the Clerks), vol. 8, p. 206b.

40. Ibid., pp. 211a, 212b.

41. Ibid., p. 212a.

42. Ibid., p. 216a.

43. Ibid., p. 224a.

44. Ibid.

45. Ibid. In his study "Messianism and Nationalism in the Teaching of R. Alcalay" (Hebrew), Jacob Katz demonstrates that the Damascus libel transformed Alcalay's concept of "the beginning of redemption" associated with the messianic aspect of the year 5600. Until then, Alcalay, like many others, believed that the determination of whether or not the Messiah would come that year depended on the usual measures of Torah study, prayer, and acts of charity. But with the success of Montefiore's and Cremieux's efforts to undo the blood libel, he concluded that it was political activity in a

real-life plane that would bring about the return of Israel to its Land. That, according to Katz, is true inner meaning to be drawn from the Damascus libel and its connection to 5600.

46. *Iggerot ha-Peqidim* (Letters of the Clerks), vol. 5, p. 60a.

47. Ibid., p. 233b.

48. Ibid.

49. In a letter to Israel of Shklov dated 27 August 1833, Ẓevi Hirsch Lehren discusses messianic matters in light of the mission of Barukh ben Samuel to the Ten Tribes and appears to be reacting to a letter in which Israel of Shklov had expressed reservations regarding 5600 as the year of redemption. Lehren writes: "May it be [God's] will that the complete redemption be sooner, as we hope to be redeemed each day, and by the grace of Heaven let it not be delayed beyond the year 5600. And I am troubled by the talk that it may continue to [. . .], but what can we do. And we, as well as the *kolel* of *Perushim*, may God save and protect them, can undertake to pay debts until the aforesaid year [5604], even if our righteous Messiah comes earlier." *Iggerot ha-Peqidim* (Letters of the Clerks), vol. 5, p. 140a.

50. Ibid., vol. 10, p. 38a.

51. Ibid., p. 22b.

52. M. Eliav, *Jewish Settlement in the Land of Israel Through the Perspective of German Politics, 1842–1914* (Tel-Aviv, 1973), p. 4 (Hebrew).

53. *Iggerot ha-Peqidim* (Letters of the Clerks), vol. 11, p. 181.

54. Ibid., p. 300.

55. P. Grajewski, *Zikkaron le-Ḥovevim ha-Rishonim*, booklet 8 (Jerusalem, 1938).

56. See A. Morgenstern, "Examining the Renewal of the Sacrificial Cult and the Rebuilding of the Temple in the Run-up to the Year 5600," *Cathedra* 82 (1997), pp. 200–202 (Hebrew).

57. See Ḥayyim Hillel Ben Sasson, *Continuity and Change* (Tel-Aviv, 1984), p. 270 (Hebrew).

58. M. Benayahu, "The Famine in Jerusalem in 5606 [1846]," *Quarterly for the Study of Jerusalem and Its History* 2, 1–2 (1949), pp. 72–88 (Hebrew). In his pamphlet *The Tobiansky Movement Among the Jews: A Messianic Episode* (Jerusalem, 1933) (Hebrew), A. Z. Eshkoli describes an odd incident linking the "messianic" movement of Andreas Tobiansky and his messenger, the Jewish apostate Gershon Romm of Vilna, with Anschel Rothschild and the Lehren family in Amsterdam. According to the sources found by Eshkoli, Gershon Romm visited Jerusalem as Tobiansky's emissary and, on 29 January 1845, addressed some sixty Jews in the "Midrash" [?] synagogue. In his account, Romm told the Jews: "God has given me the privilege of enabling me to tell those gathered here, in so holy a place, the joyful good news coming from God, which our people have anticipated for so many generations. Four years have elapsed since the appearance on European soil of the man of God [Tobiansky], and by God's command he has informed the other nations, and our Jewish brethren, that God has had mercy on us. . . . The man of God brings us, by authority of the Lord, the living word. His task is: to lift from our people the burden that has weighed on them for so long, to unite nations in brotherhood, to redeem Israel . . ." (Eshkoli, *Tobiansky Movement*, pp. 34–35). The absence of parallel sources mentioning the incident makes it impossible at this stage to verify Gershon Romm's version. But if he spoke truthfully, it can be explained only against the background of an acute messianic expectation that continued at least until 1846. My thanks to Elḥanan Reiner for calling this source to my attention.

59. Moses Maggid ben Hillel of Shklov died on 23 August 1846. Nathan Neta ben Menaḥem Mendel died on 12 October 1846. Nathan Neta ben Sa'adyah died on 31 December 1848. *Toledot Ḥakhmei Yerushalayim*, vol. 3, p. 224.

60. Ibid., p. 180. E. Bregman died outside the Land of Israel on 8 April 1852.

61. External conditions, such as the Crimean War, also had a role in these changes.

62. *Sha'arei Ẓedeq le-Zera Yiẓḥaq* (Aviezer), p. 7a.

63. Ibid., p. 40b.

64. Ibid., p. 24a.

65. Ibid., p. 24b.

66. Ibid., p. 31a.

67. P. Grajewski, *Mi-Ginzei Yerushalayim*, 13 (Jerusalem, 1931), p. 3.

68. Ibid., p. 4.

69. Baron, "Aspects of the History of the Jewish Settlement in Jerusalem," p. 304, n. 2: "And the awakening above depends on the awakening below, and how long shall our holy land remain ruined, desolate, and uninhabited."

70. Ibid., pp. 304–306.

71. M. Weinstein, "Programs for the Reform of the Jerusalem *Yishuv* During the First Half of the Nineteenth Century" (Hebrew), *Sefer Bar-Ilan* 6 (1968), pp. 339–356.

72. Ibid., p. 356.

73. Ibid., p. 354.

74. Ibid., p. 349.

75. Lunz, *Jerusalem*, vol. 9 (1911), p. 20.

76. "A voice calls out from Zion, to our brethren who seek the peace of Jerusalem . . . that they not dare to ascend the mountain; except for the elderly scholars of the generation . . . with no dependants . . . so as not to deny food to those who deserve it of right . . . and so as not to be, God forbid, as suicides and those causing harm to others." Similarly: "On your walls, O Jerusalem, I have posted watchmen [Isa. 62:6]; a voice from the sanctuary announcing an awesome admonition . . . to declare aloud . . . that they should not go up to the holy [place] from this day forward . . ." Anonymous, untitled notices printed at the press of Israel Baeck, Jerusalem, 1869 (Hebrew).

77. "Their loins quaking, young and old alike cry out for bread, but there is no one to take pity. Who heard of such a thing; they have begun to cheat and devour and steal one from another. . . . Who ever saw such . . . a father sought to sell his son to a gentile nation for a loaf of bread. "*Dim'at ha-Ashuqim*" in *Shomer Ẓiyyon ha-Ne'eman*, Altona, no. 175 (7 April 1854), p. 349b.

78. "Have you heard, our brothers and our people? Multiple evils have befallen us these days! A powerful famine of a sort not previously known, and, moreover, the glory has been taken away from our home. The staff of food that has come from our brothers in Russia and Poland has been broken, every source of support for bread or for water, for the decree of the tyrannical ruler overcame them, forbidding them from providing sustenance to our brothers who are attached to the Lord's estate." "*Qol Nehi mi-Ẓiyyon*" in *Shomer Ẓiyyon ha-Ne'eman*, Altona, no. 180 (23 June 1854), p. 359a.

79. M. Wallenstein, "Ms. Gaster 975: A Memo of the Sefardic *Kolel* in Jerusalem From the Year 5615 [1855]," *Zion* 43 (1978), pp. 75–96. So, too, I. Bartal, "Marginal Clarifications on the Memo of the Sefardic *Kolel* in Jerusalem From the Year 5615," ibid., 97–118 (both Hebrew).

80. "No one works, no one plows, there is no activity or labor. There is no commerce—not because of laziness or idleness; they do not shy away or withhold their hands from work . . . but the land is destroyed. It is abandoned, with no ruler or

judge. . . . Who will be employer and who employee? Who will sustain and who will be sustained? The entire nation is in sorry straits, a city in which all are severely impoverished . . . and they cannot support one another. . . . But despite all this, I will present before you today more than one hundred Ashkenazi men, residents of Jerusalem, even the weakest of whom will say I am a mighty worker and laborer . . . and who will enable us to toil and accomplish and eat our fill of bread through the sweat of our brows and the toil of our hands." "*Kol Nehi mi-Ẓiyyon,*" in *Shomer Ẓiyyon ha-Ne'eman,* Altona, no. 180 (23 June 1854), p. 359b.

81. N. M. Gelber, "Dr. Albert Kohen and His Visit to Jerusalem," *Riv'on le-Ḥeqer Yerushalayim ve-Toledotehah* [Quarterly for the Study of Jerusalem and Its History] 2, 1–2 (1959), pp. 175–195 (Hebrew).

82. A. R. Malakhi, "On the History of Montefiore's Weaving Factory in Jerusalem," in *Aspects of the History of the Old Yishuv* (Tel-Aviv, 1971), pp. 150–168 (Hebrew).

83. A. M. Lunz, "The House of Rothschild and Jerusalem" in *Pathways of Zion and Jerusalem,* selected and edited by G. Kressel (Jerusalem, 1970), pp. 297–310 (Hebrew).

84. Y. Yellin, *Memoirs of a Native of Jerusalem, 1830–1918* (Jerusalem, 1928), p. 113 (Hebrew). [The Hebrew wording here has an ironic twist not apparent in the English. Reversing the priorities in the original rabbinic adage, the remark states, when read literally, "the life of the hour [in this earthly world] is greater than the life of the eternal world."—***translator***]

85. It is possible that Meir Auerbuch's use of the phrase "and many with them" alludes to Maimonides' words in the *Iggeret Teiman* (*Epistle to Yemen*): ". . . pretenders and simulators will appear in great numbers at the time when the advent of the true Messiah will draw nigh, but they will not be able to make good their claim. They will perish with many of their partisans.

"Solomon, of blessed memory, inspired by the holy spirit, foresaw that the prolonged duration of the exile would incite some of our people to seek to terminate it before the appointed time, and as a consequence they would perish or meet with disaster. Therefore, he admonished and adjured them in metaphysical language to desist, as we read, 'I adjure you, O daughters of Jerusalem, . . . ' Now, brethren and friends, abide by the oath, and stir not up love until it please." Moses Maimonides, "Epistle to Yemen" [*Iggeret Teiman*], translated by Boaz Cohen, reprinted in Isadore Twersky, ed., *A Maimonides Reader* (West Orange, N.J., 1972), p. 461.

86. *Ha-Levanon,* 1, no. 8 (3 September 1863).

87. *Ha-Levanon* 8, no. 43 (3 July 1872), pp. 338, 346.

88. Sapir, *Yemenite Journey,* p. 157. The Kabbalah of the Vilna Ga'on and his disciples has not yet been the subject of an authoritative, scientific study. When such a study is done, it will have to examine not only the kabbalistic concept itself but also the effects of the debacle of 1840 on that concept and on its standing in the eyes of succeeding generations. Another area to be considered by any such study is the effect of the calamity on attitudes toward Kabbalah and its study and on the Hasidic movement and its attitude toward the Land of Israel. In light of the messianic expectations and the ensuing crisis, it is worthwhile to reexamine the reasons for Menaḥem Mendel of Kotzk's lengthy seclusion, which lasted from 1840 until his death in 1859.

89. *Mikhtevei R. Shelomoh Hershel Berliner mi-London,* film no. 29459.

90. The redemption's failure to come as predicted is grappled with by the author of *Ner Mosheh,* a book apparently written in Jerusalem in the early 1850s: "From the time I came into the sacred place, my thoughts have never known quiet or tranquility. . . . Whose misdeed spoiled the redemption, and all ask one another what can

we do, then, to advance the time of redemption? . . . Why are the appointed times delayed . . . and the prophesied promises are not seen and do not come?" The author responds: "Because by that means [i.e., the study of the *Zohar*], salvation will come sooner." R. Moses Slatki, *Ner Mosheh* (Jerusalem, 1885), author's introduction.

91. See the remarks of Meir Auerbuch in n. 86 above. Only at the beginning of the twentieth century did the descendants of the Vilna Ga'on's disciples begin to write the history of the early-nineteenth-century immigration. See T. H. Rivn, *Ḥazon Ẓiyyon* (The Vision of Zion) (Tel-Aviv, 1947), p. 9.

Bibliography

MANUSCRIPTS

Ateret Baḥurim ve-Hilkhot Olam. Rosenthaliana Library, Amsterdam, HS-Ros-54.

Derashot min-ha-Me'ah ha-19. By a student of R. Ḥayyim of Volozhin. Rosenthaliana Library, Amsterdam, HS-Ros-445.

Derashot R. Abraham Prinz. Rosenthaliana Library, Amsterdam; Israel National Library, Manuscript Photocopy Institute, 3818.

Even Shemu'el. Rabbi Aryeh Leib Frumkin. Israel National Library, Manuscript Institute, 4°32.

Ḥibbur al Shenat 5600 (Essay on the Year 5600). R. Moses Turgeman. Jewish Theological Seminary of America, New York, 1982; Israel National Library, Manuscript Photocopy Institute, 11080.

Ḥishuvei Qeẓ. R. Mattityahu ha-Kohen Mizraḥi (Matthias ben Samuel ha-Kohen). Israel National Library, Manuscript Institute, 4°1065.

Iggerot ha-Peqidim ve-ha-Armarkalim mei-Amsterdam (1826–1870) ("Letters of the *Pekidim* and *Amarkalim* [Clerks and Administrators] in Amsterdam"; referred to as the "Letters of the Clerks"), 15 vols. Yad Ben-Zvi Library, Jerusalem.

Iggerot mi-Yerushalayim. Central Archive for the History of the Jewish People, Jerusalem Unit, section J.

Iggerot Shederim (Rabbinic Emissaries). Israel National Library, Manuscript Institute, 4°199.

Iggerot Yehudim mei-Ereẓ Yisra'el le-Mosheh Montefiori. London, Montefiore Archive, ms. 574; Israel National Library, Manuscript Photocopy Institute, 6190.

Letter from the Kolel of Perushim to Moses Montefiore, summer, 1849 (Hebrew). London, Montefiore Archive, ms. 577(2); Israel National Library, Manuscript Photocopy Institute, 6193.

Mifqad Montefiori be-5599. London, Montefiore Archive, ms. 528; Israel National Library, Manuscript Photocopy Institute, 35115.

Mikhtavim mei-Izvono shel R. Shelomoh Paḥ. Israel National Library, Manuscript Institute, 4°1468.

Mikhtevei R. Shelomoh Hershel Berliner mi-London. Jewish Theological Seminary of America, New York, 3619; Israel National Library, Manuscript Photocopy Institute, 29424.

Peirushei Nakh le-ha-Ga'on mi-Vilna. Rabbi Elijah ben Solomon of Vilna. National Library, Department of Hebrew Manuscripts, No. 8°3426.

Pi Mosheh (The Mouth of Moses). R. Moses Turgeman. Israel National Library, Manuscript Institute, Manuscript Institute, 8°4424.

Pinqas Biqqur Ḥolim (Sick Visitation Register) *Perushim* 5597. Israel National Library, Manuscript Institute, 4°764.

Pinqas Qehillat Brod (*Brody Journal*). 5568–5572 (1808–1812). Ms. 76004, Jewish Theological Seminary, New York; Israel National Library, Manuscript Photocopy Institute, 29842.

Pinqas Zikkaron shel Mishpaḥat Lehren. Rosenthaliana Library, Amsterdam; Israel National Library, Manuscript Photocopy Institute, 3473.

Qol Mevasser (A Voice Brings Tidings). R. Mattityahu ha-Kohen Mizraḥi (Matthias ben Samuel ha-Kohen). San Francisco, Sutro Library, 136; Jerusalem, Yad Ben-Zvi Library, 2672 (microfilm).

Qol Qore le-Ezrat Bonei ha-Ḥurvah. ms. Sasson. Jerusalem, Yad Ben-Zvi Library, file no. 285.

Sefer ha-Zikhronot. Mordecai Samuel Girondi. Ms. Montefiore no. 58, Jews' College Library, London.

Shemu'ah al Ma'aseh bi-Yerushalayim 1835. London, ms. Sassoon 672; Israel National Library, Manuscript Photocopy Institute, 8959.

PRINTED PRIMARY MATERIALS

Aderet Eliyahu. Commentary of R. Elijah ben Solomon of Vilna on the Bible. Halberstadt, 1859.

Afiqei Yehudah. R. Judah ha-Levi Edel. Zolokow, 1803.

Ahavat David. R. Elazar ben David [Plekelsh]. Prague, 1800.

Alfei Menasheh. R. Menasheh ben R. Joseph of Ilya. Vilna, 1822.

Alim li-Terufah. R. Elijah ben Solomon of Vilna. Minsk, 1836.

Aliyyot Eliyahu. R. Joshua Heschel Levin. Vilna, 1856.

Amud ha-Yemini. R. Abraham ben Asher Anschel. Minsk, 1811.

Ateret Yosef. Jerusalem, 1899.

Be-Har Yeira'eh. R. Eliezer Bregman. Jerusalem, 1977.

Be-Lev Qashuv. R. Eliezer Bregman. Ed. A. Bartura. Jerusalem, 1983.

Ben Porat. Mordecai ben Solomon of Polnigon. Vilna, 1858.

Binah le-Ittim. R. Elyaqim ben Abraham. London, 1795.

Darkhei Yosef. R. Joseph Eliezer Leib ha-Levi Edel. Part 2. Johannesburg, 1861.

Derash Avraham. R. Nissim Abraham Ashkenazi. Salonika, 1852.

Derekh ha-Melekh. R. Pinḥas ben R. Judah of Poltsk. Grodno, 1804.

Derishat Ẓiyyon. Frankfurt-am-Oder, 1806.

Emunah ve-Hashgaḥah. R. Samuel ben Abraham of Slutsk [Moltzen]. Slutsk, 1864.

"Epistle to Yemen" [*Iggeret Teiman*]. R. Moses Maimonides. Translated by Boaz Cohen;

translation reprinted in Isadore Twerksy, ed., *A Maimonides Reader*, pp. 437–462. West Orange, N.J., 1972.
Evel Mosheh. Eliezer Lippman of Solish. Offen, 1840.
Even Shelomoh. R. Samuel ben Abraham Moltzen. Vilna, 1873.
Fez ve-Ḥakhamehah (Fez and Its Sages). Vol. 2. Ed. R. Ovadiah David. Jerusalem, 1979.
Ḥamishah Qunteresim. R. Nathan Naḥman Koronel. Vienna, 1864.
Ḥibbat Yerushalayim. R. Ḥayyim Horwitz. Jerusalem, 1844.
Hilkhot Yemot ha-Mashiaḥ (Laws of the Messianic Age). Eliezer Sinai Kirschbaum. Berlin (?), 1822.
Hillel ben Shaḥar. R. Hillel of Kovno. Warsaw, 1804.
Ḥizzuq Emunah (Strengthening Belief). Isaac ben Abraham of Troki. Altdorf, 1681; reprinted Jerusalem, 1845.
Iggerot Ereẓ Yisra'el (Letters of the Land of Israel). Ed. Abraham Yaari. Tel-Aviv, 1943.
Iggerot ha-Peqidim ve-ha-Armarkalim mei-Amsterdam (Letters of the *Pekidim* and *Amarkalim* of Amsterdam; cited as Rivlin and Rivlin, *Letters of the Clerks*). Vols. 1–3. Ed. J. J. and B. Rivlin. Jerusalem, 1965–1979.
Iggerot Soferim. S. Sofer. Vienna-Budapest, 1929.
Iqrei Emunah. Part 1. Mordecai Dov Friedenthal. Breslau, 1916.
Kitvei ha-Ga'on Rabbi Menaḥem Mendel (Writing of the Ga'on, R. Menaḥem Mendel). Jerusalem, 2001.
Kitvei ha-Rav Yehudah Alqal'ai (The Writings of Rabbi Judah Alcalay). Vol. 1. Ed. Yiẓḥaq Refael. Jerusalem, 1975.
Kur Miẓraf ha-Emunot u-Mar'eh ha-Emet (The Crucible That Refines Beliefs and Shows the Truth). R. Isaac Lopes. Metz, 1847.
Ma'ayanei ha-Yeshu'ah. R. Moses Katzenellenbogen. Frankfurt, 1859.
Magen ve-Ẓinah. R. Isaac Ḥaver. Amsterdam [n.d.].
Margaliyot ha-Torah. R. Ẓevi Hirsch of Samyatitsch. Parisk, 1788.
Mas'ei Noẓrim le-Erez Yisra'el (Christian Journeys to the Land of Israel). Ed. M. Ish-Shalom. Tel-Aviv, 1966.
Mas'ot Ereẓ Yisra'el. Ed. Abraham Yaari. Tel-Aviv, 1946.
Meḥqarim u-Meqorot. Ed. Yitẓḥaq Ben-Ẓevi. Jerusalem, 1969.
Me'ora'ot Ẓevi. Anonymous. Warsaw, 1838.
Mevasseret Ẓiyyon. R. Abraham Menaḥem Mendel Mohr. Lemberg, 1847.
Mevasseret Ẓiyyon. R. Elyaqum Karmuli. [Brussels], 1841.
Midrash Tanḥuma (Eshkol edition). Jerusalem, 1975.
Migdal Oz. Ed. J. Mondshain. Jerusalem, 1980.
Miqdash Melekh. R. Shalom Buzaglo. Amsterdam, 1750.
Miqveh Yisra'el. Menasheh ben Israel. Shklov, 1797.
Mishmeret ha-Berit (Preservation of the Covenant). R. Aviezer ben Isaac of Ticktin. Jerusalem, 5606 [1846].
Misped ha-Mishneh. R. Wolf Hamburg. Fürth, 1823.
Naḥalat Avot. R. Me'ir ben Elijah. Vilna, 1836.
Ner ha-Ma'arav. Ed. Y. M. Toledano. Jerusalem, 1911.
Ner Mosheh. R. Moses Slotki. Jerusalem, 1885.
Oholei Yehudah. R. Judah ben R. Solomon ha-Kohen. Jerusalem 1843.
Oẓar Binah. R. Aaron Ẓevi Ashkenazi. Izmir 1841.
Oẓar Genazim. Ed. Y. M. Toledano. Jerusalem, 1960.
Pe'at ha-Shulḥan. R. Israel of Shklov. Safed, 1836.

Pirqei de-Rabbi Eli'ezer (Eshkol edition). Jerusalem, 1973.

Qehalot Ya'aqov. R. Jacob Ẓevi Yellish (of Dynow). Lemberg, 1870.

Qol Bokhim. R. Israel ben Leivush of Krotchin. [Breslau], 1838.

Qol Bokhim (Eulogy for Meshullam Zalman Cohen). R. Wolf Hamburg. Fürth, 1820.

Qol David. R. David Joseph Ayash. Leghorn, 1821.

Qorot ha-Ittim le-Yeshurun be-Ereẓ Yisra'el. R. Menaḥem Mendel of Kamenetz. Vilna, 1840.

Seder Eliyahu (Commentary of the Vilna Ga'on on the Passover Haggadah). Prague, 1813.

Sefer Dor Yesharim. New York, 1903.

Sefer Ḥalomot Qeẓ ha-Pela'ot. Kapost, 1814.

Sefer ha-Taqqanot ve-ha-Haskamot u-Minhagim ha-Nehugim be-Ir ha-Qodesh Yerushalayim. Ed. A. Ḥ. Gagin. Jerusalem, 1842.

Sefer Ḥatam Sofer, Resp. Even ha-Ezer. R. Moses Sofer. Part 1. Pressburg, 1858.

Sefer Ḥatam Sofer, Resp. Yoreh De'ah. R. Moses Sofer. Pressburg, 1860.

Sefer ha-Taqqanot ve-ha-Te'udot le-Bet Midrash Eliyahu. Ed. Eliyahu Landau. Jerusalem, 1897.

Sefer ha-Zikkaron. R. Moses Sofer of Pressburg. Jerusalem, 1957.

Sefer Shir ha-Shirim, Peirush ha-Ga'on he-Ḥasid Eliyahu mi-Vilna. R. Elijah of Vilna. Warsaw, 1842.

Sefer Torat Mosheh. R. Moses Sofer of Pressburg. Vienna, 1913.

Sha'ar ha-Kavvanot. R. Ḥayyim Vital. Tel-Aviv, 1962.

Sha'arei Arukhah. R. Jacob Abuḥaẓeira. Jerusalem, 1884.

Sha'arei Yerushalayim. R. Moses Reiser. Warsaw, 1868.

Sha'arei Ẓedeq (Gates of Righteousness). R. Abraham Danzig. Vilna, 1812.

Sha'arei Ẓedeq le-Zera Yiẓḥaq (Gates of Righteousness). R. Aviezer ben Isaac of Ticktin. Jerusalem 1843.

Sheluḥei Ereẓ Yisra'el. Ed. Abraham Yaari. Jerusalem, 1951.

Shem Ḥadash. R. Ḥayyim Solomon Daniel Finzo. Jerusalem, 1843.

Shivat Ẓiyyon. A. J. Slutsky. Warsaw, 1892.

Shorshei Emunah. R. Shalom ha-Kohen. London, 1815.

Siddur ha-Gra. Part 2. Ed. Naftali Hertz Ha-Levi. Jerusalem, 1891.

Sifra de-Ẓeni'uta. Commentary of R. Elijah ben Solomon Zalman [the Vilna Ga'on]. Vilna, 1820.

Siḥah bein Shenat 5560 u-Shenat 5561, Prague, 1801.

Simlat Binyamin. Part 2. R. Wolf Hamburg. Fürth, 1841.

Sippur Ḥalomot ve-Qeẓ ha-Pela'ot. Anonymous. Lemberg, 1804.

Statutes and Documents of the "Eliyahu" Study Hall in memory of the Ga'on Rabbi Elijah, may the memory of the righteous and holy be for a blessing, established in the year "Aderet Eliyahu" ["Elijah's cloak"; the letters of the Hebrew term have the numerical value 657, indicating the year 5657 (1897)] *in Jerusalem, the one-hundredth year since Elijah's ascent heavenward* (Hebrew).

Taqlin Ḥadtin. Rabbi Israel ben Samuel. Minsk, 1812.

Tevu'ot ha-Areẓ. R. Jehosef. Ed. A. M. Lunz. Jerusalem, 1900.

Tiferet Maharal. R. Judah Yudel Rosenberg. Pyetrikov, 1912.

Toledot Ḥakhmei Yerushalayim (*History of the Sages of Jerusalem*). Vols. 1–4. R. A. L. Fumkin and A. Rivlin. Jerusalem, 1928–1930.

Tuv Yerushalayim. R. Isaac Farḥi. Jerusalem, 1843.

Yad Eliyahu. R. Elijah Rogoler. Warsaw, 1900.

Yemot ha-Mashiaḥ. R. Ḥayyim El'azar Shapira. Jerusalem, 1970.

Yismaḥ Mosheh, part 1. R. Moses Teitelbaum. Lvov, 1848; reprinted (with different arrangement and pagination) New York, 1947.
Yis'u Harim Shalom. Sila and Eliezer Bregman. Ed. A. Bartura. Jerusalem [1968].
Yoman Masa ve-Iggerot. Yad Izhak Ben-Zvi. Jerusalem, 1974.
Zekher Ẓaddiq. R. Eliezer Katzenellenbogen. Vilna, 1879.
Ẓeror ha-Ḥayyim. R. Abraham Lowenstam. Amsterdam, 1820.
Zeved Tov. R. Ze'ev Wolf Altschul. Introduction by the author's son, Elyaqim Getzel Altschul. Warsaw, 1814.
Zikhronot Ereẓ Yisra'el. Ed. Abraham Yaari. Tel-Aviv, 1947.

NEWSPAPERS AND PERIODICAL PUBLICATIONS

Annual Report of the Committee of the London Society for Promoting Christianity Amongst the Jews. London, 1809–
Der Orient. Leipzig, 1840–1851.
Ha-Levanon. Jerusalem, Paris, Mainz, 1863–1886.
Jewish Expositor. London, 1816–1830.
Jewish Intelligence. London, 1830–1835.
Jewish Repository. London, 1813–1815.
Me'asef Ẓiyyon. Jerusalem, 1926–1934.
Monthly Intelligence. London, 1835–1866.
Shomer Ẓiyyon ha-Ne'eman. Altona, 1845–1854.
Tevinah. Kovno, Frankfurt am Main, Lodz, Jerusalem, 1922–1941.

STUDIES AND OTHER SECONDARY MATERIALS

In Hebrew

Abir, M. "The Claims of Safed Jewry After the Lootings of 1834." *Sefunot* 7 (1964), pp. 269–274.
Abir, M. "The Rebellion Against Egyptian Rule in the Land of Israel in 1834 and Its Context." Master's thesis, Hebrew University, 1961.
Alfasi, Y. "Documents About the History of the Old Settlement." *Bar-Ilan Yearbook* 3 (1965), pp. 216–224.
Alfasi, Y. *Gur, the Founder; the Author of* Ḥiddushei ha-Rim. Tel-Aviv, 1954.
Assaf, D. "From Volhynia to Safed: The Image of Abraham Dov of Averitch as a Hasidic Leader in the First Half of the Nineteenth Century." *Shalem* 6 (1992), pp. 223–279.
Barnai, Y. "Changes in Nineteenth-Century Jerusalem." *Sinai* 81 (1977), pp. 151–155.
Barnai, Y. "The History of a Jerusalem Family." *Cathedra* 55 (1990), pp. 59–62.
Barnai, Y. "The 'Mughrabi' Community in Jerusalem in the Nineteenth Century." In *Chapters in the History of the Jewish Community in Jerusalem: Jerusalem in the Early Ottoman Period, Jerusalem in the Modern Period.* Ed. Aharon Kedar and Ben-Zion Yehoshua, Vol. 1, pp. 132–135. Jerusalem, 1973.
Barnai, Y. "Trends in the Study of the Jewish Settlement in the Land of Israel in Medieval and Early Modern Times." *Cathedra* 42 (1987), pp. 87–120.
Baron, S. "History of German Jews in the Land of Israel." In *Minḥah le-David* (David Yellin Memorial Volume), 116–128. Jerusalem, 1935.
Baron, S. "Aspects of the History of the Jewish Settlement in Jerusalem." in *Sefer Klausner,* ed. N. H. Torczyner, A.A. Kabak, A. Tcherikover, and B. Shochetman (Jerusalem, 1937), pp. 302–312.

Bartal, I. "Marginal Clarifications on the Memo of the Sefardic Kolel in Jerusalem from the Year 5615." *Zion* 43 (1978), pp. 97–118.

Bartal, I. "Messianic Expectations in the Context of Historical Reality." *Cathedra* 31 (1984), pp. 159–171.

Bartal, I. "Messianism and Historiography." *Zion* 52 (1987), pp. 117–130.

Bartal, I. "'Old *Yishuv*' and 'New *Yishuv*': Image and Reality." *Cathedra* 2 (1977), pp. 3–19.

Bartal, I. "Settlement Proposals During Montefiore's Second Visit to the Land of Israel, 1839." *Shalem* 2 (1977), pp. 231–296.

Bartura, A. *With a Listening Heart: The Life of Eliezer Bregman of Jerusalem*. Jerusalem, 1983.

Bashan, E. "The Attachment of Maghrebi Jews to the Land of Israel and the Messianic Hope in Christian Writings of the Seventeenth Through Twentieth Centuries." *Bar-Ilan Yearbook* 14–15 (1977), pp. 160–175.

Ben-Arieh, Y. *A City Reflected in Its Times: Jerusalem in the Nineteenth Century*. Vol. 1: *The Old City*. Vol. 2: *Emergence of the New City*. Jerusalem, 1977, 1979.

Ben-Arieh, Y. *The Rediscovery of the Holy Land in the Nineteenth Century*. Jerusalem, 1970.

Ben-Arieh, Y. "The Writings of Nineteenth-Century Western Travelers to the Land of Israel: A Historical Source and a Cultural Phenomenon." *Cathedra* 40 (1986), pp. 159–188.

Benayahu, M. "The Ashkenazi Experience in Jerusalem." *Sefunot* 2 (1958), pp. 151–153.

Benayahu, M. "Document by R. Joseph David Ayash About Distributing Money from Germany in the Land of Israel." *Sura* 1 (1954), pp. 103–155.

Benayahu, M. "The Famine in Jerusalem in 5606 [1846]." *Quarterly for the Study of Jerusalem and Its History* 2, 1–2 (1949), pp. 72–88.

Benayahu, M. "A Response to R. Benjamin Mordecai Navon." *Sinai* 24 (1949), pp. 205–214.

Ben-Jacob, A. *Jerusalem Between the Walls*. Jerusalem, 1977.

Ben Sasson, Ḥ. H. *Continuity and Change*. Tel-Aviv, 1984.

Ben-Sasson, Ḥ. H. "The Personality and Historical Influence of the Vilna Ga'on." *Zion* 31 (1966), pp. 39–86, 197–216.

Ben-Zvi, I. "Events in Safed from the Lootings of 1834 to the Druze Attacks in 1838." *Sefunot* 7 (1964), pp. 277–322.

Berur, A. "Early Use of Extraterritorial Rights by Jews in the Land of Israel." *Zion* 5 (1940), pp. 61–69.

Bet ha-Levi, Y. D. *History of the Jews of Kalish*. Tel-Aviv, 1965.

Davis, M. "Letters of the Clerks' Organization: A New Source for the Study of Ties Between American Jewry and the Land of Israel." In *Salo Wittmayer Baron Jubilee Volume on the Occasion of His Eightieth Birthday*, ed. Saul Lieberman, pp. 91–109. Jerusalem, 1975.

Dembitzer, Ḥ. N. *Book of the Defenders of the Land of Israel*. Lemberg, 1852.

Dinberg, B., ed. *Seferha-Ẓiyyonut: Mevaserei ha-Ẓiyyonut*. Jerusalem, 1944.

Dinur, B. Z. "The Question of Redemption and Its Ways During the Early Enlightenment and the First Controversy over Emancipation." In *Be-Mifneh ha-Dorot*, ed. B. Z. Dinur. Jerusalem, 1972.

Dinur, B. Z. "From the Archives of Chief Rabbi Ḥayyim Abraham Gaugin." *Zion* 1 (1926), pp. 85–121.

Elyashar, E. "Synagogues Named for Rabban Yoḥanan ben Zakkai." In *Aspects of the*

History of the Jewish Yishuv in Jerusalem, ed. J. Ben-Porat, A. Kedar, et al., vol. 1. Jerusalem, 1977.
Eliav, M. "The Jews of Holland and the Jewish Settlement in the Land of Israel During the Nineteenth Century." In *Studies in the History of the Jews in Holland*, vol. 2 (Jerusalem, 1979), pp. 139–157.
Eliav, M. *Jewish Settlement in the Land of Israel Through the Perspective of German Politics, 1842–1914*. Tel-Aviv, 1973.
Eliav, M. *The Land of Israel and Its Yishuv in the Nineteenth Century (1777–1917)*. Jerusalem, 1978.
Eliav, M. *Love of Zion and Men of HOD: German Jewry and the Settlement of the Land of Israel in the Nineteenth Century*. Tel-Aviv, 1970.
Eliav, M. *Under Austrian Imperial Protection, 1849–1917*. Jerusalem, 1987.
Elimelech, A. *Chief Rabbis*. Jerusalem, 1970.
Eshkoli, A. Z. *The Tobiansky Movement Among the Jews: A Messianic Episode*. Jerusalem, 1933.
Etkes, I. "Family and Torah Study in 'Learned' Circles in Nineteenth-Century Lithuania." *Zion* 51 (1986), pp. 87–106.
Etkes, I. *Rabbi Israel Salanter*. Jerusalem, 1982.
Ettinger, S. "Principles and Trends in the Russian Government's Policies Toward the Jews in the Wake of the Polish Partition." *He-Avar* 19 (1972), pp. 20–34.
Ettinger, S. "The Statute of 1804." *He-Avar* 22 (1977), pp. 87–110.
Falk, A. N. *History of Real Property Relationships in Egypt, Syria, and the Land of Israel in Late Medieval and Modern Times*. Jerusalem, 1940.
Fischel, H. R. Y. "Journey to Kurdistan, Persia, and Babylonia." *Sinai* 5 (1939), pp. 240–247.
Freiden, I. "*Bikur Ḥolim Perushim* in Jerusalem: From Society to Hospital." *Cathedra* 27 (1983), pp. 117–140.
Friedman, M. "The Messianic Concept of the Vilna Ga'on's Disciples in Light of a Reading of the Sources." *Cathedra* 24 (1982), pp. 70–72.
Friedman, P. "Letters From the Land of Israel, 1814–1822." *Zion* 3 (1938), pp. 267–274.
Frumkin, A. L.. "The Beginnings of the Settlement of the Ashkenazim Called *Perushim: Ha-Emet mei-Ereẓ Tiẓmaḥ*. In *Me'asef Ziyyon*, 6 vols. Jerusalem, 1926–1934. Vol. 2, 1927, pp. 128–148.
Gaon, M. D. *Oriental Jews in the Land of Israel, Past and Present*. 2 vols. Jerusalem, 1928–1935.
Gat, B. Z. *The Jewish Community in the Land of Israel (1840–1881)*. Jerusalem, 1963.
Gelber, N. M. "Dr. Albert Kohen and His Visit to Jerusalem." *Riv'on le-Ḥeqer Yerushalayim ve-Toledotehah* [Quarterly for the Study of Jerusalem and Its History] 2, 1–2 (1959), pp. 175–195.
Gelber, N. M. "The Emigration of Jews from Bohemia and Galicia to the Land of Israel, 1811–1869." In [*Sefer Peres*], ed. Michael Ish-Shalom, Me'ir Benayahu, and Azriel Schochet, pp. 243–251. Jerusalem, 1953.
Gelber, N. M. "Moshe Sachs." *Sinai* 1 (1938), pp. 568–583.
Gelber, N. M. "Napoleon I and the Land of Israel." In *Sefer Dinburg*, ed. Yiẓḥaq Baer, Yehoshu'a Guttman, and Mosheh Sova, pp. 263–288. Jerusalem, 1949.
Gelber, N. M. "The Question of the Land of Israel, 1840–1842." *Zion* 4 (1930), pp. 44–66 and appendices, pp. 1–41.
Grajewski, P. *Avnei Zikkaron* (Stones of Memory). 6 vols. Jerusalem, 1928–1929.
Grajewski, P. *Mi-Ginzei Qedem* (Documents and Sources from the Writings of Pinḥas Ben Zevi Grajewski). Ed. Israel Beck. Jerusalem, 1977.

Grajewski, P. *Mi-Ginzei Yerushalayim* (From the Hidden Treasures of Jerusalem). 24 vols. Jerusalem, 1927–1935.

Grajewski, P. *Milḥemet ha-Yehudim ba-Misyon mi-Shenat 5584 ad ha-Yom ha-Zeh* (The Jews' Battle Against the Mission, 1824 to the Present). Jerusalem, 1938.

Grajewski, P. *Pinqas Yerushalayim* (Jerusalem Journal). Jerusalem, 1944.

Grajewski, P. *Zikhronot Qedumim* (Early Recollections). Jerusalem, 1928.

Grajewski, P. *Zikkaron la-Ḥovevim ha-Rishonim* (In Memory of the Early Beloved Ones). 20 vols. Jerusalem, 1937–1938.

Haberman, A. M. "A Compromise Between Two Emissaries from Safed in Amsterdam." *Sefunot* 7 (1963), pp. 257–266.

Halamish, M, Y. Rivlin, and R. Shuchat, eds. *The Vilna Ga'on and His Disciples*. Ramat-Gan, 2003.

Halevy, S. *The First Hebrew Books Printed in Jerusalem in the Second Half of the Nineteenth Century (1841–1890)*. Jerusalem, 1975.

Hirschberg, Ḥ. J. "The Turning Point in the History of Jerusalem in the Nineteenth Century." In *Yad Rivlin: Joseph J. Rivlin Memorial Volume*, ed. Ch. Z. Hirschberg, pp. 78–107. Ramat-Gan, 1964.

Ḥisdai, Y. "Early Settlement of 'Hasidim' and 'Mitnaggedim' in the Land of Israel: Immigration of '*Miẓvah*' and of 'Mission.'" *Shalem* 4 (1984), pp. 231–169.

Hofman, Y. "Muhammad Ali's Activity in Syria." Ph.D. dissertation, Hebrew University of Jerusalem, 1963.

Horwitz, A. *The Founding Institution: History of the Kenesset Yisra'el General Committee*. Jerusalem, 1958.

Kaniel, Y. "The Dispute Between Petaḥ-Tiqva and Rishon le-Ẓiyyon Over Priority of Settlement and Its Historical Significance." *Cathedra* 9 (1979), pp. 26–53.

Kaniel, Y. "The Terms 'Old *Yishuv*' and 'New *Yishuv*' as Understood by the Generation of 1882–1915 and by Historiography. *Cathedra* 6 (1978), pp. 3–19.

Karagila, Z. "Samuel ben Israel Peretz Heller Describes the Sack of Safed 1834." *Cathedra* 27 (1983), pp. 109–116.

Kark, R. "Agricultural Land and Plans for Its Cultivation by Jews During Montefiore's Second Visit to the Land of Israel, 1839." *Cathedra* 33 (1984), pp. 57–92.

Katz, A. I. "Three Emissaries from Safed in Italy." *Sefunot* 7 (1964), p. 237.

Katz, J.. "The Historical Figure of R. Ẓevi Hirsch Kalisher." *Shivat Ẓiyyon* 2–3 (1951), pp. 26–41.

Katz, J. "Messianism and Nationalism in the Teaching of Rabbi Alcalay." *Shivat Ẓiyyon* 4 (1956), pp. 9–41.

Katz, J. "On the Year 5600 as a Messianic Year and Its Influence on the Efforts of the *Perushim* to Hasten the Redemption." *Cathedra* 24 (1982), pp. 73–75.

Katz, J. "The Ordination Dispute Between Rabbi Jacob Berab and Ralbaḥ [Rabbi Levi ben Ḥabib]." *Zion* 16 (1951), pp. 28–45

Katzburg, N. "Sources on Ottoman Law Concerning the Acquisition of Property by Foreign Citizens." In *Yad Rivlin: Joseph J. Rivlin Memorial Volume*, ed. Ch. Z. Hirschberg, pp. 151–159. Ramat-Gan, 1964.

Kedem, M. "Mid-Nineteenth-Century Anglican Eschatology on the Redemption of Israel." *Cathedra* 19 (1981), pp. 55–72.

Klausner, J. Ed. *The Zionist Writings of Rabbi Ẓevi Kalisher*. Jerusalem, 1947.

Kluger, B., ed. *Min ha-Maqor* [Anthology of Documents from Jerusalem, 1840–1940]. Vol. 1. Jerusalem, 1978.

Kokhav, S. "The Return of Jews to the Land of Israel and the English Evangelical Movement." *Cathedra* 62 (1992), pp. 18–36.

Kolat, Y. "On Studies and Students of Settlement and Zionist History." *Cathedra* 1 (1976), pp. 3–53.
Kovac, Z. "Immigration From Eastern Europe to the Land of Israel in the Mid-Nineteenth Century." *Cathedra* 9 (1978), pp. 193–204.
Kressel, G. *Planters of Hope: From Jerusalem to Petaḥ-Tiqva*. Jerusalem, 1976.
Landau, B. *The Hasidic Ga'on of Vilna*. Jerusalem, 1968.
Liebes, J. "The Messianism of R. Jacob Emden and Its Relationship to Sabbateanism." *Tarbiẓ* 49 (1980), pp. 122–165.
Liebes, J. "The Disciples of the Ga'on of Vilna, Sabbateanism, and the Jewish Essence." *Da'at* 50–52 (2003), pp. 255–290.
Lifschitz, Y. ha-Levi. *Zikhron Ya'aqov*. Kovno-Slobodka, 1924–1929.
Lunz, A. M. *Almanac of the Land of Israel*. Jerusalem, 1895–1911.
Lunz, A. M. *The Ḥaluqah: Its Rules and Organization*. Jerusalem, 1915.
Lunz, A. M. *Jerusalem Yearbook for the Diffusion of an Accurate Knowledge of Ancient and Modern Palestine*. 17 vols. Jerusalem, 1882–1919.
Lunz, A. M. *Pathways of Zion and Jerusalem*. Selected and edited by G. Kressel. Jerusalem, 1970.
Mahler, R. "American Jewry and the Concept of Returning to Zion at the Time of the French Revolution." *Zion* 15 (1950), pp. 107–134.
Mahler, R. *Hasidism and Enlightenment*. Israel, 1961.
Mahler, R. *History of the Jews: Modern Times*. Part 1, vol. 1. Merḥaviah, 1952. [Abridged English translation: *A History of Modern Jewry*. London, 1971.]
Maimon, Y. L. ha-Kohen. "Prominent Jerusalemites on Renewing the Sanhedrin." *Sinai* 32 (1953), p. 134.
Malachi, A. B. *Aspects of the History of the Old Yishuv*. Tel-Aviv, 1971.
Ma'oz, M. "Jerusalem in the Last Hundred Years of Ottoman Rule." In *Chapters in the History of the Jewish Community in Jerusalem: Jerusalem in the Early Ottoman Period, Jerusalem in the Modern Period*. Ed. Aharon Kedar and Ben-Zion Yehoshua. Vol. 1, pp. 26–272. Jerusalem, 1973.
Meisel, J. "The 1839 Register of Jews in Safed and Its Environs." *Sefunot* 6 (1962), pp. 427–473.
Mesas, R. Joseph. *Collected Letters*. Part 1. Jerusalem, 1969.
Mevorakh, B. "Belief in the Messiah in the Early Polemics Over Reform." *Zion* 34 (1969), pp. 189–218.
Mevorakh, B. "The Messianic Question in the Polemics Regarding Emancipation and Reform 1781–1819." Ph.D. dissertation, Hebrew University in Jerusalem, 1966.
Mevorakh, B. *Napoleon and His Time*. Jerusalem, 1968.
Michman, J. "The Emergence of the Organization of Peqidim and Amarkalim of Amsterdam." *Cathedra* 27 (1983), pp. 69–84.
Morgenstern, A. "The Attachment to the Land of Israel and Its Settlement in the Writings of the Vilna Ga'on and His Disciples." In *Redemption by Natural Means*, ed. A. Morgenstern, pp. 9–16. Elkanah, 1989.
Morgenstern, A. "Between Rabbi Judah Bibas and the Rabbinic Emissary of the Jerusalem *Perushim*." *Pe'amim* 40 (1989), pp. 156–159.
Morgenstern, A. "Between Sons and Disciples: The Struggle Over the Vilna Ga'on's Heritage and Over the Ideological Issue of Torah Versus the Land of Israel." *Da'at* 53 (2004), pp. 83–124.
Morgenstern, A. "The Construction of the Courtyard of 'the *Ḥurvah* of R. Judah Ḥasid' in Jerusalem." *Shalem* 4 (1984), pp. 271–305.

Morgenstern, A. "The Correspondence of the Peqidim and Amarkalim of Amsterdam as a Source for the History of the Land of Israel." *Cathedra* 27 (1983), pp. 85–108.

Morgenstern, A. "The Dispute Within the Minsk Community Regarding the Messiah's Advent in 1840." *Zion* 53 (1988), pp. 190–199.

Morgenstern, A. "Eschatology in the Writings of Israel of Shklov." *Shragai* 3 (1989), pp. 9–15.

Morgenstern, A. "Examining the Renewal of the Sacrificial Cult and the Rebuilding of the Temple in the Run-up to the Year 5600." *Cathedra* 82 (1997), pp. 200–202

Morgenstern, A. "The First Compact Between Sefardim and Ashkenazim in Jerusalem." *Asufot* 6 (1992), pp. 211–246.

Morgenstern, A. "The First Jewish Hospital in Jerusalem." *Cathedra* 33 (1984), pp. 107–124.

Morgenstern, A. "From Brody to the Land of Israel and Back: The Tale of the Monument to Malkah, Daughter of Isaac Babad." *Zion* 58 (1993), pp. 107–113.

Morgenstern, A. "Historical Reality or Wishful Thinking in Research on the Old *Yishuv*." *Cathedra* 31 (1984), pp. 12–181.

Morgenstern, A. "The Jews of Sefad, 1800–1839: Estimates and Data." *Cathedra* 49 (1989), pp. 160–172.

Morgenstern, A. "The Judah Ḥasid *Ḥurvah*: From Residential Courtyard to Community Square." *Asufot* 1 (1987), pp. 379–395.

Morgenstern, A. "Lord Joseph Amazlag: His Stature and Efforts on Behalf of Jerusalem's Jews." *Asufot* 3 (1989), pp. 397–414.

Morgenstern, A. "Messianic Expectations With the Approach of the Year 1840." In *Messianism and Eschatology*, ed. Z. Barras, pp. 343–369. Jerusalem, 1983.

Morgenstern, A. *Messianism and the Settlement of the Land of Israel in the First Half of the Nineteenth Century*. Jerusalem, 1985.

Morgenstern, A. "Moses Montefiore and the *Yishuv*: Outline of a New Understanding." In *Moses in His Generation,* ed. I. Bartal, pp. 31–36. Jerusalem, 1987.

Morgenstern, A. *Mysticism and Messianism: From Luzzatto to the Vilna Ga'on*. Jerusalem, 1999.

Morgenstern, A. "New Materials on Israel of Shklov's Effort to Restore Ordination. *Sinai* (Jubilee Volume) (1987), pp. 548–565.

Morgenstern, A. "The Nineteenth-Century Critique of Messianism." *Zion* 52, 3 (1987), pp. 371–389.

Morgenstern, A. *On a Mission from Jerusalem, 1816–1839*. Jerusalem, 1987.

Morgenstern, A. "The Organizational Unity of the *Perushim* Kolel in the Land of Israel." *Zion* 47, 3 (1982), pp. 293–310.

Morgenstern, A. "The Peqidim and Amarkalim of Amsterdam and the Jewish Community in Palestine: 1810–1840." Ph.D. dissertation, Hebrew University in Jerusalem, 1981.

Morgenstern, A. "The *Perushim*, the London Missionary Society, and the Establishment of the British Consulate in Jerusalem." *Shalem* 5 (1987), pp. 115–137.

Morgenstern, A. *Redemption Through Return: The Vilna Ga'on's Disciples in the Land of Israel, 1800–1840*. Jerusalem, 1997.

Morgenstern, A. "Two Traditions About the Origins of the *Aliyah* of the Vilna Ga'on's Disciples." *Shalem* 6 (1992), pp. 195–222.

Piekarz, M. *Hasidic Conduct*. Jerusalem, 1999.

Piekarz, M. *Polish Hasidism*. Jerusalem, 1990.

Rachelson R. "The Holy Places as a Cause of the Crimean War." Master's thesis, Bar-Ilan University, 1972.

Rivkind, I. "Listing of Those Who Perished in the Safed Earthquake of 1837." *Palestine Annual* 2–3 (1926), pp. 100–109.

Rivkind, I. *Dappim Bodedim* [Separate Pages] (Documents on the History of the Jewish Settlement in the Land of Israel in the Eighteenth and Nineteenth Centuries). In *Jerusalem (A. M. Lunz Memorial Volume)*, ed. E. L. Sukenik and I. Press, pp. 111–178. Jerusalem 1929. Also in *Zion* 5 (1933), pp. 148–163.

Rivlin, B. "The Mission of Solomon Zalman Shapira From Jerusalem to Amsterdam, 1825–1829." In *Yad Rivlin: Joseph J. Rivlin Memorial Volume*, ed. Ch. Z. Hirschberg, pp. 108–150. Ramat-Gan, 1964.

Rivlin, E. "The 1823 Regulations of the *Perushim* in the Land of Israel Concerning the *Ḥaluqah*." *Me'asef Ẓiyyon* 2 (1927), pp. 150–170.

Rivlin, E. "The Enactments Concerning Legacies in Jerusalem and the Land of Israel." In *Memorial, Part V: The Land of Israel*, ed. Y. L. ha-Kohen Fishman (Maimon), pp. 558–619. Jerusalem, 1937.

Rivlin, E. "Letter from Hillel Rivlin to His Son-in-Law, Shemariah Luria." *Me'asef Ẓiyyon* 5 (1933), pp. 141–147.

Rivlin, E. "Letter from Mordecai Ẓoref to His Father, Abraham Solomon Zalman Ẓoref, 1844." *Zion* 1 (1926), pp. 71–83.

Rivlin, E. *The Pious One, Rabbi Joseph Zundel of Salant, and His Teachers*. Jerusalem, 1927.

Rivlin, T. H. *Ḥazon Ẓiyyon* [The Vision of Zion]. Tel-Aviv, 1947.

Rivlin, Y. Y. "The Bond Between Lithuanian Jews and the Land of Israel." In *Lithuanian Jewry*, ed. N. Goren et al., vol. 1, pp. 457–488. Tel-Aviv, 1960.

Rivlin, Y. Y. "The Vilna Ga'on and His Disciples in the Settlement of the Land of Israel." In *The Book of the GRA*, ed. Y. L. ha-Kohen Maimon, vol. 2, part 4, pp. 111–162. Jerusalem, 1954.

Rothschild, M. M., *The Ḥaluqah*. Jerusalem, 1969.

Sapir, J. *Yemenite Journey*. Ed. A. Yaari. Jerusalem, 1951.

Sapir, S. "Sources on the Anglican Missionary Societies Active in Jerusalem and the Land of Israel in the Nineteenth Century to the First World War." *Cathedra* 19 (1981), pp. 155–170.

Scholem, G. *Shabbetai Ẓevi*. Tel-Aviv, 1963.

Schwartz, J. *Gates of Jerusalem*. Ed. B. Landau. Jerusalem, 1969.

Schwartzfuchs, S. "The Jews of Algeria in the North of the Land of Israel and French Protection." *Shalem* 3 (1981) pp. 333–349.

Shamir, S. "The Beginning of Modern Times in the History of the Land of Israel." *Cathedra* 40 (1986), pp. 138–158.

Shapira, M. "The Ḥabad Hasidic Community in Hebron: Its History and Image, 1820–1929. In *Vatiqin: Studies in the History of the Yishuv*, ed. Ch. Z. Hirschberg, pp. 67–116. Ramat-Gan, 1975.

Shiloh, M. "An 1842 Bequest for the Return of the Jews to Jerusalem." *Cathedra* 57 (1991), pp. 76–78.

Shischa, A. "Epistle of the Rabbinic Emissary Ḥayyim Barukh Miastro." In *Sefer Zikkaron le-Rav Yiẓḥaq Nissim*, ed. M. Benayahu. Part 4. Jerusalem, 1985.

Solomon, M. *Three Generations in the Yishuv, 1812–1913*. Jerusalem, 1951.

Spyridon, S. N. "Annals of Palestine, 1821–1841," *Journal of the Palestine Oriental Society* 18, 1–2 (1938), pp. 132–163.

Stampfer, S. *The Lithuanian Yeshiva*. Jerusalem, 1995.

Stock (Sedan) D. "On the Origins of R. Moses Sacks's Fame." *Sinai* 2 (1938), pp. 331–333.

Sukenik, E. L. and Y. Press, eds. *Jerusalem: A. M. Lunz Memorial Volume.* Jerusalem, 1928.

Tishby, Y. "Immigration to the Land of Israel for the Purpose of Raising the *Shekhinah.*" *Cathedra* 24 (1982), p. 75.

Tishby, Y. "The Messianic Idea and Messianic Trends in the Development of Hasidism." *Zion* 32 (1967), pp. 1–45.

Toledano, B. "The Origins of the Jerusalem *Yishuv.*" *Tarbiẓ* 9 (1938), pp. 119–122.

Toledano, J. M. "Journal of the Court in Safed." In *Jerusalem: Studies in the Land of Israel,* pp. 232–256. Ed. M. Ish-Shalom, M. Benayahu, Y. Peres, and E. Shochet. Jerusalem, 1955.

Vereté, M. "The Concept of Israel's Return in English Protestant Thought, 1790–1840." *Zion* 33 (1968), pp. 145–179.

Vinograd, Y. *Bibliography of the Vilna Ga'on.* Jerusalem, 2003.

Wallenstein, M. "Ms. Gaster 975: A Memo of the Sefardic *Kolel* in Jerusalem from the Year 5615 [1815]." *Zion* 43 (1978), pp. 75–96.

Weinstein, M. "Programs for the Reform of the Jerusalem *Yishuv* During the First Half of the Nineteenth Century." *Sefer Bar-Ilan* 6 (1968), pp. 339–356.

Werfel (Rafael), I. "The History of the Ashkenazi Community in the Land of Israel." *Sinai* 5 (1939), pp. 69–117.

Werte, Meir. "The Idea of Israel's Return in English Protestant Thought, 1790–1840." *Zion* 33 (1968), pp. 145–179.

Yaari, A. "Emissaries From the Land of Israel to the Ten Tribes." *Sinai* 6 (1940), pp. 163–178, 344–356, 374–382.

Yaari, A. *Journeys in the Land of Israel.* Tel-Aviv, 1946.

Yaari, A. "The Suffering of Ashkenazi Jews in Jerusalem at the Beginning of the Nineteenth Century." *Sinai* 5 (1939–1940), pp. 270–278.

Yaari, A. "The Travels of David Beit Hillel." *Sinai* 4 (1939), pp. 24–53.

Yellin, Y. *Memoirs of a Native of Jerusalem, 1830–1918.* Jerusalem, 1928.

In Other Languages

Askenazy, S. "*Pierwszy 'Syonista' Polsky.*" In *Dwa Stulecia,* II. Warsaw, 1910.

Bary, Benjamin. *Zeitgemesse Gedanken über die Emancipation des Menschen.* Königsberg, 1843.

Bonar, A., and R. McCheyne. *Narrative of a Mission of Inquiry to the Jews from the Church of Scotland in 1839.* Edinburgh, 1844.

Brinner, W. M. "A Nineteenth-Century Messiah From Azerbaizn." In *Proceedings of the Fifth World Conference of Jewish Studies,* vol. 2, pp. 6–12. Jerusalem, 1972.

Buchanan, C. *Christian Researches in Asia.* London, 1819

Crooll, J. *The Fifth Empire.* London, 1829.

Crooll, J. *The Last Generation.* Cambridge, 1829.

Crooll, J. *The Restoration of Israel.* London, 1814.

Dienstag, Israel Jacob. "Rabbenu Elijah of Vilna." *Talpiyot* 4, 1–2 (1949), pp. 269–356; 3–4 (1949), pp. 409–413; 5 (1950), pp. 861–862.

Duker, A. G. "The Tarniks." In *Joshua Starr Memorial Volume,* pp. 191–201. New York, 1953.

Egerton, F. *Journal of a Tour in the Holy Land in May and June 1840.* London, 1841.

Etkes, I. *The Gaon of Vilna: The Man and His Image.* Trans. from Hebrew by J. M. Green. Berkeley, 2002.

Ewald, F. C.. *Journal of Missionary Labors in the City of Jerusalem During the Years 1842–1844*. London, 1845.
Frankel, L. A. *Nach Jerusalem*. Leipzig, 1858.
The Gaon of Vilnius and the Annals of Jewish Culture: Materials of the International Scientific Conference, Vilnius, September 10–12, 1997. Compiled by Izraelis Lempertis. Vilna, 1998.
Gidney, W. T. *The History of the L.S.P.C.* London, 1905.
Hechler, W. H. *The Jerusalem Bishopric*. London, 1883.
Hofman, Y. "The Administration of Syria and Palestine Under Egyptian Rule (1831–1840)." In *Studies on Palestine During the Ottoman Period*, ed. M. Ma'oz, pp. 311–333. Jerusalem, 1975.
Holty, J. *A Combined View of the Prophecies of Daniel, Esdros and St. John*. London, 1815.
Hyamson, A. M. *The British Consulate in Jerusalem, 1838–1914*. London, 1939.
Irving, E. *The Signs of Time*. London, 1810.
Jowett, W. *Christian Researches in the Holy Land in 1823–4*. London, 1826.
Kobler, F. *Napoleon and the Jews*. Jerusalem, 1975.
Montefiore, J. M. *Diaries*. Ed. Dr. Loewe. Chicago, 1895.
Ma'oz, M. "Changes in the Position of the Jewish Communities of Palestine and Syria in Mid-Nineteenth Century." In *Studies on Palestine During the Ottoman Period*, ed. M. Ma'oz, pp. 142–163. Jerusalem, 1975.
Ma'oz, M. *Ottoman Reforms in Syria and Palestine 1840–1861*. Oxford, 1968.
Meyer, M. A. *Response to Modernity: A History of the Reform Movement in Judaism*. New York, 1988.
Morgenstern, A. "The Correspondence of the Pekidim and Amarcalim of Amsterdam as a Source for the History of Erez Israel." In *Dutch Jewish History*, ed. J. Michman and T. Levie, pp. 433–463. Jerusalem, 1984.
Morgenstern, A. "Dispersion and the Longing for Zion, 1240–1840." *Azure* 12 (2002), pp. 71–132.
Morgenstern, A. "Messianic Concepts and Settlement in the Land of Israel." In *Vision and Conflict in the Holy Land*, ed. J. Cohen, pp. 141–162, 182–189. Jerusalem, 1985.
Morgenstern, A. "Messianismus und Siedlung in Eretz Israel in der ersten Halfte des 19 Jahrhunderts." *Hebraische Beitrage zur Wissenschaft des Judentums Deutsch Angezeigt*, vol. 6, pp. 47–63. Heidelberg, 1990.
Morgenstern, A. "Resettlement of the Land (*Yishuv ha-Aretz*) as Viewed by the Vilna Ga'on's Circle." *Jewish Action* 49, 3 (1989), pp. 33–36.
Nadler, A. *The Faith of the Mithnagdim: Rabbinic Responses to Hasidic Rapture*. Baltimore, 1977.
Neumann, B. *Die heilige Stadt und deren Bewohner*. Hamburg, 1877.
Plaut, W. G. *The Rise of Reform Judaism*. New York, 1963.
Schmelz, U. O. "Some Demographic Peculiarities of the Jews of Jerusalem during the Nineteenth Century." In *Studies on Palestine During the Ottoman Period*, ed. M. Ma'oz, pp. 119–142. Jerusalem, 1975.
Schwartz, J. *Das Heilige Land*. Frankfurt-am-Main, 1852.
Stanislaski, M. F. *Tsar Nicholas I and the Jews: The Transformation of Jewish Society in Russia 1825–1855*. Philadelphia, 1983.
Tibawi, A. L. *British Interests in Palestine, 1800–1901*. Oxford, 1961.
The Travels of Rabbi David D'Beth Hillel From Jerusalem Through Arabia, Koordistan, Persia, and India to Madras. Madras, 1832.

Vereté, M. "The Restoration of the Jews in English Protestant Thought 1790–1840." *Middle Eastern Studies* 8 (1972), pp. 3–50.
Vereté, M. "Why Was a British Consulate Established in Jerusalem?" *English Historical Review* 85 (1970), pp. 316–345.
Wolff, J. *Journal of the Rev. Joseph Wolff.* London, 1839.
Wolff, J. *Researches and Missionary Labours.* London, 1835.

Index